TEACHING COMPUTATIONAL CREATIVITY

Teaching Computational Creativity examines the new interdisciplinary pedagogies of today's coding-intensive interactive media and design curricula. Students, researchers, and faculty will find a comprehensive overview of educational practices pertaining to innovation fields such as digital media, 3D printing, agile development, physical computing, games, dance, collaboration, teacher education, and online learning. This volume fills an important gap in the literature on creative computation, as practitioners are rarely challenged to reflect on or share their teaching practices. How do we design effective inter-, multi-, cross-, and transdisciplinary pedagogy and curricula? Brought together here are essays on the pedagogies that produce the so-called *unicorns* – graduates who can code *and* create. Here, the intertwining of (what many consider mutually exclusive) artistic sensitivities and computational skills plays an essential role, calling forth a new kind of undergraduate curriculum attuned to the interweaving of skillsets and theoretical knowledge needed to create and innovate with ever-changing technologies.

Michael Filimowicz is senior lecturer in the School of Interactive Arts and Technology at Simon Fraser University. He is director of the Cinesonika festival and academic conference, and founder of 4th Foundation, a university spinout doing curriculum development in K-12 coding and technology skills. He has published across disciplines in journals such as *Organised Sound, Arts and Humanities in Higher Education, Leonardo, Empirical Musicology Review,* and *Semiotica.* His art has been exhibited internationally at venues such as SIGGRAPH, Re-New, Design Shanghai, ARTECH, Les Instants Vidéo, IDEAS, Kinsey Institute, and Art Currents, and published in monographs such as *Reframing Photography* and *Infinite Instances.* His portfolio site is http://filimowi.cz

Veronika Tzankova is a Ph.D. candidate in the School of Communication at Simon Fraser University (SFU), with a prior M.A. from the School of Interactive Arts and Technology, also at SFU. Her research is in the area of interactive technologies within contexts of social appropriation and democratic inclusiveness. She has published articles and book chapters with the *Parsons Journal for Information Mapping*, MIT Press, and Palgrave MacMillan Publishers. Her research has also been presented at various conferences such as the Association of Internet Researchers and ACS Crossroads.

Teaching Computational Creativity

Michael Filimowicz
Simon Fraser University

Veronika Tzankova
Simon Fraser University

CAMBRIDGE UNIVERSITY PRESS

CAMBRIDGE
UNIVERSITY PRESS

University Printing House, Cambridge CB2 8BS, United Kingdom

One Liberty Plaza, 20th Floor, New York, NY 10006, USA

477 Williamstown Road, Port Melbourne, VIC 3207, Australia

4843/24, 2nd Floor, Ansari Road, Daryaganj, Delhi – 110002, India

79 Anson Road, #06-04/06, Singapore 079906

Cambridge University Press is part of the University of Cambridge.

It furthers the University's mission by disseminating knowledge in the pursuit of education, learning, and research at the highest international levels of excellence.

www.cambridge.org
Information on this title: www.cambridge.org/9781107138049
DOI: 10.1017/9781316481165

First published 2017

Printed in the United States of America by Sheridan Books, Inc.

A catalogue record for this publication is available from the British Library.

Library of Congress Cataloging-in-Publication Data

Names: Filimowicz, Michael, editor. | Tzankova, Veronika, editor.
Title: Teaching computational creativity / [edited by] Michael Filimowicz, Simon Fraser University, Veronika Tzankova, Simon Fraser University.
Description: New York : Cambridge University Press, 2017. | Includes bibliographical references and index.
Identifiers: LCCN 2016049295 | ISBN 9781107138049 (Hardback)
Subjects: LCSH: Interactive multimedia—Study and teaching. | New media art—Study and teaching. | Computer programming—Study and teaching. | Computer-assisted instruction. | Creative thinking.
Classification: LCC QA76.76.I59 T433 2017 | DDC 005.107—dc23 LC record available at https://lccn.loc.gov/2016049295

ISBN 978-1-107-13804-9 Hardback

Contents

List of Figures   *page* vii

List of Tables   xi

Notes on Contributors   xiii

Acknowledgments   xxi

Introduction: Pedagogies at the Intersection of Disciplines
Veronika Tzankova and Michael Filimowicz   1

PART I NEW FOUNDATIONS

1 Staying Current: Developing Digital Literacies for the
   Creative Classroom
   Ryan M. Patton and Luke Meeken   21

2 Teaching Interactivity: Introducing Computation
   to Art/Design Students   48
   Andrew Hieronymi

PART II CODE AS MEDIUM

3 ARRAY[ ]: Coding Slowly
   Channel TWo   75

4 Teaching for the Design Singularity: Toward an Entirely
   Code-based Design Curriculum
   Brad Tober   95

PART III PHYSICAL{LY} COMPUTING

5 A Physical Computing Teaching Initiative in Brazil
   Luiza Novaes and Joao de Sa Bonelli   107

6 Art and Technology Collaboration in Interactive
   Dance Performance
   Jinsil Hwaryoung Seo and Christine Bergeron   142

PART IV ONLINE LEARNING

7 Design Scenes of Online Code Learning Environments
   Michael Filimowicz   163

8 Between Code and Culture: Developing a Creative
   Coding Massive Open Online Course
   Mark Guglielmetti and Jon McCormack   191

PART V CRITICAL PEDAGOGY

9 Process and Outcome Paradigms in Media Arts Pedagogy
   Nancy E. Paterson   213

10 Citizens of the Cognisphere
    Daniel Sauter   229

PART VI TRANSDISCIPLINARY

11 From Growing Tools to Designing Organisms: Changing the
    Literacies of Design
    Orkan Telhan   259

12 Pedagogical Experiments in Creative Coding
    Angus G. Forbes   273

    Interviews   293

    Afterword: Toward a Curricular Synthesis   311
    Michael Filimowicz and Veronika Tzankova

    Index   317

Figures

1.1 Culture jamming project (2013)   *page* 32

1.2 Culture jamming project (2012)   33

1.3 Game card (2009)   36

1.4 Course slide (2012)   38

1.5 "Binge Inferno" screens (2012)   39

1.6 Makey Makey game controller (2012)   40

1.7 Art education student teaching games (2013)   43

1.8 Sound sculpture (2014)   43

1.9 Talking/identity mask (2014)   44

2.1 Saam: *Farm Town*   53

2.2 Saam: *Retirement*   55

2.3 Ting: *Puppet Show*   59

2.4 Ting: *Puppet Show Face-Off*   63

2.5 Michael: *AREA*   65

2.6 Michael and team: *Out There In The Void*   68

5.1 Examples of projects developed in the class *Interfaces Físicas e Lógicas*. (a) A doll that responds to one's social network status. (b) A drawing machine controlled

by the musical notes played on an acoustic guitar. (c) A game
controlled by gestures.   113

5.2 Students at work in the LIFE lab   114

5.3 Experiment in projection mapping. Software
developed in the Processing environment is used
to track the position of a red LED and use it as
a reference to place a projected image   119

5.4 A color tag is used as a tracking reference for
positioning a virtual image in an experiment using
augmented reality, Processing language, and Ketai library   120

5.5 A virtual image is precisely positioned over a drawing
on a person's skin. In this experiment, a pen drawing
over tracing paper was positioned on the user's arm
and used as a tracking reference   121

5.6 An augmented reality virtual tattoo created with
the TattooAR application   122

5.7 One of the earlier experiments created by the student
in the Physical Computing class   123

5.8 The second framing experiment was capable of
digitally controlling the emission of spray paint   125

5.9 A servo motor attached to a spool that tensions
a fishing line, used to move a can of spray paint   126

5.10 The fourth experiment, with the mechanism of
actuation of the spray paint being raised by
two motors   127

5.11 Tests made with spray paint   129

5.12 The installation in the LIFE lab   130

5.13 User testing with graffitti artist Amanda Vieira   130

5.14 The final presentation of the project at the LIFE lab   131

5.15 Color variations in glycemic index reading   132

5.16 Glycemic index result   133

5.17 The experiment made in cardboard with lens and LED light, to evaluate the possibility of reading color information using a smartphone's camera 134

5.18 The 3D printed piece and using lens and artificial light, to perform a color reading using the camera device 135

5.19 3D printing tests, using a variety of materials and equipment 136

5.20 The app interface, where the patient can monitor his glucose readings 137

5.21 App interface destined to the health professionals, where the doctor can monitor the recent glycemic readings from the patient 138

6.1 (a) Movement session, (b) dancer working on a soft circuit, and (c) LED dress research project 144

6.2 Public performance projects from the course 145

6.3 (a) *Proximity* performance and (b) diagram of the inside of the robot of *Proximity* 154

6.4 *In the Shadow* performance 155

6.5 *Zwischenkörper* performance 157

7.1 Almquist and Lupton's Venn diagram situating "use" between affordance and meaning 166

7.2 Codecademy's coding workspace located in the main browser window, next to instruction, compiler at top right 167

7.3 CodeSkulptor IDE implemented in a stand-alone (separated from instructional content) browser window 168

7.4 Wireframe of online courseware with "sublated video" 169

7.5 High encouragement and very mild reprimand on Codecademy's 172

7.6 The spatially distributed learning frames of online learning, with the expanded context shown in both print and e-book variations 179

7.7 The mono-screen scene: university computer lab 181

7.8 A distributed design scene for online code learning 182

8.1 Image applying rule no. 8 201

8.2 Animating the image by applying rule no. 11 201

8.3 Molnar (2014) Neroli Wesley 203

8.4 25-Molnar Roses (2014) Jordi Pique 203

8.5 Examples of students' works for the exercise
"draw your name" 204

Tables

1.1 Pre- and post-survey questions on students'
self-efficacy of creating images/art with a computer   *page* 42

1.2 Pre- and post-survey questions on students' self-efficacy
of knowing how to make programmable media   42

5.1 Preliminary selection of projects and crossing of
projects and criteria   117

5.2 Projects analyzed and learning processes   140

6.1 Weekly activities   151

A.1 High-level meta-pedagogical mapping of curriculum
over a 2-year period   312

Notes on Contributors

Jussi Ängeslevä is involved in academia and the design industry, and conducts his individual experimental work, focusing on embodied interfaces, experiences, and services for the public. His work as Vice Creative Director at ART+COM media design studio consistently garners international recognition in exhibitions, installations, and awards. He is an honorary professor at the Berlin University of the Art teaching Digital Media Design and has been serving as a juror, chair, or advisor in various academic and design bodies such as D&AD, ARS Electronica, TEI, and SIGGRAPH. His design ethos is leveraging hardware, software, physical, and graphic design in the search for elegance in highly specific solutions, where the meaning of a work is inseparable from the medium communicating it.

Christine S. Bergeron has been the Director of Dance Programs and Initiatives at Texas A&M University since 2008. She has a B.A. in Dance Education from the University of Akron and an M.F.A. in Choreography and Performance from Florida State University. Currently, she is working toward her Ph.D. in Dance Science from the University of Wolverhampton where she is conducting research on Pilates and its effect on dance training and performance. Choreographically she is intrigued by time and space and how the two intersect. She began working with collaborator Jinsil Hwaryoung Seo in 2011 on interactive performance including motion capture and wearable technology. Christine's vision is not to sacrifice speed or complexity of the movement for the use of LED wearables but to find a way for the technology to "keep up" with the intricacies of dance. Choreographically, her work has been presented throughout the nation in Ohio, Florida, North Carolina, New York, California, Illinois, Texas, and Wisconsin, in Mexico.

João Bonelli is a designer working in Interaction Design and Physical Computing. He is a teacher and researcher in the Undergraduate Design Program at Pontifícia Universidade Católica do Rio de Janeiro – PUC-Rio, in Brazil. Bonelli has a master's degree from New York University's Interactive Telecommunications Program (ITP) and a Ph.D. in Design from PUC-Rio.

Channel TWo (Trowbridge and Westbrook) has received a number of new media awards including a Rhizome Commission (2012), a Turbulence Commission (2011), and a Terminal Net Art Commission (2009). Channel TWo's practice involves all aspects of research and production including conceptual development, aesthetics, visual/sound design, technology development, and coding. Channel TWo is interested in luck, levels, and trespassing through the contexts of landscape, interactivity, and augmented reality. Projects intersect playful interface with critical undercurrents. Channel TWo uses media, game platforms, communication design ephemera, and mobile apps to reveal social complexity, contradictions, cognitive dissonance, and coping mechanisms. More at: www.onchanneltwo.com

Angus Forbes is an assistant professor in the Department of Computer Science at University of Illinois at Chicago, where he leads the Creative Coding Research Group within the Electronic Visualization Laboratory. His work has appeared in a variety of journals and conference proceedings, both as a lead author and in collaboration, including IEEE Visualization, ACM Multimedia, IEEE BigData, USGS Geoinformatics, and ISEA, the International Symposium on Electronic Art, among others. His media arts practice often centers on the creation of interactive narratives that explore the cultural ramifications of the contemporary proliferation of interconnected data. His artwork, performances, and multimedia installations have been shown throughout the world at festivals, conferences, and galleries, including the Beall Center for Arts+Technology in Irvine, California, the eARTS new media festival in Shanghai, China, and the National Academy of Sciences in Washington, DC. Angus is also the chair of the IEEE VIS Arts Program, a forum created to explore relationships between arts practice, design methodologies, and visualization research. He was recently appointed in the Leonardo Editorial Board and will edit a series of special sections of Leonardo, the journal of the *International Society for the Arts, Sciences and Technology* in 2015. Author's website: http://angusforbes.com

Mark Guglielmetti currently lectures in UX design in the Department of Design at Monash University. In his practice-led research, Mark critically examines new languages of digital media to create and design unnatural interfaces. Mark has presented and exhibited his research at numerous conferences and festivals including ACM Computers in Entertainment, ISEA, SIGGRAH Asia, and Ars Electronica.

Andrew Hieronymi's recent work focuses on the sensation of movement in digital games. He creates interactive installations emphasizing the physical relationship between player(s) and interface during the act of playing. He has talked and exhibited internationally in art venues and media festivals and is an assistant professor of New Media at the School of Visual Arts at Penn State University.

Jon McCormack is a research professor within the Faculty of Information Technology who has worked with computer code as a medium for creative expression for more than 25 years. He has held research positions at the University of Sussex, Goldsmiths, University of London, and the Ars Electronica Future Lab. He is currently director of Monash University's sensiLab, a transdisciplinary research center that bridges computing with other disciplines.

Luke Meeken is an artist, educator, and researcher with a B.F.A. from Carnegie Mellon University, and an M.A.E. in Art Education from Virginia Commonwealth University. His research interests include digital media and programming in art education, early childhood art education, and the relationship between art education and the development of empathy. Luke has developed and taught game-making, creative coding, and green-screen video courses for elementary and secondary learners, and has worked with students in Prague, Czech Republic, and Moscow, Russia. Luke is a founding member of Voke, an online platform for visualized art education research by emerging practitioners.

Dimitri Nieuwenhuizen (LUST). LUST is a multidisciplinary graphic design practice established in 1996 by Jeroen Barendse, Thomas Castro, and Dimitri Nieuwenhuizen, based in The Hague, Netherlands. LUST works in a broad spectrum of media including traditional print work and book design, abstract cartography and data visualizations, new media and interactive installations, and architectural graphics. Moreover, LUST is deeply interested in exploring new pathways for design at the cutting edge where new media and information technologies, architecture, and urban systems and graphic design overlap. This fascination led to establishing LUSTlab in the summer of 2010. LUSTlab is more than a new form of Research & Development. LUSTlab goes further than observing, inventing, and producing, by means of forming a platform where knowledge, issues, and ideologies can be shared. LUSTlab researches, generates hypotheses, and makes unstable media stable again. The future of digital media lies in the design of its use: humanizing the unhuman, bringing the internet down to earth, and finding the missing link between the digital and the physical. The outcomes vary from (strategic) visions to new communication tools, man–machine installations, and physical products using digital content.

Luiza Novaes is a designer working in the areas of collaborative design, inter-active media, and visual communication. She is a full-time assistant profes-sor and researcher in the graduate and undergraduate programs in Design at Pontifícia Universidade Católica do Rio de Janeiro – PUC-Rio, in Brazil. She has a Ph.D. in Design from PUC-Rio and an M.F.A. in Photography and Related Media from SVA – School of Visual Arts, New York, USA.

Nancy Paterson is associate professor at OCAD University in Toronto. She has been actively engaged with the internet since 1982 at UTZOO (University of Toronto) and since that early date she has utilized the internet in many media projects. Her background in interactive net art and media art design led to academic research in protocols and policy. Her projects can be found at: www.vacuumwoman.com and academic papers at: http://papers.ssrn. com/sol3/cf_dev/AbsByAuth.cfm?per_id=2016282

Dr. Ryan M. Patton is an assistant professor of Art Education at Virginia Commonwealth University. Dr. Patton taught high school art in the South Bronx and animation and game design with the Smithsonian Summer Associates. As part of his research in new media art education, Dr. Patton cocreated an augmented reality game called CitySneak which explores dis-rupting conventions of public space and surveillance with mobile devices. Patton also designed and produced a set of modular electronic switches intended for youth to design video game controllers. His academic writ-ing has appeared in several publications including *Studies in Art Education*, *Journal of Social Theory in Art Education*, and *Visual Arts Research*. Dr. Patton's current research interests include technology in art education, new media art, games-based pedagogy, physical computing, big data & data visualization, visual culture, socially engaged art practices, and urban education.

Daniel Sauter is an artist who creates installations and visualizations deal-ing with the cultural and social implications of emerging technologies. His research is driven by a curiosity about how the computational regime transforms geopolitics, urban spaces, and the human body. Daniel is an Associate Professor in the School of Art, Media, and Technology at Parsons

School of Design, and Co-Director of the the New School's Integrative Ph.D. Fellowship Program.

Jinsil Hwaryoung Seo is an interactive artist/researcher focusing on aesthetics of interactive experience. Currently she is an assistant professor in the Department of Visualization at the College of Architecture and a faculty fellow in the Center for Health Systems & Design at Texas A&M University. Seo received a Ph.D. in Interactive Art and Technology from Simon Fraser University in Canada and an M.F.A. in Computer Arts from School of Visual Arts (SVA). With interdisciplinary, interactive art practice, Seo investigates the intersection between body, nature, and technology. Seo has been fascinated by the aesthetic qualities of human experience, the relationships that emerge through interactions within artworks, and the underlying beauty and pattern inherent in nature. Her current research concentrates on designing for tangible and kinetic aesthetics in the contexts of performance, child development, and health. Seo has chosen interactive art for her creative practice and research in particular as it encourages immersive and embodied relationship within a work of art.

Scott Snibbe is a pioneering digital artist and entrepreneur whose work includes apps, video, and interactive installations. His art is in the permanent collections of the Whitney Museum of American Art and the Museum of Modern Art (MoMA), which in 2014 acquired his collaboration with Björk, the Biophilia App Album, as the first app in its collection. His work has been incorporated into concert tours, Olympics, museums, airports, and other major public spaces and events, and he has collaborated on interactive projects with musicians and filmmakers including Philip Glass, Beck, and James Cameron. He has received the Webby and Ars Electronica awards, and grants from the National Science Foundation, the Ford Foundation, the National Endowment for the Arts, and the Rockefeller Foundation. Snibbe currently serves as CEO of social music video startup Eyegroove, and has founded several other startups since 2000. In the 1990s, Snibbe was a staff researcher at Interval Research, performing basic research in haptics, computer vision, and interactive cinema; and was one of the codevelopers of the digital compositing software After Effects, acquired by Adobe Systems. He has held teaching and research positions at NYU's Courant Institute of Mathematics, The San Francisco Art Institute, California Institute of the Arts, and U.C. Berkeley. Snibbe currently serves as an advisor to The Institute for the Future and the Sundance Institute. He has published numerous articles and academic papers, is an inventor on more than 20 patents, and a regular worldwide public speaker.

Orkan Telhan is interdisciplinary artist, designer, and researcher whose investigations focus on the design of interrogative objects, interfaces, and media, engaging with critical issues in social, cultural, and environmental responsibility. Telhan is assistant professor of Fine Arts – Emerging Design Practices at University of Pennsylvania, School of Design. He holds a Ph.D. in Design and Computation from MIT's Department of Architecture. He was part of the Sociable Media Group at the MIT Media Laboratory and the Mobile Experience Lab at the MIT Design Laboratory. He studied Media Arts at the State University of New York at Buffalo and theories of media and representation, visual studies, and graphic design at Bilkent University, Ankara. Telhan's individual and collaborative work has been exhibited in venues including the 13th Istanbul Biennial, 1st Istanbul Design Biennial, Ars Electronica, ISEA, LABoral, Archilab, Architectural Association, the Architectural League of New York, MIT Museum, Museum of Contemporary Art Detroit, and the New Museum of Contemporary Art, New York.

Brad Tober is assistant professor of design and visual analytics at Boston University, and is a designer, educator, and researcher whose work explores the potential of emerging code-based and interactive visual communication technologies, with the objective of developing applications of them to design practice and pedagogy. His practice-led research entity, the Experimental Interface Lab, is characterized by a speculative approach to design (a manifestation of pure research) that recognizes that forms of and methodologies for contemporary practice that span design and technology are best developed through fundamentally flexible and exploratory processes. Brad holds an M.Des. from York University, a B.F.A. in graphic design from the Savannah College of Art and Design, and a B.A. in mathematics from the University at Buffalo.

Adam Trowbridge [Channel TWo] is currently an assistant professor in the College of Computing and Digital Media, School of Design, DePaul University, Chicago, IL. He is currently researching cybersecurity design, biobehavioral interface design, mobile health, programming pedagogy for designers, and geolocated augmented reality. He received an M.F.A. in Electronic Visualization from the University of Illinois at Chicago, Chicago, IL (2008) and a B.F.A. in Art (sculpture and painting) from the University of Central Florida, Orlando, FL (1996).

Jessica Westbrook [Channel TWo] is currently an associate professor in the College of Computing and Digital Media, School of Design, DePaul

University, Chicago, IL. She teaches research and studio courses in graphic, interaction, and game design. Westbrook uses design to negotiate and organize the joys and struggles of information and understanding. Her research involves visual and language systems, complexity, and contradictions. She received an M.F.A. in photography from Temple University, Tyler School of Art, Philadelphia, PA (1998) and a B.F.A. in art (photography) from the University of Central Florida, Orlando, FL (1996).

Acknowledgments

We would like to acknowledge and thank the Institute for the Study of Teaching and Learning in the Disciplines (ISTLD) at Simon Fraser University for five years of generous grants and support for our research into new pedagogies which we have applied in the School of Interactive Arts and Technology (SIAT). This has been a vital base for our publications and presentations in the theories and methods of teaching interactive media and design.

We wish to thank Monash University and in particular Professor Darrell Evans and Adrian Devey supporting the *Creative Coding* MOOC. We would also like to thank Professor Maria Garcia de la Banda, Meghan Deacon, and Linda Kalejs for their generous assistance during the development phase of the project. Finally, we would like to express our deep appreciation to Dr. Indae Hwang for his input and collaboration on the MOOC.

We would like to thank the editors of this volume for their extensive and incisive feedback.

We acknowledge TOP (Tier One Program) grant at Texas A&M University, Tiffany Sanchez, research assistant, Visualization Department at College of Architecture, and Dance Program in Department of Health and Kinesiology at College of Education and Human Development.

Introduction:
Pedagogies at the Intersection of Disciplines

VERONIKA TZANKOVA AND
MICHAEL FILIMOWICZ

Practice-based educators in the fields of interactive media and computational design are rarely challenged to reflect on their teaching pedagogies and students' learning within an academic, rather than institutional, context. The common formats within which artistic work and design creations gain conceptual and discursive dimensions are artist and curatorial statements, grant proposals, forum and blog posts, or articles produced as academic practice-based research. Where the foci of such writing are necessarily set on the productions themselves, pragmatic or aesthetic concerns, theory building, engaging the general community, or audience communication among others, teaching practices are not often of professional interest with respect to publication and research activity. On rare occasions, practice-based education and studio teaching have been studied philosophically or ethnographically by a handful of scholars such as Donald Schön (1983) or Nigel Cross (2006). However, the kinds of tacit and discursive learning essential to new media and design processes have yet to be comprehensively discussed in light of reflection on current pedagogies. The present anthology addresses this gap in the literature by initiating a new scholarly discussion in the fields of computational creativity.

Today's creators of interactive media "switch hardware and software tools like colors of paint."[1] As fascinating as such fast "switches" are, they also pose fundamental pedagogical and practical problems in tertiary education. How do we design effective inter-, multi-, cross-, and transdisciplinary pedagogy and curricula? In this volume, we bring together essays on pedagogies that produce the so-called *unicorns* – graduates who can code *and* create. Here, the intertwining of (what many consider mutually exclusive) expressive sensitivities and computational skills plays an essential role

---

[1] To cite an interview with Matt Cottam in Joshua J. Noble's *Programming Interactivity*, 2nd edn. (Beijing; Sebastopol, CA: O'Reilly, 2012).

in media and design education. This calls forth a new kind of undergraduate curriculum which adds to the already existing pedagogical challenges such as (1) maintaining a balance between breadth and depth of skills and knowledge; (2) developing fluency in coding along with advanced technological creativity; and (3) establishing the role of logic and numeracy in visually dominated media.

A multiplicity of technical skillsets – animation, graphic design, electronics, computer vision, web development, sound design, 3D printing, and algorithmic thinking among many others – contributes to an equally diverse set of professional fields, such as user experience design, virtual worlds, web applications, project management, creative directing practices, game programming, storytelling, industrial design, communication design, and beyond. This rich combination of skillsets and possible roles is profoundly cross-pollinating and thus triggers continuous shifts in professional contexts. Within this contextual framework, this anthology asks: what does it mean to teach students for computational creativity?

Almost all of the current publications in the subject area of "creative coding" feature showcases and compendiums of art and design works integrating computational or "new media" processes. However, finding texts that address pedagogy, curriculum, and educators' professional development in the richly diverse fields of computation and creative making is challenging, because teaching and learning are considered to be marginal to the prevailing discourses. In our courses, we have faced this problem on numerous occasions. Whether in the process of applying for teaching grants, or in moments of need for sources in the literature that explore relevant teaching practices, or during office hours when students come with the simple question "What should I do?," we have come to realize the scarcity of works that deal with the pedagogies of computational media and design from practical and interdisciplinary perspectives. Thus, the purpose of *Teaching Computational Creativity* is to identify specific conceptual frameworks, lines of inquiry, methods and strategies for teaching and to

1. provide an opportunity for educators to reflect in an academic context on their teaching practices, as opposed to their research and creation interests more typical of academic publications.
2. support an answer to the question: how do we define and explicate areas intersected by a multitude of platforms that cut across design, media, fine art, and informatic practices?

An impetus that contributes to this gap in the literature is the increasing diversification of disciplines and their epistemes, key concepts, methodologies, and skillsets which combine in the new hybrid practices. Additionally, the barriers to nontechnical specialists have been substantially revised, and individuals with diverse scholarly backgrounds can play key roles on multidisciplinary teams, especially with regards to the setting of technical systems within human contexts. The history of usability could be said to have begun with Frederick Taylor's *Scientific Management* (1911), which introduced processes of rigorous measurement in the work setting, and later led to developments such as operations research – the forming of large interdisciplinary teams assembled for complex technological systems design during World War II – and evolved into a conception of "human–machine coupling." With the growing integration of computers in the workplace, these empirical approaches developed into human factors research and the elaboration of new cognitive and psychometric approaches in the disciplines of human–computer interaction (HCI). The idea of giving voice to the ordinary user in an everyday setting has a history dating back at least to the 1990s with researchers such as Jakob Nielsen (1995) who proposed 10 usability heuristics for user interface design. It was with the development of the World Wide Web that user studies began to integrate more qualitative and interpretive research designs grounded in ethnography or phenomenology, for instance. We can see that it is a relatively recent development that nontechnical specialists have been included as potentially integral to interactive media and design teams.

After suffering a series of failures and development of progressively user-unfriendly software products, Silicon Valley has come to realize the importance of the humanities as an input for innovation. As much as we need engineering or scientific knowledge to practically build new technologies, nontechnical and socially oriented thinking is vital to the creation of user-centered, sustainable, and future-envisioning interactive technologies. As one headline has it, " 'Useless' liberal arts degrees have become Tech's hottest ticket" (Anders, 2015), where the article goes on to explore how graduates from arts and humanities backgrounds have become a force for creative innovation in the tech sector of the economy. Whether from philosophy, theater, literature, history, or art backgrounds, nontechs working in the tech business "provide users with extra bits of surprise and delight" (Anders, 2015, para 2). Today the development of interactive technologies includes sociocultural dimensions which the so-called "third-wave" of HCI has termed "the phenomenological matrix" (Harrison, Tatar, and Sengers, 2007). Observing these powerful shifts, we are in a position to notice how domains previously reserved to computer scientists and engineers have opened up to prioritize innovation in the fullest range of human contexts.

This diversification of practice, however, comes at a certain price – such as deciding what media and design skills *not* to cover in the curriculum any longer – and involves a series of challenges which can be summed up in the question: what do we teach to whom, with which methods, and to what effect?

Despite the rapid growth of new media and design programs in recent years, there is no comprehensive exploration of the pedagogical aspects of the richly diverse fields of computation and creative making. These new interdisciplinary programs often face definitional issues, strategically piecing together unique school names such as "interactive arts and technology"[2] or "design media arts,"[3] or perhaps distinguishing units such as "film, video, new media, and animation" from "art and technology" or "architecture, interior architecture, and designed objects"[4] in the same institution. These disciplinary separations, however, sometimes provoke forum questions such as "What is the difference between Carnegie Mellon University's Interaction Design and HCI Master's degrees?"[5] Scott Snibbe, one of the creators of Adobe's 2D animation and visual effects software, After Effects, addresses the disappearance of clear-cut boundaries in the following terms:

> If one's job can be clearly defined, then it's likely it can be immediately outsourced to Pakistan or India via oDesk, eLance, etc. To be a first world creative worker, one needs to be a synthesizer of information and fields. I read this great blog post by AJ Kessler, that was titled "If You Can Easily Describe What You Do, You're Fucked." He said, "The people that will thrive are the ones who can figure out what needs to be done next and why." So, it's good that you can't explain the meaning of your program – you're on the right track to creating people who can think on the fly and fill holes that don't exist yet.

Technological developments and intersections proceed at a pace indifferent to academic curricula or administrative unit names. As Ray Kurzweil (2011) has famously noted, our intuitions are local and linear but technology moves at an exponential rate and on a global scale. To address these complexities through the lens of pedagogy, this anthology engages with the

---

[2] Simon Fraser University.
[3] UCLA.
[4] School of the Art Institute of Chicago.
[5] www.quora.com/What-is-the-difference-between-CMUs-Interaction-Design-and-HCI-Masters-degrees

definitional problems of the field, and the complex interactions generated by the abundance of platforms and their interrelations.

Existing scholarship has conceptualized various aspects of interactive media and design's theoretical and practical foundations ranging from simple applications, processes, codes, and technical specifications to social impacts, working practices, and expressive potentialities (see, e.g., Bogost, 2007; Kwastek, 2013; Miller, 2008; Reas and Fry, 2007). In addition to the relatively obvious practical production skillsets, interactive technologies are also exemplary in relation to art and visualization practices (see Ferster, 2013; Popper, 2007). There are often clear scholastic divides in the management of digital cross-pollination. In the scarcity of works that deal with the pedagogy of interactive technologies, we can sense a strong separation between perspectives of: (1) technicality as expressed in computation, coding practices, and hardware configuration on one side and (2) digital humanities represented by a theoretical rhetoric "distant and apart from the work people have done and are doing" (Keramidas, 2012, para 2). This collection challenges these divides in the way that all applied practical activity – in this case, teaching – undermines detached theoretic positions which "battle" each other on abstract planes of mere argument. We can note, from our more integrative stance, that both digital humanities and HCI are currently articulated as being in their "third waves" (Berry, 2011; Bødker, 2015). Perhaps, a fourth wave will soon emerge which dispenses with the current divisions between human interpretations (digital humanities) and uses (HCI).

The authors here defy Charles Percy Snow's classic distinction between the "two cultures," or the culture of technoscience and the culture of the humanities. This hallowed division is to a great extent still instituted in the organization of our universities into faculties that segregate the study of literature and art from the study of science and engineering, for instance. Yet the worlds of interactive media and design combine elements of both cultures intimately and inextricably. The design of apps or interfaces for devices such as smartphones can itself be an interface between aesthetic considerations, narrative design, and computer code. Given the hybridity of practices involved in computational media and design, today's creators need to be as "agile" in their thinking as in their software development. Creative computation calls for participation in what has variously been called "the third culture" (Brockman, 1995), or what Buchanan called "a new liberal art of technological culture" or an "epistemology of design" (Loh, Chai, Wong, and Hong, 2015, p. 2) based on abductive reasoning that is distinct from the methodologies and ways of thinking in the arts and sciences (Cross, 2001). Karl Popper's notion of "World 3" (1978, p. 144) is also relevant:

> By world 3 I mean the world of the products of the human mind, such as languages; tales and stories and religious myths; scientific conjectures or theories, and mathematical constructions; songs and symphonies; paintings and sculptures. But also aeroplanes and airports and other feats of engineering.

Computational creativity does not cross disciplines merely for the sake of it, but because these hybrid practices require "the ability to synthesize knowledge from a variety of sources" (Loh et al., 2015, p. 3) and thus are perhaps better understood as transdisciplinary rather than interdisciplinary. In the disciplinary model proposed by Moore and Lottridge (2010), (1) *multidisciplinarity* is the coming together of multiple disciplines around a common problem, remaining intact, autonomous, and eventually "going their separate ways"; (2) *interdisciplinarity* is two or more disciplines coming together to forge a new discipline, as in biology and chemistry forming the field of biochemistry, or mechatronics, which is an interdiscipline formed out of electrical, mechanical, and software engineering; and (3) *transdisciplinarity* is the coming together of multiple disciplines to define a new generative context for the production of new problems and knowledge. It is clear from the chapters gathered here that the curricular space being explored and defined is this third model of "generative transdisciplinarity" which Moore and Lottridge define as "dynamic, flexible, transient, generative, reflexive and social" (p. 2738), and thus "transdisciplinary" is also the name of our last part of this book.

Moore and Lottridge argue that in the university setting, with its departmental formations around disciplinary lines and its career reward systems based on traditions that define what counts as legitimacy in knowledge production, transdisciplinarity proves the most challenging to institute while at the same time promising the greatest possibilities for innovation. They take up several brief case studies that link to the notion of 3rd Wave HCI as examples of new innovative research that has as one of its institutional features the contribution of humanities and social science lenses brought to bear on the development of new technologies. In their view, disciplined transdisciplinarity fundamentally involves collaboration and teamwork. Also, these new transdisciplinary academic units have to institutionally and professionally negotiate the validity of their research methods and perspectives relative to the more traditional disciplines.

Additionally, the chapters transgress the division between high and low culture that separates "art" from useful everyday objects. The creative intuitions and skills involved in artistic activity are also required in the design of our networked material environment today. The academic specialties that treat the different aspects of interactive media and design must come together in the mind and practice of the student. They are not assimilated into a single discipline but become differentiated resources at the command of skilled creators or teams who are proficient in coding skills as a new overlay onto the traditional requirements of art, media, design, and informatic knowledge. The relations between disciplines in the new practical work take the form of new connections between different levels of the object or system. For example, the designer has an aesthetic or practical intuition (or both) which must function as lines of code in a program, go through design process stages of variation, revision, iteration, and testing, and ultimately be instantiated in a robust artifact either as a working prototype or finished piece of technology operating in real environments which are also human contexts and subject to differing interpretations and uses. Constant conceptual movement oscillating across the boundaries between disciplines is required, integrated with the acts of making.

All of the chapters presented engage with the pedagogical techniques and principles for acclimating students to these diverse domains of knowledge and skills that can be described as neither science nor art, neither high nor low, neither culture nor commerce, but potentially mixing all at any time. This new organization of technical and cultural production at this point in its development needs a firmer conceptualization of its pedagogical practices, which is the need that this volume addresses.

Teaching Computational Creativity includes international contributions from educator–practitioners who are developing a new "scholarship of teaching and learning" (SoTL) in the fields of code-based media and design. Rather than attempt only a general framework for conceptualizing today's skillset demands[6] or "competencies"[7] to use the contemporary parlance, this collection incorporates and interconnects a mix of practical and theoretical perspectives and approaches to provide a multidimensional understanding of what matters for the disciplinary complexity of today's computational media and design curricula. We have aimed to reflect the diversity in contemporary teaching practices rather than create an artificial

---

[6] For example, narrowly defined professional training based on notions of current industry demands or "hot" labor market skills.

[7] http://edglossary.org/competency-based-learning/

sense of particular "schools of thought" somehow more or less dominant or important across differing contexts. Despite this diversity in perspectives, the collection is far from "eclectic" as the reader will note many recurring themes throughout the chapters which create a surprising sense of unity given the range of topics and technologies broached, enough unity in fact to allow us to propose a curricular synthesis in the Afterword.

As educators, our motive for developing *Teaching Computational Creativity* is pedagogic, as we teach courses on code-based design, audio-visual production and postproduction, installation, performance, narrative, media and cultural theory, information design and communication design among others. To date, no book-length academic works have discussed and analyzed the problems of pedagogy within this "multi-field" in ways that are comprehensive, practical, holistic, and directly transferable to the classroom. There are no established models for unifying curricular concepts across the involved disciplines. Thus, this anthology seeks to provide practical guidelines to educators in the disciplines of computational media and design, and to initiate new and relevant discussions. Accordingly, the anthology contains six parts, each of which explores a significant pedagogical theme acknowledging not only the heterogeneity of the fields but also many teaching and learning perspectives accompanying creative coding and computational media. Following the chapters, we present interviews with noted artists and designers who have significant professional practices and who provide an opportunity to step out of academia into the industry and contemporary studio practice as a position from which to reflect back into the educational context.

NEW FOUNDATIONS

Computational media have no distinct point of origin and as such merge within themselves a plethora of perspectives, skills, and paradigms. As much as the fields of creative coding, design, and interactive media have benefited from nontechnical, socially oriented knowledge, computational skills have now become foundational in art education. Joining the traditional notions of "2D, 3D and 4D" as a requisite skillset for any creative field, programming knowledge is beginning to be considered as a form of literacy necessary for contemporary societies and creative practice. Coding theory now joins graphic design, photography, and even art history (e.g., in the form of computer art history) as an essential formal grounding for new practitioners. Procedural logic and numeracy, traditionally not emphasized in studio education, take on new roles as in the visual modeling of organic motion and other natural phenomena in Processing, a popular coding environment used in art and design pedagogy (Greenberg, 2007, pp. xxii–xxiii).

In the first chapter, Ryan M. Patton and Luke Meeken survey the introduction of preservice art educators to programmable media, where programmable media is defined as both an expressive art form and a curricular tool. The authors present a curriculum that frames digital art and interactive design concepts through image manipulation, web design, video production, game design, and physical computing assignments. The implementation of metaphorical processes from traditional media practice inflects art education students' ability to make conceptual linkages between game design mechanics and nondigital artworks. Patton and Meeken make recommendations for curricular and policy changes to the teaching of technology in K-12 classrooms and in teacher preparation programs, providing a roadmap for the multiplicity of technological platforms used in new media art education.

Introducing coding is further discussed in Chapter 2, where Andrew Hieronymi provides a first-person case-study account. Hieronymi investigates the learning dynamics that take place during the creation of expressive interactive experiences such as digital games, interfaces, art installations, and mobile applications. Despite students' passion for interactive media, they are often intimidated by the steep learning curve of acquiring programming literacy. In his chapter, Hieronymi describes the methods he implements to assist students in overcoming these challenges and supports his strategies by looking at the work of three of his students.

CODE AS MEDIUM

Code is a text, but of a specific kind – a text that produces causal chains in machines rather than intertextual effects of encultured associations. Ina Greenberg humorously notes that "When I tell people I write code as my main artistic medium, they smile politely and quickly change the subject" (2007, p. xxii). Greenberg's observation suggests that the interpretive traditions associated with the "text" propagated by literary studies have missed code as a medium of creativity and artistic expression.

Chapter 3, written by Channel TWo, conceptualizes code as an organic medium of a pervasive, invisible material that drives our contemporary-mediated environment. From the electricity flowing through landscapes, to the models of environmental collapse, code is pervasive in our realities and is no longer marginal to mainstream art worlds, or to popular media such as cinema and games. Channel TWo argue that despite some students' resistances to coding, contemporary art and design practices cannot dispense with it, and discuss their teaching of "slow coding" as an instructional strategy.

In Chapter 4, Brad Tober examines another critical aspect of treating code as a medium – the democratization of design production. He argues that at the forefront of this phenomenon stands the contemporary maker movement which promises to extend the means of code-based fabrication to nearly everyone. Such democratization however prompts a questioning of the role of those who had previously (and exclusively) engaged in design production. If nondesigners enter the design sphere, then what are the new roles for professional designers? Tober's chapter positions an argument for developing design curricula that are "entirely code-based." Code-relevant principles and activities inform the entirety of the design processes students are exposed to. Design and code share core structural features that enable the use of code as a medium for both teaching and executing design.

PHYSICAL{LY} COMPUTING

Contrary to the widespread beliefs in the "immateriality" of the digital, practitioners are well aware of its materiality and regularly exploit it, whether in the form of embodied performances or in the circuit-based analogs of the body, namely the hardware connecting sensors and actuators to microprocessors. Physical computing presents a somatic and even visceral dimension to a medium that is generally conceptualized as lacking in physical properties, being entirely informatic in an almost disembodied sense (for a detailed discussion, see, e.g., Sanchez-Vives and Slater, 2005). Recognizing the somatic potential of computing subverts the definitional hold of "computation" as a sequence of calculative, logical, and generally mathematical procedures. Understanding this physical dimension initiates attentiveness not only to the embodied conditions of human users, but also to dispositions in relation to our increasingly informatic material contexts.

The complex relationship between computing and situated bodies is the subject of Chapter 5. Luiza Novaes and Joao de Sa Bonelli present a teaching initiative of Interaction Design and Physical Computing that is currently under development at Pontifícia Universidade Católica do Rio de Janeiro in Brazil. The relationship between the theory of design and its practice is considered in light of the seminal works of Donald Schön, Herbert Simon, and Nigel Cross. Today designers are not simply users of digital interactive systems, but are an integral part of interface development teams responsible for the mediation between computer systems and their human users.

In Chapter 6, Jinsil Hwaryoung Seo and Christine Bergeron present a longitudinal interdisciplinary collaboration between the Visualization, Dance, and Computer Science Departments at Texas A&M University. The project has provided participating students with opportunities for engagement in art and technology communities, where the context of interactive performance promotes collaboration among faculty, undergraduate, and graduate students. The authors notice that students' collaborative work leads to the development of a common language and expression which both art and computing science majors can relate. They observe that through continuous and active collaboration, students can overcome the challenges presented by communicating with individuals from vastly different scholarly backgrounds.

ONLINE LEARNING

Recent economic, social, and technological developments have triggered the reconsideration of traditional educational formats and the institutions of knowledge. Small enrolment, face-to-face studio settings in the areas of computation, art, and design are often problematic for properly accommodating the needs of an increasingly mature – and often working – student population, where demographic shifts are leading to an increasing proportion of learners from nontraditional backgrounds, i.e., learners who are not right out of high school. Many see a solution to these emerging needs in the concept of "flexible learning" generally and online education in particular (see, e.g., Arfield, Hodgkinson, Smith, and Wade, 2013; McKeough, Lupart, and Marini, 2013). Massive open online courses (MOOCs) overturn traditional studio practices of small cohorts centered around a guru-mentor. As a kind of anti-studio, online learning invites experimentation with technology at global scale, unmentored and at one's own pace. Where MOOCs introduce a potent framework for supplying autonomy to individual students within a relatively deinstitutionalized learning environment, its specific practices, technologies, and content tools are still very much under development.

In Chapter 7, Michael Filimowicz pursues these problems by situating an autoethnographic exploration of popular online code learning platforms within frameworks from distributed and multimedia cognition. Filimowicz's approach instigates a rethinking of the lab component of undergraduate courses and also suggests new strategies for furthering the design of multimedia code learning content. What emerges from Filimowicz's analysis is the notion of a "three screen scene" which articulates the spatially distributed cognitive tasks of programming work space, note taking, and expanded context. The distributed local space of learning is conceptualized as its own design frame for the development of curricular content and learning experiences.

Since the introduction of MOOCs in 2011, online learning has been exponentially gaining momentum. Numerous platforms such as Coursera, EdX, FutureLearn, Kadenze and Udacity have enabled academic educators to develop and manage courses that often enroll vast numbers of learners ~43,000 on average (Ferenstein, 2014). These platforms provide a unique range of instruments to embed discipline knowledge and skills into the development of courses. In Chapter 8, Mark Guglielmetti and Jon McCormack examine their MOOC course, *Creative Coding*, which they created for the FutureLearn platform. They explore the historical contingencies through which algorithmic thinking and coding literacies are becoming ubiquitous across many cultural spheres of activity. The authors explore the "technical and cultural prism" that coding literacies are filtered through. These contingencies and literacies are manifested within the production process of the *Creative Coding* MOOC course.

CRITICAL PEDAGOGY

The concept of the "critical" has migrated from its traditional home in the humanities and liberal arts studies to scientific, technical, and design disciplines. Rather than attempting a succinct historical account of the notion of "critique," we would like to propose a dialectical model that connects with the role of the critical in creative production and design. We can say that "existing situations" – to borrow Herbert Simon's well-known term (1996) – are analogous to the "thesis" phase of dialectic, or the current state of affairs. Critique can be understood as a "negation" of the thesis or the antithesis; however, as a negation it is merely potential and abstract. To "negate the negation" and become synthesis – which ultimately is a new thesis that both completes one dialectic and begins another – the critique (as negation of the thesis or current state of affairs) needs to be integrated back into the concrete through a new material production, creating what Simon would call the "preferred situation." Critique challenges us to examine the underlying values and concepts of our engagement with both technologies and our students. Critical pedagogy articulates the broader issues surrounding computational media and design through consideration of the dense and complex historical, social, cultural, political, and technological networks we act within.

In Chapter 9, Nancy E. Paterson explores process-oriented and outcomes-based paradigms in media arts pedagogy. Where process-based approaches to education have been dominant since the early twentieth century, outcomes-oriented education has been ascendant in recent times with the new administrative regimes of performance metrics and the new focus on measuring learning goals. Patterson draws on Reinhold Niebuhr for a fuller conception of education's "outcome," namely active engaged citizenship in cyberspace. Patterson argues that project-based learning enables students to become agents of their own goals and learning agendas, since ICTs provide platforms for individually tailored interactive learning experiences and the contextualization of knowledge.

Daniel Sauter articulates a more technologically inflected and imaginative perspective on critical pedagogy in Chapter 10. Sauter explores how joining the citizenry of what he calls the "cognisphere" requires a "modified intellectual immune system" with the social and cultural competencies to resist forms of domination embedded in technical affordances – a form of "anthropotechnic autoimmunity." Sauter argues that a liberal arts education which provides coding and machine learning capacity alongside humanistic competency prepares students to perform daily Turing tests on automated systems that have the capacity to learn, evolve, and reflect on how humans are interpolated and disciplined by machine cognizers. Sauter emphasizes that the computational regime transgresses geopolitical sovereignty because it transcends governmental structures and systems of control. The variety of praxes discussed here examine computational thinking through scientific breakthroughs such as CRISPR, geopolitical jurisdiction exemplified in the case of Safe Harbor, and telematic control systems. He concludes that the social and cultural competencies of the humanities remain key to education, and must step up to the technological issues of our time.

TRANSDISCIPLINARY

As a coherent expression of a multidiscipline, curricula in computational creativity do not easily reduce to a small and clearly defined subset of disciplines brought together in the way that engineering, for example, can be said to be comprised of math, physics, and an assembly of other particular fields as needed for the production of a specific system.[8] Can computational creativity be defined as simply as informatics + science + art + design? Persistent reflection on pedagogies naturally broaches more encompassing

---

[8] Thanks are here expressed to Dr. John Dill, Professor Emeritus of SIAT, for this succinct definition of engineering.

questions around curricula, which is the total expression at the program level of what pedagogy is at the course level.

In Chapter 11, Orkan Telhan discusses ways in which pedagogy can be augmented and opened up to a broader understanding of design – design that can address and accommodate the challenges of contemporary times such as social inequality, environmental pollution, food scarcity, and climate change among others. Rather than reinforcing common professional paradigms used to educate the conventional professions such as product design, architecture, or graphic design, Telhan proposes a literacy-oriented pedagogy centered around knowledge acquisition, methods, and skills developed across different disciplines. Telhan argues that media production methods, computational thinking, and research-oriented learning are literacies that cannot be framed within a singular approach; instead, they have to be studied as foundational domains of knowledge that help designers orient their interests, find their own voices, and decide on their skill specialization.

In the final chapter, Angus G. Forbes discusses pedagogical experiments developed for a series of creative coding courses taught over the last 6 years and recently used in interdisciplinary classes at the Electronic Visualization Laboratory at University of Illinois at Chicago. Although all courses implement different materials, they are designed to provide students with the technical ability and creative opportunity to think critically about contemporary technology–culture intersections. Forbes brings awareness to the challenges of teaching interdisciplinary courses: students come from various backgrounds and have different interests, technical and creative proficiencies, and may or may not have experience or enthusiasm for working collaboratively. In addition to providing the motivations for particular pedagogical choices, Forbes provides specific, pragmatic classroom exercises that have sparked successful research activity and student portfolio projects.

Interviews and Afterword

We follow the chapters with interviews that provide a look back at pedagogy from the perspective of some leading interactive media and design practitioners. Scott Snibbe – an interactive media artist, researcher, and entrepreneur; Jussi Ängeslevä – a designer, artist, and educator; and Dimitri Nieuwenhuizen – a multidisciplinary artist and designer and principal of the firm LUST provide a bridge to contemporary professional practices. "Successful" design studios are often the focus of today's pragmatically minded and employment-oriented students, many of whom may be unaware of the deep connections between design practice and art exhibition as complementary forms of creative activity. Alternately, today's fine art students may not have in the foreground of their future plans the multifaceted ways that fine art disciplines can translate into "making a living," as their education tends to prepare them for working with curators or collaborators rather than clients. These interviews give a rich picture of the intersection of not just art, design, and computation, but also business and educational practices as expressed in three different career trajectories.

In the Afterword, we summarize and synthesize many of the themes in the preceding parts by proposing a high-level concept map that integrates the curricular constructs of Technical Domains, Discursive Skills, and Transdisciplinary Studio as a coherent scheme that integrates the competing and variegated demands of today's technologically saturated hybrid production practices.

Finally, the title of this volume is worth some comment and reflection. To some, the term "computational" may be too redolent of artificial intelligence and computer science discourses; perhaps a bit too "engineering" in tone as well. Wouldn't another term such as "interactive" make better sense? In our view, the terms "interactive media" and "interaction design" are components of a larger field of teaching and learning activity, which the scope of this collection makes clear. Moreover, important new developments such as 3D printing or additive manufacturing are not clearly "interactive" in the usual sense of the term as one's actual interaction may in fact be limited to downloading a file from the internet and clicking "print" on the software that comes with the device. Interactivity usually implies much more than this, whether in terms of the organization of system inputs and outputs, or a user's activities, agency, and experiences.

Another notion available to us is that of "creative coding." Similarly to the conceptual challenges with interaction, creative coding itself is but one of the many topics broached in this volume. The term "coding" is also somewhat reductive and tends to be associated either with Integrated Development Environments (IDEs) and text editors on one side or specific tools such as Processing – a programming language designed specifically for making coding accessible to art and design students – or OpenFrameworks which, as claimed on its website,[9] aims for a functional parity with Processing in C++ on the other. "Coding" has also come to be a contemporary shorthand in politicized media discourse around "skills gaps" in the labor force, or the need to roll out the so-called "coding curricula" in

---

[9] http://openframeworks.cc/

K-12 education as part of general economic development policy. Accounting for these distinct associations, we felt that the word "coding" would be too narrow a concept for the themes and ideas of this collection.

Similarly, we have settled on the term "creativity" rather than its more applied and commercial counterpart "innovation" to avoid purely market or industry-oriented implications. Through our title, we mean to invoke many ways in which computational thinking – code, recursion, conditions, algorithms, databases, procedural logic, modularity – has come to inflect current art, design, and media pedagogy and practices. Perhaps, it is time that the notion of the "computational" loses some of its overly ontological cast (the inner workings at the "gut" of the machine) and takes on more praxeological dimensions at the interface of the machine with us – the creative meaning making humans enmeshed in the informatic environments that have become our world.

REFERENCES

Anders, G. (2015, July 29). That "useless" liberal arts degree has become tech's hottest ticket. *Forbes*. Retrieved from www.forbes.com/sites/georgeanders/2015/07/29/liberal-arts-degree-tech/#3ade8b335a75. Accessed online March 3, 2016.

Arfield, J., Hodgkinson, K., Smith, A., and Wade, W. (2013). *Flexible learning in higher education*. London: Routledge.

Berry, D.M. (2011). The Computational Turn: Thinking about the digital humanities. *Culture Machine* 12, n.p. Retrieved from www.culturemachine.net/index.php/cm/issue/view/23. Accessed online March 3, 2016.

Bødker, S. (2015) Third-wave HCI, 10 years later – participation and sharing. *Interactions* 22(5), 24–31. DOI: http://dx.doi.org/10.1145/2804405 Retrieved from http://interactions.acm.org/archive/view/september-october-2015/third-wave-hci-10-years-later-participation-and-sharing. Accessed online March 3, 2016.

Bogost, I. (2007). *Persuasive games: The expressive power of videogames*. Cambridge, MA: MIT Press.

Brockman, J. (1995). *Third culture: Beyond the scientific revolution*. New York: Simon & Schuster.

Cross, N. (2001). Design cognition: Results from protocol and other empirical studies of design activity. In C.M. Eastman, W.M. McCracken, and W.C. Newstetter (Eds.), *Design knowing and learning: Cognition in design education*. Oxford, England: Elsevier.

(2006). *Designerly ways of knowing*. London: Springer.

Ferenstein, G. (2014, March 3). Study: Massive online courses enroll an average of 43,000 students, 10% completion. *Techcrunch*. Retrieved from http://techcrunch.com/2014/03/03/study-massive-online-courses-enroll-an-average-of-43000-students-10-completion/. Accessed online March 3, 2016.

Ferster, B. (2013). *Interactive visualization: Insight through inquiry*. Cambridge, MA: MIT Press.

Greenberg, I. (2007). *Processing: Creative coding and computational art.* Berkeley, CA; New York: Friends of Ed. Distributed to the book trade worldwide by Springer-Verlag.

Harrison, S., Tatar, D., and Sengers, P. (2007). The three paradigms of HCI. *Proceedings of the conference on human factors in computing systems* (CHI 2007). San Jose, CA, 1–18.

Keramidas, K. (2012). The DML and the digital humanities. *Journal of Interactive Technology & Pedagogy* (2). Retrieved from http://jitp.commons.gc.cuny.edu/afterword-the-dml-and-the-digital-humanities/. Accessed online March 3, 2016.

Kurzweil, R. (2011). The law of accelerating returns. Retrieved from http://bigthink.com/in-their-own-words/the-difference-between-linear-and-exponential-thinking. Accessed online March 3, 2016.

Kwastek, K. (2013). *Aesthetics of interaction in digital art.* Cambridge, MA: MIT Press.

Loh, H.L.K., Chai, C.S., Wong, B., and Hong, H.Y. (2015). *Design thinking for education: Conceptions and applications in teaching and learning.* Singapore: Springer ebook.

McKeough, A., Lupart, J.L., and Marini, A. (Eds.) (2013). *Teaching for transfer: Fostering generalization in learning.* London: Routledge.

Miller, C.H. (2008). *Digital storytelling: A creator's guide to interactive entertainment* (2nd edn.). Amsterdam; Boston, MA: Focal Press.

Moore, G. and Lottridge, D. (2010). Interaction design in the university designing disciplinary interactions. *Proceedings of the conference on human factors in computing systems (CHI 2010)*, Atlanta, GA, 2735–43. Retrieved from https://tspace.library.utoronto.ca/bitstream/1807/24390/1/p2735.pdf

Nielsen, J. (1995, January 1). 10 Usability heuristics for user interface design. Nielsen Norman Group. Retrieved from www.nngroup.com/articles/ten-usability-heuristics/. Accessed online March 3, 2016.

Noble, J.J. (2012). *Programming interactivity* (2nd edn.). Beijing; Sebastopol, CA: O'Reilly.

Popper, F. (2007). *From technological to virtual art.* Cambridge, MA: MIT Press.

Popper, K. Three worlds. The Tanner lecture on human values. Delivered at the University of Michigan April 17, 1978. Retrieved from http://tannerlectures.utah.edu/_documents/a-to-z/p/popper80.pdf. Accessed online March 3, 2016.

Reas, C. and Fry, B. (2007). *Processing: A programming handbook for visual designers and artists.* Cambridge, MA: MIT Press.

Sanchez-Vives, M.V. and Slater, M. (2005). Opinion: From presence to consciousness through virtual reality. *Nature Reviews Neuroscience*, 6(4), 332–9. Retrieved from http://doi.org/10.1038/nrn1651. Accessed online March 3, 2016.

Schön, D.A. (1983). *The reflective practitioner: How professionals think in action.* New York: Basic Books.

Simon, H. (1996). *The sciences of the artificial* (3rd edn.). Cambridge, MA: MIT Press.

PART I

NEW FOUNDATIONS

1

Staying Current: Developing Digital Literacies for the Creative Classroom

RYAN M. PATTON AND
LUKE MEEKEN

Abstract: The majority of art educators come from a non-digital art background, possessing knowledge of art processes in ceramics, darkroom photography, and painting, but having limited experience in new media art – particularly using computer code as an expressive medium. The authors of this chapter address the challenge of introducing preservice art educators to programmable media by defining it as both an expressive artform and a curricular tool through a digital art education curriculum. Such a curriculum frames digital art and interactive design concepts through image manipulation, web design, video production, game design, and physical computing assignments. Borrowing metaphorical language from traditional media practice becomes essential to art education students' building conceptual links between formal game design mechanics and non-digital artworks. In conclusion, the authors make recommendations for curricular and policy changes to the teaching of technology in K-12 classrooms and art teacher preparation, providing a roadmap for 1,000 technological platforms of new media art education.

Keywords: K-12 art education, interactive multimedia programming, game design, physical computing, bricolage, preservice art education, culture jamming, guerrilla communication

INTRODUCTION

Many art teachers and students in compulsory education engage daily with digital systems – from the operating systems of their smartphones, to the social networks that frame their relationships, to the proprietary systems for entering and monitoring students' grades. However, the opacity of these digital systems often makes it difficult for individuals to understand how these systems operate and how they are designed (Rushkoff, 2010), which can make it difficult for school teachers and students to recognize the digital as an art medium with potential creative uses rather than simply a set of tools for representing received knowledge (Hokanson and Hooper, 2000). The majority of university students preparing to become K-12 art teachers in our courses are from non-digital art backgrounds, possessing knowledge of art processes such as ceramics, darkroom photography, and painting, but with limited experience in new media art – particularly using computer code as an expressive medium. These trends are exacerbated within a predominantly female profession when one takes into account the problematic and alienating gender representations endemic in digital media such as video games (Williams, Martins, Consalvo, and Ivory, 2009), the significant gender disparity in the computer science and game design fields that produce and market popular digital media (Hill, Corbett, and Rose, 2013; Miller, 2013), as well as underrepresentation of women in university-level new media arts courses (Garber, Sandell, Stankiewicz, and Risner, 2007). Self-reported data from our undergraduate student population shows preservice art educators abstaining from digital activities like playing video games – a pervasively preferred activity by the K-12 students they will teach.

To address the expressive and digital media-literacy needs of twenty-first century K-12 art students, this chapter argues that today's compulsory art education should introduce K-12 students to new media art and digital art practices – and that, in turn, postsecondary art education programs should introduce preservice teachers to critical and contemporary new media practices. Recent initiatives of teaching K-12 students computational thinking and the connections between science, technology, engineering, art, and math (STEAM) may require art educators to quickly expand their digital knowledge base to match – let alone surpass – these educational technology initiatives (US Congress, 2015). Parents, students, teachers, and principals see a demand for K-12 students' learning more advanced computer skills; however, school districts prioritize subjects with required standardized testing and also often lack funds or teachers to teach computer science-related courses (Google & Gallup, 2015). University students working toward their K-12 art education certification are usually required to take one technology course; either a course in instructional technology, a digital studio, or a course that speaks to both studio practice and instructional technology (Patton and Buffington, 2016). Similar to art teachers already working in compulsory education, most preservice art educators do not include new media art in their personal artistic practice and are unfamiliar with established new media art and artists. We believe this presents an opportunity for a new generation of art teachers going into K-12 schools to address some of the technological gaps found in schools by providing instruction in the new media arts.

In this chapter, we discuss the development and execution of an undergraduate university course for preservice art educators, which was designed to address these challenges. In our university's program, preservice art educators must take a Technology in Art Education course at the beginning stages of their art education degree where they are also concurrently learning how to write lesson plans while having their first experience instructing K-12 students. In our undergraduate program, preservice art educators taking the Technology in Art Education course typically still have more than two upcoming years of studio, art history, general education, and art education courses before they complete a student teaching residency in K-12 schools. By offering this technology course early in the art education degree sequence, students are able to apply what they learn in subsequent art education experiences – for instance, including new media in curricula created in their curriculum development courses, or including new media projects in their practicum lessons. In this chapter, we also address the challenge of introducing undergraduate preservice art educators to programmable digital media by defining it as both an expressive artform and a curricular tool. We detail the impact of digital art education course design which scaffolds learning for preservice art teachers, building upon the preservice educators' prior knowledge of art content and practice with a variety of digital new media art skills and concepts over the course of a semester (Ninio and Bruner, 1978; Piaget, 1962; Vygotsky, 1977).

The design for this course framed digital art and interactive design concepts through image manipulation, web design, video production, game design, and physical computing assignments. Such praxis includes metaphorical language borrowed from traditional art media practice to encourage preservice art educators to draw conceptual and formal links between new media and non-digital artworks. Students also engaged in peer-teaching through skillshares, and instructing middle-school students at an after-school technology club. We conclude our discussion with a reflection on the impact of the course on the pedagogical practices and experiences of both the preservice art teachers who completed it, and upon the authors themselves in the years since first developing and teaching the course. This impact is discussed both in terms of measurable qualitative self-reported data collected from the preservice teachers, and anecdotal accounts of the professional practices of alumni of the course who have since become art educators.

DEVELOPING THE SYLLABUS – FUTURE PROOFING THE COURSE

In 2012, the National Coalition for Core Arts Standards taskforce published a position paper supporting the inclusion of media arts instruction (e.g., animation, video games, virtual design) in schools across the country through the next generation of arts standards (National Coalition for Core Arts Standards, 2012). However, the media standards resulting in 2014 have neither been enforced by the US Department of Education nor been linked to specific K-12 teaching requirements or teaching licensure (Patton and Buffington, 2016). Thus, this media arts education policy has been developed without a mechanism for its implementation. For the course we describe in this chapter, we were mindful of the ways media arts can be taught from a visual arts perspective.

In K-12 art education, students working in traditional media are regularly introduced to technical concepts and practices that contribute to their skills related to understanding and critically referring to a variety of media. Detailed records of the forms of visual art instruction provided in K-12 schools across the United States are not readily available; however, the state of Ohio provides the most detailed descriptions of its statewide offerings in their 2013 report, *The Status of Arts Education in Ohio's Public Schools* (Ohio Alliance for Arts Education, Ohio Arts Council, & Ohio Department of Education, 2013). The report notes that general visual arts courses, followed by drawing, painting, ceramics, and photography, are the most common forms of visual art taught in schools. Darkroom photography – a medium that has lost significant market share in the photography business – is still found in high schools across the United States (Dern, 2014). From our experience as art educators, this data is representative of what we have seen in classrooms ourselves. K-12 art students learn the technical knowledge to fire ceramics, develop photographs chemically, and create structurally sound sculptures, as well as learn how to leverage this technical knowledge in their critical evaluation and interrogation of artworks. Students at all levels use smartphone apps, social media, or video games in their daily lives, yet they are not taught the skills to critically interrogate how the source code behind these programs supports their interactions, nor how the intentions or biases of the code's author(s) shape the interaction (Jenkins, Clinton, Purushotma, Robison, and Weigel, 2009). Traditional forms of technical and critical knowledge are living in the art classroom, but are these the only forms of technical and critical knowledge necessary for a twenty-first century artist or art educator?

Media and technology theorist Doug Rushkoff (2010) warned that the ways we traditionally teach and use technologies in the classroom (including the art classroom) reinforce a consumerist mindset, beholden to hardware and software makers, rather than encouraging students to be creative producers. If artists act as innovators by raising questions about the accepted practices of society, then art educators must be open to learn about, explore, and critique the objects and behaviors that contemporary society overwhelmingly engages in – *digital* objects and the behaviors mediated by them. Individuals who use technology, but do not engage with the underlying principles behind technology's functions, allow themselves to become passive, uninformed consumers. *Educators* who adopt this uncritical, receptive stance toward technology tend to use digital media as a tool for the more efficient re-presentation of old-media pedagogical experiences – e.g., tests and quizzes, or illustration and collage projects – in ill-fitting new media skins, failing to capitalize on the full pedagogical potential of new media (Hokanson and Hooper, 2000), and likewise failing to engage students in the full expressive potential of new media art. While this mode of practice may be a more efficient or less messy way to administer traditional assessments or classroom activities, it fails to provide students with genuinely new, interesting, or challenging ways of engaging with subject matter, and in the arts such practice can introduce or reinforce a bias in students that digital artforms are necessarily compromised or less authentic facsimiles of "traditional" artforms such as painting, photography, or collage (Lu, 2005). New media artforms have their own set(s) of aesthetic properties distinct from various traditional art practices, including procedurality (Jenkins et al., 2006; Paul, 2012; Reas and Fry, 2006), multimodality (Paul, 2012; Peppler, 2010), interactivity (Peppler, 2010), immateriality (Paul, 2011), dynamic responsiveness to real-time changes in the physical or informational environment (Paul, 2002), and ease of appropriation and remix (Jenkins et al., 2006; Ng, 2012). In this chapter, we argue that to best prepare twenty-first century art students, teachers must provide education in forms of digital art making which leverages these distinct aesthetic properties and engages with the conceptual and practical challenges entailed in them. Artists working in traditional media often make use of specific technical and scientific knowledge in their practices – like sculptors knowing basic engineering principles, painters knowing anatomic proportions and color theory, and ceramicists knowing thermodynamics. These forms of scientific knowledge are embodied in art practices and developed in the manipulation and mastery of materials. The artist's technical knowledge base may be amateur, a form of bricolage that does not follow prescribed protocols or processes, allowing the artist to question staid practices and procedures, and propose innovative or alternative methods (Knochel and Patton, 2016).

This bricolage approach to the accretion and application of technical knowledge is also relevant in new media arts, despite digital tools' reputation of often being alienating, esoteric, and prescriptive in their use. New media artist and theorist Simon Penny (2009) outlined a digital art pedagogy that emphasizes precisely this bricolage approach to new media art education. Penny's theories around new media art education emphasize a need for cultivating creative thinkers capable of working in interdisciplinary and open-ended ways in the digital arts (Penny, 2003). Artist, critic, and media theorist Olia Lialina (2012) outlined her ideal of a "General Purpose User" of digital technology, who eschews prescriptive mastery of a specific piece of commercial software in favor of inventive and eclectic repurposing of digital tools. Such users can "write an article in their e-mail client, layout their business card in Excel . . . find a way to publish photos online without flickr, tweet without twitter, [and] like without facebook" (Lialina, 2012, para 39). In short, they "know how to open doors without knobs" (para 59). This bricolage approach, which applies artistic problem-solving strategies to digital creative problems, not only serves to empower students to use digital media on their own creative terms, but also serves the practical purpose of demonstrating how teachers can provide authentic new media explorations even in environments where expensive commercial software like the Adobe suite is unavailable. In the same way art teachers often make inventive use of limited physical materials when planning traditional art explorations, art teachers can creatively use (or *mis*use) a variety of free or at-hand digital tools when planning digital art experiences for their students (fine art exemplars perhaps including David Byrne's Powerpoint-based artworks, or Rosa Menkman's "glitched" images created by opening JPEGs in Notepad). We have observed this bricolage conceptualization of hands-on art making and knowledge-building engenders internalized understanding of the materials and methodology regardless of the discipline or art medium (be it "new" or "old" media).

In the spring of 2012, we were tasked with redesigning the syllabus for a "Technology in Art Education" course intended for undergraduate pre-service art educators. One of the difficulties of developing this course was the vast range of topics it could cover, and the inherent limits on how many of these topics could be addressed in a single semester course. Many universities have entire departments and degree programs devoted to teaching digital art making as forms of studio practice, educational technology as a field that teaches the effective use of technological tools in learning, and new media theory and history courses. Conversely, most (if not all) US K-12 art education teacher preparation programs require only *one* course focusing on digital art and/or teaching (Patton and Buffington, 2016). The nature of these digital art/teaching courses varies according to the philosophical positions of myriad university programs supporting the varied state teaching licensure requirements. Some universities may offer a general educational technology course required for all K-12 licensure candidates, focusing on teaching with technology rather than digital artmaking, or new media art history and theory. Fortunately, teaching in an Art Education department, we had the freedom in the development of our course to weave together threads of new media art practice, digital pedagogy, and critical new media theory.

K-12 art educators are expected to have generalized knowledge of the field of art, so the course we developed kept this generalist perspective in mind. In creating the syllabus, we believed preservice art educators should have a broad understanding of new media art making, theory, and history, and be able to apply that knowledge through educational technologies which also serve as tools for digital art creation. The design for the course needed to scaffold digital learning, leading preservice art educators to apply their technical knowledge toward multiple digital literacy aims: to teach about digital art, use digital tools to teach, and be able to create digital artworks.

The makeup of our classes reflected a number of demographic and statistical realities endemic to art education and to new media education – realities that presented a number of potential challenges as we constructed our course. Our classes of preservice art educators were almost entirely comprised of women, an unsurprising fact as it matches the national demographic breakdown of K-12 art educators (Galbraith and Grauer, 2004). At the beginning of the year, the preservice art educators largely reported primarily working with traditional media such as painting, ceramics, photography, and drawing in their personal artistic practices, with little personal experience or interest in new media art making. The preservice art educators were exposed to digital video production through their freshman Arts Foundations coursework the previous year, but reported low levels of knowledge, experience, and confidence with creative practices such as digital image manipulation, web development, or video game design. This was also foreseeable, as young women and girls are frequently discouraged from engaging in digital and technical practices, and are systematically underrepresented in STEM disciplines (Hill, Corbett, and Rose, 2013) and postsecondary new media art programs (Garber, Sandell, Stankiewicz, and Risner,

2007). Many of these preservice art educators played video games in their childhood; however, the majority self-reported that they no longer engaged in this activity. Again, this information was unsurprising, given issues of representation of women in the game industry (Miller, 2013) which have led to alienating and inequitable representations of women in the majority of games themselves (Williams, Martins, Consalvo, and Ivory, 2009). Most of the preservice art educators in our classes reported having social media accounts and smartphones, so consumption of digital media through these channels was not unfamiliar or unusual.

These realities informed the shaping of our objectives for the course: not only were we charged with instructing students to be productively and critically engaged with digital art and culture – but also we had to make digital art and culture relevant to students for whom it played no part in their personal artistic practice and who were in many cases alienated or intimidated by digital tools, media, and the culture(s) surrounding them. What conceptual connections could we draw between meaningful new media art practice and practice in traditional media? How could we go beyond the canon of largely male new media artists, and beyond the ubiquitous commercial use of digital media in apps, ads, and AAA video games, to expose students to a wide of variety creative producers who leverage digital tools in multifarious creative ways?

Over the course of the semester, 30 preservice teachers completed projects in image manipulation, web design, video production, and video game production. To reduce the learning curve associated with the less familiar code-based artforms, the course was designed to break apart programming-focused projects like web design and game design into smaller pieces dispersed throughout the semester, and interleaved with more familiar, visually oriented projects such as image manipulation and video editing. For example, students were asked to make a simple, functional website early in the semester to post their reading responses for class. Later in the semester, after having more experience using HTML, CSS, and JavaScript, and opportunities to critique and examine the design and underlying code of several artists' portfolio sites, the preservice art educators expanded their personal site to include a portfolio webpage of personal work and an educational webpage on a new media artist. Because of their traditional visual arts backgrounds, many students were motivated to independently learn more complex HTML, CSS, and JavaScript code to visually match their websites with their aesthetic values, and strategies for this kind of independent artistic research (such as viewing the source code of other pages, or finding JavaScript tutorials online) were discussed in class.

The software used in the course was selected to address a variety of – sometimes contradictory – factors. While we wanted to acquaint the pre-service teachers with industry-standard software they may encounter in some public education environments (such as the Adobe suite), we also wanted to prepare the preservice teachers to be able to teach these contemporary concepts and practices in schools where freeware or consumer-grade software are the only options. We were also teaching the course in a university computer lab equipped with Macs, while preservice teachers are likely to enter a K-12 environment where most computers are Windows-based (Gray, Thomas, and Lewis, 2010), so our choices of software needed to be cross-platform, or have readily available analogs on other platforms. Another consideration was that our preservice teachers were seeking a K-12 art teacher certification, and the tools they would encounter in the course should be developmentally appropriate, or readily adaptable, for a variety of age groups. Adobe Photoshop was used in the university computer lab for image manipulation, but the preservice teachers were acquainted with free alternatives, including GIMP and Pixlr, and were challenged to teach lessons using GIMP on PCs during our partnership with a local public middle school. iMovie was used because its interface was appropriate for a variety of K-12 age levels and because it was more likely to be encountered in a school setting than professional-grade editing software, but the preservice teachers also became familiar with Windows Movie Maker when working with the middle-school students. Game design was taught using Yo–Yo Games' GameMaker Free for Mac software, because its 2D game-making environment was suitable for novices and extensible for more experienced students. Also, compatible versions of GameMaker are available across platforms, and, unlike other prosumer game design tools like Unity, the free versions of GameMaker are genuinely free for educational use, making it a likely candidate for use in even the most budgetarily constrained school environments. Web design was taught using Adobe Dreamweaver, because its combination of "What You See is What you Get" (WYSIWYG) design and hands-on HTML/CSS coding options were useful to scaffold visually oriented beginners toward use of code, and extensible to allow more experienced creators to use code entirely. Freeware analogs such as BlueGriffon or Microsoft ExpressionWeb were introduced and, again, preservice teachers were challenged to use free tools when teaching HTML-based art lessons with our partnering middle school.

Course readings covered new media art history, and relevant issues in art and art education relating to digital media. Topics like the history of Internet art (Greene, 2000), use of social media in the K-12 classroom

(Walsh, 2010), control and privacy (Conlin, 2011; The Institute for Applied Autonomy, 2005), copyright and fair use (Ferguson, 2010; Lessig, 2009), interactive design (Bilton, 2011; McKinley, 2011; Rosenberg, 2011), and games in art and education (Bogost, 2011; Getsy, 2009; Salen, 2007) were covered over the course of the semester. These articles and chapters were chosen to introduce students to ideas and examples of digital media, policy, and culture they may not have been aware of. Through discussion and reading responses, many students communicated they had been previously unfamiliar with or unaware of the issues presented in the articles. One topic of debate was balancing societal rules of public decency and security on school Internet networks, under the justification of student safety, versus the ability to access any information on the web for the sake of education (Conlin, 2011). A few art education students supported the idea that school systems should restrict Internet access at school by blocking certain websites. As one student stated, "all of the distractions and dangers that the world wide web can possibly cause to school children is a problem." Other students felt schools should not limit Internet access for students and teachers, arguing that K-12 teachers should be free to determine what content to use, and students should be held accountable for their actions online. Another student wrote:

> I remember going to a public high school in XXX it was almost impossible to do research for a project on the school computers, let alone access most images on Google. I'm not sure if all school systems are so strict, but it definitely impeded my ability to get a lot of work done at school, resulting in an increased homework load, and causing loads of frustration.
>
> It is necessary for the school systems to draw a clear line. If they want to block social networking sites, and monitor the student's web access, then they should be able to do so. However, they need to realize the breadth of knowledge and opportunity that the Internet holds for this new age of students, and respect their desire to explore it.

Debates like these translated into class discussions about safety and access to information outside of schools and how these issues of censorship and the common good connect to the greater society.

PROJECTS – WHAT WE DID AND WHAT WE MADE

The first project, designed to teach preservice art educators image manipulation, was a culture-jamming project, drawing upon the work of Banksy, Adbusters, Shepard Fairey, the Wooster Collective, The Decapitator, Princess Hijab, and guerilla advertisers as examples of this tactical media form.

The aims of this project were to conceptually demonstrate to the students how digital media could be leveraged to produce socially relevant art, and to practically demonstrate how digitally generated images could be brought into – and even interfere with – physical space. Students were asked to create an image or series of images with Photoshop and bring the images into the physical world by printing them out and inserting them into or adhering them onto an intended physical space or surface. Many students chose to make political statements with their Photoshopped images, commenting on the campus environment or signage found throughout the city. For example, one student chose to comment on Chick-fil-A's corporate efforts against gay rights (Severson, 2011). The art education student believed that Chick-fil-A should support gay marriage, and placed a removable sticker stating this position next to the informational sign at the campus restaurant location (Figure 1.1). Later, a passerby saw how the sticker juxtaposed with Chick-fil-A's public statements, and posted a photo on social media commenting on how this image made them feel.

Another student created multiple editions of a set of paper dolls with gendered outfits, and installed them in public men's and women's restroom stalls on campus to see if students of particular genders or majors were more or less likely to attire the dolls in gender normative ways (Figure 1.2). In the project critiques, students acknowledged the culture-jamming project that made them more aware of images around them in their daily life and thinking about their ability to create work that has an impact by speaking directly to the public. While this project was being completed, students were asked to multitask, gradually building up their knowledge of game making through the video game development software GameMaker and beginning their website projects by learning the basics of HTML to make a simple page for posting–reading responses.

We believe that the twentieth-century art educators and art students should be able to creatively produce programmed systems and environments, but not just to consume them. Consequently, in addition to visually focused projects like the Photoshop culture jam, our course introduced preservice educators to code-based media through web design and game development. Art education students were tasked with developing a website over the course of the semester which would serve as a repository for written responses to class readings, a portfolio of the artistic and teaching practices, and a digital resource about a chosen new media artist. The web design assignment was structured to encourage student autonomy. A few basic tutorials in HTML and CSS, a WYSIWYG program (Dreamweaver), and an FTP program started the students on the path to create their own

FIGURE 1.1. Culture jamming project (2013)

FIGURE 1.2.   Culture jamming project (2012)

websites. Students were also taught the practice of viewing the source code of other sites, or finding JavaScript snippets online, so that they could independently discover more complex types of code and functionality, and apply them to their sites without rewriting complex scripts from scratch. In addition to affording more student autonomy, and thus more individuality and variety in their final products, this way of practicing helped students draw parallels between the standard contemporary art practices of bricolage and remix and the standard coding practices of researching, excerpting, and adapting preexisting code. Students were shown a variety of websites by artists like Paper Rad, JODI.org, Miranda July, and Kehinde Wiley to see how the web could be used as a portfolio for a variety of new media and traditional media artists, as well as a space for artists who used the web itself as a medium of expression. Students were required to write – and sometimes wrestle with – HTML and CSS code. CSS templates and blogging software like Wordpress or Weebly were not allowed. This option was removed and so students could experience how web code works, requiring them to develop a basic understanding of how webpages are made and uploaded to the Internet. We recognize most preservice art educators will not teach web design or become web designers, but developing an understanding how content is created and shared on the Internet is an important knowledge for them to have to develop their digital literacy as makers. Moreover, this knowledge is important to impart to their future students who engage regularly with programmed virtual spaces on the Internet but who are often not aware of the human hand behind the code (Rushkoff, 2010). In the course management system, we posted links to HTML and CSS tutorials and examples that would be of use to the preservice art educators. Outside of class, students networked with each other to learn how to develop their websites further, and observed what their classmates accomplished during mid-project critiques. In the final evaluations, students expressed that it was difficult to develop a website to appear and function exactly as they imagined; however, they also appreciated learning the skills and knowledge necessary for web designers and developers.

Over the course of the semester, each preservice art educator gave a 20-min presentation on a new media artist. The preservice art educators were given a list of new media artists to choose from, but if a student could justify using another artist within the context of the course they were given that option. Most of the preservice art educators were not familiar with the artists they selected, but found them to be interesting and relevant to the course and their growth as artists themselves. This mirrors the authors' experiences with presenting contemporary new media art at the precollege level. While all art educators must face the challenges of presenting unfamiliar and sometimes opaque or alienating contemporary artwork to students, new media art is in many ways uniquely suited to address this challenge because of its close relation to contemporary visual culture and to popular cultural forms like video games, smartphone apps, and Tumblr gifs. As part of the new media artist assignment, and as an extension of the website assignment, students developed a webpage about their artist, including it as part of their personal website. Each student was expected to think critically and aesthetically about the presentation of media and information about their artist on their website, and thoughtfully consider both the interaction of the user/reader with their site and the aesthetics of the artist being represented. One preservice teacher made an ambitious website about Daniel Rozin, an artist whose work consists largely of "mirrors" comprised of small objects which rotate and shift to create a larger, ever-changing image. Her site design reflected Rozin's work, taking the form of a "memory" game, where a large image of one of Rozin's pieces was actually several smaller square images which flipped when moused-over to reveal images, links, and information about the artist. To create the page, the student independently researched the dynamic CSS and JavaScript to make elements "flip," and used Photoshop skills developed in the previous unit to resize and split apart the large image into squares.

Of the artforms discussed and practiced in the course, the preservice art educators were most familiar with video production, a new media skill they developed in their freshman year during their art foundations courses. Students had few restrictions for this assignment: only technical limitations like the length of the video, a minimum number of camera angles, and the inclusion of additional sounds – the latter two restrictions put in place to ensure experimentation with editing and juxtaposition of footage and sound. We also asked students to connect the beginning of their video to the end of another classmates' video to create an exquisite corpse loop, necessitating collaboration between teams during the storyboarding process. Students were asked to use iMovie rather than the more complex and professional video editing software they used in their art foundations course. We made the decision to use a more simplified video editing program based on the reality that elementary school students would also be able to use these tools. This helped us achieve our dual aim of expanding the new media skills of our preservice art educators, while fulfilling their practical need to become acquainted with tools available and age-appropriate to their own future K-12 students.

To engage preservice art educators with the notion they can create programmed interactive media, we included video game creation as part of the course. Most of the preservice art educators were not avid game players, yet they recognized the popularity and excitement K-12 students have for the medium. Video game production teaches preservice art educators a number of new media skills and techniques (including programming, image manipulation, and audio design), and contributes to an interest-driven curriculum that takes into account the knowledge, experiences, and interests of twenty-first century K-12 students.

As mentioned earlier, GameMaker was chosen for the course because of the instructors' previous experience using the software with students as young as 8 years old (Patton, 2013), and its free availability making the software a likely candidate for inclusion in school computer labs regardless of budget concerns. The GameMaker software environment is flexible enough to support learning for both young students and university students. Prior to teaching this course, we each taught game design to elementary and secondary students, using a game curriculum designed for younger children, with specific game programming instructions created as modular handouts which a K-12 student could follow for self-directed learning. Each of these handouts, or "game cards" teach students how to create a single common game element, such as a health bar, artificial intelligence, or gravity (Figure 1.3). We repurposed these cards as a way to scaffold the preservice teachers'

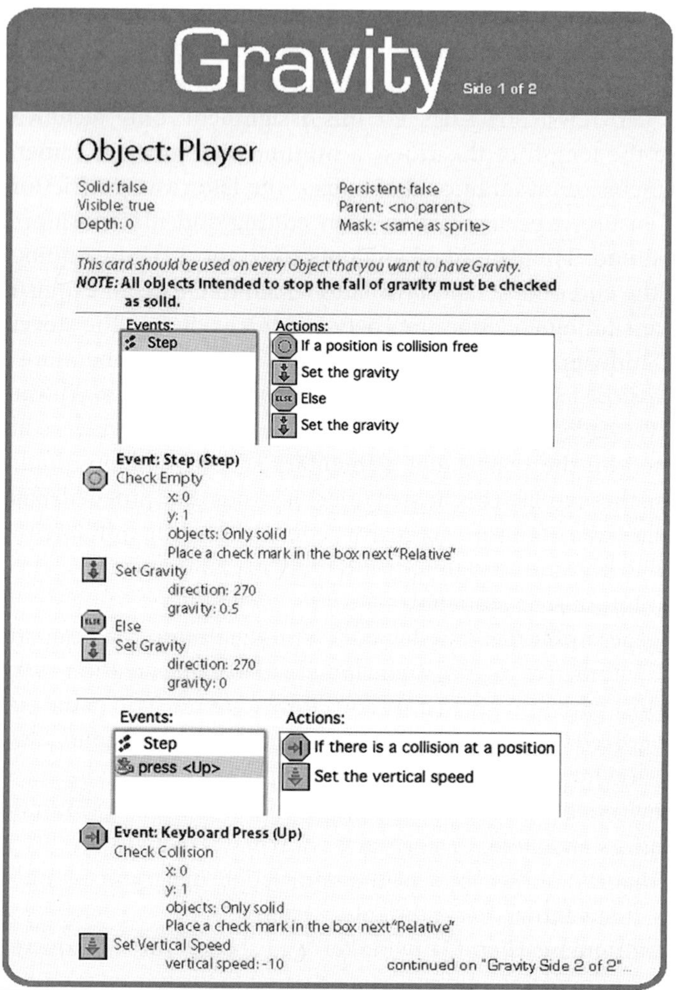

FIGURE 1.3.   Game card (2009)

learning by spreading out the relatively complex game development concepts over the course of the semester, teaching it in parallel with the other projects and discussions. At the beginning of the year, our preservice art educators each signed up to teach a single game card to the rest of their class in the form of a peer-teaching presentation. Only one or two of the peer-teaching presentations were delivered each class period, allowing the students to learn the information gradually. As student-led activities, these peer-teaching assignments were small enough that a student could master the content they were teaching in a short amount of time, allowing them to focus on their ability to teach the material to their peers. If problems arose, the course instructor, who was also present, could provide additional technical assistance. The course instructor also provided some basic computer science concepts such as debugging, variables, and loops to these peer-teaching experiences as students slowly learned how the game code worked.

As students delivered their peer-teaching presentation, they were asked to present a connection to a non-video game artist. The artist could be a painter, performance artist, photographer, etc. from any art historical period. For example, one student chose the performance artist Bas Jan Ader and works from his *Falling* series (1970–1) to connect to her peer-teaching on programming gravity. Another student chose Christian Marclay's *The Clock* (2010) for the peer-teaching presentation on creating in-game timers. This extension of the assignment allowed students to include artists and mediums they were more familiar with, drawing connections between digital and traditional mediums through conceptual links.

During the course, preservice art educators were introduced to less commercial games or "art" games. Works like *Dys4ia* (2012) by Anna Anthropy, *Machinarium* (2009) by Amanita Design, *The Artist is Present* (2011) by Pippin Barr, *LIM* (2011) by Merritt Kopas, and *Hot Throttle* (2011) by Jonatan Söderström were used to show students a variety of concepts, mechanics, and visual styles for the games they would be designing in class. Most of the preservice art educators in our class were somewhat familiar with commercial games produced by large companies, but introducing them to these "'nontraditional" or "art" games helped them relate to games as an expressive artform, and to game-makers as creative individuals. Formal and conceptual components of games were framed aesthetically as *verbs* articulated by a *mechanic* to create an *aesthetic experience/feeling* (Figure 1.4). Students were challenged to create games with new verbs, other than "jump" and "shoot," and ultimately created games with a variety of visual and ludic aesthetics, as well as conceptual/narrative cores.

By the time the preservice art educators completed teaching all of the peer-teaching presentations, the semester was more than half over, and image-making, HTML, and video-editing projects had all been completed. Students kept adding the game card components to a test game, allowing them to see how the programmable game elements fit together. When students completed all of the game cards and other art projects, and accrued a broad body of knowledge and skill with both GameMaker and other digital artmaking tools, the final "new verb" game assignment was introduced.

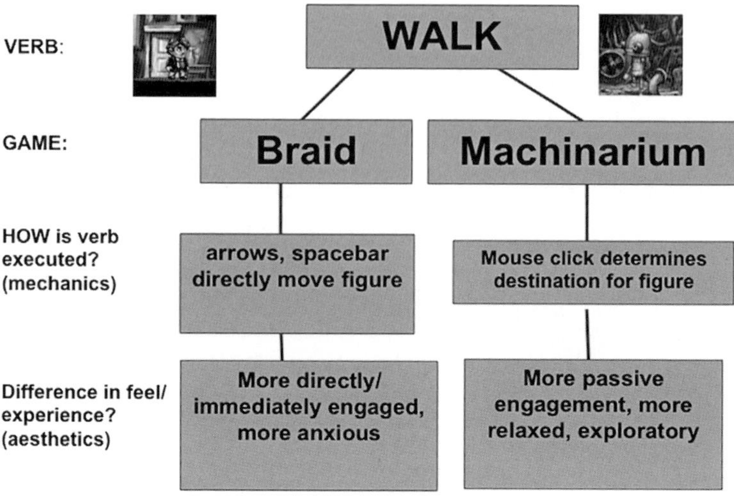

FIGURE 1.4. Course slide (2012)

The discussion of art games that explored more personal subject matter, as well as the challenge to create a game with a new "verb," resulted in a number of unconventional games made by the preservice teachers. For example, one student built her game around the verb "binge" (Figure 1.5), creating a series of levels which metaphorically articulated different aspects of her relationship to food as a child, adolescent, and adult. Each level was filled with colorful food items reminiscent of traditional video game collectables/power-ups, the collection of which raised the player's score. One level, set at her home, featured the parents as "bosses" hurling fatty foods at the player character to reflect the enabling "clean plate" and "comfort food" values enculturated at home, while another level, set at school, had the player accosted by swarms of nosey students, representing her anxiety about being seen eating in public. Intermittent "binge" levels played at an increased speed with saturated colors, and the player frantically ran from left to right collecting fast food and accumulating massive amounts of points. The game concluded with a screen which subverted the conventions of the "high score" mechanic, shaming the player by saying "All points are calories so you really haven't won anything. You're out of control! This is the HALL OF SHAME! All you can do is start over and try again." This personal facet of the preservice teacher's life had not come up in class discussions, or in her other artwork – the task of designing a meaningful game gave the student the opportunity to publicly and comfortably explore and share this issue.

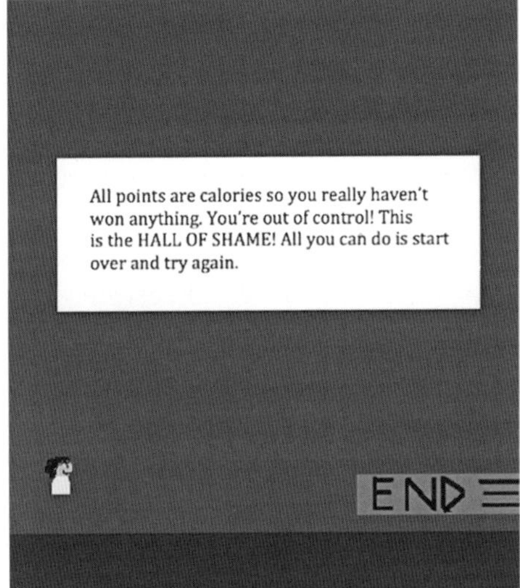

FIGURE 1.5. "Binge Inferno" screens (2012)

As part of the final game assignment, students were given the option of using a physical computing device to control their game. Students were introduced to the Makey Makey – an Arduino microcontroller device mapped to the computer keyboard. The Makey Makey is marketed as a way to create a physical computing game controller through simple circuits enabled by the human body's conductive properties. Essentially, students could create buttons out of any conductive material – tinfoil, a banana, graphite, or even their own bodies. With the Makey Makey, students from sculpture and installation backgrounds were afforded a toehold to apply a physical form to their game projects. For example, one student, whose personal artistic background was in sculpture and installation, and who had initially felt daunted by the complexity of both the GameMaker software and several of the example games played in class, made a piece which articulated both her initial intimidation by these seemingly opaque and complex systems and her ultimate feeling of mastery over them. Her "game" was a series of anarchic screens the player had to navigate by manipulating a dizzying array of tinfoil inputs, which snaked out from the computer terminal and which were connected to arbitrary keypresses (apart from the ones deliberately not actually connected to anything). Playing the "game" was initially stressful and intimidating for anyone who tried – but through perseverance and experimentation, someone could master the system and reach a "win" state (Figure 1.6).

After graduating from the university, most preservice art educators will be pursuing careers teaching in K-12 classrooms. To provide some

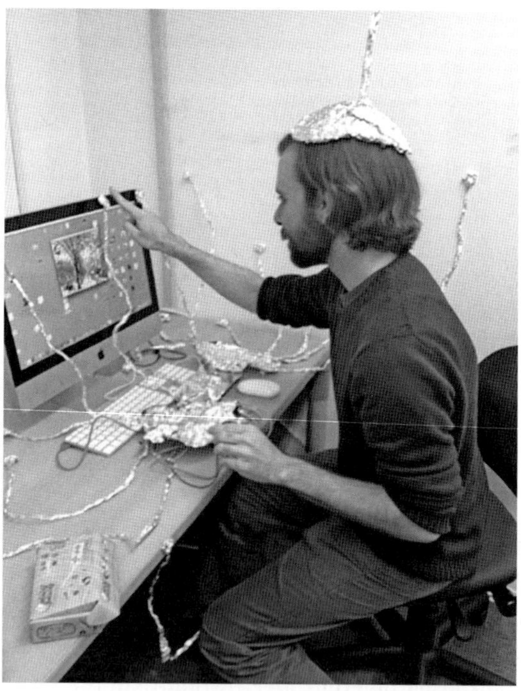

FIGURE 1.6. Makey Makey game controller (2012)

real-world experience in how digital media can be learned and taught in those classrooms, we capitalized upon a partnership our department had established with a local middle school near the university campus. The partnering school primarily serves African–American students who receive free and reduced lunch assistance. Our class specifically worked with the school's Technology Student Association (TSA) chapter, and preservice art educators paired up to teach an hour-long lesson during TSA after-school club meetings during the second half of the semester. As stated earlier in this chapter, we made a conscious effort to use free or open-source software, or commonly available commercial art software, like the Adobe suite or iMovie. In the middle school, however, we were more limited with software and hardware availability. The Adobe suite was unavailable and we were unable to install other software on the school's machines. These forms of constraint are typical in K-12 teaching environments, particularly in large school districts, and creatively working around these systemic limitations was an instructive experience for the preservice art teachers. Some students retaught themselves photo-editing skills using the free program GIMP, while others researched how to load "portable" versions of some free programs onto USB drives which could run on the school's computers without installation. The middle-school students were taught a variety of new media skills and technologies in 14 lessons over the course of 7 weeks. The preservice art educators received content requirements for their lessons; however, they had freedom in developing their lesson plans. The preservice art educators applied what they learned over the semester, teaching middle-school students digital photography and editing, website creation, video production, and game design. In doing so, the preservice teachers solidified their own knowledge of these skills, while developing lesson-planning and teaching skills. For several students, this class was taken before either elementary or secondary practicum, and constituted their first formal teaching experience. This teaching opportunity introduced preservice art educators to expanding their digital literacy to the experience of teaching digital technology to K-12 students, providing the space to see how new media art making can be taught to middle-school students.

FUTURE IMPACT OF THE COURSE DESIGN

Overall, the structure of the course proved to be successful, based on the changes in students' self-reported efficacy in course surveys, and the later employment of art education students teaching digital media. Since 2012, we have asked art education students in the course the pre/post questions: "Are you good at creating images with the computer?," and "I know how to make programmable media" on a five-point Likert scale of "strongly agree," "agree," "neither agree nor disagree," "disagree," and "strongly disagree" (see Tables 1.1 and 1.2). From the data, students each year are reporting dramatic shifts in their confidence using the computer for art making and creating programmable media over the duration of the course.

The vast majority of the preservice art educators achieved or exceeded the course expectations and completed all of the assignments. In the student evaluations, most of the art education students believed that the course was appropriately demanding, with only 16 percent of the students reporting that the course was excessively demanding. Students with no previous experience or interest in teaching digital media taught at a later stage

TABLE 1.1. *Pre- and post-survey questions on students' self-efficacy of creating images/art with a computer*

BEFORE THIS CLASS, I was good at creating images/art with a computer	2012	2013	2014	SINCE THIS CLASS, I am good at creating images/art with a computer	2012	2013	2014
Strongly agree	0	1	2	Strongly agree	3	2	2
Agree	4	4	2	Agree	4	7	8
Neither agree nor disagree	0	5	4	Neither agree nor disagree	2	4	5
Disagree	5	2	4	Disagree	0	0	1
Strongly disagree	0	1	4	Strongly disagree	0	0	0
Unanswered	1			Unanswered	1		

TABLE 1.2. *Pre- and post-survey questions on students' self-efficacy of knowing how to make programmable media*

BEFORE THIS CLASS, I knew how to make programmable media (IE games, websites, apps)	2012	2013	2014	SINCE THIS CLASS, I know how to make programmable media (IE games, websites, apps)	2012	2013	2014
Strongly agree	0	0	0	Strongly agree	3	1	3
Agree	1	0	0	Agree	6	12	11
Neither agree nor disagree	0	1	0	Neither agree nor disagree	0	0	2
Disagree	3	10	3	Disagree	0	0	0
Strongly disagree	5	2	12	Strongly disagree	0	0	0
Unanswered	1		1	Unanswered	1		

game design and new media art classes to K-12 students through summer camps and other afterschool or nonprofit arts programs (Figure 1.7). Many of these same preservice art educators also developed new course content from their experience teaching digital media. For example, the sculpture student discussed earlier, who created the anarchic "game" piece with the Makey Makey, recently pioneered a new summer course for 8–14 year old students using the Makey Makey to create interactive, sound-based sculptural and wearable artworks (Figures 1.8 and 1.9). For ourselves, observing how preservice art educators understood and demonstrated their

FIGURE 1.7. Art education student teaching games (2013)

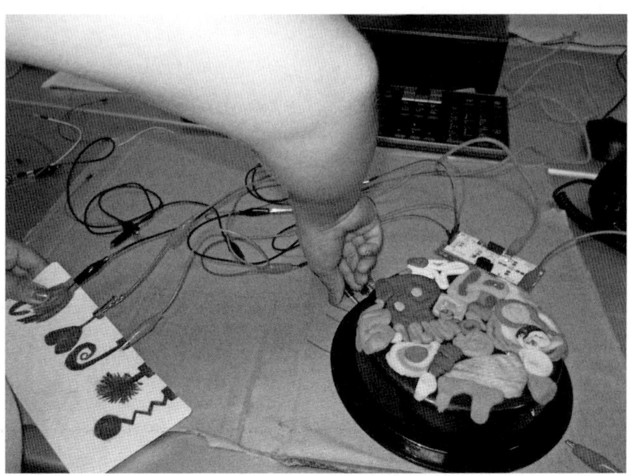

FIGURE 1.8. Sound sculpture (2014)

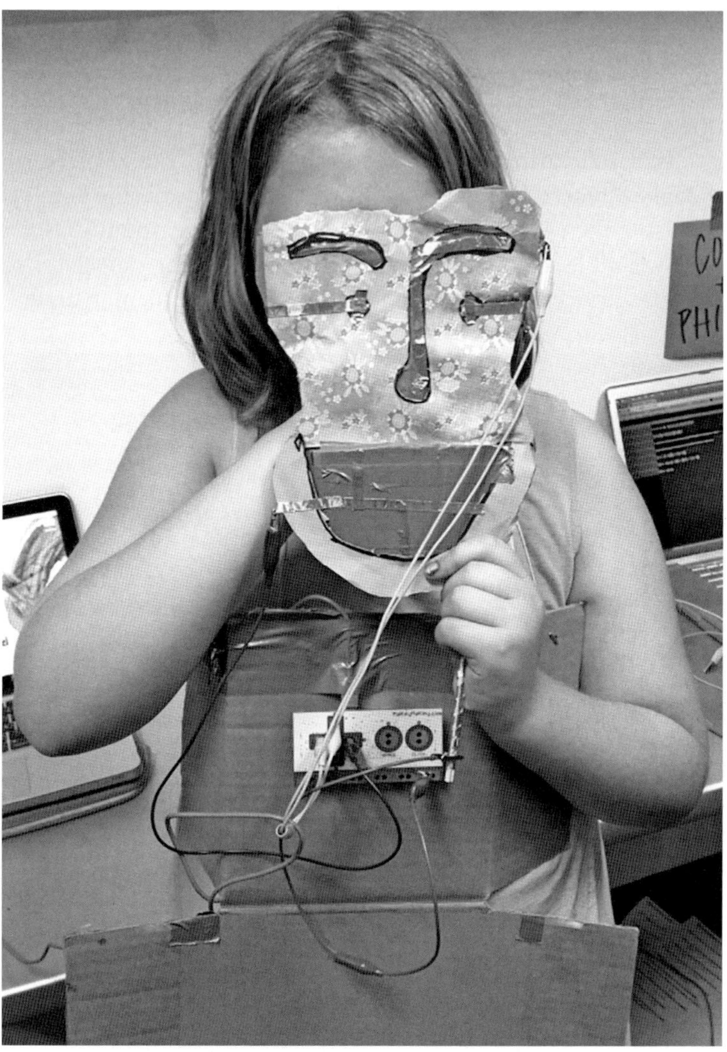

FIGURE 1.9. Talking/identity mask (2014)

knowledge in their coursework, and applied it teaching middle-school students, informed further development of the undergraduate curriculum, and a game curriculum for practicing art educators across the state (Patton and Meeken, 2013). Through theory, creative making, and teaching practice, we believe this course design impactfully contributes to efforts in the field of art education for bridging the digital literacy gap between art educators, art students, and contemporary society.

REFERENCES

Amanita Design (2009). *Machinarium*. Retrieved from http://machinarium.net/. Accessed online January 16, 2016.

Anthropy, A. (2012). *Dys4ia*. Retrieved from http://auntiepixelante.com/?p=1515. Accessed online January 16, 2016.

Barr, P. (2011). *The Artist is Present*. Retrieved from www.pippinbarr.com/games/theartistispresent/TheArtistIsPresent.html. Accessed online January 16, 2016.

Bilton, N. (2011, March 16). Arduinos provide interactive exhibits for about $30. *The New York Times*. Retrieved from www.nytimes.com/2011/03/17/arts/design/arduinos-provide-interactive-exhibits-for-about-30.html. Accessed online January 16, 2016.

Bogost, I. (2011). *How to do things with video games*. Minneapolis, MN: University of Minnesota Press.

Conlin, J. (2011, September 2). Students find ways to thwart Facebook bans. *The New York Times*. Retrieved from www.nytimes.com/2011/09/04/fashion/students-find-ways-to-thwart-facebook-bans.html. Accessed online January 16, 2016.

Dern, D. (2014, June 17). Darkroom over digital: Film photography still popular at some local schools. *Boston Globe*. Retrieved September 21, 2015 from www.betaboston.com/news/2014/06/17/darkroom-over-digital-film-photography-still-popular-at-some-local-schools/. Accessed online January 16, 2016.

Ferguson, K. (Producer). (2010). *Everything is a remix* [Video file]. Retrieved from http://everythingisaremix.info/blog/everything-is-a-remix-part-1. Accessed on January 16, 2016.

Galbraith, L. and Grauer, K. (2004). State of the field: Demographics and art teacher education. In E.W. Eisner and M.D. Day (Eds.), *Handbook of research and policy in art education* (pp. 415–37). Mahwah, NJ: Lawrence Erlbaum and the National Art Education Association.

Garber, E., Sandell, R., Stankiewicz, M., and Risner, D. (2007). Gender equity in visual arts and dance education. In S.S. Klein (Ed.), *Handbook for achieving gender equity through education* (pp. 359–80). Mahwah, NJ: Lawrence Erlbaum.

Getsy, D. (2009). Pedagogy, art, and the rules of the game. In M.J. Jacob and J. Baas (Eds.), *Learning mind: Experience into art* (pp. 125–35). Berkley, CA: University of California Berkley Press.

Google & Gallup (2015). *Searching for computer science: Access and barriers in U.S. K-12 education*. Retrieved from http://services.google.com/fh/files/misc/searching-for-computer-science_report.pdf. Accessed online January 16, 2016.

Gray, L., Thomas, N., and Lewis, L. (2010). Educational Technology in U.S. Public Schools: Fall 2008. *U.S. Department of Education, National Center for Education Statistics*. Washington, DC: U.S. Government Printing Office.

Greene, R. (2000). Web work: A history of Internet art. *Artforum International*, 38(9), 162–90.

Hill, C., Corbett, C., and St. Rose, A. (2013). *Why so few? Women in science, technology, engineering, and mathematics*. Washington, DC: American Association of University Women. Retrieved from www.aauw.org/files/2013/02/Why-So-Few-Women-in-Science-Technology-Engineering-and-Mathematics.pdf. Accessed online January 16, 2016.

Hokanson, B. and Hooper, S. (2000). Computers as cognitive media: Examining the potential of computers in education. *Computers in Human Behavior*, 16, 537–52.

Jenkins, H., Clinton, K., Purushotma, R., Robison, A.J., and Weigel, M. (2009). Confronting the challenges of participatory culture: Media education for the 21st century. Retrieved from https://mitpress.mit.edu/sites/default/files/titles/free_download/9780262513623_Confronting_the_Challenges.pdf. Accessed online January 16, 2016.

Knochel, A.D. and Patton, R.M. (2016). If art education then critical digital making: Computation thinking and creative code. *Studies in Art Education*, 57(1), 21–38. Retrieved from www.tandfonline.com/doi/pdf/10.1080/00393541.2015.1 1666280. Accessed online November 21, 2016.

Kopas, M. (2012). *LIM*. Retrieved from www.gamesforchange.org/play/lim/. Accessed online January 16, 2016.

Lessig, L. (2009). *Remix: Making art and commerce thrive in the hybrid economy*. New York, NY: The Penguin Press.

Lialina, O. (2012). Turing complete user. Contemporary Home Computing. Retrieved from http://contemporary-home-computing.org/turing-complete-user/. Accessed online January 16, 2016.

Lu, L.-F.L. (2005). Pre-service art teacher negative attitudes and perceptions of computer-generated art imagery: Recommendations for pre-service art education programs. *Visual Arts Research*, 31(60), 89–102.

Marclay, C. (2010). *The Clock*. Retrieved from www.moma.org/calendar/exhibitions/1308. Accessed online January 16, 2016.

McKinley, J. (2011, December 7). Central park, the soundtrack. *The New York Times*. Retrieved from www.nytimes.com/2011/12/08/arts/music/bluebrains-app-central-park-listen-to-the-light.html. Accessed online January 16, 2016.

Miller, P. (2013). Industry in flux: The 12th annual GD Magazine salary survey. *Game Developer Magazine*, 20(4), 15–21.

National Coalition for Core Arts Standards. (2012). The inclusion of media arts in next generation arts standards. Retrieved from http://nccas.wikispaces.com/file/view/NCCAS_%26_Media_Arts_7-28-12%20FINAL.pdf/355528606/NCCAS_%26_Media_Arts_7-28-12%20FINAL.pdf. Accessed online January 16, 2016.

Ng, W. (2012). Can we teach digital natives digital literacy? *Computers & Education*, 59, 1065–78.

Ninio, A. and Bruner, J.S. (1978). The achievement and antecedents of labelling. *Journal of Child Language*, 5, 1–15.

Ohio Alliance for Arts Education, Ohio Arts Council, & Ohio Department of Education (2013). The status of arts education in Ohio's public schools. Retrieved from www.oac.state.oh.us/MakingTheCase/PDF/2013%20Status%20of%20Arts%20Education%20in%20Ohio's%20Public%20Schools.pdf. Accessed online January 16, 2016.

Patton, R.M. (2013). Games as an artistic medium: Investigating complexity thinking in game-based art pedagogy. *Studies in Art Education*, 55(1), 35–50.

Patton, R.M. and Buffington, M. (2016). Keeping up with our students: The evolution of technology and standards in art education. *Arts Education Policy Review*, 117(3), 1–9. DOI 10.1080/10632913.2014.944961.

Patton, R.M. and Meeken, L. (2013). Currentlab. Retrieved from http://currentlab. art.vcu.edu/. Accessed online January 16, 2016.

Paul, C. (2002). Renderings of digital art. *Leonardo*, 35(5), 471–84.

(2011). New media in the mainstream. *Artnodes*, 11, 102–6. Retrieved from http:// artnodes.uoc.edu/index.php/artnodes/article/view/artnodes-n11-paul/art-nodes-n11-paul-eng. Accessed online January 16, 2016.

(2012, October). *FEEDBACK: New media art histories*. Lecture conducted from Virginia Commonwealth University, Richmond, VA.

Penny, S. (2003). Adequate pedagogy: The missing piece of digital culture. In L. Goodman and K. Milton (Eds.), *A guide to good practice in collaborative working methods and new media tools creation*. Barnsley, UK: Oxbow Books. Retrieved from www.ahds.ac.uk/creating/guides/new-media-tools/penny. htm. Accessed on January 16, 2016.

(2009). Rigorous interdisciplinary pedagogy: Five years at ACE. *Convergence*, 15(1), 31–54.

Peppler, K. (2010). Media arts: Arts education for a digital age. *Teachers College Record*, 112(8), 2118–53. Retrieved from http://kpeppler.com/wp-content/uploads/2010/10/2010_Peppler_Media_Arts.pdf. Accessed online January 16, 2016.

Piaget, J. (1962): *Play, dreams and imitation in childhood*. New York, NY: Norton.

Rosenberg, K. (2011, July 28). MoMA's "Talk to Me" focuses on interface. *The New York Times*. Retrieved from www.nytimes.com/2011/07/29/arts/design/momas-talk-to-me-focuses-on-interface-review.html. Accessed on January 16, 2016.

Rushkoff, D. (2010). *Program or be programmed: Ten commands for a digital age*. New York, NY: OR Books.

Salen, K. (2007). Gaming literacies: A game design study in action. *Journal of Educational Multimedia and Hypermedia*, 16(3), 301–32.

Severson, K. (2011, January 29). A chicken chain's corporate ethos is questioned by gay rights advocates. *The New York Times*, p. 16. Retrieved from www.nytimes. com/2011/01/30/us/30chick.html. Accessed online January 16, 2016.

Söderström, J. (2011). *Hot Throttle*. Retrieved from www.adultswim.com/games/web/hot-throttle. Accessed online January 16, 2016.

The Institute of Applied Autonomy (2005). Engaging ambivalence: Interventions in engineering culture. In G. Cox and J. Krysa (Eds.), *Engineering culture: On the author as (digital) producer* (pp. 95–103). Brooklyn, NY: Autonomedia. Retrieved from www.data-browser.net/02/. Accessed online January 16, 2016.

U.S. Congress. (2015). *STEM to STEAM Resolution. 114th Cong. 1st sess. H. Res. 247. 114 Cong. Rec. H2783*. Washington, DC: GPO.

Vygotsky, L.S. (1977). Play and its role in the mental development of the child. In J.S. Bruner, A. Jolly, and K. Sylva (Eds.), *Play: Its role in development and evolution*. New York, NY: Basic Books.

Walsh, K. (2010). 100 ways to teach with Twitter. *Emerging Education Technology*. Retrieved from www.emergingedtech.com/2010/02/100-ways-to-teach-with-twitter/print/. Accessed online January 16, 2016.

Williams, D., Martins, N., Consalvo, M., and Ivory, J.D. (2009). The virtual census: Representations of gender, race and age in video games. *New Media & Society*, 11(5), 815–34.

2

Teaching Interactivity: Introducing Computation to Art/Design Students

ANDREW HIERONYMI

Abstract: I teach undergraduate and graduate art/design students how to create expressive interactive experiences such as digital games, interfaces, art installations, and mobile applications. A core skill they need to acquire is computational literacy, which is a two-step process. The first step requires an ability to understand and modify code. The second step translates ideas and concepts into code. The transition from the first to second step is challenging for many students. The majority of my students have an art background but little or no knowledge of programming. Despite their passion for interactive media, students are often put off by the relatively steep learning curve of programming. Regardless of the topic I teach, my courses are structured around a series of assignments of varying length (1–6 weeks). Students learn programming by developing projects for these assignments either individually or in small teams. To motivate students and better help them understand the interactive design process, projects are always based on students' original ideas. In this chapter, I describe how this process takes place in the courses I teach by looking at the work of three students.

Keywords: interactive design, computation literacy, game design, agency, simulation, procedurality, flow

INTRODUCTION

The ability to "read" in a medium means you can *access* materials and tools created by others. The ability to "write" in a medium means you can *generate* materials and tools for others. You must have both to be literate. In print writing, the tools you generate are rhetorical; they demonstrate and convince. In computer writing, the tools you generate are processes; they simulate and decide.

(Alan Kay, User interface: A personal view, 1990, p. 193)

> Ideas have to be treated like potentials already engaged in one mode of expression or another and inseparable from the mode of expression, such that I cannot say that I have an idea in general. Depending on the techniques I am familiar with, I can have an idea in a certain domain, an idea in cinema or an idea in philosophy.
>
> (Gilles Deleuze, What is the creative act?, 2006, p. 312)

I teach computer programming in a college level visual arts and design program. In my courses, students learn to write code to create expressive interactive experiences such as digital games, interactive stories, mobile applications and art installations. My teaching has two main goals: (1) guide students to become computationally literate and (2) help them discover the expressive potential unique to interactive media. As Deleuze notices, this process is "inseparable from the mode of expression" (2006, p. 312), which becomes apparent to students through an understanding of the limitations and affordances of coding and interactivity in shaping ideas. This understanding represents a possible first step toward developing an idea – as Deleuze puts it – "in" the interactive medium. Ideally, it creates a spark for students, a turning point in their learning process, when they suddenly realize the creative potential of computation.

The leap from assimilating programming fundamentals to becoming a creative coder is a complicated one. In his influential essay, "User interface: A personal view," Alan Kay (1990, p. 193) compares computational literacy to natural language literacy – a two-step process where we first learn to read and then learn to write. The majority of art/design students are able to take the first step, by understanding the basics of programming through breaking down and modifying short code examples. They often have a harder time succeeding at the second step – the writing part – and have difficulty translating their ideas into code.

Alan Kay explains the process by which he developed the original graphical user interface (GUI) at Xerox Parc in the 1970s, which eventually led to the modern desktop interface of the Apple Macintosh and later Microsoft Windows. In his essay, he credits psychologist Jerome Bruner in helping him understand the process young children undergo when they learn new things. This process has three core elements: "enactive," "iconic," and "symbolic." Kay used these three modes of learning in his GUI by integrating the mouse (enactive), icons and windows (iconic), and Smalltalk, an early programming language (symbolic). I believe that this model of integrating three forms of learning can be applied to the teaching of interactive design. Bruner (1996) describes the enactive mode as vital in guiding skilled activity that has a specific purpose, and in the case of art/design students this involves teaching computational language and skills. It is the iconic mode that art/design students feel an affinity toward because of the way images refer to both particular items such as objects, as well as general things such as ideas. With this strong background in iconic understanding, students in my classes are able to integrate the procedural thinking characteristic of the enactive mode and the symbolic mode (programming) to communicate meaning through the digital projects they create. Bruner calls this integrated learning process "knowing as doing" (1996, p. 150). In the case studies that follow, I describe how this learning process happens.

Throughout this chapter, I use the term "expressive interactive experience." In the context of my courses, I define it as an interactive project for which students design both form and content. Projects are not utilitarian but instead meant to communicate an original idea, a personal feeling, or provide a playful challenge to one or multiple users through an interactive experience. It also happens that the expressive element and the interactive element are at odds with each other. As a first step, all projects require students to brainstorm an original idea using a set of constraints. Students who learn to program by developing projects based on their original ideas are motivated and better prepared to understand the process of creating interactive projects. One constraint imposed on these original ideas is the relatively short period of time required to experience the project. Students shape their ideas in the form of a core concept expressed through the interactive experience. To develop this core concept, students follow a similar series of steps regardless of the subject matter. First, they respond to the specific constraint of an assignment description. Within these limits, they generate an idea and describe it in a written document. They translate that idea into an interactive project, by writing code, creating assets, and integrating the assets into an interface, both with user inputs (mouse, keyboard, or custom devices) and system outputs (sounds, animations, and/or physical actuators). The projects are demonstrated, discussed, and revised before final submission.

This design process has demonstrated a number of benefits: students learn to produce projects on their own from start to finish following tight deadlines; they are encouraged to brainstorm original ideas easily translatable into code; and they become proficient in communicating concepts through code and interactivity. As a result, students produce a series of small applications and they can use them in their portfolios demonstrating their vision as artists | designers, as well as in a variety of skills such as game design, interface design, graphic design, and programming. The projects are evaluated based on two criteria: concept and execution. The technical aspect is secondary to the quality of the concept and the look and feel of the interactive experience. In the studio examples that follow, I describe the work of three students, two undergraduates (Saam and Michael) and one graduate (Ting), with little or no programming experience and how they are able to develop computation literacy and produce expressive interactive experiences using a variety of programming environments and scripting languages, such as Flash (ActionScript), Processing (Java), and Unity (C#). In each case, I discuss two projects: beginner and advanced. Students also responded to a questionnaire about learning programming in my courses. Excerpts about their experiences are included throughout this chapter.

These three case studies address two questions:

How can art/design students navigate the challenge of becoming computationally literate?

How can they achieve an "expressive interactive experience" by creating ideas unique to interactive media?

SAAM

Saam is an undergraduate student majoring in game design. I describe two of his early interactive applications as well as the context in which they were developed. They were created in an introductory course on interactive design taught in an interactive and game design program in an art college. Typically, game majors take this course in their second year. The course is organized sequentially into three parts: animation, interface design, and game design. Each part comprises lectures, studio time for project development, and class critique. Assignments include exercises and projects. Development time for these assignments vary: 5 days for exercises, 1 week for the first project, 2 weeks for the second, and 3 weeks for the last. The prerequisite for the course is prior working knowledge of software application tools for 2D design. For the majority of students, this course is their first introduction to interactive design as well as to using a scripting language. Using Adobe Flash, the course introduces students to fundamentals of expressive interactive design using an animation toolkit and a scripting language.

The typical Flash workflow is as follows: users import or create visual assets (vector graphics) using the built-in tools, organize those assets on a 2D plane (stage), and create animations using a timeline. Scripting can be used at all levels of the project. Then the application is compiled and a stand-alone file is created. This file can be seen using the Flash Player, a small application running either on the desktop or in a browser.

Despite Flash's waning popularity (it was renamed Adobe Animate in 2015), partly because of its poor support on mobile platforms such as Apple iOS and declining usage on websites, it is an ideal environment for introducing art/design students to interactive design. Flash was introduced as a vector graphics animation tool for the web in the mid-1990s first without scripting capabilities. It allowed users to draw and import visual and audio assets and create lightweight sophisticated animations. A proprietary scripting language (ActionScript) was eventually introduced to allow users to develop more complex interactive applications. When introducing interactive design with Flash, animations can still be created with the timeline, while ActionScript can be reserved to create user input. This provides for a gentler learning curve than other introductory programming environments such as Processing, in which both user input and animation have to be handled with code.

Farm Town

In the first part of the course, I introduce students to the asset creation and animation tools of Flash. The first ActionScript code is introduced early on to let the user control starting and stopping animations at run-time. A block of code, written in the ActionScript editor, references a button on the stage and when the user presses the mouse over the button, the code triggers a command either to start or stop the animation. Students are expected to understand what the code does and use it in the applications they develop. Early game designer and educator Chris Crawford (2003, p. 76) compares the interactive cycle to a conversation. The computer "listens" to user input, "thinks" using computational algorithms and procedures, and then "answers" through visual, audio, or physical output.

The exercise in the second part of the course asks students to develop an interface representing a coherent world in which buttons, when pressed, start and stop animations. At first, the world should be completely still, and as the user triggers animations, it should become gradually more chaotic and agitated. The user should then be able to bring the environment back to stillness. In Saam's *Farm Town* (Figure 2.1), the world is a cartoonish view of a field with a barn, a tree and an axe, a farmer, a cow and some hay bales, and a small garden plot. At the bottom of the screen is a button saying "share." The user can click on various elements of the environment and trigger short timeline animations: the axe will cut the tree, the garden plot will show flowers growing, and the hay bale will make the cow moo. If the user clicks the "share" button, another screen shows up with the

FIGURE 2.1. Saam: *Farm Town*

following message: "Congratulations. You clicked on some stuff. Good for you." Below the message, another button labeled, "Tell all my friends" brings you back to the previous screen. In this exercise, Saam applied skills learned during course lectures. He created visual assets using the built-in tools of Flash and created short "motion tween" timeline animations. For instance, for the cow animation, the head of the cow rotates and the words "moo" fade in and out. Finally, he added on the stage a pair of clickable hot spots (start/stop) tied to the animations using ActionScript sample code.

Conceptually, *Farm Town* references and parodies farming simulation social network games, such as *FarmVille*, by the game company Zynga (a precursor to *FarmVille* is actually named *Farm Town*). In *FarmVille*, players manage their farms by tending to them using simple mouse click interactions. Saam's exercise satirizes those games by showing their lack of depth, due in part to the limited interactions possible. He deconstructs a game mechanic based on this simplistic form of interactivity, the mouse click, by first letting the player click and trigger animations, and then on a second screen serving them a message mocking their eagerness to click. In describing his satirical social game, Cow Clicker, game designer and theorist Ian Bogost mentions compulsion as one contemporary behavior directly related to digital activities such as online gaming.

> Today, much of digital life is compulsive. Checking email to see if something – anything – new has arrived. Refreshing blog posts to see if new comments have appeared. Consulting web traffic logs. Reloading Twitter feeds in hopes of a new mention. We're increasingly obsessed with more and more obsessions. (2010)

Saam demonstrates with this exercise the various contradictions and tensions that can potentially arise with user interfaces. He shows that he is able to create a working application within Flash with buttons and animations. He is also able to create a consistent visual world in which a user might be compelled to click on those buttons to trigger animations. Finally, he emphasizes the mechanisms involved in compulsive clicking by referencing social media Flash games such as *FarmVille*.

Retirement

As students learn additional programming techniques with ActionScript, their projects increase in complexity and the range of expressive possibilities widens. For their final project with Flash, students are asked to design a point-and-click adventure game with a topic: the game has to be based on the passage of time. Time can be expressed either in a linear or in a nonlinear way, literally or allegorically. They have 3 weeks to complete the game, starting with a design document, followed by a prototype, and finally a complete game. To assist students in developing their adventure game, I introduce additional programming techniques. The first is the usage of variables. Variables are empty holders in computer memory from which a program can store and retrieve data. With a variable, the program can remember the value of a given element or attribute throughout the game, such as the status of a key (has it been found or not) or the current age of an elderly man. In addition to variables, I introduce conditional logic. This important programming technique allows, for example, different scenarios to play based on the status or value of a given variable. ActionScript uses syntax close to English (if . . . then . . . else) and can therefore be easily assimilated by beginning programmers.

To facilitate the development of the game, students are given a 2D scrolling engine to work with. This engine displays a placeholder as an empty rectangular area taking up the whole stage. It shows four directional arrows on each side. When clicking on an arrow, the rectangle scrolls in the opposite direction of the pointing arrow and reveals another rectangle corresponding to another area. Based on their game level designs, students decide a specific layout of areas linked with these arrows and organize them in Flash during authoring time. Each area can be referenced in code with a number. Students can then copy–paste blocks of "if . . . else" statements to organize the logic of the area layout. With this simple engine, students can focus on their level design and navigation logic without having to write code from scratch.

Saam's game, *Retirement* (Figure 2.2), puts the player in control of an elderly man who has just been put in a retirement home by his family. As the man stares out of the window, he sees a blooming flower outside of his room. He decides to get to the flower by navigating his way out of the home. Along the way, the player will need to help other elderly people in the home in order to leave. The man's face is displayed on the top right corner of the screen. Each click on a navigational arrow adds a year to the man, gradually aging him and giving the player a visual cue of the time left to leave the home. Throughout the game, players also collect various items they store in an inventory that can be seen at the bottom of the screen. Some of these items, such as a key, or medicine needed by a patient, need to be collected to open restricted areas. Ultimately if the player successfully manages to lead the elderly man outside of the home and within reach of the flower, he succumbs to a heart attack

FIGURE 2.2. Saam: *Retirement*

and dies. The game ends with the patients he helped putting flowers on the man's tombstone.

> I felt pretty proud of my game "Retirement," I had a limited set of tools and scope, but felt that I executed on the vision I had. The beginning started with how the narrative would fit then came the puzzles and finally the visuals and implementation. It was satisfying because it was the first game I made. From that point on I knew it was possible to make games by myself and that I could execute on a vision I had. (Saam)

Retirement is reminiscent of independent game designer Jason Rohrer's 2007 *Passage*, both in its general theme (the passage of time, the inevitability of death) and in its visual design (8-bit style graphics). In *Passage*, the player controls a character in a 2D scrolling environment starting on the left side of the screen. The character can go up, down, and right but cannot go left. As the character moves around exploring the environment, his appearance changes and he gets older. By the time he reaches the right side of the screen in a matter of minutes, the character dies of old age and the game ends.

What Ian Bogost defines as a proceduralist game when describing *Passage* could apply to Saam's *Retirement*: a game in which the main character, as an old man, dies at the end despite the player successfully accomplishing the goal of the game.

> Proceduralist games are oriented toward introspection over both immediate gratification . . . The goal of the proceduralist designer is to cause the player to reflect on one or more themes during or after play, without a concern for resolution or effect. (2009)

Let us take a look at Saam's progress. With his first interactive exercise – the animated environment of *Farm Town* – he is introduced to the interactive loop as a conversation with the computer: speak, listen, and respond. Saam learns to read, understand, and modify a basic script to start and stop a timeline animation. In this instance, code is used only for user input and controlling the timeline's play-head. In the final project of the course, the adventure game, *Retirement*, Saam is given more complex code to work with: variables, conditional logic, and a game engine to modify. He creates a more sophisticated application, a full game with navigation, puzzles, and a story. One of the main concepts learned through these projects is *agency*. This is the ability to provide the user with a sense of control based on constant reinforcement and communication of his sense of space, time, and action: where he *is* (visual communication), where he is *going* (clarity of interface), what he is supposed to *do* (consistency of overall user experience).

The understanding of agency presented Saam the ability to explore unique affordances of the interactive medium. The first exercise, *Farm Town*, communicates the feeling of click compulsion that can be triggered by social games such as *FarmVille*. In the second project, *Retirement*, Saam explored procedurality. What does it mean for the old man to die as he is about to get the flower? How are users supposed to feel about this conflicting ending they generated through their action? Agency, click compulsion, and procedurality are unique to computation and the interactive medium. In his interview, Saam mentions how satisfying it felt to be able to express himself with these newfound skills:

> I wanted to learn programming because I felt I was limited in my skills and wasn't properly able to communicate my ideas. I felt like a painter without a paintbrush or a canvas, all I had were ideas, but I couldn't actually bring them to life until I learned to code. Coming up with original ideas for projects felt pretty natural, I would take the lessons learned and try to shape an experience around them. (Saam)

TING

> I like to learn things with an idea first. When I start a project, the first thing I consider is "what results [do] I want to present?" I will think about how to use programming to build the projects after I have the ideas. (Ting)

Ting is a graduate M.F.A. student in interactive design. In this section, I describe two of her projects. The first is based on an interface design assignment she did in an introductory course *Scripting for Interactivity*. The second is a revision of that project done as her final project in a physical computing course.

Puppet Show

In the scripting course students are introduced to programming fundamentals with Flash using ActionScript, Adobe's proprietary scripting language. The structure of the course is similar to the course on Interactive Design described in the previous section in that it has three parts: animation, interface design, and game design. The difference is that the content of the scripting course puts an emphasis on learning to write custom code. The lectures are about understanding fundamentals of programming using ActionScript and the exercises and projects apply those fundamentals toward developing expressive interactive experiences.

In the first part, animation, students learn to create animations using code. They learn about how to control with ActionScript the changing values of the properties of visual objects such as horizontal or vertical position, scale, rotation, alpha value, etc. They learn how to change those values over time to create animations. To control the starting and stopping of animations, students learn about conditional logic. With "if . . . else" statements, they can write conditional statements asking the program every frame if an object has reached its destination. In pseudo code, they write down in English the algorithm's logic: to move an object from the left side of the stage to the right side, increasing the horizontal value (x) of the object by increments of 10 will move it horizontally at the rate of 10 pixels per frame. At 24 frames per second (fps), the object will move 240 pixels per second. If the x value of an object is bigger than 240 pixels, then stop incrementing it so that the object stops moving. Moving from pseudo code, they have an easier time writing the correct statements in ActionScript. By the time students reach the second part of the course, *interactive design*, they have also learned to work with functions, loops, and arrays. A function is a block of related lines of code that can be called upon and reused at will. With functions, the code becomes more modular and helps reduce errors. An array is a list used to group similar type of variables. A loop is a code structure meant to repeat a block of code a set number of times, for example to sort through an array of variables.

In the second part, *interface design*, the main assignment asks students to create a custom navigable interface with clickable buttons triggering transition animations between the different sections of the interface. The aesthetic of the transitions and buttons needs to match the content of the interface; for example, designing a jukebox where selecting records brings you to different sections of the interface, or a galaxy with planets where the planets represent the different sections of the interface. As a starting point, students are given an application with navigational buttons. The buttons have four states, "up" (default state), "over" (when the mouse is over the button), "down" (when the mouse button is depressed on the button), and "on" (when the section corresponding to the button is displayed). The buttons are animated, shrinking and growing between the various states, as well as changing colors. If a button is "on" and another button is pressed, the former button goes back to an "up" position. This last behavior requires buttons to check each other's current state, a feature using a "for" loop and an array. This sample code application is developed as a tutorial during lecture time. Students take turns sitting in front of the class and typing in the code while the rest of the class gives suggestions. Students are given 2 weeks to develop their project, with two deliverables: a design document and the Flash application. The design document requires a project description, rationale, architecture (flow chart, site map), and visual comprehensives.

For this assignment, Ting developed a project titled *Puppet Show* (Figure 2.3). *Puppet Show* recreates the experience of a mechanical puppet theater (Ma Jun) in Flash. The entire stage is comprised of a wooden theater with three subsections. At the top are the faces and hands of two puppeteers, each controlling two puppet-hands. In the middle is the central stage with curtains in the background. At the bottom on the left is a dynamic text field displaying contextual information and on the right is a coin slot with a coin to be inserted. When the application starts, two wooden panels conceal the puppeteers and the stage is dark. The text field at the bottom suggests the user to insert a coin. When the user clicks on the coin, it animates and enters the slot. The wooden panels at the top scroll both left and right, revealing the puppeteers, and the stage lights up, revealing an empty stage. The user can begin activating the hands of the puppeteers. Each hand controls one character, Nick "the cute boy," Emma "the girl," John "the frank boy," and Zada "the monster."

FIGURE 2.3. Ting: *Puppet Show*

Pressing on one puppet-hand activates an animation where the corresponding character slowly descends on the stage. Pressing the hand again retracts the character. Each hand can make a puppet appear or disappear. Depending on which character is already on the stage, it leads to different situations. Pressing one button leads to the characters introducing themselves. Pressing two buttons leads to two characters being on the set with six different scenarios. Pressing three buttons leads to three characters on the set with three different scenarios. And pressing four buttons leads to all four characters with one scenario. Using four clickable sets of hands controlling four puppets, Ting created a dozen different animated scenarios depending on the combination of characters present on the stage.

The vertical animated appearance of puppets is entirely controlled with ActionScript. As each puppet-hand triggered a dedicated character, they each had variable with a true or false value (Boolean) associated with it. Before the scene starts, the program checks all four Boolean variables using conditional statements and depending on their value it triggers different animations. With this simple setup, the theater accommodates all possible permutations of the four buttons and 14 different possible scenarios. Scenarios are not set sequentially, so users can trigger them in any order. Instead of creating smooth animations, Ting created two-frame animations to mimic the jerkiness of mechanical puppets. The visual look of the theater is reminiscent of an old puppet theater and the puppets are quite expressive despite their limited motions.

Historically, puppet shows are an early form of interactive media. Puppeteers traditionally ask their young audience to vote on the outcome of the story unfolding on stage. The mechanical puppet theater is an extension of the original puppet theater. Ting's project, with the technical limitations and constraint of the assignment (basic user input with buttons, basic animations), managed to effectively simulate an older form of interactive media. As media theorist Bolter and Grusin write, "what is new about new media comes from the particular ways in which they refashion older media" (1999, p. 15).

Puppet Face-Off

> To combine the "traditional" and "technological" is one of my interests . . .
> The main challenge of "Puppet Face-off" is to create a device that bridges
> the visual and real world. (Ting)

A year later, Ting enrolled in my Physical Computing course. This course introduces students to developing interactive installations using open-source software and hardware. It is divided into technical lectures, student presentations of digital artists, and studio time for project development. Students are given a series of assignments tied to specific technologies that culminates in an open project in which they are free to combine the technologies learned in the course. Students are expected to have programming experience when they take this course. The two main programming environments are *Processing* and *Arduino*. Processing is an open-source Integrated Development Environment (IDE) developed specifically for artists and visual designers. It is a subset of the web programming language Java and has an active community of users and developers. Arduino is a sister project to Processing and is also open source. Arduino is comprised of a microcontroller and has a similar IDE as Processing. Its scripting language is a subset of the programming language C.

First, Processing is introduced along with basic computer vision techniques. For their first projects, students develop interactive installations using a camera as an input device. Basic algorithms written in Processing allow students to detect motion, presence, and color in real time and use this alternative form of input in interactive installations. Then I introduce the Arduino microcontroller and the Arduino programming environment. We cover the basics of electronics, how to create a circuit, use resistors to control the current, and hook up basic sensors, both digital (e.g., push-buttons) and analog (e.g., potentiometers), and actuators (e.g., light-emitting diodes [LED], motors). Students develop installations using digital and analog input and output. An example of a simple circuit is a button controlling the blinking of an LED. When the button is pressed, the current goes through and the LED turns on. When the button is depressed, the LED turns off.

As her final project in the course, Ting decided to revisit the project she had developed in *Scripting for Interactivity*, *Puppet Show*. This time, she decided to create a different kind of experience. She built a small physical wooden stage that could accommodate a monitor screen, displaying the theater stage with two digital puppets. Puppeteers stand behind the wooden stage and, using puppet-hands attached to strings, control the animation of digital puppets on the stage. The faces of the puppets are snapshots of the puppeteers or members of the audience taken with a webcam located above the screen. Ting started by using the Arduino microcontroller connected to switches attached at the end of the puppeteer hand. Moving the hand would turn the switch on or off, sending a value (digital input) to the microcontroller, which would then be sent to a Processing program via a serial connection going through a USB cable to a computer. That value is again checked by a conditional statement and triggers the animation of the puppet. This time the focus of the project is not interactive storytelling. Instead, it provides the audience and participants with a blend between physical input and digital output. The participant's input corresponds to the actual movements of puppeteers, while controlling digital animations with the display of the faces of participants on the puppets. Ting in her interview mentions her ultimate goal with *Puppet Face-Off*:

> The most exciting part of this project is that players not only control the puppets, but also "become" the puppets, which creates an immediate association between the players and the project. (Ting)

There are two main goals in the physical computing course. The first is to introduce students to alternative input and output approaches to computer interaction beyond traditional mouse, keyboard, and monitor. The second is to encourage them to create interfaces engaging the full body of users. This second goal ideally can lead students to experience a central paradigm of interactive art installations: the tension between the simulated mediated world and the physical world of the interaction space. Media historian Kate Mondloch calls this

> a self-consciously dual spectatorship – one simultaneously caught up in the space of illusionist representation and made aware of the material condition of the viewing experience. While spectators are allowed to partially immerse themselves in illusionist, virtual times and spaces, they must concurrently recognize their embodied presence in the here and now of the exhibition space. (2010, p. 62)

In *Puppet Face-Off*, the duality between immersion in a digital space and awareness of the physical space is not meant to create conflict or tension for the users experiencing the installation piece. Unlike Saam's *Retirement* game in which the procedural design was meant for the player to reflect on his actions, the experience of *Puppet Face-Off* is more fluid and less critical. It is instead the nature of the mediums used, both physical and digital, that creates this oscillation between immersion and awareness.

Let us recap on Ting's work. In *Scripting for Interactivity*, she learned to write code for user interaction. She learned to create animations with code by incrementing the values of visual asset's properties such as their horizontal (x) and vertical (y) positions. These incremental values are regulated by conditional logic constraining them within a given range. In *Physical Computing*, she learned to work with basic electronics, building circuits between switches, and an Arduino microcontroller to trigger animations in Processing. Even though the programming environment and input/output devices were different in both courses, Flash/ActionScript and Processing/ Arduino, the logic of digital input/output was similar. Conceptually, it made sense for Ting to rework her puppet project in a new context.

The core element of the computational medium that she explores in both projects is simulation. With her first project *Puppet Show*, Ting emulated a mechanical puppet theater. With her second project *Puppet Face-Off*, she emulated an actual live puppet theater but added the faces of participants to the puppets, a feature that could only be created through computation.

As media theorist Lev Manovich writes:

> But what happens when we simulate different media in a computer? . . . The appearance of new properties may be welcome as they can extend the expressive and communication potential of these media. (2013, p. 70)

Using simulation, she explored two unique affordances of the interactive medium. In *Puppet Show*, it was interactive storytelling. How can one create a nonlinear story using 4 buttons with 14 unique combinations? In *Puppet Face-Off*, she explored embodiment (Figure 2.4). How can players experience an installation that engages them both on a physical and digital level?

FIGURE 2.4. Ting: *Puppet Show Face-Off*

MICHAEL

Michael is an undergraduate major in an interdisciplinary design degree. In this program, students receive a general education in digital art and design. In their sophomore year, they take an introduction to scripting course. It is a prerequisite for more advanced courses, such as game design, physical computing, and touch screen design. In this section I describe two games Michael designed, one individually in the introduction to scripting course, and the other as part of a team in the game art course.

AREA

In Introduction to Scripting, I introduce programming fundamentals using the Processing environment. As seen in the previous section, it is an ideal language for interfacing with Arduino but it is also ideal for teaching programming fundamentals. Unlike Flash, Processing does not provide a set of designer tools for asset creation or animation. Instead, everything in Processing relies on scripting. After about 6 weeks (of a 15-week semester), and when all the fundamentals have been covered, students are given a digital game design assignment.

The game they have to design has to be asymmetrical, player 1 using the mouse and player 2 the keyboard. The game can be cooperative or competitive. Students have to strive for an original game experience using this constraint. They are encouraged to take into account the affordances of both input devices: analog, spatial for the mouse, digital, continuous for the keyboard. Students have 3 weeks to complete the assignment. During the first week, they write a design document with a full description of the game. During the second week, they develop a prototype for the game and have the third week to finish and test the game.

For this assignment Michael created a two-player coöperative game titled *AREA* (Figure 2.5). In *AREA*, he relies on the display, transformation, and interaction of circles. Circles in this game scale move and collide.

> The visual design was largely beholden to the limitations of my coding skill, so I decided on an aesthetic that embraced the simple mechanics. The only visuals on screen (player character, enemies, and collectibles) are circles that vary their size. (Michael)

Player 1 is responsible for movement and Player 2 for scaling. Players control a small blue circle displayed on a square stage with a black background. When Player 1 moves the mouse, the blue circle follows it. When Player 2 presses the up or down keys on the keyboard, the diameter of the

FIGURE 2.5. Michael: *AREA*

circle increases or decreases. Every 2 seconds, another circle is spawned at a random position on the stage, and starts moving in a linear motion, bouncing against the edges of the stage. The circles are randomly assigned a color, either light red or green. At their center, a small circle of corresponding solid color (red or green) slowly grows until it matches the diameter of the light-colored circle. When the diameter of the inner circle with the solid color matches the diameter of the outer circle, the circle becomes "active." Collisions between an active green circle and the blue circle add a point to the main score and remove the green circle from the stage. The score briefly appears as a flashing number in the center of the screen. Collisions with an active red circle end the game. The goal of the game is to collect as many green circles as possible thus increasing the score while avoiding a collision and instant death from a red circle. In the revision of the game, Michael added in the background a large display in dark gray of the highest score giving an additional incentive for players to reach a high score.

For this project, the first thing covered in the course is basic game algorithms: using a timer, collision detection between simple shapes, object movement using trigonometry, and an object following a mouse. This is the first time these students are involved in coding an application based on a preliminary idea. We look at how to break down a project into small, manageable parts. After having developed a game idea with a setting, rules, and player controls, students create a flow chart that describes all the decisions made in the game, by both the players and the system. Then the game is broken down in individual behaviors and a list is created using pseudo code written in English. In the case of Michael's game, for example, the list includes: the user's control of the circle; the timer necessary to time the pace of the circles appearing on the screen; the collision between circles; and so on.

These parts are all developed first in separate Processing sketches and then incorporated in individual classes. A class is a single document that can be used to generate individual instances of objects. For example, a circle class with a description of the visual look of the circle and its behavior can generate both red and green circles. They both share similar behavior in that they have a core solid color circle growing, but based on their color the collision with the blue circle will have different consequences. Once all the classes have been developed individually, they are assembled in the final program. In the course textbook, Daniel Schiffman describes this process in detail giving a full tutorial of a small game (2008, p. 167).

This method has a number of advantages. Breaking down the project into a set of classes means students are not overwhelmed by the complexity of a project because each individual class can be developed separately. If a given class requires a challenging algorithm, it can be identified early. This modular approach allows for scaling complexity and if followed successfully can help prevent students from getting overwhelmed when writing code.

The last thing we discuss is basic game design principles. The main goal of this particular assignment is to create a game that can lead to a "flow" state for its players. Flow is a theory that was developed by psychologist Mihaly Csikszentmihalyi (1991). It can be reached while performing a task and corresponds to an ideal state of mind between boredom and challenge. When applied to game design, it involves creating a game that is not too easy and not too hard. As players learn the game and become more accustomed to it, their skills evolve and the game has to increase its difficulty. If achieving this outcome is successful, then players get into a state of flow. To achieve this state, players need to be in a constant balance between reward and punishment. They need to feel that they are making meaningful decisions as they play, and that if they fail it is their fault and not because of the unfairness of the game.

In week 2 of the assignment, Michael had a working prototype of his game. In his original design document, he had given Player 1 an additional rule:

> As the circles bounce, their diameter changes relative to their proximity to the blue circle. They shrink when close and grow when far.

After working with the prototype, he realized he had to add another rule for Player 2:

The increase of the diameter of the blue circle decreases the speed of the green and red circles. The decrease of its diameter increases their speed.

Ultimately, the game achieved balance and provided an opportunity for players to reach a state of flow. It also possessed the characteristics of what game designer Jesse Schell defines as elegance in game mechanics:

We call simple systems that perform robustly in complex situations elegant. Elegance is one of the most desirable qualities in any game, because it means you have a game that is simple to learn and understand, but is full of interesting emergent complexity. (2008, p. 197)

Out There In The Void

One of the advanced courses students can take after introduction to scripting is Game Art, in which students study game design as an artistic medium of expression. In the course they are exposed to *avant-garde* art movements of the twentieth century such as dada, surrealism, and fluxus, as well as indie games and art games. They are also introduced to Unity, a programming environment and game engine for creating 2D and 3D games, as well as C# (pronounced "C sharp"), the scripting language used with Unity. The course is divided into three sections In the first section, students design board games and paper prototype games, and in the second section they are introduced to Unity and C# where they create mods based on existing Unity game prototypes. In the third section, students form teams and work together on a project modifying a dungeon crawling prototype in which a character navigates the rooms of a dungeon fighting monsters and looking for treasures. During lectures, I walk students through the process of how the prototypes are created and discuss the Unity interface as well as the code.

For the final assignment, students select an *avant-garde* movement as a starting point for their idea. A team of four students, Megan, Michael, Matt, and Drew, worked together on a game titled *Out There In The Void* (*OTITV*) (Figure 2.6). They had 6 weeks to complete the project. The game was developed using the Unity game development environment. The game prototype is a single-player dungeon crawler. In it, the player controls an avatar from a top–down view using the mouse. Holding down the left button of the mouse and dragging makes the avatar follow the cursor. At the beginning of the game, the avatar finds itself in a room enclosed by walls.

FIGURE 2.6.   Michael and team: *Out There In The Void*

It has to find a way to an opening and move through it. The environment is bigger than the stage and scrolls as the avatar navigates the space. As it moves through the opening, the avatar is teleported to the opening of the next room. The openings can be used to navigate back and forth between the rooms of the dungeon. Various spells in a left side bar can be clicked and triggered to perform attacks on various monsters populating the rooms of the dungeon.

To understand how the prototype works so students can reverse-engineer it for their own game, we recreate the game prototype in class. The functionality of the existing code is discussed section by section as new classes are added to the prototype and the different features of the game are implemented.

In the course textbook, Brian Schrank defines various art game genres. One of these genres, "complicit formal" is defined as using

> performativity and the body to blend games with theatrical art. A contemporary "art experience" freely mingles with a familiar "game experience." Where do the games end and the performance hacks or traditional gallery spaces begin? (2014, p. 95)

OTITV is a single player game with "audience participation" that could be defined as "complicit formal" according to Schrank's definition. It is played in front of an audience comprised of at least one person. The player controls a hand-drawn doodle in the shape of a circle with two dots representing eyes. This doodle finds itself in an environment with a similar structure as the dungeon crawler, a series of rooms accessible through a portal circumvented with a maze-like wall organization. The doodle can be guided using the keyboard from room to room. The environment represents a lined piece of paper with vast unlined areas. The only threat to the doodle is a slowly increasing number of pink erasers chasing it. The doodle can fight back by shooting a cloud of ink toward the erasers to delete them. The doodle can only shoot ink on the areas of the stage with lined paper and as it moves from room to room increasing areas of the lined paper are disappearing.

As a player attempts to make his/her way from page to page, a member of the audience can participate. At the top of the stage are four sentences next to a colored circle, yellow, blue, red, and green. These four-colored circles correspond to four buttons on a Microsoft Xbox videogame console wireless gamepad. With the gamepad, the audience member can select one of the sentences. These sentences are commands given to the player. Examples of commands are: "Don't move down," "Defend yourself," "Find an eraser," "Move forward," "Talk about your experience so far," "Step off the page," "Stay in the void," "Always be moving up," "Maneuver around erasers," "Stay next to a wall," "Survive as long as you can in the void," "Pause the game." These commands are not enforced by the software but instead are understood as rules the player has to obey in front of the audience.

As an inspiration for this project, the team referenced Flux artist George Maciunas's *Flux Ping-Pong* (1976). In that project, audience members are encouraged to play table tennis on a modified ping-pong table. One side of the table is slanted in its middle at a 30° angle and the other has a large hole carved at its center. Audience members attempting to play a game are severely hindered by the modified table. The modifications bring forth the affordances of the game on a regular table. In *OTITV*, by having audience members intervene during the game and add arbitrary challenges to the player, the game gets closer to an interactive art piece, as art historian Katja Kwastek writes:

> Aesthetic experience manifests itself in a process of oscillation between flow and reflection, between absorption in the interaction and distanced (self)-perception, and between cathartic transformation and cognitive judgment. (2013, p. 162)

Let us recap on Michael's computational learning. In *Introduction to Scripting*, after learning programming fundamentals, he learned to write down the behavior of his game as pseudo-code, then how to take advantage of the object-oriented programming paradigm, by breaking down complex processes into discrete algorithms embedded into separate classes. In *Game Art*, Michael's understanding of object and classes helped him reverse-engineer a game prototype with help from his teammates. The core element he learned in both courses is the inherent tension between transparency and reflection in the digital medium and how to take advantage of it in his projects. With *AREA*, Michael created an immersive experience that could lead players in a state of flow, getting them absorbed in the game. In *OTITV*, he created a more complex and ultimately flawed experience, a combination of procedurality and embodiment, in which players are constantly disrupted in their play by the audience interfering with their digital experience. These two projects, at opposite end of the flow/reflection spectrum, provide a glimpse of what is at the core of all interactive applications. As media theorists Bolton and Gromala write in their book *Windows and Mirrors*, "every digital artifact oscillates between being transparent and reflective" (2003, p. 6).

CONCLUSION

The works of Saam, Ting, and Michael present just three cases among many students I have taught over the years. They instantiate cases where computation "clicked" and they were able to experience something unique to the medium through their learning. In the introduction of his book *Mindstorms*, Seymour Papert (1980) describes his early childhood fascination with car parts and, most specifically, gears. As a 2-year old, he merely enjoyed rotating wheels. A few years later, he actually understood how they worked. Pappert explains that the abstract model of gears he developed in his head helped him understand early mathematical concepts in elementary school. What he suggests is that developing an affective relationship with technology generates intellectual models that can help solve complex abstract problems. This seems to be the key from my experience teaching computation to art/design students. The vast majority have already developed an affect for creativity. Making visual work gives them satisfaction. Art/design students learn by caring for what they make. Learning computational skills to create interactive experiences is challenging and requires a different creative mindset to the more common media expressions they are used to. What is common, however, is the desire to achieve working control over the content and form of their ideas. In the digital studio, students translate their ideas into code, which facilitates the process of assimilating and applying a new way of thinking through an intrinsic motivation to see their ideas take shape. Once they have control of that motivation, they are willing to push themselves and take the extra steps necessary to become creative coders.

REFERENCES

Bogost, I. (2009). Persuasive Games: The Proceduralist Style. Retrieved from www.gamasutra.com/view/feature/132302/persuasive_games_the_.php. Accessed online February 16, 2016.

(2010). Cow Clicker: The Making of Obsession. Retrieved from http://bogost.com/writing/blog/cow_clicker_1/. Accessed online February 16, 2016.

Bolter, J. and Grusin, R. (1999). *Remediation. Understanding New Media*. Cambridge, MA: MIT Press.

Bruner, J. (1996). *The Culture of Education*. Cambridge, MA: Harvard University Press.

Crawford, C. (2003). *Chris Crawford on Game Design*. Berkeley, CA: New Riders.

Deleuze, G. (2006). What is the creative act? In Lapoujade, D. (Ed.), *Two Regimes of Madness: Texts and Interviews 1975–1995* (pp. 312–24). Los Angeles, CA: Semiotexte.

Kay, A. C. (1990). User interface: A personal view. In Laurel, B. (Ed.), *The Art of Human–Computer Interface Design* (pp. 191–207). Reading, MA: Addison-Wesley Publishing.

Kwastek, K. (2013). *Aesthetics of Interaction in Digital Art*. Cambridge, MA: MIT Press.

Maciunas, G. (1976). *Flux Ping-Pong*. Retrieved from http://wgfluxus.tumblr.com/post/1331395914/image-george-maciunas-flux-ping-pong-1976. Accessed online February 16, 2016.

Manovich, L. (2013). *Software Takes Command: Extending the Language of New Media*. London: Bloomsbury Publishing.

Mondloch, K. (2010). *Screens: Viewing Media Installation Art*. Minneapolis, MN: University of Minnesota Press.

Papert, S. (1980). *Mindstorms: Children, Computers, and Powerful Ideas*. New York: Basic Books.

Rohrer, J. (2007). *Passage*. Retrieved from http://hcsoftware.sourceforge.net/passage/. Accessed online February 16, 2016.

Schell, J. (2008). *The Art of Game Design: A Book of Lenses*. Amsterdam: Elsevier/Morgan Kaufmann.

Schrank, B. (2014). *Avant-garde Videogames: Playing with Technoculture*. Cambridge, MA: MIT Press.

Shiffman, D. (2008). *Learning Processing: A Beginner's Guide to Programming Images, Animation, and Interaction*. Amsterdam: Morgan Kaufmann/Elsevier.

PART II

CODE AS MEDIUM

3

ARRAY[ ]: Coding Slowly

CHANNEL TWO

Abstract: Code is the pervasive, invisible material that drives our contemporary mediated environment: the electricity flowing through our landscapes, the models of environmental collapse, and billions of dollars spent distracting people from considering what that collapse might mean. Code is not merely on the backend of the actual mainstream art worlds of cinema and video games; it has become a driving aesthetic. While our students may detour through galleries and museums, they carry around intensely powerful, networked, code-driven devices and soon return to larger screens to further engage with software and social media. The foundation of contemporary art and design practices is code. Teaching and learning the code underlying all new media is challenging. Mere access to information does not prompt students to teach themselves. The introduction of code to first-year postsecondary students can occur through critical discourse and be connected to more than future job prospects. Who can read and write code right now? What kind of programs are they writing? What kinds of questions are being asked? Whose voices are present? Are critical perspectives about code happening in art and design worlds? Are radical, boundary-pushing queries being made? ARRAY foregrounds code literacy and agency for artists and designers in an effort to address these questions.

Keywords: creative coding, learnable programming, agency, computational literacy, art and design foundation, critical coding

ARRAY[ ]: CODING SLOWLY

Mere access to information does not prompt students to teach themselves. This fantasy, however, frequently forms the basis of pedagogical approaches to new media. While the abundance of online tutorials can augment some subjects, new media processes are complex and the multiple approaches to any given topic are difficult to navigate. We believe that agency with new media comes from learning foundational skills in safe, structured, and responsive environments. In this chapter, we introduce ARRAY[ ], discuss code as a priority in art and design foundations, evaluate the current climate surrounding code in art and design, and present "Coding Slowly," the first project in our code curriculum.

ARRAY[ ] is a web repository of entryways into new media craft, processes, materials, cultures, and contexts specifically geared toward beginners. Casually, we have described it as an online textbook with "teachers edition" notes. Projects on the site are organized and searchable through key concepts and provide detailed lesson plans that include instructional narratives, new vocabulary, material for students, example files, and relevant links. ARRAY[ ] is neither a Massive Open Online Course nor a software tutorial site. It is an evolving collection of new media curricula designed by new media instructors with years of experience in teaching first-year college students in foundations-level classrooms and studios. We created a set of guiding principles that reflect our motivation to differentiate the site from other online education approaches.

ARRAY[ ] is

- independent and noncorporate. Our editors, developers, advisers, contributors, and organizers are all teachers and professors deeply invested in education.
- free of financial barriers.
- a repository of knowledge based on the idea that the "foundations" of new media are constantly shifting, negotiated, contested, and divergent.
- focused on art and design students, because these are populations that can operate outside the limits of acceptable behavior.
- resistant to uncritical approaches to teaching contemporary media practices.
- suspicious of concepts like "access," "innovation," and "evidence-based strategies."
- counter to cultures of training and certification.
- interested in sociopolitical factors of interface, media, and distribution systems.
- conscious of the complexity of learning over time.
- intended to assist teachers and learners in reducing fear, and increasing agency.

ARRAY[ ] currently includes project scenarios, essays, and blog entries that can be referenced as starting points for learning. Unlike a conventional printed textbook, ARRAY[ ] uses the flexibility of the web platform to grow, change, and respond to shifts in art, design, and education. Our projects can be modified at any time as contributors test and refine their projects in studios and classrooms, or updated as philosophies, circumstances, and technologies change. Contributor essays and blog entries capture current thoughts and accumulate over time to reveal patterns and trends in thinking and activity. The title ARRAY[ ] is inspired by a concept common to programming languages that means, "a systematic arrangement" or "a variable that can be indexed." ARRAY[ ], true to its namesake, is a flexible container of elements related to new media foundations for art and design education.

CODE IS NOT EASY

The word "easy" occurs regularly throughout papers and talks regarding programming pedagogy. In "A Pedagogical Pattern for Teaching Computer Programming to Non-CS Majors," Zhen Jiang, Eduardo Fernandez, and Liang Cheng claim that "advanced materials can be transparent, making them easy to learn and to practice" (2011, p. 3). There is also a generally accepted outlook that students would learn programming easily if programming languages could provide instant results. Students are framed as impatient consumers who need simple, visual results quickly, lest their attention span wander. In an article in Infoworld (Bartimo, 1984), Alan Kay – an object-oriented programming pioneer and Smalltalk co-creator – described testing programs and machines for ease of use at Xerox's Palo Alto Research Center: "I thought children would be pretty good because they have no strong motivation for patience." Designing for students as if they are impatient children runs throughout Bret Victor's essay "Learnable Programming" (2012). Victor is quite explicit that code should be easy to learn. His assessment of existing pedagogical languages and approaches is based on this idea in nearly every case. Programming, and learning to program, must be easy, and it must also be immediate where "The environment must be designed to get something on the screen as soon as possible, so the programmer can start reacting."

Bret Victor, by his own account, was an early designer for iPad user interface concepts. In our initial ARRAY[ ] proposal (Trowbridge and Westbrook, 2011), we explicitly pointed to the iPad as a device which trained students to use technology as consumers rather than creators. The "appification" of technology – which brings access via immediacy and ease of use at the expense of agency – cannot be uncoupled from either Kay or Victor's approach to conceptualizing people's ways of interacting with computers. Designing easy-to-use programming languages moves students away from understanding how computers work and creates more consumers of already developed software. Thirty-eight years before the iPad, Kay described his vision of pedagogical computers in A Personal Computer for Children of All Ages (1972).

> A better "book," one which is active (like the child) rather than passive. It may be something with the attention grabbing powers of TV, but controllable by the child rather than the networks. It can be like a piano: (a product of technology, yes), but one which can be a tool, a toy, a medium of expression, a source of unending pleasure and delight . . . and, as with most gadgets in unenlightened hands, a terrible drudge!!

While Kay would later criticize the iPad (Greelish, 2013) for its tight control of sharing content, he imagined his Dynabook as a device driven by paid, controlled consumption. He explained how information could be purchased via vending machines that would allow the user to see the full information after paying for it.

Brett Victor also turned to a children's toy, arguing that programming languages should be like a bucket of Lego that can be dumped out onto the floor so that people new to programming can "create-by-reacting." How this might work is not clear but it is driven by the idea, repeated throughout "Learnable Programming," of moving students out of a mode of thinking in their heads and, instead, acting immediately. The irony of using Lego as a model is perhaps only evident to parents who grew up with Lego and have bought Lego for their children recently. The toy is no longer simple, clever building blocks that fit Victor's metaphor. The most popular Lego sets are made up of very specialized pieces that allow children to easily, if not instantly, get outside their head and recreate scenes from the popular big-budget movies and television.

Bret Victor's description of a potential "learnable" programming language is much more vague than Kay's description of the Dynabook, and thus likely never to come about. Many of his ideas do not seem plausible. A telling example is his desire for code that would draw a rectangle to the screen before the programmer had finished specifying the size and ratio of the rectangle, a Platonic ideal rectangle that the programmer, now more of a user, could then customize. These approaches attempt to address a perceived need for students to see something immediately. Like Kay, Victor assumes students have no patience. However, he extends this beyond children to anyone who wants to learn to program. "Learnable Programming" is an outline for a strange approach to programming that is instantly visible to a student who flows through it visually comprehending what she has not yet thought out. While this might be a huge leap forward in the way some people would like to interact with computers (if it were at all possible), it also sounds very much like an alternative to learning to use code instead of an improvement on writing code and creating programs. The layers of abstraction necessary to implement Victor's learnable programming language would result in code that is far removed from the binary math behind the code, obscuring and even mystifying how the computer works.

The arc of Apple Computers from a computer marketed for education, and framed as a tool for creative production, to an "ecosystem company" (Jackson, 2014) focused on seamless access to movies, television, and music, has influenced many educators' outlook on the relationship between pedagogy and computers. While many factors led to the decision to found ARRAY[ ], two important things happened with Apple that serve as reasons that new media art and design students should be critical of any attempt to make things easy and immediate: Apple radically changed Final Cut from a professional to a consumer-oriented video editing tool, and they locked out software created by anyone other than paying Apple Developers by default in OS X 10.8. New media art and design departments had come to rely on Apple for professional video editing and for creating and running art software. Relying on one company for so much art and design studio practice, curriculum, and pedagogy was never wise but there was little choice when the assumption was that artists and designers want to immediately express themselves using a computer. This assumption requires software that is as simple and as removed from the hardware as possible.

The current climate surrounding code and computing, and the attachment to "easy," has a detrimental influence on the integration of code as a foundation for art and design. It keeps faculty and potential students waiting for other people to produce the perfect, immediate, visual approach to programming. Without a radical change to the underlying hardware, Victor's learnable programming would need to be designed and coded by people who are able to program in complex, low-level (and thus, unlearnable, by his standards) languages. By arguing for these simplifications as a necessary step toward programming pedagogy, Victor promotes removing agency from students, making them once again reliant on *actual* programmers.

Faculty with no experience in programming are unable to differentiate between complex programming that has been labeled as easy, unrealistic proposals like Victor's and scaled-down tools that provide easy results but reduce agency beyond simple results. All too often, these uninformed faculties are making curricular decisions. Their knowledge is based on experience with consumer tools used for digital imaging and video, trending "educational technology" (Stager, 2012), and seduction by, or rejection of, current media hype.

RESISTANCES TO CODE IN NEW MEDIA ART AND
DESIGN FOUNDATIONS: CODE.EDU HYPE

"Learnable Programming" is a strange, fever dream manifesto compared to the rational, career-focused code push spawned by the intersection of entrepreneurial, education startups and the sharp focus on science, technology, engineering, and mathematics (STEM) in K-12 education in the United States. The resistance to this within higher education, especially in humanities and the arts, is based on a suspicion or rejection of what Bill Joy (2000) described as "our attitude toward the new . . . our bias toward instant familiarity and unquestioning acceptance." It is easy to become suspicious of any move toward code literacy when the overriding (i.e., well-funded) dialogue is centered on job training ("What's wrong with," n.d.). In an article titled "How Big is Coding Right Now? A Programming School Just Sold for $36m" (Finley, 2015), code is so big that commercial education is buying whatever bits they can get and venture capital is funding whatever it can. It is "the growing 'code literacy' market." The "Year of Code" (CNN Money, Code Year, 2012) came and went in 2012, and it returned in 2014. "Over the course of the year we will signpost national and community tech events, crowdsource funding to help parents, pupils and educational organizations. We will commission detailed polling and analysis on how we can take coding far and wide" (Year of Code, 2014). It is difficult to see a difference between this description of teaching code and the language used by technology incubators.

Our students, learning to code slowly, are not driven by a desire to join a startup company or found the next online service company. An example of what really holds their interest is an intersection of biology, code, and capitalism, in the form of the retail store Target (Duhigg, 2012). In 2002, Target began investigating how they could use their massive collection of customer data to discover whether a customer was pregnant. As part of a discussion of loops, we consider the power of iteration cycles of code. The Processing void draw() loop runs again and again, 60 times per second and, as we accentuate in class, will continue to do so as long as the computer has power. Ada Byron, Countess of Lovelace, wrote of Charles Babbage's Analytical Engine (King, 1843):

> *A cycle* of operations, then, must be understood to signify any *set of operations* which is repeated *more than once. It is equally a cycle, whether it be repeated twice* only, or an infinite number of times; for it is the fact of a *repetition occurring at all* that constitutes it such. In many cases of analysis there is a *recurring group* of one or more *cycles*; that is, a *cycle of a cycle, or a cycle of cycles.*

Our students' firsthand experience with automation via cycles of code becomes literacy with the ways in which corporations and governments are able to use data for control. These cycles enable the collection and logging of metadata by the National Security Agency (NSA), facial recognition for security theater, and invasive marketing. When the recurring cycles include code that connects a set of consumer behavior that indicates pregnancy, Target is able to market to women who may not have shared with anyone that they are pregnant. In the case of a Minnesota teen, Target not only invaded her privacy but also inadvertently announced her pregnancy to her father when it sent her coupons. Working with loops, students can begin to extrapolate even more situations where capturing this kind of data will infringe on privacy and be used for tighter control by both corporations and governments.

If students are impatient, as Kay and Victor believe, it is because they live in a capital-oriented culture that encourages the impatience that serves and drives entire markets. Billions of dollars in advertising and entertainment discourage criticality and encourage people to react immediately, emotionally, and impulsively. Educators do not need to cater to this approach in order to reach students. Our experience has been that most students are willing to be patient when they are presented with a meaningful approach to a complex topic. They are not impatient children but have learned to resist things that seem like marketing, including pedagogical approaches.

Reading and writing code, the definition of programming, requires intense practice over a long period of time. The intense need for practice is shared between code and other art and design media, particularly drawing. However, first-year art and design students arrive with a great deal of experience in mark making and virtually no experience with code. A drawing instructor can generally assume students can use a pencil, based on a lifetime of experience. From early childhood on, students have been making marks with chalk, crayons, and graphite. Students understand a great deal about pencil use:

- It is held in the dominant hand and is useful both in a specific, supported way and in a multitude of other potentially useful applications.
- Results from holding it in the nondominant hand can be amusing.
- It makes marks on paper and other surfaces but not all surfaces.
- These marks are a combination of how it is moved and what pressure is applied.
- Too much pressure results in an error in which the mark making material breaks.
- Pencils can be misused in a variety of ways, they stick in ceilings, and one pencil will break another.

These same students, born in the 1990s or later, have typically spent their entire lives using digital devices ("Millennials Tech-Dependent," 2010), yet they have little to no idea how the devices work. Compounding this illiteracy, the phrase "digital native" (Prensky, 2001) is applied to them, a popular sentiment that refers to a competent consumer of technology products. In art and design departments, the belief that students already know how to use (Sadowski, 2014) computers intersects with an existing faculty that lacks experience with new media. This results in inertia that prevents the introduction of any new media in foundations, particularly code. When introduced to code, students are not aware of their digital native status. Many describe themselves as "dumb with" or "terrible with" computers. Their fluency only applies to using interfaces and, even then, their native tongue involves near-random clicking on icons that might seem helpful.

The introduction of code to first-year postsecondary students can be critical and connected to more than future job prospects. Anastasia Salter (2011) wrote that "a student who is only familiar with what others' programs can do, and used to working within those systems, might never consider a solution outside those boxes." A critical approach introduces students to code in ways that suggest not only thinking outside the box but also thinking about how the box is constructed, who makes the box, and their current role in the box. When this approach is brought into art and design foundations, new boxes and power structures emerge.

RESISTANCES TO CODE IN NEW MEDIA ART
AND DESIGN FOUNDATIONS: (MERELY)
"A SPECIALIZED FIELD OF ITS OWN"

In the first "Year of Code," 2012, art historian and critic Claire Bishop wrote "Digital Divide" (2012), describing the lack of new media art in the "mainstream" art world. The essay quickly glosses over decades of new media art history in multiple art worlds, labeling new media as "a specialized field of its own," so that Bishop can return to the mainstream and build the case for a "divide." The absurdity of this maneuver was likely invisible to the mainstream art world readers but it sent ripples through new media art worlds and communities – not because it was surprising, but because it made visible what we always suspected, new media is intentionally excluded from conversations regarding the (imagined) mainstream art world. In many circles, including academia, people are ignorant about the practice of new media art and design. This includes people teaching in, and administrating, art departments. The situation in the field of design is more complex. There is a longstanding relationship between technology and process in design fields. The early success of Apple and Adobe are tied into their use for desktop publishing, and the mechanical processes in design became software-based. However, in many design studios and companies, and in most academic design departments, there is a wall between the people who design and the people who write code. Web design and interactive design become "front end" and "back end," with design departments focused only on the former.

Bishop's short description, and it is not unique, points to "commercial galleries, the Turner Prize, national pavilions at Venice," a collection of specialized art worlds that only a very small number of people would consider mainstream. We are well past any interest in the discussion of high and low art required to believe that this small, privileged art world represents, via audience or (their primary anchor) financial measures, any sort of mainstream. The most popular art forms, by both measures, are cinema and the emergent form of video games. Both are intensely reliant on code.

If code is considered outside the mainstream art and design worlds, is it outside the foundations of art and design? Code is the pervasive, invisible material that drives our contemporary-mediated environment: the electricity flowing through our landscapes, the models of environmental collapse, and the billions of dollars spent to distract people from considering what that collapse might mean. Code is not merely on the backend of the actual mainstream art worlds of cinema and video games, it has become the driving aesthetic. While our students may detour through galleries and museums, they carry around with them intensely powerful, networked, code-driven devices and soon return to larger screens of some sort. Code holds a predominant critical and conceptual position in the mainstream world but is only a "specialized field" in the imagined mainstream art world. Foundation classes are not limited to addressing the specialized field made up of "commercial galleries, the Turner Prize, [and] national pavilions at Venice." The foundation of contemporary art and design practices, outside that specialized world, is code.

Where and how code fits into the predominant art world is a distraction to increasing the number of new media artists and designers who are using code, as is the hype from entrepreneurial education. If anything, they point to why there is a need for more art and design instructors, and administrators, who understand code working in foundations programs. As art and design faculty who understand code, we know that there is no need to indoctrinate or entice students, only to offer them structured opportunities to encounter programming as a creative practice. Coding slowly is a step toward that.

CODE AS CONTEMPORARY ART AND DESIGN MEDIUM

We believe that it is the responsibility of foundations art and design departments and programs to introduce code as an art and design medium. Art and design students should learn to read and write code because they are a population that can operate outside of the bounds of acceptable behavior. ARRAY[ ] is a prompt for artists and designers to think critically and push the boundaries of contemporary life. Unfortunately, new media integration at the foundations level has in recent years been co-opted and limited by professional interests and trapped in a yearly cycle of training students to use and adopt Adobe Creative Suite tools. This trend leaves students with little more than an introduction to software-based digital imaging and video editing. ARRAY[ ] intentionally foregrounds code as an imperative in foundations curriculum.

Foundation studio instructors and administrators might think of code as something that happens in Internet start-ups and in the computer science department. This may be true currently, but using material native to other fields, industries, or in other areas of academia is not new to art and design. Borrowing and appropriating tools, ideas, and methods from science, engineering, math, literature, anthropology, and history for use in art and design curriculum has been a standard practice for sometime. While welding is taught in sculpture classes, it is neither part of an education in engineering, specifically, nor an attempt to move the students toward becoming a Certified Welder. In academia, programming is still primarily taught in the computer science department. However, code education in art and design foundations does not necessarily mean teaching computer science. The areas covered by computer science are fairly new and the boundaries are contested. Paul Graham (2003), in discussing affinities between art and programming, suggests that computer science is also a complex mixture of approaches:

> I've never liked the term "computer science." The main reason I don't like it is that there's no such thing. Computer science is a grab bag of tenuously related areas thrown together by an accident of history, like Yugoslavia. At one end you have people who are really mathematicians, but call what they're doing computer science so they can get DARPA grants. In the middle you have people working on something like the natural history of computers – studying the behavior of algorithms for routing data through networks, for example. And then at the other extreme you have the hackers, who are trying to write interesting software, and for whom computers are just a medium of expression, as concrete is for architects or paint for painters. It's as if mathematicians, physicists, and architects all had to be in the same department.

Graham describes a desire to build "beautiful software," which hints at entry points for code within art and design. Instead of using tools made by programmers to create beautiful images and objects, art and design students can engage with the aesthetics and politics of code as code, a contemporary art and design medium. We cannot predict what this will look like as a widespread practice. There are too few artists in new media programming their own work and too many artists outside new media hiring programmers to make new media art. The mainstream art world promotes pairing (and thus dividing) artists and technologists, from the 1966 "9 Evenings: Theatre and Engineering" ("9 Evenings," n.d.) to the recent Seven on Seven Conference (Connor, 2015), organized by Rhizome. Introducing code at the foundations level is intended to provide a basis for change across the curriculum, and, at minimum, provide students an introduction robust enough that they understand that it is a medium that they do not need to become a computer scientist, or hire one, in order to use.

AN EXAMPLE FROM ARRAY[ ]: CODING SLOWLY

If more people, different people, could write code, what kinds of programs might be written? What sort of questions could be asked, or answered?

We invite first-year art and design instructors to consider the state of things in the contemporary world. Is everything okay? Are things settled, fair, sustainable, inclusive, beautiful? The programmers are programming. The products are being developed. The programmers are programming. The data is being captured. The programmers are programming. The information is being parsed. The programmers are programming. The patterns are being identified. The programmers are programming. The logistics are being refined. The programmers are programming. The products are developed. Code is being developed continuously but very few people are talking about who is developing that code:

Who can read and write code right now?
What kinds of programs are they writing?
What kinds of systems are being put in place?
What kinds of questions are being asked?
Whose voices are present?
Are critical perspectives about code happening in art and design worlds?
Are there radical, boundary-pushing queries being made?

Art and design students are a complicated set of people, often uncoupled from clear career direction but curious, inventive, and inclined to find and push boundaries. This is especially true at the foundation level. ARRAY[ ] was founded in the hope that these people will write programs, and question the present from a code-literate perspective. We hope they will create a critical, fair, sustainable, inclusive, beautiful future.

The project below is our initial introduction to code. Our approach uses the Processing programming language, which was developed by artists and designers as "a flexible software sketchbook and a language for learning how to code within the context of the visual arts" (Processing, 2015). Like all ARRAY[ ] projects, it is written for an audience of instructors, at the high school to first-year college level. Our subsequent project, titled "From Here to There and Back Again: Loops, Variables and Conditionals in Processing," forms a sequence that creates a complete introduction to fundamental programming for art and design students. However, ARRAY[ ] also includes code introductions and projects from other instructors. These projects are all intended to serve faculty who are already teaching new media at the foundations level and faculty who need to learn. The writing on ARRAY[ ] is intentionally more informal and conversational in tone than textbooks and academic publications and the project below is presented here as it is on the site.

CODING SLOWLY (INTRO TO BASIC PROGRAMMING WITH PROCESSING)

Project Narrative

This project sequence introduces code as a material for art and design practices. Like all projects in ARRAY[ ], Coding Slowly is an effort to distill a complex practice into a foundational experience. This project can be used as a starting point for learning. Its authors will likely continue to refine and update the project over time.

The approaches presented here have been developed based on observations and evolving questions including: How can code be introduced to beginners within a context of art and design foundations? How can art and design methods be referenced or integrated in creative coding edu? How can pedagogy interrupt and address gender, race, and class discrepancies in code-based art and design practices?

Starting Points

Code underlies most forms of contemporary art and design: architecture, data visualization, electronics, fabrication, graphics, imaging, kinetic sculpture/objects, media, modeling, output, sound, visual communication design/publication, video games/interactive spaces, web-based art/design.

Any process involving software, electronics, digital fabrication, or the Internet involves code. Code sensibilities and skills are immensely useful and transferrable. Code literacy leads to agency. Agency becomes options. Options translate to flexibility for artists and designers. Creative outliers in sustainable situations ask questions and push boundaries.

Intentions

Code is not easy. "Coding Slowly" provides a flow of commented samples presented along with relatable visual art and design references, themes, topics, and activities. "Slowly" is used in the project title to communicate, with intention, that being careful is okay (and encouraged). Learning is not a race. While code concepts should be considered and mapped, starting in preschool, this integration is not yet the norm. Late learners need time to get used to new concepts. Some learners need to experiment, some need regular practice, some need a project to get started. Some people need time alone, others need group dynamics. Progress is relative. Programming is not easy for most artists and designers. Ask programmers how long it took for them to internalize and translate the concepts. A frequent response is "years!"

Artists and designers do not usually gravitate toward the study of computer science. Material (even code) needs qualities, context, and meaning that artists and designers can study and manipulate. This might be accomplished through individual experience, or may need to be shaped through curriculum and pedagogy. "Coding Slowly" can be directed toward the traditional, formal concerns of art and design foundations (drawing, color, 3D structures, time-based media), or it could be attached to contemporary practices. For example, if the teacher/learner is interested in sociopolitical themes, code-based practices can reference recognition/ surveillance systems, data scenarios, Internet [history/politics/darknet], or other under-explored or invisible territories. Screening the Hello World! Processing Documentary [https://vimeo.com/60735314] will reveal a lack of diversity in the field of creative-coding, illustrating some common gender/ race discrepancies in technology-oriented fields. Digging into game design/ mechanics/cultures and problematic entertainment tropes/stereotypes will reveal some pervasive patterns in terms of representation and audience in code-generated media. Less sociopolitical approaches might involve associating code-based practices with everyday life experience like language, routines, seasons, and cultural artifacts and activities. Find everyday life correlations (i.e., comfort zones) described as follows.

Potential comfort zones: Associating code-based practices with everyday life

There are many ways to conversationally weave in, parallel or reference familiar activity when introducing programming concepts. This may help put some people at ease.

Connecting with rules: All human languages use rules to constrain behaviors/outcomes/meanings. How many letters do we have? How do you end a sentence? When do we start a new paragraph? All programming languages use rules too.

Connecting with procedure: Even the most mundane human activities/routines involve order of operations (e.g., getting dressed, making food, brushing teeth). How would you describe the steps involved in making a sandwich or preparing a bowl of cereal? All programming languages use order too.

Connecting with variables and conditions: Cultural activities like cooking and playing games involve variations (dynamic information) and situations (if). Recipes have ingredients and process, games have inventory and mechanics. All programming languages use variables, and conditionals too.

Connecting with iteration or looping: Cultural activities like knitting and weaving, and rhythms and beats use repeating patterns (again and again) that begin and end when a condition is met. Most life systems – from biology (e.g., breathing, living, dying) to weather (time, seasons) involve cycles. All programming languages use iteration too.

Potential anxiety zones: Experience, conditioning, words, alienation, expectations

Consider experience: Students have been drawing, assembling physical objects, dressing themselves, and watching movies since they were toddlers. They have developed instincts and literacies. Show them a painting, a sculptural installation, performance, or video art, and they have some understanding of the process, some agency, based on a lifetime of related experience. Is code part of a lifetime of experience? Not currently.

Consider conditioning: There are many cultural factors (in the United States) that might contribute to the anxiety of learning. Pervasive testing culture, schedule-oriented lifestyles, and closed apps/consumer devices are a few norms that remove abstract thinking, procedural/problem solving skills, critical thinking, and inquiry from daily life.

Consider words: The words code, program, and hack can have negative connotations (or aggressive associations). Code can mean secret. Program can mean control. Hack can mean cut. Semantics matter.

Consider feelings: Programming involves the abject or uncanny use of common English symbols (consider what happens when symbols change meaning). What happens when you see familiar letters and words doing strange things, or little pieces of punctuation behaving very differently than expected? Is it agitating, alienating, disorienting? Humans might be more wired to reject than rationalize fear or unknowns.

Consider expectations: Sharing inspiring, high-profile works when introducing new themes or topics in college-level art and design classes is a tradition and convention. Most code-based art and design (online, in exhibitions, museums, and galleries) involved a collaboration of people with a range of skills and years of experience. It is not uncommon for "technology" artists and designers to outsource the code work by hiring programmers, without transparent attribution. Is it fair to present these examples as something that can be accomplished? Or does it set students up for disappointment?

Vocabulary

boolean, code, coordinate, hsb, IDE, iteration, logic, program, programming language, pixel, procedural thinking, rgb, software, syntax, variable, vector

Structure and Timing

Review the Instructional Narrative below. Download Processing and gather the downloadable content files (Step 01: 2D shapes, Step 02: 3D shapes, Step 03: colors, Step 04: variables, Step 05: conditionals, Step 06: iteration, Step 07: functions, Step 08: input, Step 09: output, Step 10: images, Step 11: text, Step 12: arrays, Step 13: objects).

"Coding Slowly" can be spread out over weeks/integrated in courses or modified for a 1–2 day workshop. Experiment with timing. Pay attention to the group needs and dynamics. Humans need to move. Interrupt screen-time. Repeat material as needed.

Instructional Narrative

Getting Started/software installation: Download, extract, and install Processing. www.processing.org/download/?processing

Classroom/workshop: This may be something students can do on their own time, or it may be something you want to do as a group. If downloading en masse is problematic (Internet issues), an option is to distribute the software via a portable usb drive. Once the software is obtained, students should move the extracted Processing Application icon to: HD > Applications (note: this is Mac-oriented, operating systems vary). Remind/ inform students that they should never run software from the download directory or from the desktop because of the likelihood of problems. Processing sketches use a nested directory structure (for files and assets like images and fonts) so it is a good idea to keep Processing organized/ situated properly from the start.

Getting Started/software orientation: Preferences, Menus

Menu – Processing > Preferences: It is always a good idea to look at the preferences when you are getting your bearings with new software. With Processing, you want to decide where your files and assets will save (this is file management). By default, Processing saves all of your sketches (files) to something like this sketchbook location – /User/Documents/Processing.

Menu – File > Examples: These are very useful for intermediate and advanced learners. We discourage beginners from borrowing/appropriating because they will rely on the skills, experience, and intentions of another author. Students new to this material will not have the skills to fix their own problems they should attempt to modify existing works above their skill set. This could lead to frustration, learned helplessness, and disengagement.

Menu – Sketch > Import Library: These are very useful for intermediate and advanced learners, but will not pertain to beginners right away. (Note for a more experienced future: libraries extend/expand the functionality of Processing so that Processing can do more complex things with media, hardware, etc.)

For future reference, there are currently three levels of libraries:

1. From the menu, select a library that is already installed (dxf down through video): These are vetted and standard libraries already installed and bundled in the current version of Processing. When one of these libraries is selected, Processing will place a piece of code (text) in your sketch telling your sketch to import the library package.

2. Add Library: These are contributed libraries that have to be down-loaded before they are bundled with your current version of Processing. Because this is Open Source software, contributed libraries are in con-stant development. Note: this is a great time to have a conversation contrasting the development of commercial software and open source software, a new concept to most beginners currently. Once you "Add Library" that library will be listed and selectable through the Import

Library just like dxf, etc. You can also use "Add Library" to remove an installed library from your software.

3. Find more contributed Libraries, install them manually: www.processing.org/reference/libraries/ and how to install instructions: https://github.com/processing/processing/wiki/How-to-Install-a-Contribut

Getting Started/software anatomy (or Processing Development Environment): file name, toolbar, mode, tabs, text editor, error messages, console, line number

Sketch file name/software version: The default name is actually the sketch creation date; use "save as" to name sketches more specifically. Note: .pde file extension means "processing development environment."

Sketch mode: Mode selection is based on the final output or platform; Java is the default and where this project flow starts. Java mode is useful for standalone applications that will launch on an individual's computer (run launches locally); JavaScript is useful for translating Processing for web (run launches browser); there are additional modes for more advanced learners.

Toolbar: The current visible/actionable buttons are run sketch, stop sketch, open a sketch, save this sketch, export (again, Processing is in Java mode by default).

Tab organization (advanced): As sketches grow in complexity, they can be organized into multiple tabs as a means to separate functionality and make editing easier; this is an advanced feature but something to be aware of, especially if students are looking at published samples and examples. With beginners, multiple tabs are often a red flag that they are modifying appropriated/borrowed material.

Code text editor: All this white space gets filled with lines of code which form a program; when the "run" button is activated, the code entered in the text editor is "compiled" (or translated to something your computer can use and understand). Processing then generates visual feedback, a display window showing the code in its visual form.

Code error messages: These are very useful! Introduce students to the error as a friendly helper and nothing to be alarmed by. Even the most advanced Programmers spend a significant portion of their time evaluating errors. This never-ending process is called debugging code.

Console (or output information): This area is useful for receiving error details, and useful for getting data feedback from programs using variables.

Line number: This number shows where your cursor is in the code text editor area.

Getting Started/the display window (launched via the run or play button): The *x, y* coordinate plane is new to many students and it takes time and practice to internalize it. Never assume the coordinate plane is a familiar concept or will come naturally. Sometimes gestures or physical activity helps students internalize information or form pneumonic devices. If it is a good time to stretch and feel weird, have students form an x with their body and move across the space/horizon line; then have them form a y with their body and jump up and down on an imagined vertical. You could even craft event scores in small groups. Alternative activities might include: plotting/ drawing shapes on wide-ruled graph paper, or preparing physical manipulative and doing a bingo-type game calling out coordinates.

The rest of this ARRAY[ ] project is made up of well-commented Processing sketches, available for download on the project page. The code below is an example of one of the many short examples.

```
// loop with a while [do while true!]
// this sketch uses ellipse geometry to demonstrate
any geometry can
// be used in a while loop
// variable is in the x position so the horizontal
position is dynamic
// when the test is false, the program exits curlies,
continues through stack,
// returns to draw();
// comparing approaches to repetition:
// conditional: if the expression is true, a
conditional runs
// ONCE then goes to top of the draw
// while loop: if the expression is true, a while runs
// FOREVER until it proves false, then goes to top of
draw

int i=10;

void setup() {
  size (300, 200);
  background(50);
  stroke(255);
  noFill();
}
```

```
void draw() {

  while (i<300) {
    ellipse (i, height/2, 50, 50);
    i=i+30;
  }
}
```

CONCLUSION: THE FUTURE, SLOWLY, NOW

Given the current pervasive code-based state of things, there should be no need to describe or detail why art and design students should be introduced to code in the foundation year. However, art and design foundations are lagging behind. We need to instigate critical new directions. There is no simple, easy solution to the integration of new media pedagogy into foundations art and design programs. Teaching and learning the code underlying all new media is challenging in the short term and extremely rewarding in the long term. ARRAY[ ] is designed for those who seek foundations of new media developed by focused, invested peers. While not all teachers and learners introduced to code will take it up, they will have the kind of literacy urgently needed in contemporary practice and in critical discourse.

REFERENCES

"9 Evenings: Theatre and Engineering" (n.d.). Retrieved from http://monoskop. org/9_Evenings:_Theatre_and_Engineering. Accessed online December 7, 2016.

Bartimo, J. (1984). "'Smalltalk' with Alan Kay." *InfoWorld Jun 11, 1984*, 6(24): 58.

Bishop, C. (2012). "Digital Divide." *Art Forum*, September 2012(7): 434–42.

CNN Money (January 6, 2012). "Code Year Draws 200,000 Aspiring Programmers." Retrieved from http://money.cnn.com/2012/01/06/technology/code_year/. Accessed online December 7, 2016.

Connor, M. (2015). "Eight Big Ideas from Seven on Seven." Retrieved from http://rhizome.org/editorial/2015/may/4/seven-seven-2015/. Accessed online December 7, 2016.

Duhigg, C. (2012). "How Companies Learn Your Secrets." Retrieved from www. nytimes.com/2012/02/19/magazine/shopping-habits.html. Accessed online December 7, 2016.

Finley, K. (2015). "How Big Is Coding Right Now? A Programming School Just Sold for $36M." Retrieved from www.wired.com/2015/01/pluralsight-code-school/. Accessed online December 7, 2016.

Graham, P. (2003). "Hackers and Painters." Retrieved from www.paulgraham.com/ hp.html. Accessed online December 7, 2016.

Greelish, D. (2013). "An Interview with Computing Pioneer Alan Kay [Online interview]." Retrieved from http://techland.time.com/2013/04/02/an-interview-with-computing-pioneer-alan-kay/. Accessed online December 7, 2016.

Jackson, E. (2014). "Apple Isn't A Hardware Or Software Company – It's An Ecosystem Company." Retrieved from www.forbes.com/sites/ericjackson/2014/06/03/apple-isnt-a-hardware-or-software-company-its-an-ecosystem-company/. Accessed online December 7, 2016.

Jiang, Z., Fernandez, E.B., and Cheng, L. (2011). "A Pedagogical Pattern for Teaching Computer Programming to Non-CS Majors." Retrieved from www.hillside.net/plop/2011/papers/E-22-Jiang.pdf. Accessed online December 7, 2016.

Joy, B. (2000). "Why the Future Doesn't Need Us." [Online article] Retrieved from http://archive.wired.com/wired/archive/8.04/joy.html. Accessed online December 7, 2016.

Kay, A.C. (1972). "A Personal Computer for Children of All Ages." *ACM '72: Proceedings of the ACM Annual Conference*, Volume 1, Article 1.

King, Augusta Ada Byron. (1843). "NOTES BY THE TRANSLATOR" in *Sketch of the Analytical Engine invented by Charles Babbage,* Esq. by L.F. Menabrea, of Turin, Officer of the Military Engineers. Retrieved from http://psychclassics.yorku.ca/Lovelace/lovelace.htm. Accessed online December 7, 2016.

"Millennials Tech-Dependent, But Not Necessarily Tech-Savvy." (2010). Retrieved from www.millennialmarketing.com/2010/04/millennials-tech-dependent-but-not-necessarily-tech-savvy/. Accessed online December 7, 2016.

Orlowski, A. (2014). "Unexpected Termination Error at Year of Code: Chief Dumps Venture for Other UK.gov Riches." Retrieved from www.theregister.co.uk/2014/06/25/year_of_code_chief_quits/. Accessed online December 7, 2016.

Prensky, M. (2001). "Digital Natives, Digital Immigrants." *On the Horizon* 9(5): 1–6.

Processing. (2015). Retrieved from https://processing.org/. Accessed online December 7, 2016.

Sadowski, J. (2014). "The 'Digital Native,' a Profitable Myth." Retrieved from http://thebaffler.com/blog/the-digital-native-a-profitable-myth/. Accessed online December 7, 2016.

Salter, A. (2011). "Program or Be Programmed." Retrieved from http://chronicle.com/blogs/profhacker/program-or-be-programmed/37448. Accessed online December 7, 2016.

Stager, G. (2012). "Dumbing Down." Retrieved from http://stager.tv/blog/?p=2691. Accessed online December 7, 2016.

Trowbridge, A. and Westbrook, J. (2011). "Free and Open Source TextBook/ToolKit for Art Foundations." Retrieved from http://rhizome.org/commissions/proposal/2599/view/. Accessed online December 7, 2016.

Victor, B. (2012). "Learnable Programming [Online Essay]." Retrieved from http://worrydream.com/LearnableProgramming/. Accessed online December 7, 2016.

"What's Wrong with this Picture?" (n.d.). Retrieved from https://code.org/stats

"Year of Code." Retrieved from http://yearofcode.org/. Accessed online December 7, 2016.

4

Teaching for the Design Singularity: Toward an Entirely Code-based Design Curriculum

BRAD TOBER

Abstract: We can all attest to the fact that digital technologies of all kinds – both hardware and software – are becoming increasingly integrated into both our individual lives and society as a whole. At the forefront of this phenomenon is the contemporary maker movement (a "design singularity" of sorts), which promises to democratize and extend the means of design production to nearly everyone with interest. This movement, however, has significant implications for the profession of design, as the democratization of technologies prompts a questioning of the role of those who had previously (and exclusively) engaged with those technologies. If the conventional means of design production are made accessible to non-designers, then in what activities should the professional designer be engaged? As one potential response to this question, this contribution to Teaching Computational Creativity begins to establish an argument for developing design curricula that are "entirely code-based," referring to the high degree to which code-relevant principles and activities inform the entirety of the design processes students are exposed to. Design and code are uniquely positioned for forming this curricular relationship, as they share a number of key core elements that would potentially enable the use of code as a medium for both teaching and executing design.

Keywords: code, interaction design, integrated curriculum, democratization of technology, role of designer, design-build, high-fidelity prototype, design process

The *Singularity* evokes concerning visions of robots with artificial intelligence exceeding our abilities as *homo sapiens sapiens* – effectively allowing them to claim their rightful places as our overlords. In the first chapter of his book, *The Singularity is Near* (2005), Ray Kurzweil summarily explains this impending reality as due to the fact that "the pace of change of our human-created technology is accelerating and its powers are expanding at an exponential pace" (p. 24). We can all attest to the fact that digital technologies of all kinds – both hardware and software – are becoming increasingly integrated into both our individual lives and society as a whole. This can be attributed to at least three distinct factors at play: the increasing accessibility in terms of cost and computational power of technology, the increasing number of devices we interact with on a daily basis, and the growing interest in the culture surrounding technological entrepreneurship.

These factors culminate in the contemporary maker movement, which promises to democratize and extend the means of design production to nearly everyone with interest. This movement (a "design singularity" of sorts), however, has significant implications for the profession of design, as the democratization of technologies prompts a questioning of the role of those who had previously (and exclusively) engaged with those technologies. If the conventional means of design production are made accessible to non-designers, then in what activities should the professional designer be engaged?

This question is not a new one – designers have historically struggled in identifying and asserting their relationship with new materials, methods, and technologies. The 1984 introduction of the Macintosh personal computer is but one example. In this case, non-designers gained increased access to a tool that enabled the conventional process of professional designers, enabling them to create work that (on a surface level, at least) performed the same functions as the work of a professional. This use of digital technology, in its infancy, was so contentious that those designers who embraced it were referred to as "the new primitives" (Meggs and Purvis, 2006, p. 490). Part of the profession's response at the time included a focus shift from production to concept; that is, while the tools of production were no longer exclusive to professional designers, the ability to develop and communicate powerful and meaningful messages was still highly dependent on a professional designer's experience.

A contemporary design response to the democratization of (production) technologies can be found in the process and practice of *meta-design*. While still emphasizing concept, meta-design represents a shift back to a designer's engagement with production. Meta-design involves the transformation of the role of the designer from one in which s/he is primarily concerned with the design of individual artifacts to one where s/he also creates or develops new tools, systems, and methods for design. Here, the meta-designer is acting as a facilitator or mediator of the design process of other designers.

Working together, the meta-designer and the designer present an idealized vision of the imminent future of design. For these two roles of the designer to work together successfully, they both require fluency in a variety of both ideational and executional platforms – the number of which easily reaches into the thousands (at a minimum). Teaching technical proficiency in even some single-digit percentage of these platforms is neither logistically possible nor desirable, as any technological platform is bound for ultimate obsolescence, whether intended or not.

Instead, meta-design requires proficiency in a new (to many designers, at least) language of communication – computer code. This is not without its own challenges, however. As Donald Knuth (1986), creator of the METAFONT font description language, notes, "Meta-design is much more difficult than design; it's easier to draw something than to explain how to draw it" (p. 1). This points to coding/programming ability as not merely a technical skill designers should have; rather, it represents a higher-level conceptualization of a comprehensive and cohesive approach to designing for and with technology. Additionally, computer code is characterized by a much longer functional lifespan and is not tied to a corporation or other provider in the same way as proprietary software, making it an ideal skill that serves to "future-proof" designers and empowers them to more faithfully execute their ideas. Contemporary (and future) design curricula must respond to this fact by empowering design students with the knowledge base necessary for engaging with current and yet-to-come technological platforms, whether they are creating or using these platforms. A comprehensive integration of code both in the foundation of and throughout a design curriculum, given that code is often a commonality across platforms, would provide students the flexibility necessary to achieve this objective.

While, at first glance, such a focus on code represents a departure from the core tenets of the maker movement as described previously, both endeavors seek to engage with some fundamental material of creation. For the maker movement, these materials include (but are not limited to) the various processes of and forms of media used with 3D printers and laser cutters. While the use of code is certainly an essential component of the maker movement – after all, 3D printers and laser cutters need specialized software to run – in most cases, the maker movement is not interested (primarily) in the process of making using code directly. Instead, the maker movement looks to enable a particular form of creation using various high-level purpose-built tools. A code-based approach to meta-design, in contrast, has a much broader imperative. Here, code represents a low-level tool that can be used in the creation of other facilitative and design-oriented tools. This distinction is perhaps best seen by analyzing the output of these tools – a 3D printer very specifically produces 3D models/prototypes, while code can be used to implement a vast array of diverse applications.

To be clear, the curriculum envisioned here is distinct from teaching a superficial characterization of computer science, and it should not be confused with certain approaches to teaching new media or interactive art. Design and code are uniquely positioned for forming this curricular relationship, as they share a number of key core elements that would potentially enable the use of code as a medium for both teaching and executing design (Tober, 2012). Some design educators have begun to explore ways to leverage this unique relationship in the classroom. One example is "Programming Design Systems," a graduate course taught by Rune Madsen in the Interactive Telecommunications Program at New York University. Madsen describes the course as "focus[ing] on the intersection between graphic design and code," noting that his students "work to write software that [abstracts design theory] into code, and [then] print the output on paper for design critique" (Madsen, 2014).

Madsen's course is an insightful take on relating code-based principles to conventional graphic design practice. The author has similarly developed a foundational design project, *200 lines: in space/of code*, that "addresses the new and emergent by re-framing the existing and established" by engaging first-year undergraduate art and design students with the principles and elements of design through a formal exercise using *Processing*, an environment for what has become known as creative coding – the programmatic creation of images, animations, and interactive experiences (Tober, 2015). Of course, it is not adequate to only fully incorporate code into curricula at the graduate level, nor is a single-course assignment an accurate representation of what is possible in terms of integrating design and code. What, then, does an "entirely code-based design curriculum" look like?

Historically, many designers have specialized in one particular area of design practice, such as print design or web design. This is no longer the case, as contemporary designers are increasingly expected (in professional practice) to be able to engage with technology to at least some degree, regardless of whether their focus or interest is in designing for it. Accordingly, developments in curricula focusing on interaction design are of particular importance to a discussion of design and code. In this context, "code-based" does not imply that code is the exclusive medium through which design is executed; rather, it indicates the high degree to which code-relevant principles and activities inform the entirety of the design process.

Interaction design – a discipline concerned with the creation of strategies for human engagement with dynamic, often digital, systems – might be considered a type of hybrid discipline, encompassing aspects of what are fundamentally considered graphic design, industrial/product design, computer science, and human psychology (among other areas). This particular conceptualization of interaction design points to areas of significant overlap with architecture; one might argue that architecture, in a broad sense, is a discipline concerned with the development of strategies for human engagement with constructed/built systems.

Howard, Culley, and Dekoninck (2008) identified four distinct phases of a process framework characterizing many of the creative disciplines: analysis, generation, evaluation, and (most notably) communication/implementation. In disciplines like interaction design and architecture, this implementation phase is often disconnected from the rest of the process, perhaps due to the impression that the necessary skills are too far removed (and often technically oriented) from those typically held by the practitioner. Increasingly, contemporary characterizations of these disciplines are recognizing that this is not the case, and that by also engaging with the implementation phase of the creative process, practitioners can ensure a heightened degree of appropriateness and cohesion in their final output. Architecture recognizes this using terminology such as "creating–making" and "design–build" to intrinsically link the roles of both the designer and the constructor.

Interaction design is less terminologically explicit in its recognition of this form of practice. Professional practice increasingly demands that interaction designers – even those tasked primarily with the planning aspects of creation – hold at least some level of technical proficiency in the tools used to implement dynamic digital systems (in the form of software; i.e., websites, desktop and mobile applications, etc.), and so it is often assumed that many of these designers are, in fact, designer–developers. However, this characterization is less about linking the roles of designer–developer and more about optimizing and increasing the efficiency of the interaction design process.

Implicit in the framework phases identified by Howard et al. is a primarily linear characterization of the creative process (i.e., evaluation follows generation, which follows analysis). While this is true in a broad sense, some of these phases may be repeated one or more times. For example, a negative evaluation of a product of the generation phase would prompt another repetition of the generation phase. This characterization forms the basis of how process has traditionally been taught in the context of many of the creatively oriented disciplines, yet it has become somewhat inappropriate for many contemporary design areas in particular.

In software development, an area closely engaged with interaction design – this type of linear process characterization is known as the *waterfall* model –described as such because the sequential nature of the approach makes implementing changes or corrections to earlier phases particularly challenging (in the same way that water cannot travel in reverse up a waterfall) (Ambler and Holitza, 2012). This holds true for interaction design as well, where constantly changing project and client requirements necessitate a process that is dynamic and able to respond appropriately to these realities. In this situation, the waterfall process model would require a designer to repeat process phases for every change that needed to be implemented, regardless of the scale of the change. Some related interaction design methods associated with these phases include rough sketches (hand-drawn or digital), wireframes (drawings typically intended for demonstrating the structure of a design's layout), and static refined design mock-ups. Only at the very end of the process, when a fully planned design has already been created, would the design be developed into its final functional form. This correlates with a "design-then-build" paradigm, maintaining separation between the roles of designer and developer.

The software development response to the waterfall process model – referred to as an *agile* model – is also relevant to interaction design. The agile model first emerged in 2001 following the publication of the *Manifesto for Agile Software Development*. This brief statement emphasizes four core values: "individuals and interactions," "working software," "customer collaboration," and "responding to change" (Beck et al., 2001). Two of these values, in particular, are of most use when considering the interaction design process: working software (or design) and responding to change. Mapping the agile software development model to the interaction design process recognizes that designing for dynamic digital systems requires an approach that is both equally dynamic and able to implement alterations to a design in an efficient manner. The waterfall process model suggests that a series of methods must be repeated for every incremental alteration to a design; that is, new sketches, wireframes, and mock-ups must be produced. This is, of course, labor-intensive and not very responsive to change.

Agile principles are easily applied to areas of design practice involving technology (such as web and interaction design), given their development out of and relationship to engineering contexts, but a broader conceptualization of design can potentially benefit from an agile perspective as well. Notably, awareness of the relevance of this perspective to design in general is not necessarily a new thing – design professionals have previously written on this topic, some at least as early as 2008 (Bowles, 2008). Along with the contemporary focus of design on users of designed works (whether or not such a design process is specifically that of user experience design), there is also an increased interest in relating agile principles to user-centered design (Hussain, Slany, and Holzinger, 2009). Regardless, all design is process-based, and an agile perspective on design represents a different view of that process – one that emphasizes and promotes flexibility, functionality, and responsiveness.

While not specifically inherent to the agile model, there are other interaction design methods that are arguably more relevant and appropriate for it – those that may be considered forms of high-fidelity (and rapid) prototyping. In general, prototyping refers to the production of models and guides that inform the final production/implementation of a design. Fidelity refers to the degree to which a prototype reflects the final design: low-fidelity prototypes are simple and rudimentary, while high-fidelity prototypes may be difficult to distinguish from the final design. Sketches, wireframes, and mock-ups are typically considered forms of low-fidelity prototyping, while higher-fidelity options include semi-functional and interactive demonstrations of the targeted final design.

Even within the realm of high-fidelity prototyping are a range of viable methods, each with particular advantages and disadvantages. This range of methods is often highly variable in terms of the technical skills needed by the designer in order to implement the high-fidelity prototype. One category of prototyping approaches that is less technically demanding involves the use of tools that transform a series of static mock-up images into an interactive demonstration of a design through the linking of "hotspot" areas on the images. Along with basic animations, these sorts of tools can be used to quickly put together a demonstration of a particular path, or series of user interactions, through a design that is visually reflective of the ultimate objective of the designer. While options such as these can be considered high-fidelity prototyping tools, they exist more on the low end of high fidelity since they act more as an extension of low-fidelity methods. In order to use these types of tools, the designer must produce an adequate series of static mock-up images, which typically are preceded by wireframes and sketches in the waterfall process model. This means that these tools are not as responsive as they can or should be to changing project and/or client requirements. However, they are effective in demonstrating dynamic functionality that would otherwise be difficult to communicate through low-fidelity methods alone.

The most flexible and most high-fidelity prototyping methods, however, also address the other agile value of interest – working software/design. In terms of the final output of the interaction design process, these two are one and the same, meaning that by implementing approaches to high-fidelity prototyping that address the creation of working software/design, the role of the designer is transformed into that of the designer–developer.

The use of code presents a unique opportunity for a truly agile conceptualization of the interaction design process, particularly due to the way in which some contemporary code-based tools for interaction design incorporate and compress the ideational phases of the creative process into the phases that focus on the production and output of a final design. Perhaps the best example of this is Processing, which uses the term *sketch* to refer to the software programs it facilitates the creation of. The implication here is that the ideational sketching phases of the interaction design process are, in fact, the same as those in which the implementation of a design happens. Since code, in the form of some type of software, is the medium of the final design, it only makes sense that the most appropriate and authentic ideation-related activities also happen through the use of code. In practical terms, this can help to ensure that a designer's ideas are actually viable prior to reaching the implementation phase, which ends up saving a great deal of time and effort.

While Processing is an extremely open and flexible tool for interactive design, examples of more specialized code-based prototyping tools exist as well. A variety of web-based frameworks exist for building high-fidelity prototypes of mobile applications using HTML, CSS, and JavaScript. Designers use a library of pre-built interface components, along with others that can be custom-coded, to build a functional prototype of a mobile application in very much the same way one might design and develop a typical website. This type of building block approach requires more technical knowledge as a foundation, but it is far more flexible in comparison to a "hotspot" prototyping tool. In addition, the prototypes created using these tools are extremely high fidelity – to the point that, in many cases, these prototypes can be transformed into a final application for release through the use of a native mobile platform wrapper like Apache Cordova. Cordova allows a designer to insert an application developed using HTML, CSS, and JavaScript into a code structure that can be built and deployed to the various app stores for each major mobile platform.

While the use of code enables the production of very high-fidelity prototypes, the pursuit of such a degree of fidelity in the first place represents the greatest potential for the application of a design–build approach to interaction design. In the two code-based types of tools discussed, the division between a strictly design phase of a project and a strictly build (or development) phase has been significantly blurred. In Processing, ideation and design happens through "sketching," which is accomplished through writing and engaging with code; a Processing "sketch" may very well be a final design. HTML/CSS/JavaScript mobile prototyping tools similarly concatenate several phases of the conventional design process, as the prototypes produced using these tools can transform directly into a final design. An agile code-based approach to interaction design no longer recognizes designing and building as distinct, yet related, activities; rather, the dash in design–build represents a fusion of the two into a new, hybrid form of practice.

Preparing today's students for professional success in an environment that recognizes the benefits of a design–build approach to interaction design requires a curricular structure that comprehensively considers the proficiencies – both technical and conceptual – from the very beginning of a student's undergraduate career. In many university undergraduate design programs, an explicit focus on the development of technical skills is often taboo, as it is often seen as a more effective and efficient use of time and resources to emphasize conceptual development. It is expected that technical skills develop incidentally on students' own time in response to the individual requirements of particular assignments. However, fully integrating agile methods into a design curriculum requires an explicit focus on technical skills early on – one might say that the foundation of a design program characterized, at least in part, by a design–build approach is purely technical. This is because a high level of technical proficiency in code-based design tools forms the basis for conceptual development through high-fidelity prototyping later on in a student's education.

Most transitional periods are marked by a number of challenges, and implementing agile methods into a design curriculum is no exception. Hesitance to new ideas and change is to be expected, but shifting experienced design students to agile approaches to design can be a particular challenge as it often represents a negation of many of the principles they have learned previously. Design curricula typically emphasize the importance and relevance of process, and conventional curricula make heavy use of sketches, wireframes, and mock-ups as ideational forms – those which the agile model aims to replace with high-fidelity prototyping. Those students who have grown attached to conventional process approaches may find it difficult to fully embrace the agile model out of fear that it is not a valid approach to design. Transitional curricula may need to recognize this by incorporating elements of both conventional and agile process.

Interaction design is both a burgeoning field and a dynamic practice, and as such, its supporting process must adequately accommodate continually changing project (and, in a professional context, client) requirements. Conventional process forms, such as rough sketches and static mock-ups, are typically inappropriate for interaction design, as they are highly inefficient when subjected to the degree of iteration inherent to interaction design. Agile methods, such as high-fidelity prototyping, are much better suited for manifesting the interaction design process. Code-based tools, in particular, not only enable the production of high-fidelity prototypes, but also hold the greatest potential for demonstrating the application of a design–build approach to interaction design. This approach is what needs to be considered in the establishment of an entirely code-based (generalist) design curriculum, one which treats code as a critical pedagogical component from foundational-level studies through to advanced coursework. Such a curriculum will foster code-proficient designers who, far from merely being technically focused developers, will be able to speak the language(s) and design for the media of tomorrow, ultimately ensuring the continued relevance of the professional designer.

REFERENCES

Ambler, S.W. and Holitza, M. (2012). *Agile for Dummies*. Hoboken, NJ: John Wiley & Sons.

Beck, K., Beedle, M., van Bennekum, A. et al. (2001). *Manifesto for Agile Software Development*. Retrieved from http://agilemanifesto.org. Accessed online December 7, 2016.

Bowles, C. (2008). Getting Real About Agile Design. *A List Apart*. Retrieved from http://alistapart.com/article/gettingrealaboutagiledesign. Accessed online December 7, 2016.

Howard, T.J., Culley, S.J., and Dekoninck, E. (2008). Describing the Creative Design Process by the Integration of Engineering Design and Cognitive Psychology Literature. *Design Studies*, 29(2), 160–80.

Hussain, Z., Slany, W., and Holzinger, A. (2009). Current State of Agile User-Centered Design: A Survey. *HCI and Usability for e-Inclusion*, 416–27. Berlin, Germany: Springer-Verlag.

Knuth, D. (1986). *The METAFONTbook*. Boston, MA: Addison-Wesley.

Kurzweil, R. (2005). *The Singularity is Near: When Humans Transcend Biology*. New York, NY: Penguin.

Madsen, R. (2014). *Programming Design Systems*. Retrieved from http://printingcode.runemadsen.com. Accessed online December 7, 2016.

Meggs, P.B. and Purvis, A.W. (2006). *Meggs' History of Graphic Design*. Hoboken, NJ: Wiley.

Tober, B. (2012). Making the Case for Code: Integrating Code-Based Technologies into Undergraduate Design Curricula. *Proceedings of Catch 22: 2012 University and College Designers Association Design Education Summit*. 224–9. Retrieved from https://ucda.com/des_proceedings.lasso. Accessed online December 7, 2016.

(2015). *200 lines: In Space/of Code*. Retrieved from www.arrayproject.com/content/200-lines-space-code. Accessed online December 7, 2016.

PART III

PHYSICAL{LY} COMPUTING

5

A Physical Computing Teaching
Initiative in Brazil

LUIZA NOVAES AND
JOÃO DE SÁ BONELLI

Abstract: In this chapter, we present the teaching initiative of Interaction Design and Physical Computing that is currently under development at Pontifícia Universidade Católica do Rio de Janeiro – PUC-Rio in Brazil, within the class called *Interfaces Físicas e Lógicas*, and in the LIFE Lab – *Laboratório de Interfaces Físicas Experimentais*. A discussion about the emerging area of Physical Computing in the field of Interaction Design is conducted from the conceptual framework of its practice and teaching initiatives in the Design school used for the study. In this context, thoughts on Design Thinking and Reflective Practice by theorists such as Donald Schön, Herbert Simon, and Nigel Cross are brought into the scene, as part of a learning methodology proposal, exploring the relation between the theory of Design and its practice. To expand the discussion, Weiser's ubiquitous computing concept is added as one more approach. In this sense, the idea that we live surrounded by digital interfaces embedded in objects that assist us in activities related to communication, information, entertainment, safety, health, and wellbeing becomes each day more present. Thus we are witnessing the rise of a new area of Design practice, in which designers, besides being users of the digital interactive systems, are involved in the process of development of the interfaces that are responsible for the mediation between the computer systems and men. This emerging area of Design is called Interaction Design, an area that has the discipline known as Physical Computing – in Brazil, *Interfaces Físicas* – as a key content. The discipline explores the relationship between the physical world and computer systems. Another author, who is brought to the discussion, is O'Sullivan, who advocates that through the use of software, hardware, electronics, sensors, microcontrollers, automation systems, and motors, the Physical Computing devices are digital interactive systems that sense and react to the physical world. Even though there is undeniable growth of the Interaction Design field globally, in Brazilian Design Courses there are still few academic initiatives concerning its teaching, especially at the undergraduate level. In this context, the Interfaces Físicas e Lógicas class from PUC-Rio's Design-Digital Media course has been – since 2010 – among the first Physical Computing classes offered in a Brazilian undergraduate Design program. This teaching–learning initiative has come together with the conception of a laboratory, designed as a space for the practice of Physical Computing. The LIFE Lab is an initiative of PUC-Rio's Department of Arts & Design that aims to provide students with the appropriate environment and technology for the practical development of Physical Computing projects. The lab is integrated to the other labs of the design program such as the product design lab, and the graphic production lab, favoring interdisciplinary and multidisciplinary projects, as well as the interchange between cultures and languages of Design. Occupying 36 square meters of floor space, the lab is equipped with computers, open source software, electronic components, Arduino boards, and a small library. Ever since the implementation of the LIFE Lab, a growing variety of Physical Computing projects have been developed. The projects quite often reveal a thorough design thinking process, in which the reflective practice with Physical Computing tools leads to a variety of creative and innovative Design solutions. One selection of these projects – along with a brief description and analysis of the individual design processes – is presented at the end of the essay. For more information, please visit www.life.dad.puc-rio.br

Keywords: physical computing, interaction design, reflective practice, design thinking, design learning

INTRODUCTION

In this chapter, we present the teaching initiative of Interaction Design and Physical Computing that is currently under development at Pontifícia Universidade Católica do Rio de Janeiro – PUC-Rio[1] in Brazil, within the class called *Interfaces Físicas e Lógicas*,[2] and in the LIFE Lab – Laboratório de Interfaces Físicas Experimentais.[3] Physical Computing as an emerging

---

[1]   PUC-Rio – Pontifical Catholic University of Rio de Janeiro: www.puc-rio.br
[2]   Interfaces Físicas e Lógicas – Physical and Logical Interfaces.
[3]   LIFE – Laboratory for Experimental Physical Interfaces: www.life.dad.puc-rio.br

area of Interaction Design is discussed from the framework of its concept, practice, and teaching initiatives in the Design school mentioned.

Additionally, thoughts on Design Thinking and Reflective Practice by theorists such as Donald Schön, Herbert Simon, and Nigel Cross are brought into discussion as part of a learning methodology proposal, exploring the relation between the theory of Design and its practice.

We live today surrounded by digital interfaces embedded in objects that assist us in a number of activities related to communication, information, entertainment, safety, health, and wellbeing among others. Computer technology has indeed become ubiquitous in our lives. In the Design field, the emergence of interactive technologies opened new opportunities for designers, to say for instance motion graphics in the graphic design area, interface design for automated processes in the product design area, and experience design, which draws from many other disciplines. Considering a broader context, we are witnessing the rise of a new area of Design practice. Designers, besides being users of the digital interactive systems, have been involved in the process of development of the interfaces that are responsible for the mediation between the computer systems and men. This emerging area of Design has been called Interaction Design.

A key subject in the Interaction Design field is the discipline known as Physical Computing – in Brazil, *Interfaces Físicas* – which explores the relationship between the physical world and computer systems. Through the use of software, hardware, electronics, sensors, microcontrollers, automation systems, and motors, Physical Computing devices are digital interactive systems that sense and react to the physical world (O'Sullivan and Igoe, 2004).

Even though there is undeniable growth of the Interaction Design field globally, in Brazilian Design courses there are still few academic initiatives concerning its teaching, especially at the undergraduate level. According to the Brazilian Ministry of Education, there are currently 325 undergraduate Design courses in Brazil, but the vast majority of them are focused on the more traditional Graphic Design and Product Design careers. Only 9 of these 325 courses have majors in Digital Design or Interactive Media.[4] One of these very few courses is the Design-Digital Media course at PUC-Rio, where this study is conducted.

---

[4] Source: e-MEC undergraduate teaching institutions database from the Brazilian Ministry of Education (Ministério da Educação-MEC): http://emec.mec.gov.br

In this context, the Interfaces Físicas e Lógicas class from PUC-Rio's Design-Digital Media course is, since 2010, among the first Physical Computing classes offered in a Brazilian undergraduate Design program.

This teaching initiative has come together with the conception of a laboratory, designed as a space for the practice of Physical Computing. The LIFE Lab is an initiative of PUC-Rio's Department of Arts & Design that aims to provide students with the appropriate environment and technology for the practical development of Physical Computing projects. The lab is integrated into the other labs of the design program such as the product design lab, favoring interdisciplinarity and interchange of Design cultures and languages.

Ever since the implementation of the LIFE Lab, a growing variety of projects have been developed in the premises of PUC-Rio's Design program. These projects quite often reveal a design process where the reflective practice with Physical Computing leads to a number of different creative and innovative Design solutions. A significant selection of projects – along with a short description and analysis of the individual design processes – will be presented here.

Our goal is to study the characteristics of reflective practice through the development of Physical Computing projects and its results, in a learning environment of Design project. We believe that one of the reasons that the majority of Design Courses are not yet investing deeply in the Physical Computing sector is that there is a lack of professionals well prepared to act in the frontier between artistic and technological aspects, in a conciliation of abilities.

PHYSICAL COMPUTING

In the practical field of Interaction Design, as noted earlier, one main subject is the discipline known as Physical Computing, which explores the integration of computer systems with the physical (real) world. Physical Computing can also be described as the integration of computer systems with sensors and actuators. In this context, sensors are mechanisms that translate the physical world information into electronic information that will be processed by the computer system. Buttons, light sensors, temperature sensors, or pressure sensors are examples of sensors. Actuators, in their turn, are devices that are controlled by a computer system and act on the physical world, for example, motors, LEDs, and speakers.

The term Physical Computing was coined in the realm of the Interactive Telecommunications Program (ITP) from New York University.[5] Since 1971, the graduate program has been home to some of the most significant

---

[5] NYU ITP: http://itp.nyu.edu

research in the area. Widely known technologies such as QuickTime VR, the Processing programming language, Arduino, and the first interactive television were developed there. The current chair Dan O'Sullivan is internationally recognized as the creator of the term Physical Computing, and is the author, with Tom Igoe, of the pioneering book *Physical Computing: Sensing and Controlling the Physical World with Computers*. In the introductory chapter of the book, they state:

> We believe that the computer revolution has left most of you behind. Steve Jobs had similar thoughts when he founded Apple Computer and set out to build "computers for the rest of us." The idea was to enable people who were not computer experts – like artists, educators, and children – to take advantage of the power of computing. The graphical user interface (GUI) popularized by Apple was wildly successful, widely copied, and is now the standard interface of almost all personal computers . . . Now we need to make "computers for the rest of you." We need computers that respond to the rest of your body and the rest of your world. GUI technology allows you to drag and drop, but it won't notice if you twist and shout. It's made it easy to open a folder and start a program, but we'd like a computer to be able to open a door or start a car. Personal computers have evolved in an office environment in which you sit on your butt, moving only your fingers, entering and receiving information censored by your conscious mind . . . We need to think about computers that sense more of your body, serve you in more places. And convey physical expression in addition to information.[6]

In Brazil, PUC-Rio is the first university to include Physical Computing content in an undergraduate Design program. Since 2010, the Design-Digital Media course of this university includes classes of *Interfaces Físicas e Lógicas*, dedicated to the teaching of Physical Computing. For a better understanding of the context, the PUC-Rio undergraduate Design program is structured as a 4-year, eight-academic semesters program and offers four majors: Visual Communication, Product Design, Fashion Design, and Digital Media Design. Although the student chooses one major to begin with, since the program is structured and based in a credit system, it is possible for the student to navigate between majors according to his/her interests. In consonance with the striking presence of humanistic orientation that guides the courses at PUC-Rio, the program seeks to provide solid formation that is defined not only by the amount of knowledge and information acquired by the student, but also by the development of his/her ability to think, understand, and recreate nature and society. More than

---

[6] O'Sullivan and Igoe (2004, p. 7).

only preparing professionals for the market, PUC-Rio aims to be an environment for the production, conservation, and construction of knowledge. The program is committed, above all, to the formation of a designer with humanistic values, capable of theoretical reflection and criticism, a professional with strong basis in planning, project, and development in the area of Design. In this sense, since the beginning of the course the student is encouraged to: have a proactive and entrepreneurial attitude, work in teams, evaluate the market demands, and be aware and updated on economical, social, cultural, technical, and technological trends.

Specifically in the curriculum of the Design-Digital Media course, four classes cover Interaction Design subjects: *Hipermídia* (Hypermedia); *Design e Expansão dos Sentidos* (Design and Expansion of the Senses); *Design de Objetos Inteligentes* (Design of Smart Objects); and *Interfaces Físicas e Lógicas* (Physical Computing).

In the realm of the *Interfaces Físicas e Lógicas* class, the students acquire the skills necessary for the practical experimentation with Physical Computing projects. This is a mandatory class, planned for students attending the seventh semester of the eight-semester Digital Media major. Being senior students, they are already aware of the issues related to Interaction Design, and have a wide understanding of Design processes and methodology, since at this point of their courses, they are expected to have already developed at least six Design projects, within mandatory project classes.

In the *Interfaces Físicas e Lógicas* class, the students learn – by practicing – coding, electronics, and how to use sensors and actuators. The requirement for the conclusion of the class, after one academic semester, is that the student develops and presents a physical interaction project, in the level of a working demo. For the development of the projects, the students need to learn specific techniques required to build them. Often the students need to collaborate with other areas of knowledge such as Engineering and Computer Sciences. It is noteworthy that the PUC-Rio campus favors these collaborations, because it is a campus where different areas of knowledge are situated very close to each other and with a tradition of research that makes people receptive to challenges that are presented to them (Figure 5.1).

The syllabus of the *Interfaces Físicas e Lógicas* class includes:

- Introduction to programming in the Processing language
- Electricity and electronics
- Use of sensors and actuators
- Arduino development for sensors and actuators

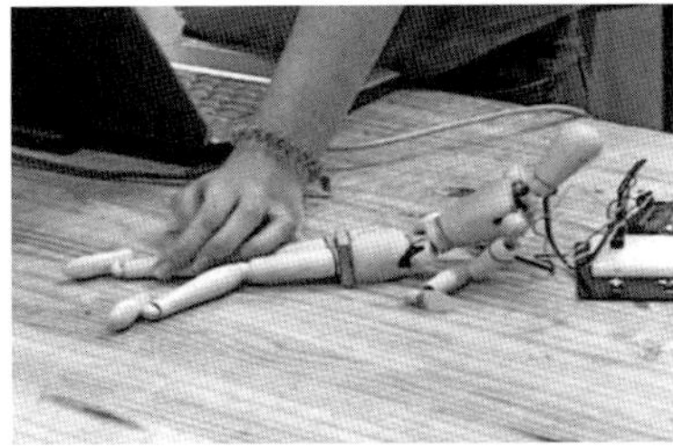
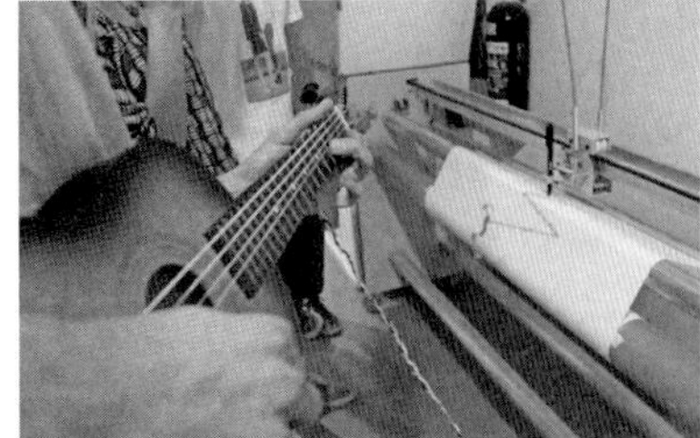

FIGURE 5.1. Examples of projects developed in the class *Interfaces Físicas e Lógicas*. (a) A doll that responds to one's social network status. (b) A drawing machine controlled by the musical notes played on an acoustic guitar. (c) A game controlled by gestures.

- Computer vision
- Mobile development
- Interaction design project development

LIFE LAB

The laboratory LIFE is an initiative aimed at providing an appropriate environment for practical experimentation and development of Interaction Design and Physical Computing Projects. The lab, established in 2010 and expanded in 2013, has 36 square meters of floor space and is equipped with computers, open source software, electronic components, Arduino boards, and a small library among others. The lab is planned to be a space dedicated to the creative experimentation in Interaction Design. The goal is to provide computational and electronic resources in order to allow for innovative Physical Computing and Interaction Design projects (Figure 5.2).

Ever since the implementation of the lab, a variety of projects have been developed in its premises. The three projects selected to illustrate this chapter are examples of projects developed within this lab environment.

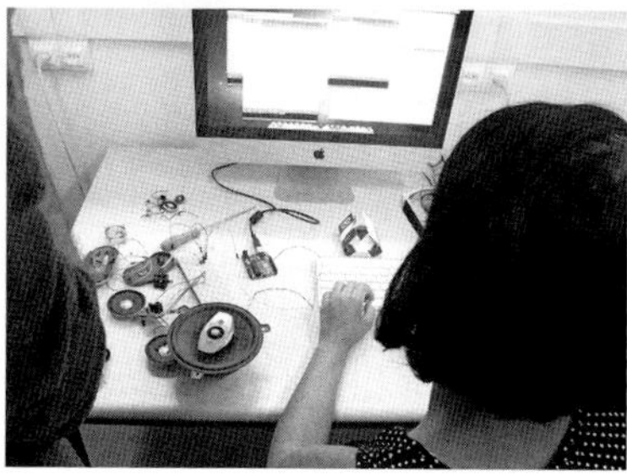

FIGURE 5.2. Students at work in the LIFE lab

REFLECTIVE PRACTICE LEARNING EXPERIENCE

What designers know about their own problem-solving processes remains largely tacit knowledge – i.e. they know it in the same way that a skilled person "knows" how to perform that skill.

(Cross, 1982, p. 224)

Many researchers have studied the practice of Design, its characteristics, and peculiarities. What exactly defines the designer's practice? How do designers work and how do they think? A first step toward understanding design as a discipline is by trying to establish relationships between Design and the major areas of knowledge. By doing that, would you classify Design as part of the Human Sciences, Exact Sciences, or the Arts?

Since the beginning of the twentieth century, several attempts toward making design more scientific happened. Cross (2001) identifies a search for scientific design in thinkers such as Le Corbusier, who supported the concept of the house as a "machine for living." Later, in the 1960s, he identifies a search for scientific processes in design influenced by the application of scientific and computational methods developed during the Second World War, from which came civilian developments such as operations research and management decision-making techniques. In addition, the 1962 "Conference on Design Methods," in London, is considered a mark in defining design methodology as a scientific field of knowledge, while Buckminster Fuller proposed a "Design Science Revolution": science, technology, and rationalism to overcome the human and environmental problems that he believed could not be solved only by politics and economics.

Moreover, Herbert Simon (1996), in his book *The Sciences of the Artificial*, states: "The natural sciences are concerned with how things are . . . design on the other hand is concerned with how things ought to be." For Simon, we can call overall activities of design research "the sciences of the artificial" – a body of intellectually tough, analytic, partly formalizable, partly empirical, teachable doctrine about the design process.

Equally important are Horst Rittel and Melvin Webber (1973), pioneers in the idea that scientific principles would not apply perfectly to the practice of design, architecture, and urban planning. In the seminal article "Dilemmas in a General Theory of Planning," the authors define the problems of design project as "wicked problems," fundamentally unnamable to the techniques of science and engineering, which dealt with "tame" problems.

Cross as well has addressed the issue of the wicked problems as a starting point to the investigation about designer's unique way of thinking and working. In the essay called "Designerly ways of knowing," he states:

> It is also now widely recognized that design problems are ill-defined, ill-structured, or "wicked." They are not the same as the "puzzles" that scientists, mathematicians, and other scholars set themselves. They are not problems for which all the necessary information is, or ever can be, available to the problem-solver. They are therefore not susceptible to exhaustive analysis, and there can never be a guarantee that "correct" solution-focused strategy is clearly preferable to go on analyzing "the problem," but the designer's task is to produce "the solution."

Donald Schön suggests an approach for the teaching of design and architecture based on its practice, a concept he named Reflective Practice. Schön identifies that there is a component of artistry in the practice of the professionals whom we recognize as being successful in their careers – in several areas, not only in design. He relates this talent to the capacity to deal with "complex problems that escape the canons of rationality." In his words, "there is a central nucleus of artistry in the practice of the professionals that we recognize as being the most competent" (Schön, 1998, p. 22).

Schön advocates that practical experimentation with the real situations encountered in the professional practice is the best way to prepare a future professional, a concept that he called "reflective practice," based on the ideas of "knowing-in-action" and "reflection-in-action."

According to the author, knowing-in-action is "the type of knowledge that we reveal in our intelligent actions" (1998, p. 31). When we do something intelligently, the act of knowing is in the action done. For example, when we are riding a bike, we are not aware of the theory of how to ride a bike. We are not consciously aware of the complex movements of our body to compensate and balance our weight in motion. To learn how to ride a bike it is necessary to try it, until your body does it in a tacit manner.

Schön based his study in the concept of "tacit knowledge" coined by philosopher Michel Polanyi. In the book *The Tacit Dimension* (1966), Polanyi writes about "knowing more than you can tell" and of tacit knowledge, defined as "the formation of experience in the search of knowledge" (Polanyi, 1966, p. 4).

Schön also cites British philosopher Gilbert Ryle when trying to establish a relationship between the act of designing and doing:

> "Thinking what I am doing" does not connote "both thinking what to do and doing it. When I do something intelligently, I am doing one thing and not two."(Ryle, 1949, p. 29)

Schön describes reflective practice as a "reflective conversation with the situation" where each move might produce – happily or unhappily – consequences other than those intended. When this happens, the designer may form a new understanding of the situation: "He shapes the situation in accordance with his initial appreciation of it, the situation talks back, and he responds to the situation's back-talk" (1983, p. 79). The designer responds to the situation's back-talk by reframing the problem. When the designer reframes the problem, he conducts what Schön calls a frame experiment to test his reframing of the situation.

> When the practitioner finds himself stuck in a problematic situation which he cannot readily convert to a manageable problem, he may construct a new way of setting the problem – a new frame which, in what I shall call a "frame experiment," he tries to impose on the situation. (1983, p. 63)

To the author, reflective practice can be described as a process of problem-setting rather than a process of problem-solving. The reframing of the problem is a key element in the way that practicing professionals (not only designers) deal with the complex problems of their practice.

METHODOLOGICAL CONSIDERATIONS

What are the benefits of teaching computer programming to designers? What are the benefits of enabling designers a reflective practice experience of Interaction Design by using computer programming? In the following section, we present three case studies (Yin, 2009) representative of the design projects developed within the Design-Digital Media course at PUC-Rio, in the period from 2013 to 2015 inclusive, with a focus in the analysis of Interaction Design.

The cases were selected among a preliminary list of eight Interaction Design projects developed as final projects in the undergraduate Design program. The study was concentrated on the final projects, because they are the works in which the students incorporate all the knowledge acquired during the 4-year formation. These final projects, usually developed along two academic semesters, are the more complex projects that the students develop in the course.

The following criteria were adopted in the selection of the projects studied:

(a)   If the project was considered a Physical Computing Project
(b)   If a reflective practice methodology was adopted in the development process
(c)   If the project was developed in the environment of the LIFE Lab

The crossing of the projects and the criteria can be seen in Table 5.1.

The projects selected for analysis were the ones that satisfied all the defined criteria. The data analyzed were collected from the objects/products themselves, and the projects documentation produced by the

TABLE 5.1.   *Preliminary selection of projects and crossing of projects and criteria*

Year	Project	Criteria		
		a	b	c
2013	TattooAR	X	X	X
2014	Core	X		X
2014	Ohm		X	X
2014	Tinta Solta	X	X	X
2014	CPCBN		X	X
2014	Sango	X	X	X
2015	Pitaco			X
2015	Coolab		X	

students, which includes the theoretical foundation and description of the development process. Additionally, qualitative semi-structured interviews were conducted with the students. The interviews were made in the environment of the LIFE Lab and were recorded in video. The focus of the analysis was in the resulting products of the design process and their conceptual, formal, and functional characteristics, linking them to the knowledge acquired by the student in the Design-Digital Media course at PUC-Rio.

CASE STUDY

Project 1: TattooAR[7]

The thesis project TattooAR, developed by Gabriela Schirmer Mauricio as part of the requirement for graduation in the undergraduate Design-Digital Media course at PUC-Rio, uses augmented reality (AR) technology to create a virtual tattoo (Schirmer, 2014; Schirmer et al., 2015). Gabriela proposes a tattoo that can be viewable in mobile devices, and shared in social networks. As a starting point, the student wished to explore the body as a surface for artistic expression. Gabriela was aiming at designing a technology that would allow people to virtually draw over the skin, without the permanence of a real tattoo ink. At first the student conducted an experiment using Projection Mapping technologies, as a way to position a digitally projected image onto a person's skin (Figure 5.3).

In a process of reflective conversation with the situation, the material talked back to the designer, presenting her a problem of which she was not aware before. The results of the experiment seemed viable, but it was not a portable solution – which would limit the audience of the project. To the designer, one very important aspect of the project was to have the possibility to be used in the urban environment (the streets) as a feature, just like it happens with a real tattoo.

In this moment, the practitioner reframed the problem, suggesting a new direction for the project, by reshaping of the situation. Gabriela started searching for a mobile solution for her project and encountered the technology of AR available in smartphones. She used it to overlay a virtual image over a real image, captured by the device's camera and visible in the screen of the mobile device. The AR opportunity was considered more appropriate, because it did not depend on a video projector to form the image on the skin, and the mobile platform already allows the desired portability and embodiment.

---

[7] www.life.dad.puc-rio.br/projetos-english/TatuAR-english.html

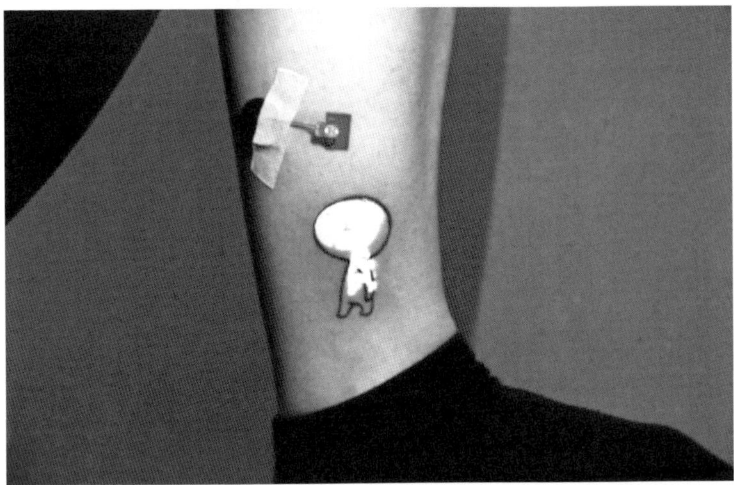

FIGURE 5.3. Experiment in projection mapping. Software developed in the Processing[8] environment is used to track the position of a red LED and use it as a reference to place a projected image

With this reframing of the situation, the project changed from a projection-mapping installation into an AR mobile application. When reflecting upon her own design process, the student stated:

> I wanted the project to be used by people. And how many people have a digital projector at home, or have access to this technology? The project would become something like an installation for the tattoo to happen. Then I migrated to mobile and Augmented Reality as an app, nothing distant from what people use.

So, her next framing experiment consisted in developing an AR application that would run on a smartphone – which she could achieve by using the Processing development environment, the Ketai[9] Sensor Library, and Google Android[10] mobile platform (Figure 5.4).

This reframing of the problem changed the situation, inspiring a new set of reflections. The experiment was indeed successful in the task of positioning a virtual image layered over a real image, but it still had the undesirable need of using a color marker as a reference to the positioning of the virtual image.

---

[8] Processing: https://processing.org
[9] Ketai Sensor Library: https://code.google.com/p/ketai/
[10] Processing for Android: https://github.com/processing/processing-android/wiki

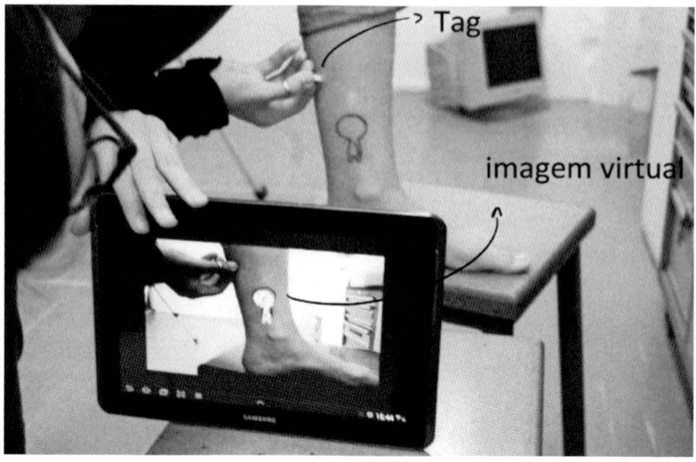

FIGURE 5.4.   A color tag is used as a tracking reference for positioning a virtual image in an experiment using augmented reality, Processing language, and Ketai library

In a new reframing of the problem, the student shifted to using the more complex Java[11] programming language, available in the Android[12] Development Toolkit, using the Eclipse[13] development environment, and becoming able to work with the Metaio[14] Augmented Reality Library in order to experiment her concept of AR Tattoo:

> For someone who doesn't know programming, it's not simple to say: "I'll make an Augmented Reality." From my research, the Metaio software was the easier to understand and easier to work with. It was didactic; they had a tutorial that was simple to start working with and which was the basis for my final software. So it worked out.

The student was already proficient in the Processing programming language, which is based on the Java programming language, and because of that, she was able to move to the Java development environment.

> But the process was complex. Processing works in one window. The Eclipse interface is composed of many files and folders, if you change something in one file, you then have to change something in another file to make it work. It's all interconnected, and I had to make a map to make things work. And it worked, but the process was complex.

[11] Java: www.java.com
[12] Android developer: http://developer.android.com
[13] Eclipse: www.eclipse.org
[14] Metaio: www.metaio.com

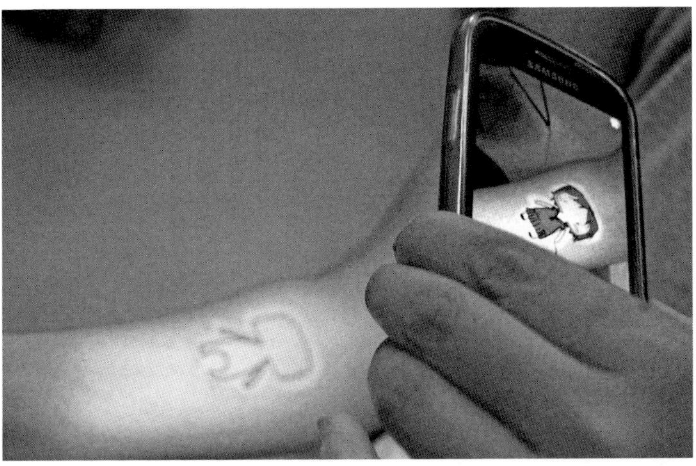

FIGURE 5.5. A virtual image is precisely positioned over a drawing on a person's skin. In this experiment, a pen drawing over tracing paper was positioned on the user's arm and used as a tracking reference

So, her next software experiment was capable of tracking a shape – that was drawn on the skin – and precisely positioning a virtual image on a smartphone's display (Figure 5.5).

For the development of the tracking component – the part drawn on the real skin – the young designer experimented with different graphic techniques such as rubber stamp, cutout images, adhesive label, and removable tattoo. The removable tattoo was chosen, because it allowed a more precise image tracking (Figure 5.6).

For the final presentation of the project, the student demonstrated her Android mobile application that allows users to visualize and choose from previously stored tattoo art that can be seen on the skin without the permanence of real tattoo ink. The software also allows users to take pictures that can be saved on the device's gallery and also shared in social networks.

Project 2: Tinta Solta[15]

The project Tinta Solta, developed by the student João Whitaker in 2014, was presented as his final project in the Design-Digital Media course. The

---

[15] www.life.dad.puc-rio.br/projetos-english/TintaSolta-english.html

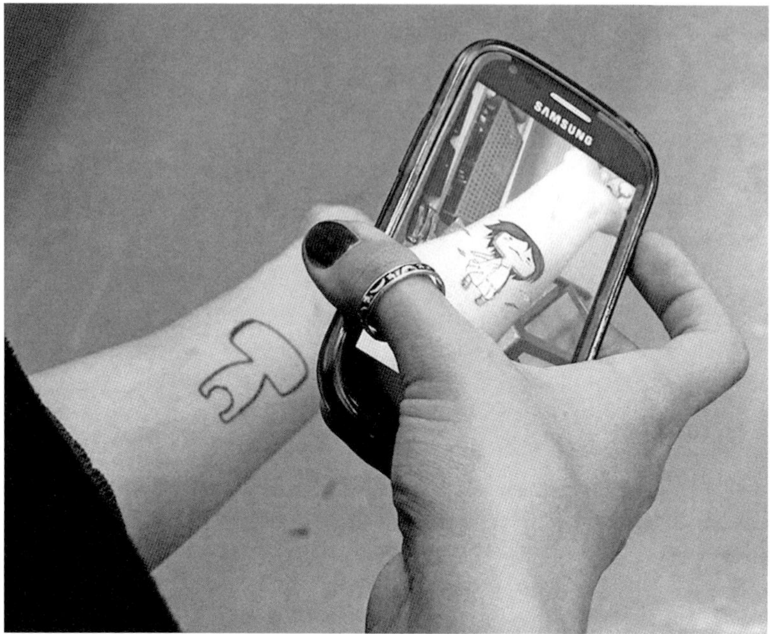

FIGURE 5.6. An augmented reality virtual tattoo created with the TattooAR application

project is an interactive installation that interprets the user's gestures into a robotic graffiti painting. The project addresses conceptual issues such as the presence of graffiti in the streets and in art galleries; its appreciation and criminalization as well as the value of handmade versus mechanically produced art. Tinta Solta prompts reflection about graffiti as an artistic expression through the use of Physical Computing technology. The motivational starting point for the project was the student's personal experience with graffiti painting. Being already a graffiti artist, he wanted to merge his artistic practice with digital media practice.

At the beginning of the project, the student was also enrolled in the *Interfaces Físicas e Lógicas* class. In one of the first assignments for the class, he produced a robot that made drawings through the use of a pen and motors controlled by a light sensor connected to an Arduino board. This experiment inspired a new and unexpected direction for the project (Figure 5.7).

The student described the process:

The first drawing machine was a car. It was my first contact with motors, actually. For this first car that I made, I didn't control anything, I just

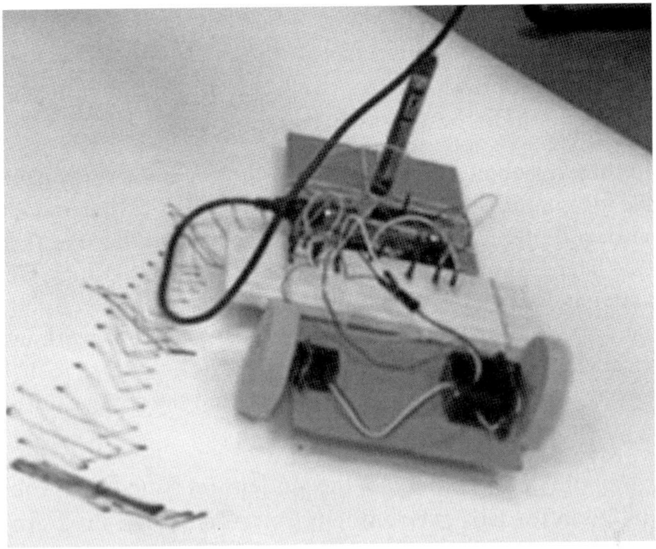

FIGURE 5.7. One of the earlier experiments created by the student in the Physical Computing class

used some basic code that the monitors in the lab helped me to build, and the motor started spinning, and I said: "that's it, I'll put it to spin and I'll make some kind of structure to hold a pen." Then I went to the modeling lab to cut a piece of foam and tied it to the motor. It kept spinning, a very rudimentary car, but it was my first contact with electronics. I mean, it didn't look like a car. I just call it a car because it had wheels. But it was the first drawing machine.

This framing of the situation revealed a new possible direction to the project:

It was important because I saw that I could make something interactive. I wasn't thinking about using it in the project. In the first moment, it was just an assignment for the discipline, and it was very good to know that it was possible to use code and do something with motors. Because when you say "I'm using motors" for someone who has never used them, it sounds too far ahead. Today I look at this experiment and say "It's very basic" but on that moment it was "Wow, it's cool, a car that draws with a light sensor."

Next, in a process of reflective conversation with the situation, the student then started to investigate the possibilities of creating a drawing machine.

Inspired by the works of the Graffitti Research Lab[16] and So Kanno,[17] he conducted a framing experiment to test the possibility of controlling the emission of spray paint. The student reflects on the difficulties he had to face when he was conducting the experiment:

> I started thinking about a way to press the button of the spray paint, and I had the idea of making some kind of lever. At first I tried to do it with cardboard, and I remember showing it to people, and they didn't understand that later I would build it with wood or some other material. And when I cut it in wood, it was all crooked, we had to use wedges, and when I put the motor it didn't work well because it's difficult to work with the cylindrical shape of the can. It didn't fit. We didn't know how to make the lever. One other time the mechanism locked and the spray paint started flowing and intoxicating us, so we had to stop.

After these difficulties emerged, the student reframed the problem, and started looking in the labs environment from the Design Program at PUC-Rio for the practical knowledge that had become necessary for the conduction of the experiment:

> It was natural for me to arrive in the modeling lab with a spray can and say "I have to make something that will hold this paint can and press this button somehow." I received help from Cid, the Lab supervisor. He taught me: "measure it this way, use a caliper rule." During this part of the process, I spent more time in the modeling lab because I didn't know how to do it, so I learned by doing it.

After some trials, the student managed to build a mechanism that was capable of controlling the emission of paint by using a servomotor controlled by an Arduino board (Figure 5.8).

So, at this point in the development of the project, the reframed question became: how can this mechanism be used to produce a drawing? The next experiment was also developed in the *Interfaces Físicas e Lógicas* class, and was inspired by the technology used in another installation developed at the LIFE Lab:

> We continued developing the project in the class. At this time there was the Arpoador installation here, and I could see it had a spool that tensioned a fishing line. So we thought about trying to do something similar in our project. The intention was to see if we could make a structure to

---

[16] Graffitti Research Lab: www.graffitiresearchlab.com
[17] So Kanno, Senseless Drawing Bot: http://kanno.so/senseless-drawing-bot/

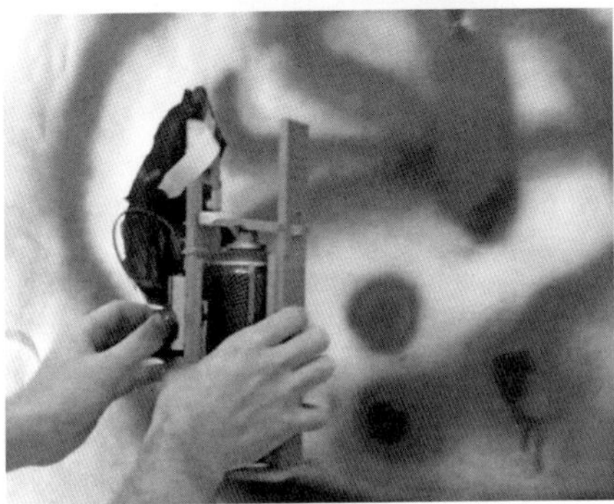

FIGURE 5.8. The second framing experiment was capable of digitally controlling the emission of spray paint

rise and move a spray can. Let's see what the issues are: if it will handle the weight of the can, if we will be able to establish a communication between three motors. The experiment consisted in borrowing a piece from the Arpoador project and see if it would be able to raise the can. And then it started spinning and we could see it raising the spray can.

This experiment showed that it would be possible to move the spray can with the fishing line attached to motors (Figure 5.9). In a process of reflective conversation with the situation, questions about the interface responsible for the movement of this mechanism emerged:

I said: "I'll have to program these motors. How will I interact with them?" It was natural; someone suggested the use of a joystick to control the movement as if it were a videogame.

Consequently, the next experiment had the goal of combining the components that were, until now, separated: the printing mechanism (developed in experiment 2) and the movement system (experiment 3). For its

FIGURE 5.9. A servo motor attached to a spool that tensions a fishing line, used to move a can of spray paint

realization, it became necessary to build a structure to support the drawing and its components (Figure 5.10).

This experiment has shown that it would be possible to make a drawing using mechanically controlled spray paint. To reflect about the use of his project, the student tested it intensively:

> The joystick was working: we put it up, it went up; we put it down, it went down. We were controlling it, and it was generating some very interesting drawings. We were able to draw with the joystick.

In the reflective conversation with the situation, the material talked back. In the practical experimentation with his drawing machine, new questions emerged:

> At this time, the motors were ready, the structure was working, and drawings were being made. We stayed for some time asking ourselves: "What are the next steps?" We thought about making an interface with a joystick, or maybe importing a digital drawing that would be printed by the machine. But I knew it wouldn't be so interesting, because it was so much more fun if the person was controlling it dynamically.

One of the possible interactions considered was to use the artist's gestures. Among the many sensors capable of digitally interpreting someone's gestures is the Kinect sensor:

> My advisor was encouraging me to experiment with the Kinect. It's a different thing. Because we had already done it with the joystick, it was

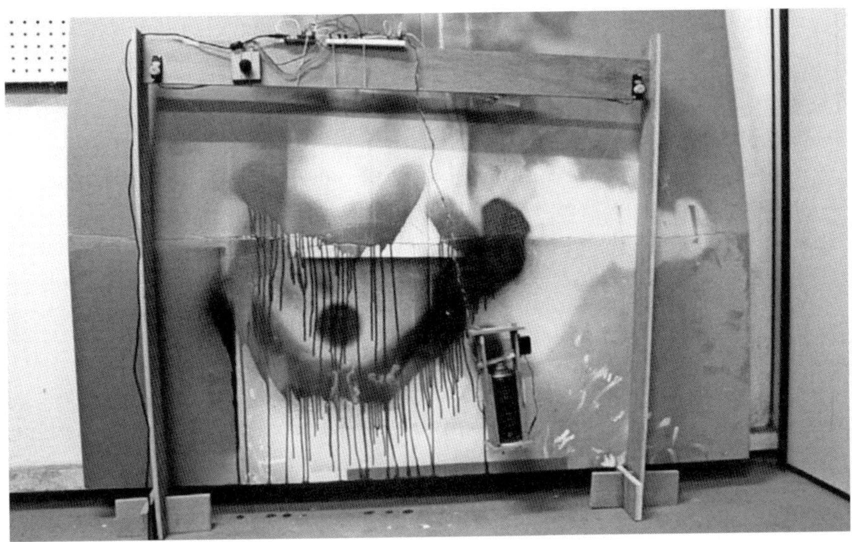

FIGURE 5.10. The fourth experiment, with the mechanism of actuation of the spray paint being raised by two motors

already there. And I don't think it made sense to do it with the joystick: it's a small gesture. With the Kinect I could try to replicate the gesture of the graffitti: you can move all your body. It's almost a performance. And the Kinect would allow this, almost like a dance.

But the student was insecure about a technology that was unknown to him and seemed complicated:

I was afraid of the Kinect. I thought it would be difficult, that I would have to hack it, and that the communication with processing and Arduino also would be very difficult.

Fortunately, in the class *Interfaces Físicas e Lógicas*, the student had a chance and was able to produce an experiment that used the Kinect to recognize the user's gestures. This was possible because he collaborated with a colleague who had prior experience with the Kinect:

At the end of the semester, we managed to do it with the Kinect. Gabriel Maia helped me. Actually, looking at it from the outside, we have already made more complicated things, but at that time I said: "this will be very difficult." But seeing him working opened a path for me to say: "If he managed to do it, and if other students in the classroom are dealing with the Kinect, it means I can also do it. But initially I was very afraid of going further with the Kinect."

By making progress in the development of the experiment in the class *Physical Computing*, the student describes the difficulty he has encountered:

> The final presentation in the class Interfaces Físicas e Lógicas went very wrong. We took it to the painting booth in the Modeling Lab, and we put it to work there, but we didn't know what would be the gesture to activate the spray, so we just set it to paint continuously, hoping it would be ok. And then the paint ended, and the lab was all dirty. In my personal vision it went wrong. At this point I thought: "this will be very difficult." I was worried about being committed to that. I was already planning excuses: "no, it will be better with the joystick," trying to convince myself.

After this frustrated experiment, the student embarked in a new process of understanding the situation. He reformulated the problem by going a few steps back, and trying to understand on his own what had been done by the colleague:

> We had made all the experiments, documented them all, explaining why we had done everything. At this time I thought: "I know it can be done, so I'll try to understand what he did, and I will do it again, this time by myself. I made thousands of tests; I stayed for hours, days and weeks in the lab drawing with it. Actually, at that time it became much more fun to draw with it than to program, so I just kept drawing. It was an evolution again: I was doing it on my own, without any help, and learning programming: "what does each line of code do? Let me create code that is mine now, that I'll know how it was done, I'll comment each part." Because it had already been done. So it was just a matter of time for me to learn how to go further with it.

Consequently, the designer finally managed to program the Kinect sensor in order to experiment with his concept of gestural interaction (Figure 5.11).

> When we started working with the Kinect, it became another interaction. It was not just pressing a key and staying there, seated, drawing. It's you doing it while standing up in front of it. So we went on to discover it. And it was a leap to see it working, to move your hand and see it moving without touching it. This was something that called my attention: to have a machine that you are controlling the movement, without touching it. It looked like magic.

The next step was to enlarge the size of the installation, so that it would reach the proportions of a real graffiti panel. In this moment, the student made a reflection (Figure 5.12):

> The next step was making the experiment bigger, and seeing what issues would come up. We had the idea to use a ladder to support the mechanism, because the ladder is also an element from the streets; the graffiti artist uses these ladders to do his work.

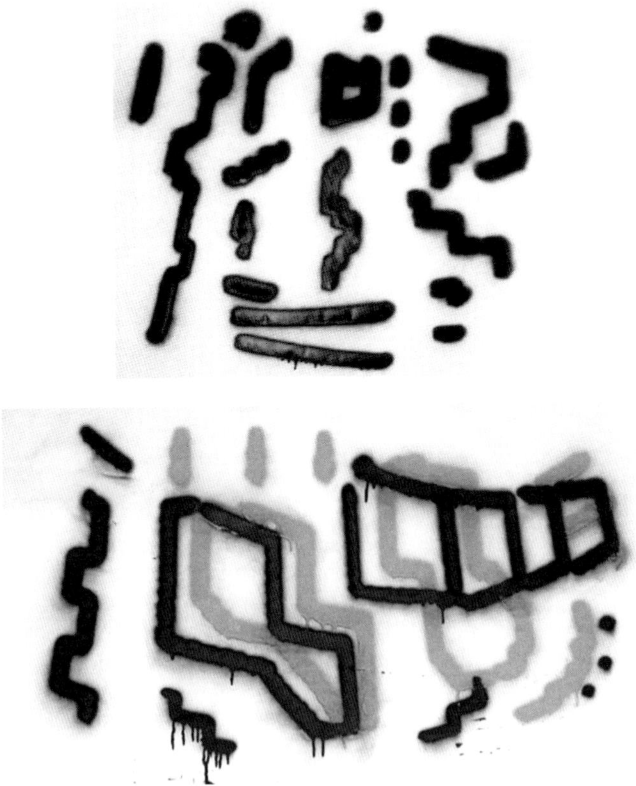

FIGURE 5.11.   Tests made with spray paint

Yet, the student reflects that he didn't have at that time a clear notion of what the project would become (Figure 5.13):

I didn't have any idea of what the project would become in the end. But when we started experimenting with it, we started discovering its language. We went on discovering what the machine would give to us. We thought: "let's try to make it not a printer, let's see what kind of drawing it will make." And this was actually very interesting: when we saw that we were incorporating the "error," it was good because we started using its language to make the drawings. The primary intention was to make a tool for the graffiti artists, which is also a good idea itself. But when we saw that it would be possible to use the imperfect to make art, this was a turning point in the project. This machine did this drawing and it can't be done in any other way. And this was a challenge too.

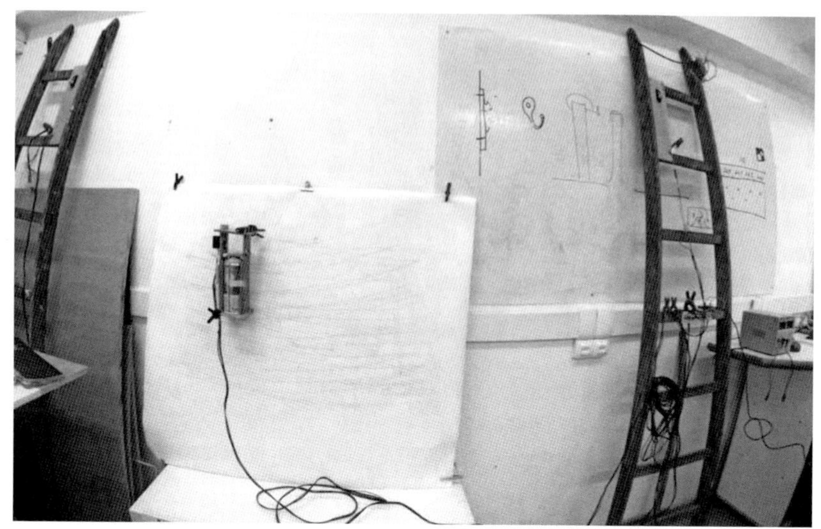

FIGURE 5.12.   The installation in the LIFE lab

FIGURE 5.13.   User testing with graffitti artist Amanda Vieira

FIGURE 5.14. The final presentation of the project at the LIFE lab

When we showed the work, people would say: "you have to correct this line," or "the ink is flowing down." Then I said: "that's its language, you have to use these drops in the drawing." At this time I was testing with Amanda, and she made this drawing that had curved lines, and the drops of ink were completely part of the drawing. And this drawing is still today one of my favorites, because she used the dropping ink to make art. When I started this project I didn't have any idea that it would create this kind of drawings.

For the final presentation, the installation was exhibited at the LIFE lab and people were invited to participate (Figure 5.14).

Project 3: Sango[18]

The Design-Digital Media final undergraduate project Sango, developed by the student Jhonnata Oliveira, is a combined hardware/software kit that monitors blood glucose level of a diabetes patient by using a smartphone. The system uses the sensors in a mobile device for the retrieval of the glucose data, thus making the project available for a significant number of people. In the start of the project, Jhonnata wanted to develop

---

[18] Sango: www.life.dad.puc-rio.br/projetos-english/Sango-english.html

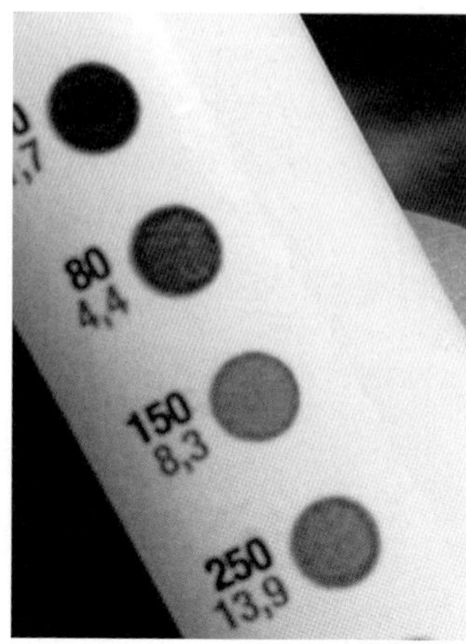

FIGURE 5.15.   Color variations in glycemic index reading

technology for the medical area that would empower and benefit less favored layers of society that cannot afford an expensive system such as the Accu-Check.[19] His research showed that in 2014, smartphones were available practically to all levels of Brazilian society, and based on this information he decided to develop a mobile application for smartphones that would empower people.

The student had a prior experience with diabetics (members of his family have the disease), and this challenged him to investigate the subject. In his research, he discovered that the reading of glucose level in many devices is based on a color system. This color is the result of a chemical reaction of a drop of blood in a glucose strip that is distributed freely in Brazilian public hospitals (Figures 5.15 and 5.16).

These initial discoveries fueled the conduction of a collaborative ideation dynamic: the student invited four colleagues to a co-creation workshop with the aim of elaborating the first steps of the project. This workshop happened in the LIFE Lab after one class of *Interfaces Físicas e Lógicas*. According to the student:

> The greatest insight of my research wasn't generated personally, wasn't generated after some profound reflection, it was generated through the interactions that I experienced in the LIFE Lab. The Lab has always been

---

[19] Accu-Chek: www.accu-chek.com

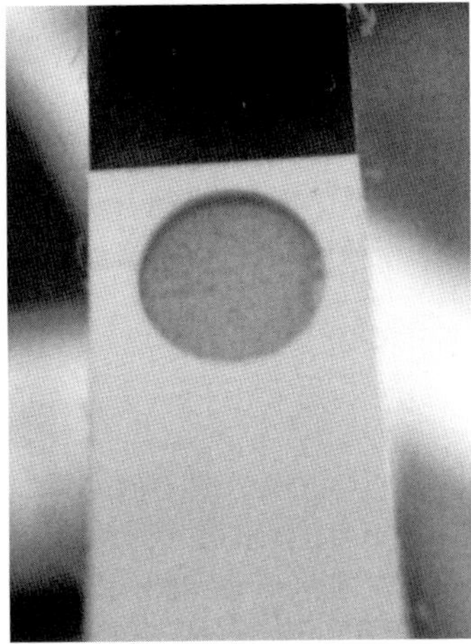

FIGURE 5.16. Glycemic index result

very well attended, by smart people, and in one of these interactions with my friends, in co-creation workshop, we arrived in a possible solution in which the camera of a smartphone could help in the reading of glucose level. And that was a turning point. This co-creation workshop happened at the LIFE Lab and was previously organized. The participants were Rafael Cirino, Rafael Mei, Gabriel Zanini, and Matheus Villaça. It was after a class of Interfaces Físicas e Lógicas, which we were all attending and made it easier. We went on generating ideas. I used a timer. We made three cycles of five minutes, and that was enough to generate many ideas. These drawings were kept with me, and the idea to use the color came from one of these drawings. It was in the second cycle of ideas when someone – I think it was Rafael Cirino – said: "Look! The color, the camera . . ." That was the turning point, as I said, the interactions in the Lab.

Effectively the camera embedded in most smartphones is capable of color information reading. At this point, the student reframed the question of the project and started exploring the development of a system, for the reading of glucose level in a diabetes patient, using the camera embedded in a smartphone. So, the student went on to conduct an experiment to test this.

For the realization of the experiment, the student figured out that he would have to create some kind of optical hardware that would make

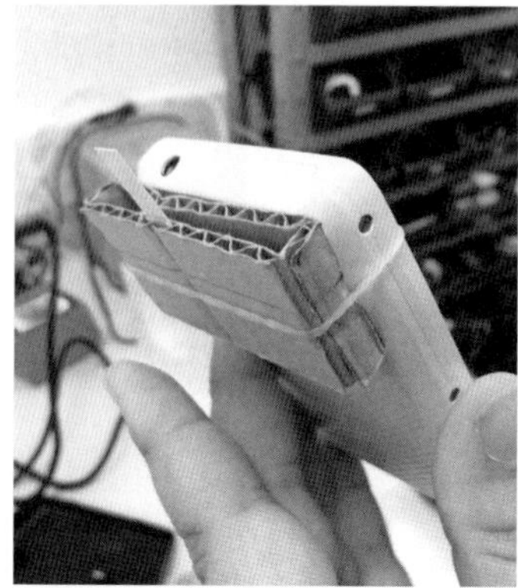

FIGURE 5.17. The experiment made in cardboard with lens and LED light, to evaluate the possibility of reading color information using a smartphone's camera

it possible for the camera the reading of the color information in the glucose strip.

In a practical process, Jhonnata experimented with lenses to enable focusing of the camera in a close distance. Consequently, it became necessary to learn concepts of optics to understand the type of lens that would allow for a short focusing distance. He also experimented with artificial lighting to generate a precise color reading. The experiment conducted – built in cardboard – had the aim of verifying whether it would be possible to read the color information in the glucose strip (Figure 5.17).

For the development of the software that interprets the color reading, the student used the knowledge he had acquired in the *Interfaces Físicas e Lógicas* classes, where he had learned to use the Processing[20] development environment to create apps that run on Google Android[21] smartphones. The Ketai[22] software library for Processing enabled the digital analysis of the color information captured by the camera embedded in the device.

Even though this experiment was successful in the task of reading the color information, its structure was fragile and unstable, generating difficulties in the reading. The subsequent experiments were oriented toward producing a hardware device that could make the color reading reliable.

[20] Processing: https://processing.org
[21] Android: www.android.com
[22] Ketai: https://code.google.com/p/ketai/

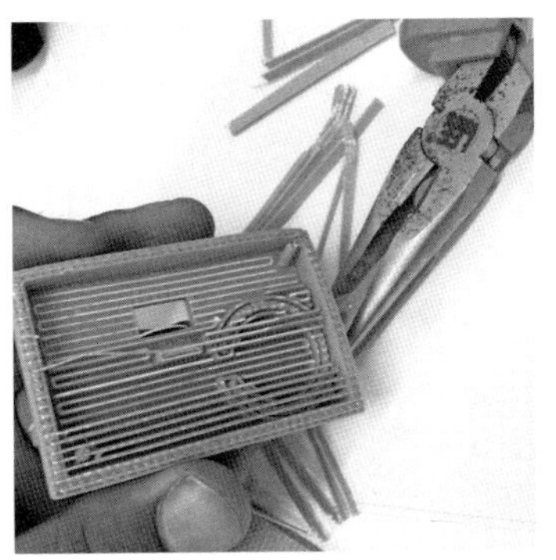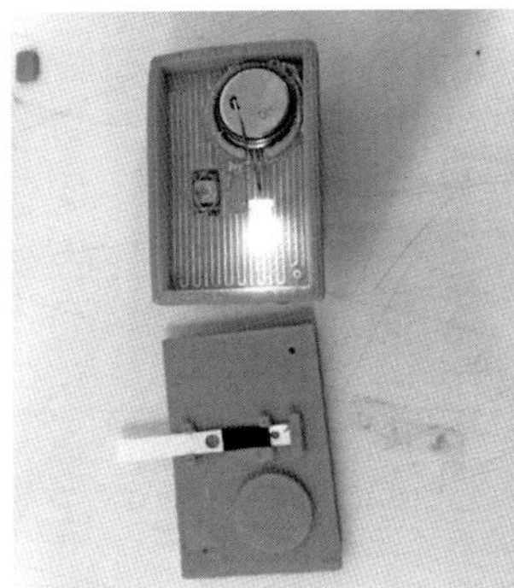

FIGURE 5.18. The 3D printed piece and using lens and artificial light, to perform a color reading using the camera device

In this sense, the student got acquainted with digital fabrication techniques that would help him build a solid and reliable hardware component. The student started experimenting with 3D printing technology, which he was able to access in the NEXT Tridimensional Experimentation Lab that is part of a whole lab environment of the Design Program at PUC-Rio (Figure 5.18).

In the practical testing with this experiment, another issue emerged: what other technological resources can enhance the project? At this moment, the student searched for references in the field of telemedicine, and was able to reframe the question of study: how can telemedicine contribute to the monitoring of glucose in the diabetes patient? As an answer, the student elaborated a new concept for the project: to use the telecommunication tools present in the smartphone to share dynamically, in real time, the information regarding the glucose level between the patient and the doctor and also with the log. Consequently the scope of the project

FIGURE 5.19. 3D printing tests, using a variety of materials and equipment

changed, from a glucose-reading app to a system that shares your glucose level dynamically with your doctor.

Even though it presented an evolution in relation to prior experiments, this experiment was still unstable and delicate. At this moment, besides looking for theory references in 3D modeling, the student also went looking among the professionals in the NEXT Lab for the practical knowledge in 3D modeling and 3D printing that he needed to acquire. For that, he received the support of Professor Guilherme Lorenzoni from the NEXT Lab team. During the process of experimentation with the 3D printing technology, the student was able to explore with different types of plastics (ABS and PLA in a variety of colors) and also with different models of printers (RapMan,[23] Felix3D,[24] and UPrint[25]) (Figure 5.19).

For the software component, this experiment was oriented toward producing a software that would not only read the glucose level but also store this log in a database that could be shared with the doctor. For that, he migrated to the Java programming language, using Eclipse development environment for Android devices. The new platform allowed the development of the interface based on standard elements from the android environment, but also the possibility of communication with a database that can be

---

[23] RapMan: http://reprap.org/wiki/RapMan
[24] Felix Printers: http://felixprinters.com
[25] Stratasys UPrint: www.stratasys.com/3d-printers/idea-series/uprint-se-plus

shared between the doctor and the patient. Consequently, the patient can access all his readings and share them with the doctor, who can also access the readings from the patients, in real time.

The development of the software in the more complex Eclipse environment demanded that the student migrated to the Java programming language, which was possible and somehow easy because the student had knowledge of programming with the Processing environment already, which is based on the Java programming language.

The student also collaborated with a colleague student from the Computer Sciences program, who helped him in the development of the software, especially in the implementation of the database, once its complexity escaped the knowledge of the designer. In a multi- and interdisciplinary process, the student was able to collaborate with a professional developer who helped him in a technologically complex software implementation.

Consequently, the software development was oriented toward two main components: the interactive environment used by the patient – where he can read and access his stored glucose levels – and the environment used by the doctor – from which he can monitor the readings of the levels of glucose of the patients (Figures 5.20 and 5.21).

On the final presentation of the project, Jhonnata demonstrated the working app in a smartphone and the hardware accessory, which were capable of reading the levels of glucose of the patient through a blood drop and sharing this information with a health professional.

FIGURE 5.20. The app interface, where the patient can monitor his glucose readings

FIGURE 5.21. App interface destined to the health professionals, where the doctor can monitor the recent glycemic readings from the patient

CONCLUSIONS

The three projects presented in this chapter illustrate the importance of the Processing programming language use as a tool to promote a reflective practical experience of computer programming by designers. Processing language is confirmed as a programming language designed and ideal to teach programming to artists and designers.

> From the beginning, Processing was designed as a first programming language. The same elements taught in a beginning high school or university computer science class are taught through Processing, but with a different emphasis. Processing is geared toward creating visual, interactive media, so the first programs start with drawing. Students new to programming find it incredibly satisfying to make something appear on their screen within moments of using the software. This motivating curriculum has proved successful for leading design, art, and architecture students into programming and for engaging the wider student body in general computer science classes.[26]

The Processing language, widely used by designers for creative coding, has also been adopted within the Design-Digital Media course at PUC-Rio.

---

[26] Processing Overview: A short introduction to the Processing software. https://processing.org/overview/

In the practice of the classes, Processing has proven to be a simple software development environment that has empowered young designers to prototype interactions. Some characteristics of its successful use that deserve attention are its uncomplicated development environment (just a simple text window for writing code); its availability as an open-source toolkit; and its compatibility with Windows, Mac, and Linux operational systems. In the projects presented in this study, even when the Processing language was not present in the final form of the project, it was used in part of the experimentation process. In the three projects studied, the use of Processing programming language empowered the young designers to experiment with technology in a reflective-practical process.

Expanding the considerations above into a broader context, one can say that in the three projects the initial computer programming knowledge – that was acquired in the classes within a single Design-Digital Media course – *Interfaces Físicas e Lógicas* – empowered the young designers to experiment with technology, not being intimidated by it, and to build artifacts that could be tested in a real-life context.

We can also conclude that the reflective practice methodology experienced by the students allowed them to live a dynamic and endless process as researchers, which certainly transformed the way they project and design solutions, as well as when they elaborate concepts, in a permanent experimentation and theoretical reflection process.

One relevant characteristic of the reflective practice process is the learning that happens during the development of the projects that sometimes knowledge is not directly applicable to the project, but one that becomes part of a repertoire for the student. It is knowledge that the students are prepared to derivate and not only to repeat. All three projects analyzed reveal a relationship between theory and practice where the theory was acquired during the process, and not before the process. The established relationship between theory and practice is notable. Instead of acquiring all the theoretical references *prior* to the development of the projects, the students go search the theory *during* the development of their projects, in order to guide their design decisions.

> "Thinking what I am doing" does not connote "both thinking what to do and doing it." When I do something intelligently, I am doing one thing and not two. (Ryle. 1949, p. 29)

Table 5.2 shows the variety of knowledge that the students faced during the process of development of their projects.

Instead of a static set of knowledge, the students were capable of looking for information, of collaborating with professionals from different areas,

TABLE 5.2. *Projects analyzed and learning processes*

Project	Learning in the process
1. TattooAR	Programming, Physical Computing
2. Tinta Solta	Product Design, Construction, Programming, Physical Computing
3. Sango	Telemedicine, Product Design, Digital Fabrication, 3D Modeling, Programming, Physical Computing

and of acquiring the knowledge that was necessary for the development of their projects.

It is also relevant to note that all the projects analyzed were developed within the area of Design, and present multi- and interdisciplinary relations with other fields of knowledge. The TattooAR presents multi- and interdisciplinary relations with the areas of Arts and Computer Sciences, as also does the Tinta Solta project. The Sango project, in turn, presents multi- and interdisciplinary relations with the areas of Medicine and Computer Sciences. We can highlight the relation with the area of Computer Sciences that is present in all of the projects, once computing is a main tool for the practice of Interaction Design, as this chapter shows.

Finally, it is important to highlight the importance of developing an Interaction Design environment for the growth of research in the area, an environment dedicated to creativity, multi- and interdisciplinary collaboration, the sharing of knowledge, and reflective practice processes. Our study considers that such a collaborative environment composed of not only the LIFE Lab, but also the Interfaces Físicas e Lógicas class, the academic collaborations within our program, the academic collaborations with other programs of the university, and the academic collaborations with other research labs, is essential to the results achieved.

REFERENCES

Cross, N. (1982). Designerly Ways of Knowing. *Design Issues*, 3(4), 221–7.
    (2001). Designerly Ways of Knowing: Design Discipline versus Design Science. *Design Issues*, 17(3), 49–55.
Oliveira, J. (2014). *Sango*. Undergraduate Design Thesis. PUC-Rio.
O'Sullivan, D. and Igoe, T. (2004). *Physical Computing: Controlling and Sensing the World with Computers*. Mason: Course Technology.
Polanyi, M. (1966). *The Tacit Dimension*. Chicago: The University of Chicago Press.
Rittel, H. and Webber, M. (1973). Dilemmas in a General Theory of Planning. *Policy Sciences*, 4, 155–69.

Ryle, G. (1949). *The Concept of Mind*. London: Hutchinson.

Schirmer, G. (2014). *TatuAR*. Undergraduate Design Thesis. PUC-Rio.

Schirmer, G., Bonelli, J., and Chagas, M.G. (2015). TattooAR: Augmented Reality Interactive Tattoos. *Lecture Notes in Computer Science*, vol. 9187. New York: Springer.

Schön, D. (1983). *The Reflective Practitioner: How Professionals Think in Action*. New York: Basic Books.

   (1998). *Educating the Reflective Practitioner: Toward a New Design for Teaching and Learning in the Professions*. San Francisco: Jossey-Bass.

Simon, H. (1996). *The Sciences of the Artificial*. Cambridge: MIT Press.

Whitaker, J.G. (2014). *Tinta Solta*. Undergraduate Design Thesis. PUC-Rio.

Yin, R. (2009). *Case Study Research and Methods*, 4th edn. London: Sage Publications.

6

Art and Technology Collaboration in Interactive Dance Performance

JINSIL HWARYOUNG SEO AND CHRISTINE BERGERON

Abstract: We present a 2-year interdisciplinary collaboration, the Interactive Technology and Arts Initiative (IATI), between the Visualization, Dance, and Computer Science Departments at Texas A&M University. The grant program provided participating students opportunities to engage in art and technology communities promoting interest in the production of interactive performance while facilitating collaboration among faculty, undergraduate, and graduate students. Throughout the program, students produced many interactive performances integrating in both traditional theatre and alternative performance settings. In terms of the students' collaborations, students have developed a common language that different parties can understand and work with. Through continuous and active collaboration, students were able to overcome the challenges presented by communicating with others from vastly different backgrounds.

Keywords: interactive performance, collaboration, interdisciplinary research, interactive dance, motion tracking, projection mapping, interactive installation, wearables, costume design, immersive environments

INTRODUCTION

We would like to introduce the Interactive Technology and Arts Initiative (IATI), a 2-year interdisciplinary collaboration between the Visualization, Dance, and Computer Science Departments at Texas A&M University. IATI introduces students to both art and technology communities in order to promote interest in the production of interactive performance while promoting collaboration among faculty, undergraduate, and graduate students. Students applied both artistic and technological methodologies to design, exploring a wide range of applications such as artificial intelligence, embodied computation, science of perception, narrative treatments, virtual worlds and tangible, wearable or immersive environments. Dancers, visual artists, and programmers alike explored the iterative process of production development in our cross-listed course entitled "Interactive Performance and Technology" and throughout other performance-related activities. Many interactive productions have been implemented in both traditional theatre and alternative performance settings, featured an outdoor performance, implemented dynamic projections onto the surface of a building, and allowed audience members to experiment with the technological framework of the performance.

The successful integration of technology into the fields of dance and performance is an ongoing creative challenge for many choreographers and computer scientists. Various past projects have demonstrated the complexity of successful and meaningful utilization of technology in the design, development, and performance of technology-infused dance. We seek to add to this continuing conversation with an approach that instills active cooperation among choreographers, visual artists, and technologists in the design and implementation of interactivity in an aesthetically holistic fashion that allows the human and technological performance.

OVERVIEW OF INTERACTIVE PERFORMANCE AND TECHNOLOGY COURSE

The course was designed for a 15-week semester, with classes occurring twice a week for 4 hours in Spring 2013 and Spring 2014. The course consisted of undergraduate dance students from the College of Education and Human Development, undergraduate and graduate visualization students from the College of Architecture, and undergraduate and graduate computer science students from the College of Engineering. Over two semesters, 40 students were involved in the course and created over 18 collaborative projects. The course consisted of three main components: teaching, research, and creative activities.

Teaching

Prior to the beginning of the semester, faculty from all three colleges convened to develop the syllabus, course calendar, and assignments. Throughout the course, these three faculty presented lectures in their area of expertise over a wide range of content including but not limited to dynamic collaboration, interactive performance, improvisation, choreography, dance production, motion capture, projection mapping, and wearable technology. Each faculty also provided mentorship and evaluation for students

FIGURE 6.1. (a) Movement session, (b) dancer working on a soft circuit, and (c) LED dress research project

throughout the semester. Students engaged in cross-disciplinary activities such as movement sessions and building circuitry. These diverse activities guided the students in the development of their understanding of the distinctive processes within their collaborative group. Open workdays were scheduled throughout the semester as well. During such classes, student groups worked together freely toward their end goals while receiving feedback from faculty in all three areas: visual art, performance, and technology (Figure 6.1).

Research

This program also directly benefited creative research in dance, visualization, and computer science disciplines. Areas of our research include dance movement capture, interactive systems, and experimental visualizations.

- Performance capture: Real-time motion capture and analysis derived from a single performer and/or large crowds using different types of sensors such as video/depth cameras and inertial sensors; acquisition and analysis of facial expression and hand gesture; audio analysis; human performance studies (kinesiology).
- Interaction: Virtual agent system design in response to audience movement and/or speech; animation and control techniques for creating responsive virtual agents/avatars; telematic performance; aesthetics of immersion in mixed reality environments; aesthetics of technological mediation in live performance; collaborative relationships among interactive contents, performers, and audience.
- Visualization: Interactive visualization technology and 3D holographic and stereoscopic technology for interactive art; virtual agent and world design and visualization; experimental projection techniques.

FIGURE 6.2. Public performance projects from the course

Creative Activities

This course enabled the creation of numerous projects, encouraged continued collaboration among faculty and students, and produced numerous successful performances. Each collaborative student group was expected to present their final projects as comprehensive performances which the public was invited to attend. Their productions were also featured in the dance program's annual concert *Perpetual Motion*, and the visualization program's annual public exhibition *Viz-a-Go–Go*. Site-specific performances occurred throughout campus using motion capture on large building structures and open spaces. The products of these successful collaborations were also represented by faculty at various conferences including the American College Dance Association's regional conference, Waco Dance Fest, and the National Dance Educator Organization's annual conference. As a result of this course, students continued to collaborate and pursue interactive performance projects independently, with many choosing to present their work in senior dance concerts (Figure 6.2).

BACKGROUND

Interactive Performance

Interactive media technologies have been producing an artistic and cultural revolution. Now, even dance has welcomed the power and immersive quality of the digital age. The practice and history of performance has a great deal to contribute to these new forms. There is an active community of dancers and choreographic practitioners who are experimenting with dance and technology integration and the use of technology to engage audiences, as evidenced by the enthusiastic participation and lively exchange on various web sites (deSpain, 2000). Within the academic research community, interactive dance has been explored with a variety of different technologies and approaches. Faver used a live video feed of dancers (Faver, 2001). Both Meador, Rogers, O'Neal, Kurt, and Cunningham (2004) and Mandilian, Diefenbach, and Kim (2008) used motion capture, silhouettes, and video filters in their dance productions. Sheppard et al. found creative ways for computer scientists to work with dancers through tele-immersive dance (Sheppard et al., 2008). In addition, the increased mobility of wearable computer technology has greatly impacted the ability to exhibit new expression effects. *QuantumSound* is the piece that expresses the movement of the performances through sounds using wearable devices and establishes synesthesia-like experiences in which audiences feel as if they are watching and listening to colors (Quantum Sound suits). *ImogenHeap* is an equipment that makes various sounds such as Vibrato by adjusting sounds using sensors and controllers located on various body parts such as the hands, arms, and back. Performers can perform like they are playing the musical instrument on the stage using this equipment (ImogenHeap). *AUDFIT* is the interactive performance piece which makes real-time sounds by gathering data on movements through the sensors. The audience can choose one out of three sound channels made from the performer's movement and can enjoy three kinds of sounds from one movement (AUDFIT, 2014).

Practice-based Research

The arts and the sciences contribute to the understanding of the human life. However, it is considered that each discipline inquires different values, aims, methods, registers, and more. Sometimes, they are often posed in opposition to one another, highlighting the largely incommensurate extremes rather than productive synergies that endeavor to serve integrated Arts + Technology ends. The main goal of our program was to identify synergies and foster collaborations between visual/performing arts and computer science. As such, we focus on practice-based and collaborative research methods throughout our program.

In contrast to scientific research emphasizing the generalizability and repeatability of knowledge, creative art research expresses a form of experience-based knowledge (Sullivan, 2005) and explores subjective qualities of experience. Artists identify researchable problems discovered in practice, and respond or solve them through professional practice. Therefore, artists know their works and the questions around the works better than any other researchers. In general, art is an artist's unique and aesthetic expression, imposing particular and embodied knowledge. Even though art is considered as research, it is widely known that artistic research cannot be easily generalized into a well-defined methodology. Rather, it entails a strong belief that the methodology should be flexible, transparent, and transferable via communication with others. According to Gary and Malins, artistic research material may not be repeatable, but can be made accessible for communication and shared understanding. From these basic philosophical positions, it is clear that an artist's attitude to research should be eclectic, diverse, open, and creative in the methodologies that are adopted and utilized. Artists are adaptable; they often develop research methods based on their artworks or investigative processes. In other words, they are capable of tailoring different research methods according to individual projects. This has involved the use of multiple media to integrate visual, tactile, kinesthetic, and experiential data into rich data. The recent interdisciplinary research culture also makes it possible to expand art practice research into collaborations with other disciplines. As long as participating individuals hold an outward-looking attitude and an awareness of other research cultures and paradigms, dynamic and creative practice-based research methods provide unique perspectives, differing greatly from traditional research. It will be beneficial to have research methods that are responsive and driven by the demands of practice (Gray and Malins, 2008).

Collaborative Research

Collaboration can be defined as a recursive interactive process (Marinez-Moyano, 2006). Many interactive artists have collaborated with scientists and engineers in various forms and new technology has been adapted to traditional performances. In addition, scientists and engineers have discovered and invented new things from creative and collaborative approaches. Interdisciplinary collaborations are based on a collective team effort, where different disciplines, such as arts, design, engineering, science, and so forth, bring in crucial conceptual aspects and research objectives from their own field of expertise. Unlike most research and development, interdisciplinary projects do not aim at problem solving or task-specific applications but focus on audience participation instead, through which they generate valuable new insights in mediated social interaction and cultural user experiences.

Essi Salonen argues that different modes of collaboration should be used as projects move through the process of development (Salonen, 2012). Working from Pisano and Verganti's "Two Dimensions of Collaboration," Salonen developed a quadrant system chart that visualizes how different types of collaboration could be utilized through the design problem-solving process. The two dimensions of collaboration are openness (open to closed) and governance (flat to hierarchical) (Pisano and Verganti, 2008). Siân Ede, Arts Director at the Gulbenkian Foundation in London, has suggested that artists have always enjoyed testing the capabilities of new materials and technologies, been alert to assessing how new scientific discoveries can alter the vision we have of ourselves, and ask awkward questions about the moral and ethical consequences of science (Ede, 2000). However, Ede identifies the mutual desire to collaborate to make new work together that reflects the interests of both parties, as a relatively new phenomenon (Wright and Linney, 2006).

Victoria Vesna is an artist, and the chair of the Department of Design | Media Arts at UCLA, School of the Arts and Architecture. She always works with researchers, artists, and scientists. NANO is one of her collaboration projects with the scientist James Gimsewski which includes nine interconnected installations at the Los Angeles County Museum (Vesna, 2004). The project seeks to provide a greater understanding of how art, science, culture, and technology influence each other. At the exhibition, participants can feel what it is like to manipulate atoms one by one and experience nanoscale structures by engaging in art-making activities. There are a lot of potentials in artists and scientists coming together, in taking a risk and introducing the unknown as an experience and an art form (Scaravaggi, 2015).

Performance art is also instinctually a collaborative form. There are many collaborative partnerships in the arts, with one of the most famous collaborations occurring between choreographer, Merce Cunningham and composer, John Cage. Their collaboration began in 1944 and continued until Cage's death in 1992. After reading the publication of the *I Ching* in the 1950s, Cunningham and Cage abandoned traditional elements of composition such as rhythmic structures, cause and effect, and climax and began to use chance as a way to develop their work. Rather than working side by side on a specific objective, they worked separately to create the result. Although the final work was presented in the same time and space they both felt that each art form, both music and dance, should stand on its own. This belief makes their collaborative work unique and different from the traditional idea of collaboration (Celant, 1999; Vaughan and Harris, 1997).

Another monumental collaboration in dance history is between choreographer and dancer, Martha Graham and sculptor, Isamu Noguchi. Their relationship began when Graham commissioned Noguchi for two portrait heads in 1929. Their first collaborative efforts came in 1935, when Noguchi created the set for Graham's solo, *Frontier*. Over the years, Noguchi created over 20 set designs for Graham's choreographic works. Some of the most notable creations are Appalachian Spring (1944), Cave of the Heart (1946), Errand into the Maze (1947), Night Journey (1947), and Embattled Garden (1958). Graham's and Noguchi's collaboration often began from a vision from Graham. She would discuss an idea, theme, or myth that she wanted to base a new work on with Noguchi. He would then create his sculptures where Graham would integrate them into her choreography, often as an extension of her own body (Benbow-Pfalzgraf and Benbow-Niemier, 1998).

INTERACTIVE PERFORMANCE AND TECHNOLOGY COURSE DESIGN

This course explores interactive art and technology practice that integrates the creative and imaginative possibilities of interactive art with its application to new technology research. It fosters innovation and the creation of new knowledge in the engagement of the body with emerging technologies within theater, dance, music, art, design, computing, communications, and other allied fields. This practice-based course investigates interactive performance as an emerging art form.

Learning Objectives

Upon successful completion of the course, the student will be able to

- Create a collaborative interactive performance project by integrating performance and technological skills that support interactive aesthetics.
- Demonstrate an increased conceptual and kinesthetic awareness of mediated environments and the ways they affect movement and performance.
- Understand emerging technologies that allow for interactivity in performance with a focus on real-time motion capture, interactive visuals, and projection mapping.
- The ability to collaboratively plan, design, and present ideas and prototypes for interactive performance.

Roles of Participating Faculty

Each faculty member from the three colleges took on specific roles throughout this process. The Visualization faculty member from the College of Architecture was responsible for managing the grant program and specialized in collaboration, interactive performance, physical computing, projection mapping, and wearable technology. The faculty member from the Dance program in the College of Education and Human Development assisted in the development of the course and conducted lectures and movement sessions on dance production, improvisation, choreography, and costuming. A computer science faculty member contributed in teaching motion-capture systems. All three faculty members attended team meetings with the students and gave feedback on their projects in their area of expertise.

Course Activities

The course was broadly divided into three parts (see Table 6.1). Within the first 5 weeks, students learned wearable techniques and attended improvisational movement sessions. Throughout the next 5 weeks, students worked on motion tracking and projection mapping. In the last 5 weeks of the course, students worked on their final projects. To develop their final projects, teams produced original code, choreographed solos and duets to highlight the technology, created visualizations, designed and constructed stage sets, costumes, and props and prepared the stage space including the use of theatrical lighting.

In regards to specific course concepts, students learned about interactive performance, collaboration, improvisation, and choreography with a focus on space, time, and energy. Students also investigated audience experience and perception, resulting in some students deciding to track the audience to change the visualizations on stage. Students also learned about specific technological concepts including camera motion tracking using the Kinect, the Wii and digital cameras, projection mapping, soft circuits, and wearable technology using LED lights, Lilypad Arduino, touch sensors and conductive thread, and the like. Students explored their ideas through small studies using the technology and concepts they learned. Each study was demonstrated through a performance of their work. Team members were responsible for all aspects of the performance such as set, costume design, construction, sound, and lighting. The final projects ranged from indoor to outdoor performances, each posing its own set of unique production needs which students were expected to consider, manage, and accommodate. For example, students had to consider the threat of inclement weather and the

TABLE 6.1. *Weekly activities*

Week 1	• Introduction to interactive performance

Sketch one: Interactive costume design

Week 2	• Introduction to interactive costume design • Team creation/roles distribution and brainstorming thematic concepts • Communication (web design, picture, video), Project management (mailing list, scheduling, booking) • Content production (choreography, sound, video, narrative development)
Week 3	• Tutorials for soft circuitry, wearable computing
Week 4	• Workdays (individual team meetings and critiques)
Week 5	• Sketch one presentations

Sketch two: Responsive environment design

Week 5	• Introduction to responsive environment/brainstorming thematic concepts
Week 6	• Motion tracking tutorial/projection mapping tutorial • Technical aspects (motion capture and tracking programming, prototyping)
Week 7	• Workdays (individual team meetings and critiques)
Week 8	• Sketch two presentations

Final project

Week 9	• Collaborative idea generation/project proposal
Week 10	• Guest artist visit/critique
Week 11	• Creative iteration/workdays
Week 12	• Technical components completed; technical demo/workdays
Week 13	• Technical rehearsals
Weeks 14–15	**Final public shows**

availability of stable Wi-Fi connections, suitable electrical power, appropriate performance flooring for the dancers, etc. when producing large-scale outdoor performances.

STUDENTS' COLLABORATIONS

Processes

Most of the students did not have experience in interdisciplinary collaborations prior to their enrollment in this course; the dancers had never made soft circuitry and the computer scientists had never created art performance. Only a handful of students, the interactive artists from the Visualization Department, did have prior experience in completing collaborative projects. However, this is mostly due in part to the inherently interdisciplinary nature of the department. Nonetheless, all students were required and encouraged to collaborate with their peers from the other departments throughout concept development, research, implementation, public show, and documentation processes.

The student groups primarily convened within the dance studio environment. The space was equipped with a typical production grade system. Working in the space allowed students to apply any stages of project testing in the final performance space. Depending on the students' role, however, some students would occasionally complete specific tasks within their own specialized departmental facilities. For instance, dance students worked on choreography and practiced dance; computer science students worked on programming for motion capture; visualization students worked on soft circuitry and implementing interactive visuals. Students would then reconvene to combine their developments and test each new iteration of their projects. Occasionally, there were notable instances of crossover; with their extensive knowledge of costume design and fabrication, some dancers were enlisted to help interactive artists within their group sew soft circuitry and wearable technology into their costumes. Throughout this collaborative endeavor, students focused on examining technology opportunities for performance art, studying art practice and the role of interactive technology.

Collaborations

Four to five students from different departments had to collaborate to create dance performances utilizing interactive technologies. In general, interactive art students took on the role of project facilitator. However, the collaboration styles and the outcomes varied based on team members' various backgrounds and experiences. Teams with an artist leader were markedly more explorative, while teams with a computer science leader were more rigid and focused on specific goals and necessity items.

The students with an artistic background exhibited very developmental and iterative approaches to their works. Essentially, this means that while they have a rough idea of what they want to achieve, their ideas constantly develop as they produce the work. Computer science students were less flexible and more goal-driven. One student reported, "Sometimes I believe I've resolved the problem with artist team members but the next time we talk it seems they meant something else. It seems that artists do not approach any problems logically and specifically." Throughout the semester, students started developing a common language that both parties could understand and work with. Many artists had to spend a great deal of time learning about the technology before they could make progress on their part; many computer science students began iteratively testing their systems with dancers on the stage.

STUDENTS' PROJECTS

Students' projects focused on the relationships between dancers' movements and embodied technologies. Some students fabricated dance costumes that were aware of the dancer's movement using an accelerometer, a touch sensor, a heart rate sensor, and LEDs. Some other students utilized a Kinect or a webcamera to capture dancers' movements and mapped with interactive visuals, sounds, or robotics. All projects have been presented at local events and both national and international conferences. We introduce four selected projects below.

Proximity

Proximity is a performance art piece that evokes a performer's improvisation based on the interaction with a robot on the stage. Students created a robotic improvisational dance partner that uses principles of interactive dance and emergent behavior to collaborate with a human dancer in live improvised dance performance. *Proximity* consists of an autonomous robot "egg" that reacts to the distance from a dancer and the qualities of the dancer's movement with a set of kinetic and sonic expressions and behaviors. The dancer and robot interact and improvise together as collaborators in this creative dance process.

Students used Arduino and Processing combined with readily available hardware and electronics to construct the *Proximity* robot. To achieve a sense of naturalistic motion, they designed the robot in an egg-like shape, with wobbling as the primary method of kinetic expression. This motion depended on carefully controlled manipulation of the robot's center of gravity, which due to the necessarily light weight of the robot could easily be upset by the addition of extra components for sensory input and output. As a result, they externalized the sensory input to an overhead webcam that used blob tracking to measure the relative distance between the dancer and the robot.

FIGURE 6.3. (a) *Proximity* performance and (b) diagram of the inside of the robot of *Proximity*

Figure 6.3(a) depicts the movement method for the robot. A weight (1) is suspended within the rounded base of the robot from an arm swung by a servo motor (2). This swinging action on the center of gravity causes the body of the robot (3) to naturally wobble.

In the Shadow

In this project, a dancer interacts with and is accosted by an elusive dancer who is only seen by his shadow. This contrasts the distance (in space, time, or mental state) between the physical dancer and the elusive shadow dancer with the closeness of the two dancers and their inability to remain apart. The projection blurs the lines between what is and is not physically in the space by playing with light and shadow, in metaphor, manipulating emotional control. There is a pervasive feeling of being dominated or followed, perhaps by a stalker, throughout the performance. These themes were derived from the black and white interactions happening both on and off the projection screens. Shadows are often unavoidable and a completely flat surface is not always the most interesting thing to project on to. This makes the ideal viewer position for shadow reduction right at the projector. The students who designed this project wanted to embrace those shadows using them as a feature-driving element to highlight the contrast between the silhouette and its surroundings.

This project is realized as an interactive dance performance where two dancers interact with front-projected visuals, using two webcams and an Xbox Kinect. The design can be broken down into the set, the visuals,

FIGURE 6.4. *In the Shadow* performance

the costume, and the choreography. The stage is designed as three panels – a larger central panel and two smaller panels to each side. The central panel is used for projection. The two side panels are used as backdrops for the webcams. The projector and Kinect are in front of the central panel, facing toward it. Each side panel has a webcam facing it. The main physical dancer performs primarily in front of the central screen, in view of the Kinect. The shadow dancer remains in front of the side panels and also travels behind the central panel. The tone of the choreography was very menacing, almost as if the shadow dancer were stalking the main dancer. However, the shadow dancer never came into physical contact with the main dancer. The image projected onto the main dancer's screen could, however, manipulate the main dancer. The dancer silhouettes are captured and used as input for the projected visuals. The black and white banding effect compliments the female dancer's cast shadow on the projection screen. The two dancer's bands interfere in a way that resembles electromagnetic fields. The interaction is complex and almost chaotic which plays to the relationship between the dancers (Figure 6.4).

Zwischenkörper

Zwischenkörper, "between bodies," is an interactive performance art piece that explores manifestation of hybrid virtual/physical synthetic dance partners and the dancers' and audience's perception thereof. It involves a dancer interacting with three hybrid entities, manifested as responsive pillows physically and as color-coded undulating meshes projected onto a screen behind her, virtually. The parallel existence of the entities in virtual and physical space creates a cognitive dissonance that mirrors and questions the inexorably developing duality of human life in the physical and virtual worlds.

The project consists of several parts working in tandem to cultivate a complete visual, kinetic, and tactile experience. The dancer interacts with three synthetic agents that have physical and virtual manifestations. The virtual manifestations are projected onto a screen behind, enclosing the performance, along with the dancers' own virtual representation, controlled through a Microsoft Kinect motion capture system. The physical forms are expressed through three interactive pillows and the dancer herself. The pillows are each equipped with Arduino Lilypad microcontrollers that coordinate touch sensors, flex sensors, and accelerometers. They communicate with the computer system controlling the virtual projection via a Zigbee Wi-Fi network. As a whole, the system represents an ambient intelligent space embodied by the dancer's movement and the sensors and feedback embedded in the interactive pillows.

Zwischenkörper has been performed on multiple occasions as both a dance performance piece and an interactive artwork that invited audience interaction. As a performance, the interaction occurred exclusively between the performer and the synthetic agents, while the audience observed. In this context, the playfully ambiguous relationship between the dancer and the entities was communicated through light and motion. As an interactive installation, the audience was allowed to interact directly with the pillows and virtual meshes and to control the dancer's manifestation in the virtual space with the Kinect. This exploratory context allowed the audience a direct subjective experience of the pillows and their tactile qualities (Figure 6.5).

CHALLENGES

Although there were many successes in this endeavor, there were also many challenges. Some of the greatest challenges included durability of technology, project timeline, iterative process, outdoor performance, and student scheduling between the three different colleges.

Using wearables created some unique problems. Foremost, it is time intensive to experiment with unfamiliar and sometimes unreliable materials such as conductive thread and thin wire. It was difficult to find materials

FIGURE 6.5. *Zwischenkörper* performance

that were flexible enough to yield to the flow of the dancer's movement yet durable enough to support the needs of the technology. Using kinetics for motion capture brought its own particular challenges. The space in which a singular kinetic could pick up the movement of the dancers was extremely limited. The use of multiple kinetics simultaneously was explored but created a new set of issues including the ability to stream multiple hard drives into one main software.

One major challenge encountered through this process was the overall timeline to develop the technology and visualizations while still allocating enough time for the creative choreographic process. Often there would be changes to the technology in the last stage of the process without the dancers having the appropriate time to adapt their choreography. For dancers specifically, this led to the necessary implementation of an improvisational approach to the performance rather than allowing them the opportunity to create a set choreography designed explicitly for the technological environment.

Outdoor installations created a whole new set of challenges. Permissions from building supervisors, unstable Wi-Fi connections, convenient accessibility to electrical power, appropriate flooring for the dancers, unpredictable weather, and defining a vast open space to become a more focused performance space were only a few of the additional challenges brought forward by outdoor interactive performances. One of the most positive outcomes and most significant advantages of this type of performance was its remarkable visibility. People unexpectedly walked into a performance and often stopped with intrigue, curiously wondering what was happening. Since the installations created large-scale visualizations on outdoor structures, audiences could view an aspect of the installation from outside the realm of the performance space. Audiences often had an interactive opportunity with these installations and were able to experience the environment for themselves at the end of the performance.

Many of the challenges that we encountered were readily expected and anticipated. There were, however, a few unexpected issues. One major concern was student scheduling outside of class for rehearsal and independent exploration. We discovered that the students from the three departments maintained contradictory schedules. Not only did availability between graduate and undergraduate students vary greatly, but it was also significantly difficult to balance the different responsibilities of their disciplines as well. Dance, visualization, and computer science all require many hours of study and preparation outside of the traditional classroom setting. Dancers had hours of rehearsals each day; visualization students spend hours in the lab designing; and the computer science students were Ph.D. candidates who were conducting their own research. This scenario caused many problems with students trying to find time to come together outside of the class period to work on their projects. Even though the course had built in workdays, interactive performance is time consuming and students involved were seeking degrees in time-intensive art forms. No matter how you arrange it, there are still only so many hours in a day.

CONCLUSION

We presented the IATI, a 2-year interdisciplinary collaboration focusing on the "Interactive Performance and Technology" course. Through the program, undergraduate, graduate students, faculty from the dance, visualization, and computer science departments collaborated to create public performances and exhibitions. The Interactive Performance and Technology course was a great success in terms of creating interdisciplinary projects, exhibiting performances, and presenting outcomes. Through continuous and active collaboration, students were able to overcome the challenges presented by communicating with others from vastly different backgrounds. Students worked on developing a common understanding of each other's intentions and vision, engaging in extensive discussions, and allowing enough time to establish meaningful relationships. Students also spent quite a lot of time learning about each other's unique disciplines.

Open and clear communication among mentors and peers is an important part of the creative process. However, art–technology collaborations have particular requirements and difficulties. As such, it is important to establish the right conditions for collaboration. We believe that successful collaboration can be learned by building on the lessons from experience and applying the results of this kind of research to ongoing situations. For successful partnerships, the establishment of long-term relationships during which trust and confidence is built up through direct application is but one of many clear advantages of this creative process.

REFERENCES

AUDFIT. (2014). https://vimeo.com/88823872 (Accessed January 15, 2016).

Benbow-Pfalzgraf, T. and Benbow-Niemier, G. (1998). *International Dictionary of Modern Dance*. Detroit: St. James.

Celant, G. (1999). *Merce Cunningham*. Milano: Charta.

deSpain, K. (2000). Dance and technology: A pas de deux for post-humans. *Dance Research Journal*, 1, 2–17.

Ede, S. (2000). *Strange and Charmed: Science and the Contemporary Visual Arts*. London: Calouste Gulbenkian Foundation.

Faver, C. (2001). Toward a digital stage architecture. *IEEE MultiMedia*, 8, 6–9.

Gray, C. and Malins, J. (2008). *Visualizing Research: A Guide to the Research Process in Art and Design*. Burlington, VT: Ashgate Publishing Company.

Heap, Imogen. www.stampthewax.com/2015/01/21/imogen-heaps-magic-gloves-couldredefine-music-making (Accessed January 15, 2016).

Mandilian, L.E., Diefenbach, P., and Kim, Y. (2008). Information overload: A collaborative dance performance. *Proceedings of the 1st ACM International Workshop on Semantic Ambient Media Experiences*, 57–60. New York, NY.

Marinez-Moyano, I.J. (2006). Exploring the dynamics of collaboration in interorganizational settings. In Schuman, S. (ed.), *Creating a Culture of Collaboration* (pp. 69–85). Hoboken: Jossey-Bass.

Meador, W.S., Rogers, T.J., O'Neal, K., Kurt, E. and Cunningham, C. (2004). Mixing dance realities: Collaborative development of live-motion capture in a performing arts environment. *Computers in Entertainment*, 2, 12.

Pisano, G.P. and Verganti, R. (2008). Which collaboration is right for you? *Harvard Business Review*, 86, 12.

Quantum Sound suits. http://sensoree.com/artifacts/quantumsound (Accessed February 15, 2010).

Salonen, E. (2012). A designer's guide to collaboration. www.designingcollaboration.com (Accessed February 15, 2010).

Scaravaggi, S. (2015). Victoria Vesna's interactive experience. www.digicult.it/digimag/issue-020/victoria-vesnas-interactive-experience (Accessed January 15, 2016).

Sheppard, R., Kamali, M., Rivas, R. et al. (2008). Advancing interactive collaborative mediums through tele-immersive dance (TED): A symbiotic creativity and design environment for art and computer science. *Proceeding of ACM MM'08*, 579–88. New York, NY.

Sullivan, G. (2005). *Art Practice as Research : Inquiry in the Visual Arts*. Thousand Oaks, CA: Sage Publications.

Vaughan, D. and Harris, M. (1997). *Merce Cunningham: Fifty Years*. New York: Aperture.

Vesna, V. (2004). http://victoriavesna.com (Accessed February 15, 2016).

Wright, A. and Linney, A. (2006). The art and science of a long-term collaboration, new constellations conference, museum of contemporary art. *Proceedings of the New Constellations: Art, Science and Society Conference*, 54–60. Sydney: Museum of Contemporary Art.

PART IV

ONLINE LEARNING

7

Design Scenes of Online Code Learning Environments

MICHAEL FILIMOWICZ

Abstract: An autoethnographic exploration of online code learning environments is situated within a context of multimedia cognition frameworks. This suggests new strategies for both the design of multimedia code learning content and facilities. What emerges from this analysis is the notion of a "three-screen scene" that articulates the spatially distributed cognitive tasks of programming workspace, note taking, and expanded context. The three-screen scene is considered as its own design frame for the development of both courseware and computer labs for self-learning coding skills.

Keywords: distributed cognition, online learning, multimedia cognition, interactive platforms, spatial information processing, HCI, e-learning, autoethnography

DCOG

Distributed Cognition (DCog) is an approach to the study and understanding of mind that takes into account the environmental situatedness of embodied subjectivity, locating cognition in the interactions between a subject and its context. The term's origin is attributed to Edwin Hutchins, whose early work was in cognitive anthropology. "Nervous systems do not form representations of the world, they can only form representations of interactions with the world" ("Overview of Distributed Cognition," n.d.). "People think in conjunction and partnership with others and with the help of culturally provided tools and implements" (Salomon, 1997, p. xiii). DCog resonates across psychology, ethnography, and design since its insights and perspectives have been generative for a range of technologies. Field observations of interactors in their specific contexts have led concretely to the development of new artifacts and technological systems, such as improved plane cockpit designs (Hutchins and Klausen, 1996) and air traffic control technologies (Fields, Wright, Marti, and Palmonari, 1998), where there are

163

high stakes in the organization of cognition, human action, and technical systems at interplay. Hutchins's (1995) "classic" in this field, *Cognition in the Wild*, is an ethnographic study of the spatial distribution of functions and knowledge throughout the departments and levels of a navy ship. Hutchins originally described this study as "naturally situated cognition."

> The choice of naturally situated cognition as a topic came from my sense that it is what cognitive anthropology really should have been about but largely had not been. Clifford Geertz (1983) called for an "outdoor psychology," but cognitive anthropology was unable or unwilling to be that. (p. xii)
>
> In particular, the ideational definition of culture prevents us seeing that systems of socially distributed cognition may have interesting cognitive properties of their own. (p. xiii)

Contra the response of Thamus to Theuth in Plato's *Phaedrus*,

> Their trust in writing, produced by external characters which are *no part of themselves*, will discourage the use of their own memory within them. You have invented an elixir not of memory, but of reminding. ("The First Critique of Writing," n.d., italics added)

From a DCog perspective, the "external characters" of writing *are* contiguous with the subject and are part of a larger integrated cognitive system, to be taken together as a unit of analysis and understanding in the manner of its distribution of representational states.

DCog informs the autoethnographic method of this case study, and is a "sensitizing concept" that shapes an inductive method such as autoethnography. Originally proposed by Blumer (1954) in sociology, a sensitizing concept

> gives the user a general sense of reference and guidance in approaching empirical instances. Whereas definitive concepts provide prescriptions of what to see, sensitizing concepts merely suggest directions along which to look. (cited in Bowen, 2006, p. 2)
>
> Social researchers now tend to view sensitizing concepts as interpretive devices and as a starting point for a qualitative study. (ibid.)

Self-observation of one's own usage of the websites for code learning can inform a range of decisions, such as selecting which sites an instructor may send students to, which features to emphasize, what factors facilitate or impede learning, or may even lead to the design of new courseware and tools. This modification of a DCog method – the shift from ethnography to autoethnography – is also germane for general research into computer-mediated learning activities, especially *self*-learning outside of the classroom. Applied DCog also allows one to move analytically from the descriptive toward the prescriptive, or concretizing the gleaned insights into new systems or content for those systems.

The concept of "affordance," used often in DCog, originated in the psychology of perception and was coined by J.J. Gibson, first appearing in *Senses Considered as Perceptual Systems* (1966, p. 285):

> When the constant properties of constant objects are perceived (the shape, size, color [etc.]), the observer can go on to detect their *affordances*. I have coined this word as a substitute for *values*, a term which carries an old burden of philosophical meaning. I mean simply what things furnish, for good or ill.

Like DCog, the notion of affordances has crossed over easily from psychological to design discourses and indeed popular parlance, as shown in this excerpt from a 2002 *New Yorker* article:

> Digital documents . . . have their own affordances. They can be easily searched, shared, stored, accessed remotely . . . But they lack the affordances that really matter to a group of people working together. (Gladwell, 2002)

Gibson claimed that any organism can directly perceive, without elaborate cognitive schematization, possibilities for action in relation to the physical properties of entities in the environment. For example, an insect may well perceive the surface of water as "walkable" in the same way that a human perceives a concrete sidewalk. Each surface exhibits, for the respective species, a specific flatness, expanse, and resistance that *affords* the possibility of walking across it. Thus affordances are not only immediate perceptions of the physical properties of the surrounding environment nor the sense of what actions a creature may take in relation to these features, but affordances themselves are relative and vary by the kind of being doing the perceiving. In design discourses, affordances have received several important modifications, for instance by Donald Norman who, in *The Psychology of Everyday Things* (1998), has framed affordance as the actions that are easily perceivable by a user in the context of interaction with a designed artifact.

Affordance theory has made more inroads into social science than into humanist discourse. In a collaborative article that offers a bridge between humanist and social science perspectives, Almquist and Lupton (2010) note,

> Humanist interpreters of design . . . tend to emphasize meaning and interpretation at the expense of affordance and use . . . For most humanists, the idea that design might have "universal" applications, or that affordances might precede or subtend cultural differences, is a species of ideology that must be exposed and "chastened." (p. 4)

These authors propose the category of "use" as an overlapping field between subjective meaning and objective affordance, which they summarize in a Venn diagram (Figure 7.1). The use of any particular technology can be analyzed according to both the affordances presented by the material object, and the intentions and meaning-world of human subjects, potentially serving multiple disciplinary perspectives simultaneously.

Hutchby (2001) has pointedly shown up the limitations of the social constructivist paradigm in sociology of scientific knowledge (SSK) studies and demonstrated the need for an understanding of affordances to counter constructivist claims about real things lacking inherent properties. While noting that "most of the work in this field [SSK] is not about technology in the abstract, but about the complex relationships between technologies and the social and interactional circumstances in which they exist and through which they attain their meaning" (p. 442), Hutchby traces instances of what one might describe as theoretical overreach in SSK claims that artifacts are lacking in inherent properties and possess instead only social accounts of such properties. "[A] new empirical perspective is possible on the nature of the relationship between technological artifacts and human practices. That perspective needs to be grounded in a conception of the constraining, as well as enabling, materiality of the technology as a worldly object" (p. 444). It is in Gibson's concept of affordances, as constraining–enabling, that Hutchby finds the conceptual resources to overcome SSK's one-sidedness with respect to physical properties.

For our purposes here, the overlap space in the Venn Diagram is highly suggestive for understanding the forms of meaning making that are

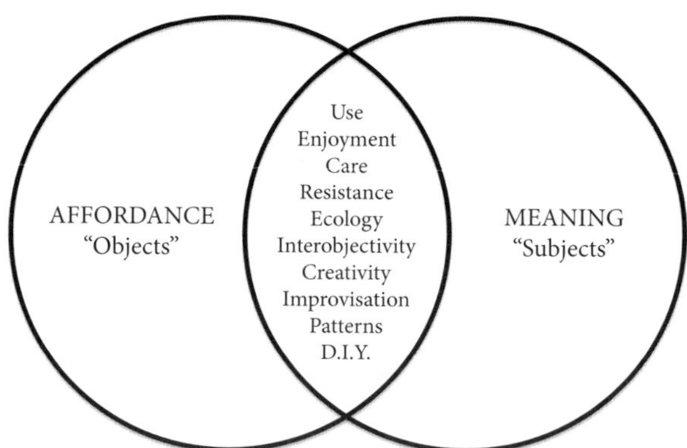

FIGURE 7.1. Almquist and Lupton's Venn diagram situating "use" between affordance and meaning

coproduced along with the use of a technology. In the analysis below, I will explore the meaning effects and forms at the intersection of users and computational platforms that can be discerned in an analysis of contemporary online code learning environments.

AFFORDANCE AND STYLE

The single screen is taken as the default configuration for online code learning. The presumption for content creation for most of these sites is to pack system features, cognitive and practical tasks into a compressed single frame topography. In the survey of code learning environments, several trends can be identified with respect to presenting the workspace and its contextualizing instructional material, as well as some interesting stylistic variations.

Coding in the Browser

Both Codecademy (see Figure 7.2) and Code School implement coding environments in the same browser as the instructional component. Codecademy keeps the bulk of the browser space dedicated to the act of coding, allowing for larger code blocks to be read and written, whereas Code School takes an almost exact opposite approach, and frames coding within a very small and narrow text area, dispensing short exercises of code writing tasks, sometimes one line at a time. Codecademy devotes a small window (upper right in Figure 7.2) for the compiler to show the results of the code, whereas

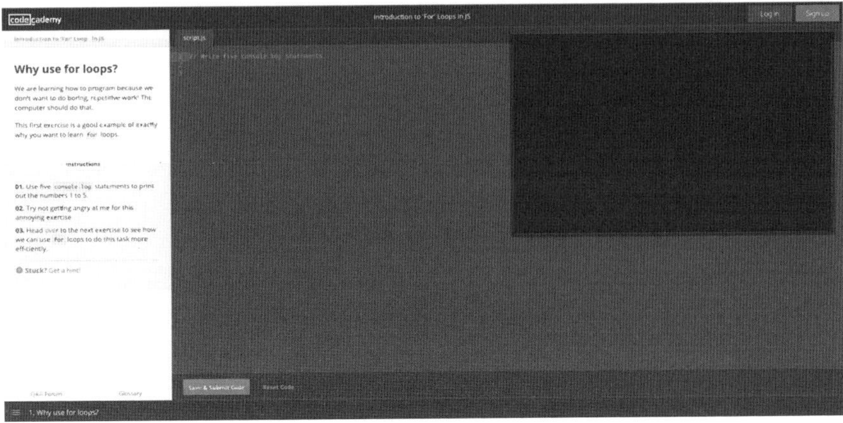

FIGURE 7.2. Codecademy's coding workspace located in the main browser window, next to instruction, compiler at top right

Code School modifies the coding text area, graying it out, and replacing it with the compiled result and showing a dark gray check mark indicating successful execution of the brief coding task. There are intertextual and multimodal elements on display as well: Codecademy utilizes a graphic element similar to ribbon style bookmarks to note completed lessons (top left in Figure 7.2), while Code School implements a more elaborate pirate and treasure hunt theme, both visual and textual, in the "Try R" course. The programming language R, which is oriented toward statistics, becomes a more pirate-like "Arrrrrrrrrrr" in its hammy humor, and given a narrative atmosphere via a giant squid on its landing page.

Coding in Another Browser Window

The Coursera MOOC course *An Introduction to Interactive Programming in Python* (Rice University, Fall 2013) implements an integrated development environment (IDE, combining both text editor and compiler) for Python called CodeSkulptor (www.codeskulptor.org) within its own web browser (see Figure 7.3), separate from the main instructional courseware. This requires two browser windows open for coding along to instruction, which in turn strongly suggests to an interactor that a two-screen desktop is perhaps more ideally suited to this kind of learning, since otherwise constant switching back and forth between the courseware and workspace is required.

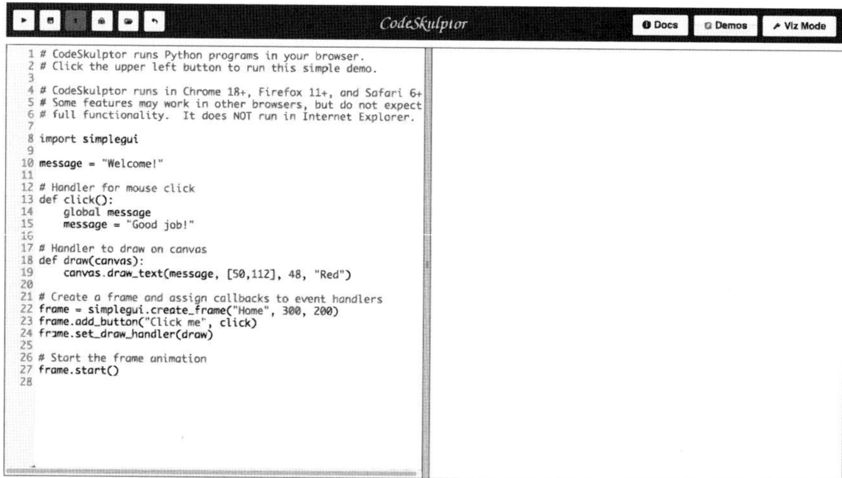


```
 1 # CodeSkulptor runs Python programs in your browser.
 2 # Click the upper left button to run this simple demo.
 3
 4 # CodeSkulptor runs in Chrome 18+, Firefox 11+, and Safari 6+
 5 # Some features may work in other browsers, but do not expect
 6 # full functionality.  It does NOT run in Internet Explorer.
 7
 8 import simplegui
 9
10 message = "Welcome!"
11
12 # Handler for mouse click
13 def click():
14     global message
15     message = "Good job!"
16
17 # Handler to draw on canvas
18 def draw(canvas):
19     canvas.draw_text(message, [50,112], 48, "Red")
20
21 # Create a frame and assign callbacks to event handlers
22 frame = simplegui.create_frame("Home", 300, 200)
23 frame.add_button("Click me", click)
24 frame.set_draw_handler(draw)
25
26 # Start the frame animation
27 frame.start()
28
```

FIGURE 7.3. CodeSkulptor IDE implemented in a stand-alone (separated from instructional content) browser window

The browser space of the courseware modulates between full-screen video and what I will term "sublated" video (see Figure 7.4), or audiovisual media reduced to a small box in the corner to supplement the textual content. There is an additional presentation style in which the courseware browser space mirrors the external CodeSkulptor programming environment for purposes of content presentation in the instruction. Offering a runtime programming environment that is set up within a browser creates a uniformity of learning experience for all interactors. Instead of having to address multiple operating systems and different download packages, and then shape all the learning materials to address simultaneously OSX, Windows, Android, Mobile, Tablets, and Linux, for example, this approach can put thousands of interactors literally on the same, albeit second, page, within an overall environment that is closer to real-world workflows in its look and feel. This uniformity of course experience is also characteristic of the first approach mentioned earlier, which however lacks the look and feel of an actual IDE.

Significantly, having a dedicated browser window for coding grants much more screen space to the compiler – where the results of the code are displayed – but requires much more screen space overall, or switching between either foreground and background or tabbed windows, to utilize. Implementing a coding environment within a browser is not without issues; namely, there are usually some technical artifacts and adjustments that

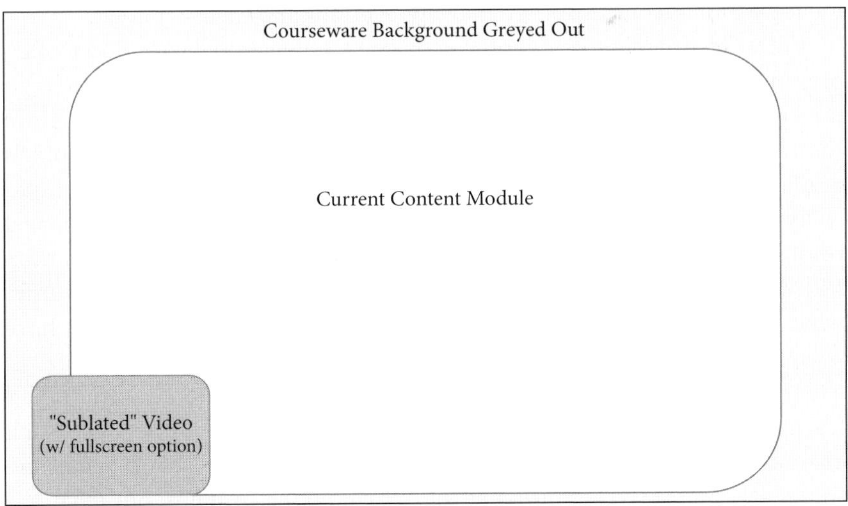

FIGURE 7.4. Wireframe of online courseware with "sublated video"

occur such that there are sometimes minor stylistic alterations that need to be learned in order to implement code building in a browser, so that the code does not run exactly as it would be in "real-world" situations utilizing regular coding tools such as IDEs.

Coding Outside the Browser

Formats produced by Lynda.com or Zed Shaw rely on interactors setting up widely used programming environments on their computer, using common text editors and IDEs (such as R studio, XCode, Processing, or Eclipse) that are the actual applications used by software developers. This requires running other applications entirely in their own windows in the vicinity of the instructional browser. Zed Shaw's instructional style is entirely text-based. His pedagogy involves having the interactor type sections of code that are dispensed in short lessons under various topic headings, concluding each lesson by asking the interactor to investigate variations on the preceding code. In his online Python course, based on his book *Learning Python the Hard Way*, code is to be typed in a text editor (TextWrangler is specified) and executed in the computer's command line application (Terminal on a Mac, PowerShell on a PC). Learners in this scenario are working with the actual tools that are used in software development, rather than a modified pedagogical version of these applications. Lynda.com, in which the primary pedagogical method is the use of video lectures, complements the video lessons with downloadable exercise files, to be worked on in tandem with the video lectures, thus requiring the simultaneous use of separate applications and their windows.

Video-recorded screen captures of code typed into text editors often present a significant difficulty when it comes to the legibility of text in the context of video lectures. Video screen resolution is 72 ppi, and since Internet-streamed video is compressed, there are often not enough pixels available for good-resolution screen capture. Thus compressed video, especially when it comes to textual legibility, is typically of much lower visual resolution than the original imagery displayed on a computer monitor. Video clips of screen-captured text are often difficult to read, and it is somewhat astounding to note how many thousands of video tutorial hours have been produced wherein no effort has been made to increase the font size in a text editor in order to make code more readable as a video lecture. When learning to code, there are crucially significant differences between such characters as [ ] vs. { } vs. ( ), or between ; vs. : or " " vs. ' ' and yet all too frequently one is left squinting at the screen trying to figure out what has actually been typed in the video when trying to follow along. There are ways to address this in the production of videos, e.g., through use of larger fonts, or inclusion of Powerpoint slides instead of video screen capture. Browser-based electronic print is typically cleaner and more legible by many orders of magnitude compared to its screen-captured video incarnations.

Multimedia Cognition

Zed Shaw likes to dispense advice:

> Programming as a profession is only moderately interesting. It can be a good job, but you could make about the same money and be happier running a fast food joint. You're much better off using code as your secret weapon in another profession.
>
> People who can code in the world of technology companies are a dime a dozen and get no respect. People who can code in biology, medicine, government, sociology, physics, history, and mathematics are respected and can do amazing things to advance those disciplines. (Shaw, n.d.)
>
> I've written tons of **code**. Some of it is here, most of it is in dead software at dead companies. I used to enjoy writing software for other people, but now I enjoy writing it for myself only. (Github, 2013)

Codecademy, Code School, and Zed Shaw utilize to a great degree casual and conversational tone. There is often an antiphonal relationship in the coupling of prosaic conversational tonalities to the ultradry scripts of coding itself. The somewhat self-referential Shaw warns his interactors to steer clear of boring coding jobs where workers are "a dime a dozen" and, using Rodney Dangerfieldesque language, "get no respect." Shaw bids his audience to connect programming skills to intellectual disciplines which they will probably find more personally rewarding. His highly autobiographical online paratexts – the first excerpt above, from an entry entitled "Advice from an Old Programmer," is placed at the end of his Python tutorials – provide an acerbic commentary on the lifeworld of coders that could very well be of high interest to those who use his lessons. The second excerpt has more the character of an autobiographical post in the blogosphere.

Another variant of informal voice, Rice University's Coursera Python MOOC, shows computer science faculty engaged in various "videatrics" that we could label "hamming and geeking it up," indeed even posing with props such as a suit of medieval knight armor in the spirit of Monty Python (from which the programming language takes its name), wearing "fun" t-shirts with mismatched ties and playing the hand game Rock Paper Scissors Lizard Spock which has also been translated as graphic icons and emblazoned on their t-shirts.

Here we can read a kind of nervous giddiness, skating light and silly over the abyssal question of what near-future disruptions await educators and academia as courses such as these proliferate on the web, at no cost whatsoever to interactors and prospective students who are now learning to expect their coding education at no cost. Additionally, of course, the team of instructors are just trying to "make code fun" while simultaneously playing up to geek stereotypes in popular culture, a combination of video antics that apparently is afforded by the fact that the course is free, and with absence of tuition comes lack of grading (though no end of online and inline quizzing), lack of credentials, no harm done to a GPA, and the hammy freedom to geek it up on video.

Codecademy and Code School also integrate a regular stream of "jokiness." One should hesitate to name these gestures "jokes" or even "banter" out respect for various traditions of humor. "Jokiness" seems apt to describe such phrases as "HTML + CSS = BFFs" or "best friends forever" ("Codecademy Forum," n.d.). This ever-present jokiness in a number of the major code learning sites constantly reminds the interactor that they are not being evaluated as happens in "real school" – where presumably a more serious demeanor prevails – despite the use by some of these sites of the words "School" and "Academy" in their domain names. With regards to evaluation, Code School shows a gray checkmark while Codecademy offers a green-colored "Way to Go!" or a red-colored "Oops – Try Again!" (see Figure 7.5) that are the only carrots and sticks held out as replacements for grades and marks.

This brings a bit of elementary school atmosphere into online code learning, which may be an intertextual artifact resulting from the fact that these websites are typically addressed to essentially *everyone*, and like what is said proverbially of newspapers, their intended audience may indeed be anyone from a third grade level of education on upward, i.e., anyone who

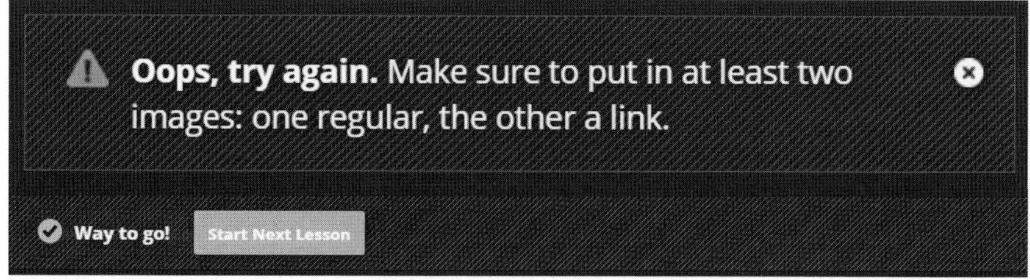

FIGURE 7.5. High encouragement and very mild reprimand on Codecademy

can read. Yet it is also true that code learning sites put the general constructs of grades, GPA, and credentials into question through the general efficacy of their format. If the whole point is *learning*, after all, and these sites *work*, why continue to bother with evaluation and degrees? Today the trends in competency-based education and micro-credentialing (e.g., badges and nano-degrees) are in part spurred by these new formats in online code learning. Still, the MOOC variation of these environments often seems anachronistic with their constant inline multiple choice quizzes and options for paid premium grading and certificates that have a ring of consumerist belonging, as can be found, for example, in Coursera's offering of "Signature Track" for paying members who want to obtain a kind of auratic diploma upon completion. According to the Coursera blog, Signature Track offers:

- **Identity Verification**. Create a special profile to link your coursework to your real identity using your photo ID and unique typing pattern.
- **Verified Certificates**. Earn official recognition from Universities and Coursera for your accomplishment with a verifiable electronic certificate.
- **Sharable Course Records**. Share your electronic course records with employers, educational institutions, or anyone else through a unique, secure URL ("Introducing Signature Track," 2013).

To rephrase Marshall McLuhan's well-known phrase about the content of new media being old media – old education becomes the content of new education. The lecture is dead; so long live the video lecture.

The conversational voice noted earlier – which McLuhan might term the "orality" of audiovisual and "global village" culture – is in fact promoted by much e-learning theory: "A teacher may need to model a lighter tone in text to promote conversation" (Haythornthwaite and Andrews, 2011, p. 21).

> [D]eeply ingrained conventions of social interaction tend to exert themselves unconsciously in human–computer interactions. These findings prompted a series of experiments that show that learning is better when the learner is socially engaged in a lesson either via conversational language or by an informal learning agent. (Clark, 2002)
>
> The view that corporate communications need to be formal is based on a misguided notion: that e-learning is designed to deliver information, rather than create an experience. Adopting a conversational style serves to create a "personality" with whom the user is more likely to engage, as opposed to an information provider. And the more engaged a user is, the more likely a better learning outcome and positive change for your organisation is. (Leo Corporate Training, Web)

There has been a significant amount of research into what the field of multimedia cognition terms the "personalization" effect or principle, which has been empirically verified using various forms of A/B testing of "personal" vs. "impersonal" learning materials that were in every other way identical except for minor word changes (Mayer et al., 2004, p. 391):

> The personalized version was identical except that in 12 places, the word, "the" was replaced with the word, "your" as is indicated by the 12 bracketed words. The only difference between the personalized and nonpersonalized presentations was that "the" (in the nonpersonalized version) was changed to "your" (in the personalized version) at 12 places in the narration. (The paper materials and the nonpersonalized version of the multimedia lesson were adapted from Mayer and Sims 1994)

However, while observance of the personalization principle tends to be widespread in online code learning, this is not necessarily the case with other principles that are well noted in the literature and listed below ("E-Learning Theory (Mayer, Sweller, Moreno)," 2016) with brief commentary. To give an idea of the application of these principles with regards to the preceding examples of online code learning platforms (italics added):

Multimedia principle: Using any two out of the combination of audio, visuals and text promote deeper learning than just one or all three.

Zed Shaw's approach, being text-only, is an outlier. In the main, code learning environments combine multiple forms of media, such as audio-visual clips, slide carousels, colorful icons like bookmarks, mock suits of armor as background props, or drawings of a giant squid to add a narrative theme.

Modality principle: Learning is more effective when visuals are accompanied by audio narration versus onscreen text. There are exceptions for when the learner is familiar with the content, or when printed words are the only things presented on screen.

An interesting variation on this principle can be found in Lynda.com tutorials, where transcripts of the audio component are available, allowing a learner to choose between listening and reading, or listen at first, and refer back to the written transcript later. Zed Shaw's text-only approach illustrates well the modality principle, presenting a single modality – visual text – to online learners, which also allows for quick oscillation between didactic instruction and personal tone.

Coherence principle: The less that learners know about the presentation content, the more likely they will be distracted by unrelated content. Irrelevant video, music, graphics, etc. should be cut out to reduce cognitive load. Learners with some prior knowledge, however, might have increased motivation and interest with unrelated content.

Should beginners trying out the statistical programming language R really be given a parallel pirate narrative as they learn how to perform statistical operations with arrays? As one progresses through the R modules one is also, in the graphic context, completing a kind of "treasure map journey" and enduring lots of pirate jokes.

Contiguity principle: Learning is more effective when relevant information is presented closely together. Relevant text should be placed close to graphics, and feedback and responses should come closely to any answers that the learner gives.

This principle would relate mostly to the workspace of coding. Codecademy's platform features high contiguity in this sense, whereas the need to open multiple windows or tabs to change between workspace and courseware can impede this. Having multiple screens ameliorates any negative effects though there is still the interesting problem of online courses that are high in both video and textual content and which require a learner to often choose one or the other, across screen areas or via window overlays onto the courseware.

Segmenting principle: More effective learning happens when learning is segmented into smaller chunks. Breaking down lessons and passages into shorter ones helps promote deeper learning.

Like the personalization principle, this is one of the most often observed design strategies used by the popular code learning platforms. Learning content is typically modular and scaffolded toward greater complexity, and learners are able to pick up where they left off.

Signalling principle: Using arrows or circles, highlighting, and pausing in speech are all effective methods of signalling important aspects of the lesson.

Codecademy is high into signaling, with its green book marks, red exclamation marks, and green check marks. Other platforms, where there is larger area devoted to coding workspace, tend to take a more subdued approach to signaling. Text editors for coding employ signaling features such as color highlighting syntax for the particular programming language being used.

Learner control principle: For most learners, being able to control the rate at which they learn helps them learn more effectively.

Like personalization and segmenting, code learning typically involves a sequence of short exercises accompanied by brief explanatory material.

Personalization principle: A tone that is more informal and conversational, conveying more of a social presence, helps promote deeper learning. Beginning learners may benefit from a more polite tone of voice, while learners with prior knowledge may benefit from a more direct voice.

Of interest here is that the personalization principle can vary by level of expertise of the learner, as with some other principles in this list, in this case "polite" vs. "direct." Note also the issues that arise, noted earlier, when a website that is designed to be kid or teen friendly has also to be used by adults, who would have to tolerate the various forms of jokey juvenalia.

Pre-training principle: Introducing key content and vocabulary before the lesson can aid deeper learning. This principle seems to apply more to low prior knowledge learners.

Like the personalization principle, stating upcoming key concepts in advance has an effect that varies by a learner's expertise.

Redundancy principle: Having graphics explained by both audio and on-screen text creates redundancy. The most effective method is to use either audio narration or on-screen text to accompany visuals.

In the case of learning to code, much of the learning occurs through doing. The design approach would then be modulated by the extent to which speech or text helps facilitate the act of coding and all that it entails, such as successful compiling of the script, going through the process of debugging, and so on.

Expertise effect: Instructional methods that are helpful to low prior knowledge learners may not be helpful at all, or may even be detrimental, to high prior knowledge learners.

All of the sites under review here are geared toward beginners. For purposes of designing code learning materials in a 4-year undergraduate program, however, this principle suggests that approaches should change in the progression through the years of study. For example, anecdotal institutional evidence suggests that video tutorial platforms such as Lynda.com are much more widely in use in undergraduate curricula compared to online e-book subscription platforms such as Safari Technology Books. The expertise effect suggests that instructors may want to consider switching from video tutorials to e-books as better modes for delivering content, in the progression from lower to upper division courses.

Note Taking

The research on divergent effects of handwriting vs. typing in the act of note taking is far from conclusive and is often contradictory. And there is much reporting and purporting to be found in the popular media with regards to the notion that writing notes by hand is "more effective" than typing them out. Typing is sometimes said to be preferable (higher number of words per minute jotted down), while writing may activate more preferable "areas of the brain" (Carroll, 2012). However, often noted in articles on this topic is that a contributing factor to issues around typing notes is the plethora of distractions afforded by connectivity (Buell, 2013). Typing is often framed as less effective than handwriting, not because of inherent properties of technique or technology, but because being online at the same time one is learning affords ample opportunities for not paying attention, via checking email, engaging in popup chats, checking notifications, or surfing websites unrelated to the learning task at hand. Through autoethnography, I can confirm that checking news sites and the email inbox are frequent diversions from learning coding online. However, the affordance of connectivity can also be framed as a way of scheduling regular breaks for the mind, based on a need for moments of respite from the demands of learning. In a traditional classroom space, one would not be in control of the pace of instruction, and any cognitive respite would likely be at the expense of missing out on important information. In a self-learning and self-*paced* situation, however, connectivity provides useful distractions, though ones that also have to be managed.

It should also be mentioned that there are differences to account for between the acts of typing notes vs. using copy/paste operations. The latter tends to be performed either when the intention is to come back to larger blocks of content at a later date, or when there is too much material to succinctly summarize. Further to this, in the course of this self-study, my autoethnography through these code learning environments led to a change in my note taking to the use of Google docs rather than in separate Word files. Separate documents running in other applications produced a visual and ergonomic clutter that was "solved" by the use of tabs in the browser, where notes could go onto a document in the cloud. Thus there is oscillation between windows, via browser tabs, that often occurs between the instructional content, the coding workspace, and the particular needs of note taking. The practice of taking notes in Google docs also allows for the insertion of images procured through taking screenshots, so that complex multimedia instructional content could be easily replicated in the virtual notebook. Note taking by typing also of course mirrors the actual activity employed in coding, and many forms of notes, such as copy/pasting URLs of important references and examples of executed scripts and projects, are more amenable to the keyboard than a notebook.

THREE-SCREEN SCENE

As we have seen earlier, there is "fierce competition" for desktop screen space in the multiplicity of cognitive and practical tasks. A browser window as a merely spatially constraining factor can be mitigated easily enough by opening up multiple browser tabs if an interactor opts to switch back and forth between instructional and programming windows, or through use of another screen. Figure 7.6 shows what I call the "three-screen scene," which is disclosed again by way of autoethnographic method. The three screens or frames encompass the following praxeological and cognitive tasks: workspace, expanded context, and note taking. Shown is the expanded context in both print and tablet variations. The notion of "expanded context" can refer to the online courseware (e.g., video clips, readings, and lecture content), or reference materials related to programming languages (e.g., W3Schools or Max/MSP tutorials).

This spatial distribution was found to be the most optimal arrangement from the viewpoint of self-learning to code in different programming languages across a variety of online platforms. The three-screen scene (or its alternative, the four-screen scene, if one wishes to combine e-books and print books) is here understood as a design frame for the distribution of cognitive load and tasks required of the code learning platforms. It is common enough to attach a laptop to an external second monitor. Perhaps less standard in general social and educational practice is utilizing an adjacent iPad as a third screen as part of a coherent field of spatially distributed learning functions.

FIGURE 7.6. The spatially distributed learning frames of online learning, with the expanded context shown in both print and e-book variations

Code learning platforms incorporate an electronic hybridization of the online classroom and the self-learning "cookbook" that has for many years been a staple of bookstore offerings (e.g., to be found in the "Computers" section at chain retailers). Because books tend to lie flat unless being held up by the reader (or being supported by book stands, which are not very common household objects), the horizontality of a book on a desk is at odds with the verticality of computer screens. Also of course, the hands are needed for typing and so are unavailable for holding a book open to the desired pages. Screens face the interactor; a book on the desk faces the ceiling; and often poor posture or bad ergonomics splits the difference. In my autoethnographic inquiry into the personal cognitive environment of self-learning coding skills, I have found it necessary to build a book stand to produce better learning conditions. The rationale for building a book stand involved a mix of aesthetic considerations (e.g., the general plastic ugliness of units on offer on Amazon or the office supply store) and the desire for a compact device at the correct angle suited to the user's embodied situation, which entailed comparing the affordances of printed volumes

     Michael Filimowicz

to e-books in the self-study. In very little time a preference for a mini iPad developed as the ideal complement to online code learning, since books were bulky, and required large clips to keep the pages viewable. A mini iPad had other affordances of value: its size is similar to the Kindle, which is also at hand as an option; it has better battery life than a larger iPad; it is a very light and portable object compared to larger tablet, and does not require lighting like many e-readers (though this has been addressed by the Kindle Paperwhite model, with backlit electronic ink technology). This suggests that print books designed for code learning in computer labs should be spiral bound, which is the approach taken by the teacher training platform 4th Foundation (discussed later).

As noted earlier, this first instantiation of a three-screen scene allows for three separate screen spaces: two for the laptop and one via the iPad. The laptop's virtual desktop is arranged top to bottom, so that a cursor traverses a virtual vertical space, rather than the more common left to right, which also conserves the overall footprint of the computer on the actual desktop. This top/bottom orientation also assists with the goal of maintaining good sitting posture and other ergonomic considerations by keeping the interactor facing forward, rather than making constant left-to-right neck movements. While any user can customize their home setup as they see fit or can afford, the distributed personal environment described here goes beyond one's mere personal preference and can be used in the creation of school-based computer labs, where footprint space is typically limited and at a premium, and where all too frequently the "mono-screen scene" predominates (e.g., mid-range iMacs, as shown in Figure 7.7) in students' computer labs. Just as online code learning platforms presuppose the single screen as the only "real estate" to design content for – and thus cramming praxeo-cognitive tasks into a multiplicity of windows – so do our education institutions' IT units typically default to a purchasing and operations model of "buy a bunch of computers and string them alongside each other (on a tight budget)."

As previously mentioned, an autoethnographic DCog orientation can shift from the descriptive to the prescriptive, and here we have allowed this to occur, not only to demonstrate and be explicit about the method employed, but also to address an important general consideration. Figure 7.7 shows why this discussion of screen space is especially important with respect to general pedagogical and institutional infrastructure considerations. The photo depicts a typical university computer lab (in this instance, at my home institution) which in standard fashion offers students a mid-sized single-screen desktop for learning. While sometimes these screens can

FIGURE 7.7. The mono-screen scene: university computer lab

be very large (as in the case of newer, premium models of iMacs), online tutorials and learning websites frequently require one window for instructional content, and other windows for enacting coding and other software operations. Given the increasing role of online learning materials in educational institutions generally, it is a serious matter to reconsider the setup of student computer spaces. We can hypothesize that providing external monitors, laptops, mobile technologies, and customized digital interactive e-books to students in place of the traditional single desktop computer with its solo screen may better support self-learning in computer labs, and could also be a better allocation of resources.

Taken as a single design frame, the three-screen scene can be diagrammed as shown in Figure 7.8.

Since the expanded context can in fact be a book, here we have modeled each screen more generally as a "frame" to link this overall design scene that has emerged out of the autoethnography to more general notions in cognition such as "spatial indexes," "oculomotor coordinates" (Richardson and Spivey, 2000), and "exploiting and supporting spatial memory" (Scarr, Cockburn, and Gutwin, 2012).

Empirical research has found that spatial information is encoded simultaneously along with semantic content in different neural pathways even though the spatial information may be semantically neutral or insignificant. There is a "special relationship between spatial information and memory"

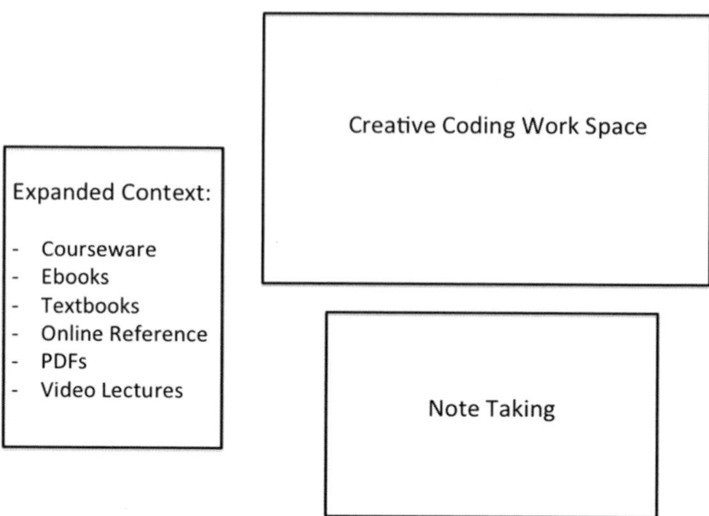

FIGURE 7.8. A distributed design scene for online code learning

(Richardson and Spivy, p. 270). "The vast majority of behavioral acts are saccadic jumps of the eye, unaccompanied by any other behaviours" (citing Bridgeman, Ibid.). "Recent research is demonstrating interesting dissociations between memory effects participants explicitly report and the implicit memory that their eye movements reveal" (p. 271). "There is strong evidence that spatial information can be learned implicitly . . . [Researchers] support 'position-special' theories of visual processing . . . arguing that an analysis of conditional probabilities in some tasks reveals that there is no object identity information without position information" (p. 287). "First, object location is encoded with a high degree of automaticity, whereas memory for word location is susceptible to task demands and, perhaps, encoded by a separate process. Second, there is some evidence that memory for item information seems to be coded fairly independently of location information" (p. 287).

> There is a large body of behavioral and neurophysiological evidence that converges on a view of the primate visual system as comprised of two subsystems or information streams... The current picture... is of a "how" and a "what" system. The "how" pathway is based on the dorsal visual pathway and is a pragmatic, action-based system controlling sensorimotor output in an egocentric reference frame . . . In contrast, the "what system in the ventral pathway utilizes an allocentric framework . . . and is concerned with recognition, categorization and other cognitive functions." (p. 289)

These citations relate to the so-called "Hollywood Squares" phenomena in which cognitive experiments have uncovered separate systems for processing semantic information and spatial position, both of which are encoded simultaneously but in different ways, even when spatial information is not semantically important. Attention to the spatial distribution of the local "egocentric" learning environment discloses the importance of the positional "how system" whereas in our pedagogy, courseware, and learning spaces we might typically focus only on the semantic "what system." This empirical research provides a descriptive base for identifying key neurological capacities that can then be utilized as general cognitive resources in the design of online code learning environments, which also entails the aforementioned shift from the descriptive to the prescriptive.

HCI is an appropriate domain to seek the prescriptive propositions that can build upon descriptive empirical understandings of our cognitive capacities in the development of new interactive systems:

> In human–computer interfaces, knowledge of the spatial location of controls can enable a user to interact fluidly and efficiently, without needing to perform slow visual search. Computer interfaces should therefore be designed to provide support for developing the user's spatial memory, and they should allow the user to exploit it for rapid interaction whenever possible. However, existing systems offer varying support for spatial memory. Many break the user's ability to remember spatial locations, by moving or re-arranging items; others leave spatial memory underutilised, requiring slow sequences of mechanical actions to select items rather than exploiting users' strong ability to index items and controls by their on-screen locations. (Scarr, Cockburn, and Gutwin, 2012, p. iii)

Scarr, Cockburn, and Gutwin develop a framework for exploiting spatial memory in interfaces, arguing that "spatial arrangements support quick revisitation" (p. 42) which are manifested in a series of general design principles such as the "principle of simultaneous presentation" (p. 38) to aid HCI designers to more effectively utilize our cognitive resources to make use of spatial frames. Other HCI spatial principles of relevance to online code learning environments are (pp. 63–4):

- Use categorizations and orderings to help novice users quickly find items.
- When multiple groups of items are displayed simultaneously, provide salient labels for groupings to encourage hierarchical search.
- Users develop an accurate memory for the locations of frequently accessed interface items.

- In training systems, forcing users to intentionally memorize item locations can increase long-term retention.
- Providing a spatial overview of an information space can improve users' ability to navigate to known locations, as well as reduce visual search.
- Allowing users to customize the interface to their personal needs can increase satisfaction.
- Adaptive systems that frequently change item locations prevent users from developing a spatial knowledge of controls. Avoid this whenever possible.
- Interfaces can avoid disrupting spatial memory by keeping existing items spatially consistent relative to a salient frame of reference, such as the window border.
- When examining spatial memory in visual interfaces, use visually homogeneous targets to avoid confounds caused by visual pop-out effects.
- HCI researchers should be cautious when generalizing results of spatial memory experiments to all user populations.

"Spatial knowledge of controls and data enables rapid interaction and information retrieval, and allows users to focus more of their cognitive resources on the task at hand, rather than on the interface" (p. 62). Instead of presuming a single frame that needs to be crammed with video lectures, online reference material, downloadable code, note taking, code editor, and compiler, not to mention the distraction windows of email, chats, Facebook, and YouTube, all navigated via multiple tabs, windows, pop-ups, or expandable screens, the designers of both online learning platforms and the computer labs where they are engaged can benefit from a different conception by considering the locally distributed spatialized set of distinct tasks and information types, namely (a) workspace, (b) note taking, and (c) expanded context, the three emergent spatial distribution categories of this autoethnographic study.

The screen or frame for what I am calling the expanded context can play a critical role in supporting exploration of the "infinite possibilities" of creative coding, as a support of the imagination, or as the space for encyclo-pedic lookup of code references. This frame for the expansion of the overall context can assume in its design a nearby frame for coding, and also a frame for note taking, as its overall distributed cognitive scene. Expanded context here can run the gamut from examples of art to inspire creativity, to deeper dives into the uses of code functions, to historical antecedents and links to other disciplines. Also in practice, additional tabs in the note-taking window support further distributions of the expanded context, depending on the complexity of the material being engaged.

DESIGN PARAMETERS

As we have seen, there is much for the creative practitioner to engage with as a general design scene when it comes to their students' self-learning of creative coding skills. Whether the creators of these code learning environments are MOOC-employed instructional designers informed by educational psychology, or self-professed experts "winging it" in a more amateur style, together they produce a variegated set of responses to the general problem, possibility, and constraint spaces of online code learning. The goal of this chapter is to present creative educator–practitioners with a well-modeled explication of the variations in practices, platforms, and design principles that will allow them to engage imaginatively and perhaps more rigorously with the pedagogies for this kind of learning, and perhaps become better content designers, for instance in their own courseware. Below I offer some general headings to aid in the design considerations of the three-screen scene:

1. *Code and Window*: Is the code and the instruction and/or explanation presented in the same integrated browser window, or is the interactor is asked to open up multiple windows, on perhaps multiple screens (e.g., instructional window, text editor, and compiler)? A distributed cognition perspective would suggest not cramming all learning tasks and information into a single-constrained spatial frame but rather to take advantage of the cognitive resources which add the automaticity of spatial processing as its own cognitive resource.

2. *Practice and Narrational Context*: Some environments offer whole paragraphs of verbal contextualization, while others offer brief snippet-like instructions and/or step-by-step piecemeal increments in the construction of larger blocks of code. Strategies may range from storytelling, extensive background histories, clever or imagistic analogies and parallels drawn, vs. more bare sets of instructions of the sort "do this, now do that."

3. *Audiovisual Complementarity*: The use of time-based media is yet another layer of affordances with its own set of action possibilities that is distinct from but of course related to textuality and codicity. Screen-captured text is typically blurry, and the more legible print is in video, indeed the less like video it is and the more like a Powerpoint it becomes. There are differences in learning styles that can be attended to, by offering readers text-based explanations on a

screen vs. listening to someone's verbal account of similar content; or reading an instructor's handwriting via use of electronic pens on a screen in a manner redolent of classroom white boards.

4. *Building and Opening*: Some environments bid the interactor to construct along with the tutorial, writing code simultaneous to the act of apprehending new concepts. Other approaches ask the interactor to open files of a preexisting, already-organized worked examples alongside of which an explanatory text fills out the context and provides guidance as to how to approach and understand the example.

5. *Gatekeeping and Browsing*: An environment can be designed so as to not let an interactor progress unless a specific task or set of tasks is accomplished successfully, according to the built-in algorithm that checks the coder's performance of the assignment. At the other end of the spectrum, tutorials can be offered in more of a freely browsable manner, to be perused at will and in any sequence by the interactor, without any features that check or inhibit the progressions through modularized content.

6. *Social In/Formality*: Some sites perform elaborate playfulness or casual conversational tangents, making intertextual references to pop culture for example or employing personal anecdotes, while others are more matter-of-fact and to-the-point in voice, perhaps assuming an older or professionally oriented audience. Indeed, the question of the audience is an interesting problematic because by default most of these platforms are aimed at anyone who can read and has an interest in coding. This suggests that one line of further development for these sites is better articulation of the presumed users' level of expertise with respect to audience address.

7. *Experimenting with the Expanded Context*: Offloading the cognitive and practical burden of the expanded context into its own spatial frame, e.g., through interactive e-books, can free up the possibilities of courseware to range more freely between historical precedents in art and design, to encyclopedic code references, to lectures written or video-recorded. By not having to "cram" everything into a presumed single or second monitor, a spatially distributed praxeo-cognitive approach allows for the formation of specific, and new, design strategies in the development of curricula and courseware. For example, historical precedents tend to be under-referenced in code learning, and a wider field of content creation devoted to the expanded context can lend itself to addressing other pedagogical considerations.

The above suggested parameters, and the preceding categorizations of designed interactions, are clearly not the only possible description of the possibility space of online code learning environments. It would be another project to refine this initial set of categories and parameters into a formal typology, in the format of a table or hierarchical scheme, for instance. Also these parameters can be combined with the e-learning principles previously mentioned to more fully map and link pedagogical to stylistic, systems, and content considerations. What should be clear is that the technological capacities of the Internet offer clearly delineable action possibilities but do not strictly determine the format, style, audience, or pedagogical approaches of these websites. Both the agency of the designers and the enabling constraints of the medium are at work and in play. The motivations of the designers are usually clearly inferable; in essence, the goal for most these providers is to "scale up," gain as much web presence and as many users as possible. However a provider like Zed Shaw appears to express a desire to be a kind of popular "code guru," but often comes across more like what one might call a "code show-off," and adds a bit of "shameless self-promoter" to his persona through the manner that he mixes personal rant and biographical backstory with his mission to bring programming to the world, and the world to his books sold on Amazon.

What this study adds to the overall design space for self-learning coding skills, and which can be of particular interest to creative practitioner–educators, is the articulation of the distributed cognitive space for self-learning code and the possibilities for a comprehensive teaching and learning approach in which skills can be more fully contextualized while also encouraging the development of stronger self-learning skills. The three-screen scene, if implemented as institutional infrastructure, suggests that perhaps computer labs should just have monitors, and students can bring their own laptops or laptops checked out from an equipment repository, and that side supports for an additional frame (book, tablet, cell phone, outlet) can be provided in a less resource-intensive lab design. It also suggests that curricular content can be dedicated to other media, such as PDFs or e-books, to be used alongside the scene of working, self-learning, and experimentation, rather than overloading a single frame via a learning management system or online video tutorial database. A better grasp of the spatially distributed learning context provides new understandings of the possibilities and constraints of creatively employing online coding platforms with an eye toward better outcomes.

CODA

This happens to be an interesting economic moment in Canada, when the decline of the Canadian dollar due to falling global oil prices has politicians rethinking economic strategy away from overreliance on natural resources. New focus on the tech sector and innovation strategies has led to direct new investment in British Columbia for certain post-secondary education (PSE) institutions to encourage the development of coding skills in more learners. With this new external and targeted funding, the School of Interactive Arts and Technology has developed an online self-paced program which explicitly incorporates the frame of the expanded context as part of the overall teaching strategy, curating open source content so as to encourage self-learning and creative exploration (www.futuresavvy.xyz). I am also applying the three-screen scene in a new social enterprise I have founded, 4th Foundation (www.4th.foundation), which develops curricula for coding and technology skills in K-12 education as governments roll out new standards around computation. As well, I invite comment and also collaboration from others interested in exploring a distributed scene of learning cognition for creative coding skills.

REFERENCES

Almquist, J. and Lupton, J. (2010). Affording Meaning: Design-Oriented Research from the Humanities and Social Sciences. *Design Issues* 26(1), 3–14.

Blumer, H. (1954). What is Wrong with Social Theory? *American Sociological Review* 18, 3–10.

Bowen, G.A. (2006). Grounded Theory and Sensitizing Concepts. *International Journal of Qualitative Methods* 5(3), 1–9.

Buell, C. (2013, July 5). Fighting Distraction in Online Courses. Retrieved from http://edcetera.rafter.com/fighting-distraction-in-online-courses/. Accessed online March 15, 2016.

Carroll, G. (2012, March 13). MidTerms 2012: Taking Class Notes: Which is Better – Typing or Handwriting? *Houston Chronicle*. Retrieved from http://blog.chron.com/torturedbyteenagers/2012/03/midterms-2012-taking-class-notes-which-is-better-typing-or-handwriting/. Accessed online March 15, 2016.

Clark, R. (2002). Six Principles of Effective e-Learning: What Works and Why. *Learning Solutions Magazine*. Retrieved from www.learningsolutionsmag.com/articles/384/six-principles-of-effective-e-learning-what-works-and-why/page2. Accessed online March 15, 2016.

Codecademy Forum (n.d.). Message Posted to www.codecademy.com/forum_questions/51ce64f47c82caca49023fa5. Accessed online March 15, 2016.

E-Learning Theory (Mayer, Sweller, Moreno). (2016, April 10). Retrieved from www.learning-theories.com/e-learning-theory-mayer-sweller-moreno.html. Accessed online March 15, 2016.

Fields, R.E., Wright, P.C., Marti, P., and Palmonari, M. (1998). Air Traffic Control as a Distributed Cognition System: A Study of External Representations. *Proceedings of ECCE-9, the 9th European Conference on Cognitive Ergonomics.* Roquencourt: France, European Association of Cognitive Ergonomics. Retrieved from: http://citeseerx.ist.psu.edu/viewdoc/download?doi=10.1.1.26.7987&rep=rep1&type=pdf. Accessed online March 15, 2016.

Geertz, C. (1983). *Local Knowledge: Further Essays in Interpretive Anthropology*, New York: Basic Books.

Gibson, J.J. (1966). *Senses Considered as Perceptual Systems*, Boston, MA: Houghton Mifflin Co.

Github, 2013 (March 18). Retrieved from: https://github.com/gulnara/markov/blob/master/zedshaw.txt. Accessed online March 15, 2016.

Gladwell, M. (2002, March 25). The Social Life of Paper. *The New Yorker.* Retrieved from: www.newyorker.com/magazine/2002/03/25/the-social-life-of-paper. Accessed online March 15, 2016.

Haythornthwaite, C. and Andrews, R. (2011). *E-learning Theory and Practice.* London: Sage.

Hutchby, I. (2001). Technologies, Texts and Affordances. *Sociology* 35(2), 441–6. DOI: 10.1177/S0038038501000219.

Hutchins, E. (1995). *Cognition in the Wild.* Cambridge, MA: MIT Press, Bradford Books.

Hutchins, E. and Klausen, T. (1996). Distributed Cognition in an Airline Cockpit. In Engeström, Y. and Middleton, D. (Eds.), *Cognition and Communication at Work.* New York: Cambridge University Press, pp. 15–34. Retrieved from http://hci.ucsd.edu/102a/readings/cockpit-cog.pdf. Accessed online March 15, 2016.

Introducing Signature Track. (2013, January 9). Coursera [blog]. Retrieved from http://blog.coursera.org/post/40080531667/signaturetrack. Accessed online March 15, 2016.

Mayer, R.E. and Sims, V.K. (1994). For whom is a picture worth a thousand words? Extensions of a dual-coding theory of multimedia learning. *Journal of Educational Psychology* 86, 389–401.

Mayer, R.E., Fennell, S., Farmer, L., and Campbell, J. (2004). A personalization effect in multimedia learning: students learn better when words are in conversational style rather than formal style. *Journal of Educational Psychology* 96(2), 389–95.

Norman, D. (1998). *The Psychology of Everyday Things.* New York: Basic Books.

Overview of Distributed Cognition (n.d.). Lecture Notes from University of California San Diego HCI Lab. Retrieved from http://hci.ucsd.edu/102a/11Lectures/DCogOverview.pdf. Accessed online March 15, 2016.

Richardson, D.C. and Spivey, M.J. (2000). Representation, Space and Hollywood Squares: Looking at Things That Aren't There Anymore. *Cognition* 76(3), 269–95.

Salomon, G. (1997). *Distributed Cognitions: Psychological and Educational Considerations.* New York: Cambridge University Press.

Scarr, J., Cockburn, A., and Gutwin, C. (2012). Supporting and Exploiting Spatial Memory in User Interfaces. *Foundations and Trends in Human–Computer Interaction* 6(1), 1–84.

Shaw, Zed. (n.d.). Advice from an Old Programmer. *Learn Python the Hard Way* [Website]. Retrieved from http://learnpythonthehardway.org/book/advice. html. Accessed online March 15, 2016.

The Benefits of a Conversational Style in E-Learning. Leo Corporate Training (2015).Retrievedfromhttp://leolearning.com/2015/04/benefits-conversational-style-e-learning/. Accessed online March 15, 2016.

The First Critique of Writing (n.d.). English Dept University of Illinois Web, Plato 275a, Retrieved from www.english.illinois.edu/-people-/faculty/debaron/482/ 482readings/phaedrus.html. Accessed online March 15, 2016.

8

Between Code and Culture: Developing a Creative Coding Massive Open Online Course

MARK GUGLIELMETTI AND JON MCCORMACK

Abstract: Since the rapid rise of the massive open online course (MOOC) in 2011, online learning has increased sharply. Various platforms such as Coursera, FutureLearn, and Udacity enable academics to develop and manage single courses that often enroll vast numbers of learners. These platforms provide a unique range of instruments for an academic to embed discipline knowledge and skills development into the course. In this chapter, the authors examine the MOOC they created for the FutureLearn platform called *Creative Coding*. They explore the historical contingencies through which *algorithmic thinking* and coding literacies are being ubiquified across various cultural spheres of activity and also the "technical and cultural prism" through which these literacies are filtered. These contingencies and literacies provided a framework for the production of the *Creative Coding* MOOC, which is discussed in the latter half of this chapter.

Keywords: MOOC, generative art, Creative Coding, history of art, programming, creativity, cultural studies, online learning

> Virtual representations derive all their powers from numerical manipulation. Timothy Binkley greatly clarifies matters when he reminds us that numbers, and the kinds of symbolization they allow, are the first "virtual reality"
>
> (Binkley, 1993, p. 93, as quoted in Rodowick, 2007, p. 9)

INTRODUCTION

The story of numbers is a human one as much as it is a technological one. Numbers have been and are a central feature in the formation of the human endeavor since the Upper Paleolithic. Early in human prehistory, homo sapiens probably developed the capacity to distinguish cardinal numbers

that denote quantity and ordinal numbers that denote ordered sequences
(Chrisomalis, 2010). More complex artifacts, known as numerical notation
and numeral systems, were invented significantly later, approximately
5,500 years ago, first in Mesopotamia 3500 BC and then in Egypt ca. 3250 BC
(Chrisomalis, 2010). Mathematical texts such as the Reisner Papyri, Moscow
Mathematical Papyrus, and Kahun Papyri date from the nineteenth-century
BC (Chrisomalis, 2010; Gillings, 2008).

Since the formation of the numerical systems in the Fertile Crescent,
hundreds of paleographic variants and over 100 different numerical systems
have been developed. In most cases variants and systems were "borrowed
wholesale" (Chrisomalis, 2010, p. 23) from preexisting structures, however,
in a small number of cases – as evidenced in Mesopotamia and Egypt but
also extended to East Asia, Mesoamerica, the Andes, and the Indus Valley –
they developed independently from any external cultural influence. The
formation of these unique technical systems reflects the cultural characteristics in which they were developed; Shang numerals in China were
first used for divinatory purposes while Mesoamerican notation systems
were developed for astronomical and calendric purposes. The formation
of numerical notations and numeral systems within these cultures is vis-à-
vis a complex mesh of sociocultural and historical contingencies through
which these technical artifacts were transformed, transmitted, and eventually declined.

In contemporary society, an array of technical systems also reflects and
refracts the cultural characteristics of our time.[1] Various technical conventions that employ numbers numerically or purely symbolically, such as
their symbolic use in programming, feature significantly in many aspects of
life not least in the sciences, and of specific interest to the authors, computer
science, and computer programming. Numbers, and the symbolic application of them through various processes, routines, and conventions, are
commonly written by a programmer (in a human-readable format) into a
series of instructions – the source code – that when compiled is transformed
into numerical machine code typically expressed as numbers in the binary
system as 0 and 1.[2] When executed, the software directs the computer to

---

[1] These cultural characteristics include features such as a modern, universal numerical
    system and the unification of logic (George Boole) with the theory of sets (Georg Cantor).
    This "unity of abstraction in modern mathematics" (Ifrah, 1998, p. 598) laid the founda-
    tion of computer science.
[2] The term "numbers" here is understood as having a vastly different meaning to its use
    in other historical contexts. For example, adepts in the Shang Dynasty used numbers

perform specific abstract operations which in turn generates further processes, inputs, and outputs. Numbers, and the abstraction of them through various processes, are instrumental in our digitally mediated world.

The point we make is that numbers and numerical systems are tightly bound to the sociocultural and sociopolitical milieu in which they are shaped. They are central to the formation of all civilizations, channeled, as it were, according to the social and political vagaries of the day. Restated, numbers and numerical systems are modeled through social, political, economic, and technical regimes; they are potently activated at the discretion of the sociocultural–sociopolitical forces that regulate them.

It is through an understanding of the rich relationship we have with numbers and their applied abstractions – the human–technical prism – that our massive open online course (MOOC) called *Creative Coding* was conceived. The authors set out to design a course that explored alternatives to what might be considered the traditional status quo in pedagogical design, that is to organize "technical systems" and "culture" into discrete pedagogies, which tends to be a standard practice in online courses on programming for creative expression. We believe that through alternatives to this traditional pedagogical structure that many creative programming courses tend to adopt, learners might more fully appreciate the *creative act of coding* and not just the technical process of coding in itself. With this in mind, we designed a course for learners to explore the creative and historical contexts of the processes and systems they would use during their course of study in *Creative Coding*. We make connections in what appears at first to be unrelated themes such as Islamic non-figurative art, the so-called "Dictum of Descartes," creativity in Renaissance Florence, and machine learning. The decision to map creative coding into a complex cultural context was received enthusiastically by the course participants (learners) and, as discussed later, contributed to the success of the course.

BACKGROUND

In contemporary life numbers resonate in nearly every activity we participate in, none more so than those that directly facilitate our digitally mediated selves. Comparable to the aforementioned civilizations, numbers – and the transformation of them through specific application such as computer

---

and writing to communicate "with the world of gods" (Gernet, 1963, quoted in Ifrah, 1998, p. 270) while programmers work with symbols to program a symbolic processing machine; numbers are a set of these symbols.

programming – interconnect with social, economic, and political domains. The propensity to strategically employ numbers and numerical systems sociopolitically is clearly evident in many levels of institutional policy making. The strategy to exploit the economic benefits a programming-literate population may advance is most evident in changes to the national school curriculum in England in 2014 in which "computing" has been added to the compulsory list of subjects pupils must study. The subject commences when pupils enter primary (elementary) school in Year 1, at the age of 5. They are taught how to create and debug programs, understand what algorithms are, and use technology creatively (Department for Education UK Government, 2013a). The learning intensifies in Year 2 when teachers are "guided" to instruct pupils, aged 6, to code "robots using instructions given in right angles" (Department for Education UK Government, 2013b, p. 99). This transformation in the curriculum heralds a new social future in which the overarching policy reform will likely enable deep transformations in all facets of the socioeconomic landscape including law, medicine, arts, design, architecture, science, manufacturing, etc.

Adopting the major policy reform in the national curriculum in England is recognition that programming is now an integral part of mainstream society much like literacy and numeracy are identified as essential features of an educated populous. This reform simply reflects the world we live in. For example in 2012, the Tiger Leap Foundation in Estonia implemented a program to teach programming to primary school pupils (Mansel, 2013) while the nonprofit organization code.org was launched in 2013 in the United States to expand access to computer science to "every student in every school" (Code.org, n.d.). In the authors' own country, politicians are also stridently arguing for policy reform to ensure programming is taught in primary school education (Sterling, 2015). Coding, it appears, is "the new black" in various strata of government and nongovernment administration.

Coinciding with trends to integrate coding into a K-12 framework is the rapid rise of the MOOC into the public educational domain (Ng and Widom, 2014). The amplification of public awareness and engagement in MOOCs is, in part, credited to the huge numbers of student enrolments into three Stanford University MOOCs on programming in late 2011. The first course *Introduction into Artificial Intelligence*, launched by Computer Science Professor Sebastian Thrun and Director of Research at Google Peter Norvig, attracted 160,000 learners with approximately 25,000 students receiving a certificate of completion (DeMillo, 2015). *Introduction into Artificial Intelligence* was followed by the launch of two more MOOCs, *Machine Learning* by Andrew Ng and *Databases* by Jennifer Widom, with both subjects attracting approximately 100,000 enrollments with 13,000 and 7,000 completions, respectively (Ng and Widom, 2014). The scalability of these MOOCs, that is the sheer numbers that are able to enroll into subjects, inspired key researchers to explore the potential of this platform as a serious alternative to classroom and lecture theatre teaching. In late 2012 Udacity, founded by Thrun, had over 750,000 student enrollments (Heussner, 2012) while Coursera, launched by Koller and Ng, had over 1.7 million students enrollments (Pappano, 2012). At the time of writing (2016), Coursera now has over 18 million registered learners. The intersection between large-scale online learning courses and subjects such as programming transformed the cultural imagination for MOOCs with *The New York Times* declaring 2012 to be "The Year of the MOOC" (Pappano, 2012).

As educators, our challenge – within this disruptive setting of MOOC ascendency and a renewed need for coding literacy at all educational levels – was to create a creative programming course with wide appeal and practical relevance. As authors such as Daniel Pink (2005) have argued, Western nations are in the midst of a new "conceptual age," succeeding the previous "information age" that began with the arrival of digital computers into business and industry in the twentieth century. In the conceptual age, traditional manufacturing and professional jobs, such as accounting, law, and software engineering, are more cost-effectively filled by workers in developing nations where labor costs are less expensive. Some analysts also predict that many of these jobs will largely be automated in the coming decades. Hence the challenge is how to innovate and maintain a viable workforce in a global context. This so-called "conceptual economy" relies on design, empathy, creativity, innovation, and divergent thinking, operating in a globally connected and competitive economic environment. A transdisciplinary creative coding course fits well into this current situation.

CREATIVE CODING MOOC

Our *Creative Coding* MOOC was conceived in 2013 with the belief that coding literacy should be as ubiquitous as other basic literacy skills such as reading, writing, and basic mathematics. Similar to the creative endeavors these literacy skills afford – poetics, intellectual enquiry, and entertainment – coding too is a creative discipline based in practice, one that stimulates our affective, intellectual engagement in the world.

While we come from a university teaching perspective, for this course our aim was to have a broad appeal, being suitable for people from all walks of life without any previous coding experience or IT background. We imagined our audience as having, at a minimum, at least some interest in a creative practice, but this was by no means a fundamental requirement. We wanted to design a course that was accessible, yet intellectually stimulating and challenging, one that confronted the status quo for teaching creative programming at the time.

Our course launched in July 2014 and was designed to run for 6 weeks with approximately 3 hours of study per week to complete. We later came to realize that this was a serious underestimation of the time needed, despite testing on several Ph.D. student volunteers.[3] We will return to this issue in the section "MOOCs as a Learning Platform" of this chapter.

The *Creative Coding* MOOC was delivered through the FutureLearn platform, a UK-based company wholly owned by the Open University. FutureLearn's university partners are primarily based in the United Kingdom, with our university (Monash University, based in Australia) being one of the first international university partners for the platform. Apart from providing a British presence among the largely US-dominated MOOC providers, strategically FutureLearn aimed to differentiate themselves in a number of ways. These included delivery platform independence (working from launch on smartphones, tablets, and desktops); an emphasis on consistent, homogeneous design and user experience across all courses; usability compliance; quality control and verification; and integration of social engagement directly into course materials. Other MOOC providers have subsequently adopted many of these features. Another important point of differentiation at the time of launch was FutureLearn's partnerships with non-university institutions, including the British Museum, British Council, British Library, and the National Film and Television School.

Our MOOC also provided an opportunity to guide learners through a process to understand algorithmic thinking as a methodological approach to conceptualizing the world. Algorithmic thinking forms a basis for understanding phenomena that occur in the world through the lens of formal logic and process specification. Developing a formal specification of a process is the first step in implementing it on a computer – the basis of all coding.

As with any complex and creative human activity, learning to code well takes many years of practice and patient study,[4] so as a 6-week course we had to tailor expectations accordingly. Most topics were introduced with custom sample code that learners had to modify rather than starting from scratch.

A good example of introducing concepts of creative algorithmic thinking is in what we called the "spinning top" example. Here, learners are

---

[3] Obviously Ph.D. students are not representative of the general MOOC learner.

[4] As with any human skill, typically around 10 years or 10,000 hours are required to obtain virtuosity (Ericsson, Krampe, and Tesch-romer, 1993; Gardner, 1993; Gladwell, 2008).

shown a spinning top moving over a sheet of paper and asked to conceptualize the movement of the top as an abstract pattern. Rather than focus on an accurate simulation of the physics (which would be too challenging for beginners), the idea was to express the concept of motion in terms of basic sinusoidal and noise-based patterns – something learners were already familiar with from previous exercises – and sample code was provided to articulate this process explicitly.

Rather than focusing on exact mimicry or simulation accuracy, learners were then asked to extend the basic code to make the virtual spinning top behave in ways that the physical top could not. This specification asks learners to think of the spinning top beyond its purely physical behavior into the realm of the imagination. But this new liberation is tempered by two things: (i) the reference to the original idea of the top moving in space and (ii) any ideas must be expressed (eventually) algorithmically in code.

This simple exercise provided learners with a pathway to explore coding creatively. The steps can be summarized as

1. start with a physical phenomena of interest;
2. conceptualize and abstract;
3. implement as code;
4. reinterpret the phenomena without the limitations of conventional physics (in the broadest possible sense), encouraging imagination and play;
5. modify the code to suit this new interpretation.

Good creative coding is also a matter of critical reflection and refinement, and we encouraged learners to critically reflect on their own code and that of others, with the aim of modifying and improving their efforts iteratively. Being a useful process, any serious refinement requires a significant time investment, which for many learners spun out well beyond the recommended 3 hours/week workload that the course initially advertised. A reappraisal of the time commitment in the second running of the course allowed for 6 hours/week rather than the original 3 hours/week. While still inadequate for some, it represented a more realistic time commitment necessary to gain sufficient understanding of the course material.

TECHNICAL AND CULTURAL PRISM

The core development team for the *Creative Coding* MOOC included the two authors and Dr. Indae Hwang, who assisted with code development, production, and graphic design for the course. While the core team was small in terms of a production unit, our collective backgrounds represent a diverse array of pedagogical traditions including filmmaking, humanities and media studies, computer science, graphic design, the visual arts, UX design, and new media art. This array of theoretical, practical, and creative orientations enabled the team to conceive of an approach to teach programming vis-à-vis mixing the unique discursive forces and grammars from these disparate domains into a single course. The decision to create this course was, in many respects, to diverge from a normative account of programming for creative practice often delivered through other MOOC courses on creative coding. These courses tended to teach the techniques of programming, including the skills required to create an output such as music, images, video, etc., without the context through which these artifacts are created. In other words, MOOCs that adopted this style of presentation tended to *train* a learner how "to do" but not to contextualize the learner's creative expression or provide historical references from which the practices arise. Another topic that we felt underrepresented was an exploration of the philosophical implications that algorithmic models give rise to as they filter through a vast range of discursive orientations, such as modeling "creativity" in machine learning systems (Saunders, 2002) or "evolution" in Artificial Life software (Langton, 1995).[5]

Making connections between programming and creative expression, technology and culture enabled us to weave disparate epistemologies into the course. The epistemological crossover is evident in the first week of the course notably when concluding the discussion on "Generative art and artists":

> Generative art in all its forms raises interesting questions about art and creativity. In Sol LeWitt's drawings for example, who is the artist? Is it LeWitt himself, who devised the instructions for making the drawings but did not create them, or is it the person interpreting his instructions to actually draw the drawing? When a computer is interpreting the artist's instructions we might be less inclined to think of it as contributing any creativity to the artwork. But as computers become more sophisticated this view might change, particularly as artists start to use techniques from artificial intelligence research in their works.

---

[5] In our approach to developing an overarching interdisciplinary framework, we embrace what Ronald Barnett (2011, pp. 63–4) describes as "supercomplexity"; "Crudely, we may say that complexity refers to an open-endedness and unpredictability in the way in which systems (whether manmade or natural systems) behave. Supercomplexity, on the other hand, refers to an open-endedness and unpredictability in concepts and ideas . . . in supercomplexity, the very terms in which complex systems are to be understood are liable to be disputed." For Barnett, and indeed for the authors, "[s]upercomplexity is characteristic of interdisciplinary work, for *there* is to be found multiple, rival and incommensurable framings of the world" (Barnett, 2011, p. 64).

To creative practitioners who already code these observations may be recognizable, perhaps superficial; however, to the novice creative coder or to the experienced programmer interested in coding creatively, the observation generated significant discussion in the comments section of the MOOC with 838 learners remarking on these conclusions on generative art.[6]

There are many exemplars, found in culture and nature, that help to explain coding while simultaneously providing the creative, intellectual, and philosophical stimulation necessary for the learner to have a rewarding experience *and* to produce unorthodox acoustic, visual, or tactile output. We draw heavily on a wide array of examples, some of which are listed below, to provide a framework to motivate the learner by making connections between the technical aspects of coding with culture.

Frequently, the examples apprehend a highly conceptual and artistic application for a specific concept, such as the concept of feedback. Feedback is an important feature in Avlin Lucier's *I am sitting in a room* (1969). In this work, a recording of Lucier's spoken voice is played back into a room and the resulting sound is re-recorded, emphasizing the acoustic properties of the room itself and the magnetic tape used for recording. The new recording is then played back and re-recorded in the same room, the process repeating 32 times until only the vaguest fragment of the original voice remains and the musical characteristics of the room dominate. Each iteration of this feedback loop is presented sequentially in the final work. Lucier's music performance example serves as a catalyst for introducing other uses of feedback in a creative project, culminating in the algorithmic concepts of feedback apparent in recursive Fibonacci functions and fractal graphics.

Other examples are didactic, serving to demonstrate a specific concept or approach to coding and the relationship between the method and the creative context in which the method may be applied. This form of instruction was introduced in the first learning "module" of the course, in a video called *What is Creative Coding?* to give the novice coder basic insight into the foundation principles of generative art. In the video, we begin by describing how processes used by programmers and coders have

---

[6] We refer to the 2015 iteration of the online course. There are two short videos that comprise the discussion on generative art that are watched sequentially, *What is Creative Coding?*, which provides historical context of generative art and *Generative Art and Artists* in which we discuss practitioners who use the technique in their practice. The number of comments given is the aggregate number of responses for both videos.

been utilized to create works of art for at least 1,300 years, as generative processes are as well refined in Islamic art and architecture[7] as they are in creating a generative design or artwork using computer-coding techniques (Alexander, 1993). We then go on to explain the basic processes used to create a generative artwork:

> The underlying principle in generative art is to create a process that generates an artwork from the process. A process might be a set of rules or series of instructions that are carried out by others or by a machine. Each rule or instruction may be written in everyday language and is usually straightforward and unambiguous to understand.
>
> The process to design a very basic Islamic pattern could be created with a number of rules: Step 1. Draw a circle 50 mm in diameter. Step 2. Draw a square around the circle. Step 3. Draw a circle half the size of the original circle around the bottom corner of the square. Step 4. Repeat steps 1–3 to the immediate right of their original position. Step 5. Repeat step 4 six times. Step 6. Repeat steps 1–3 immediately below their original position. Step 7. Repeat steps 4–5. And Step 8. Repeat steps 6–7 six times. Now three more rules will animate the generative pattern.
>
> So the first rule would be: Step 9. Increase the size of each circle and square by a given number until they are 4 times larger than they were originally. Step 10. Decrease the size of each circle and square by the same given number. Step 11. Loop steps 9 to 10. And the final step might be: add color. These instructions won't create a work of art nor is the process indicative of the historical context in which Islamic patterns were designed but it does outline the basic principles of generative art; simple local rules can create unexpected complex patterns.

This example serves four main purposes for the learner. First, it demonstrates the basic principle of generative art. Secondly, it provides the learner with a conceptual model of programming and how simple rules generate a complexity. Thirdly, it introduces the learner to a simple form of "pseudocode," the text-based description and organization of the code for implementation. Finally, it provides the learner with a creative context, in this case Islamic pattern making, so that they can contextualize the technique in question (see Figures 8.1 and 8.2).

---

[7] As is evidenced in the *Dome of the Rock* in Jerusalem completed in 691 CE (Ettinghausen, Grabar, and Jenkins-Madina, 2001).

FIGURE 8.1.   Image applying rule no. 8

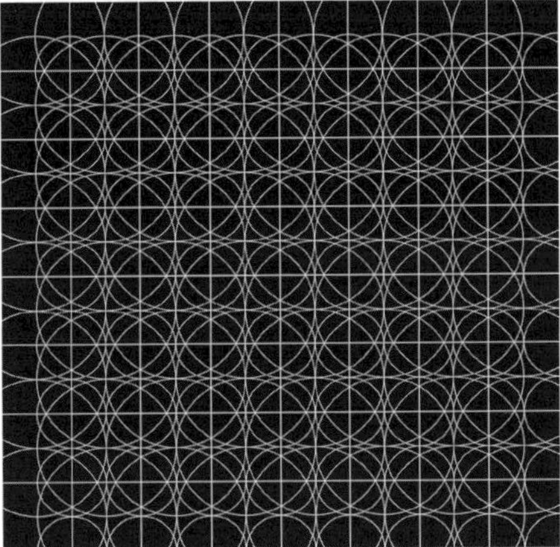

FIGURE 8.2.   Animating the image by applying rule no. 11

Social Learning

FutureLearn encourages comments from learners by building them into every step of the courseware, so they appear on each page.[8] This helps to keep the comments focused on a specific learning topic. The success in

---

[8] A lesson "step" is the smallest atomic unit within the FutureLearn system. Several steps form a module, and several modules form the course content for a week. The week is the highest division of course modularity, and the pathway through the course is always sequentially linear.

mixing the technical and cultural aspects of coding is reflected in many positive comments associated with our conceptually blended approach. Here is a brief selection of learner comments (anonomized for privacy) from the 2015 course:

> It's interesting to see how two concepts that can look and function differently when apart and together. Both bring a new dimension to the other that might never have been considered before.
>
> I had no idea that a set of rules could produce such beautiful patterns. It reminds me of when I did an art exam at school and used graph paper to ensure that all my designs (based on Arabic patterns, funnily enough) were equal. I can really see the possibility to explore more complex ideas.
>
> In less than 3 minutes we saw an example of how coding can create moving art. The original piece before the animation reminded me of 2D artwork or poster but adding the movement with the decreasing/increasing shape size transformed the art into an experience for the viewer.

The themes explored during the 6-week course included: creative coding, generative art, conceptual models of interaction, interactive media art, modalities of creativity, creativity and computer art, randomness and variation, typography, artificial life. Topics were aligned to the conceptual framework of the theme and to the practical activities learners undertook each week. For instance, in week 4 of the course the characteristics of randomness and variation were examined in relation to how they are expressed in nature and biological systems, and how they feature quite significantly in social activities, such as how randomness was entangled with chance and fate in ancient times or in financial theory where a "random walk" algorithm models fluctuating stock prices. We introduced artists who use randomness and variation in their art-making to provide the creative stimulus: Jean Erp, John Cage, Vera Molnar, Sol LeWitt, Maria Verstappen, and Erwin Driessens, among many others. In the corresponding practical activities, randomness and noise are implemented and explored in creative coding.

The decision to align a practical activity with a cultural theme was judiciously undertaken and we were conscious that it was not always desirable to map a practical exercise to an obvious theme. For example, in week 2 of the course learners were required to reinterpret Vera Molnar's *25 Squares* (1991) in the lesson on "looping and repeating" (see Figures 8.3 and 8.4). The exercise might have also been well suited to the topic "arrays" in the following week or randomness and variation in week 4.

FIGURE 8.3. Molnar (2014) Neroli Wesley

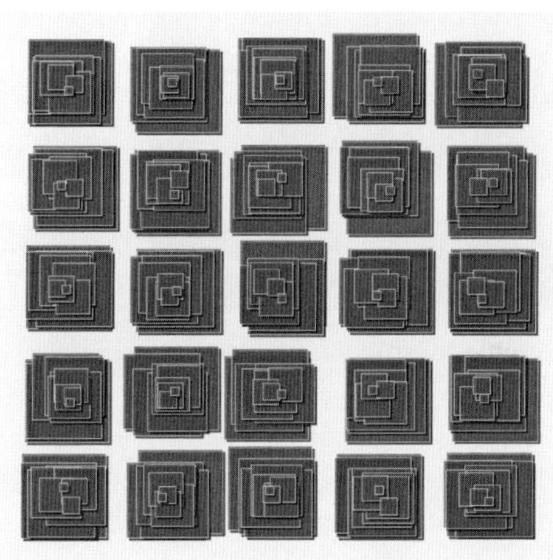

FIGURE 8.4. 25-Molnar Roses (2014) Jordi Pique

We were always mindful that the course needed to be accessible and enjoyable, especially in weeks 1 and 2 when learners new to coding might potentially struggle with algorithmic thinking. A popular activity in week 1 is "draw your name." Students are asked to "draw their name" in any way they like and post the results. They are allowed (and encouraged) to modify and experiment with the code. The beauty of this exercise is that the task is simple enough to be done in minimal time, yet it rewards experimentation

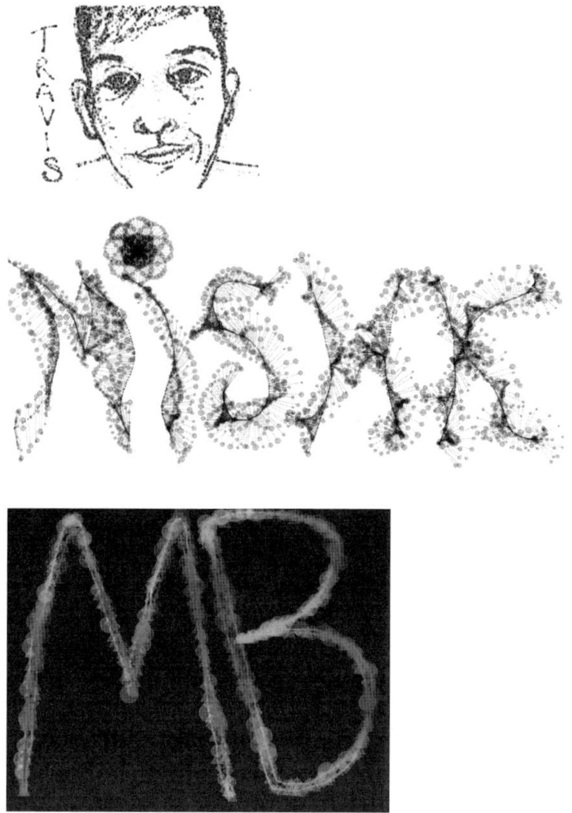

FIGURE 8.5.   Examples of students' works for the exercise "draw your name."

and creativity. There is no "wrong" answer to the activity. The code deliberately uses a modestly interesting drawing mechanism, one that provides just the right amount of interest – so that the drawing piques one's curiosity, but simultaneously encourages the user to experiment with the code to add features (such as color) or modify the way the drawing engine works. Hence the task asks for two kinds of creative thinking: the drawing and the code. Some examples of students' works are shown in Figure 8.5.

EVALUATING MOOCS AS AN EDUCATION PLATFORM

Our course has attracted a large number of learners to sign up (over 36,000 in two runs in 2014/15). This cohort carries a wide diversity across age, culture, geography, and background knowledge. The majority of people engaged in our MOOC, however, came from the United Kingdom – unsurprisingly given FutureLearn's UK base and predominantly UK-based institutional membership.

One interesting group we identified in our cohort was that people often liked to work in pairs, or small groups, often one with an artistic background and the other with a computing or engineering background. Often the groups were "virtual" with each member having a different geographic location. Matching these complementary skill sets seemed to work well for progressing through the course, as did having a partner whose expertise could be drawn from for clarification and encouragement.

Asking people to devote more than 3 hours/week becomes a difficult challenge for many learners. As we discussed in earlier parts of this chapter, having a number of open challenges, combined with the pedagogical approach of iterative critical reflection and improvement, demanded a significant time commitment from our learners. For novices, in particular, it often proved to be difficult to accommodate all the material in any given week, particularly in the middle weeks of the course where the programming demands were highest.

MOOCs as a Learning Platform

The technology for MOOC delivery is still in its infancy. The FutureLearn system offers only a linear pathway through the material and does not allow (for example) alternate pathways based on skills, preferred learning style, cognitive or academic abilities. This limits the ability of a single MOOC to reach a broader audience, because everyone must follow the same pathway regardless of their age, experience, learning style, or background. Moreover, FutureLearn presents only limited opportunities for interactive media content, with short videos and text the dominant paradigm. When developing the course, the FutureLearn authoring system limited each lesson step to have only a single title image or video and then text. It was not possible to include additional images or other media content further down the page, despite there being no technical limitations to do this.[9] A workaround was to host images on an external server and link back to them from the MOOC.

Assessment is another feature that requires further development. FutureLearn allows only simple methods of assessment: quizzes, tests, and peer review.

---

[9] Since developing our MOOC, FutureLearn have addressed this issue.

Quizzes and tests on the platform are essentially the same – multiple-choice questions that are limited to text responses. Tests allow three attempts to get the correct answer, whereas a quiz allows unlimited attempts. While useful for giving learners some basic feedback on their understanding of the course material, they are not well suited to test many creative coding concepts (most obviously you cannot write any code in a multiple-choice question). Other platforms have far superior testing and evaluation mechanisms; hopefully many of these mechanisms can be incorporated into FutureLearn too.

Peer assessment asks a learner to submit a short text (500 words or less in only plain text without formatting) which is then evaluated anonymously by other learners who are asked to respond to the text according to criteria set by the educators. Again, FutureLearn's implementation of this mechanism was somewhat crude, reducing the possibilities for how it could be effectively used within our course. It was not possible to submit an image, animation, or code for peer assessment, for example.

Our peer assessment topic focused on the cultural and philosophical implications of artificial life, which were explored in week 6 of the course. The question was designed to shift the emphasis of "artificial life" away from a purely technical or artistic apprehension of the domain into one that might reorient a learner's conceptual framework to consider what "life" is and societies as unpredictable discursive framing of it:

> Our attitudes about what constitutes life changes from culture to culture. Indeed our attitudes about life changes from person to person! Consider for a minute people who own pets. Some people are emotionally predisposed to cats, some to dogs or horses or birds or a combination of these creatures. Notwithstanding how emotionally attached we become to our pets, pets don't live in the wild; all pets live in human environments. In other words pets have artificial lives.
>
> With this in mind, would there be anything wrong with creating, then becoming emotionally attached to, an artificial life using approaches from creative coding and computer science? Would you nurture an artificial pet? Would you love and care for it? If you had a friend that was emotionally attached to an artificial pet would you let it "die" even if you had the option to keep it "alive"?

Results to our peer-review assignment were mixed. A number of students felt that the feedback they were given was either disrespectful or unhelpful. Others complimented their peers on thoughtful and insightful reviews of their submissions. Unfortunately, the FutureLearn system does not allow educators to vet reviews before they are sent (this would be impractical for any reasonably sized MOOC anyway).

Our overall impression is that these assessment technologies are currently underdeveloped, but that with work, they can become effective and engaging assessment mechanisms. A number of research projects in this area are already underway. For example, the PRAISE project developed at the University of London makes the idea of creative feedback an essential part of online creative learning. The project is specifically concerned with building computational systems that enable students to develop their own creative practice in music together in communities, and centers on *feedback* as the key mechanism.

Whereas traditionally creativity is a rather nebulous and difficult concept to pin down in assessment (despite many results from psychology suggesting otherwise), feedback is a much clearer concept to focus on and as PRAISE develops the project may give us a better understanding of how we learn our creative practice. From a coding perspective, such feedback mechanisms are also suitable. Learners can comment and highlight other's code and ask questions about how specific parts of a program work interactively. This, combined with in-the-browser code editing and compilation or interpretation, makes the online learning environment more self-contained. Many platforms, such as Code Academy (www.codecademy.com), are already well advanced in this area.

CONCLUSIONS

We believe that the most promising aspect of MOOCs is through the social learning they enable. A person struggling with material can post a question and ask for help at any time of the day and night and receive numerous helpful replies. Using principles of small-world networks, it would be beneficial to have the system connect the most competent individuals to smaller networks of others. Emerging mass-market virtual reality technologies might also fundamentally change the learning experience in creative contexts – allowing learners to simultaneously share and experience the creative examples of others in virtual space.

Even in the current, relatively simple form, the conversations and ideas shared using social media learning kept learners interested in the course and this aspect differentiates current MOOC technology from previous, similar systems such as distance education and online learning systems.

On a practical level, the platform should support the types of activities educators require. For our *Creative Coding* MOOC, the sharing of creative output and code proved difficult – the platform had no support for interactive, social sharing. We used third party sites, including Flickr (for images and animations), and processing.js (for sharing code and sketches) to work around platform limitations.

Finally, additional conceptual connections in our current course material would reinforce the pedagogical assertions we make between culture, philosophy, and technology. For example, the leitmotifs explored in week 6 of the course which figure profoundly in Artificial Life – emergence, self-organization, and "lifelike behavior" (Langton, 1989) – are, according to Laura Marks (Marks, 2010, p. 290), features in the longer genealogy of the human endeavor: "[cellular automata] artworks have a deep historical precedent in Islamic nonfigurative art, whose patterns evolve with an algorithmic liveliness that prefigures artificial life." Highlighting such relationships between human activity and technology promotes a deeper, more nuanced understanding of the cultural–technical prism we live in, and supports the creative practitioner learning how to code and the experienced programmer wanting to express themselves creatively.

REFERENCES

Alexander, C. (1993). *A Foreshadowing of 21st Century Art: the Color and Geometry of Very Early Turkish Carpets*. New York: Oxford University Press.

Barnett, R. (2011). Complexities of interdisciplinarity: Two (or three) into one will go. *Complicity: An International Journal of Complexity and Education*, 8(2), 59–66.

Chrisomalis, S. (2010). *Numerical Notation: A Comparative History*. Cambridge; New York: Cambridge University Press.

Code.org. (n.d.). About Us. Retrieved from https://code.org/about. Accessed online February 21, 2016.

DeMillo, R.A. (2015). *Revolution in Higher Education: How a Small Band of Innovators will Make College Accessible and Affordable*. Cambridge, MA: MIT Press.

Department for Education UK Government. (2013a). *National Curriculum in England: Computing Programmes of Study*. London: UK: Author Retrieved from www.gov.uk/government/publications/national-curriculum-in-england-computing-programmes-of-study/national-curriculum-in-england-computing-programmes-of-study. Accessed online February 21, 2016.

(2013b). *The National Curriculum in England: Framework Document*. London: Author.

Ericsson, K.A., Krampe, R.T., and Tesch-Römer, C. (1993). The role of deliberate practice in the acquisition of expert performance. *Psychological Review*, 100(3), 363–406.

Ettinghausen, R., Grabar, O., and Jenkins-Madina, M. (2001). *Islamic Art and Architecture 650–1250*. New Haven, CT: Yale University Press.

Gardner, H. (1993). *Creating Minds: An Anatomy of Creativity Seen Through the Lives of Freud, Einstein, Picasso, Stravinsky, Eliot, Graham, and Gandhi*. New York: Basic Books.

Gillings, R.J. (2008). *The Mathematics of Ancient Egypt Complete Dictionary of Scientific Biography* (vol. 15, pp. 681–705). Detroit: Charles Scribner's Sons.

Gladwell, M. (2008). *Outliers: The Story of Success* (1st edn.). New York: Little, Brown & Co.

Heussner, K.M. (2012). Udacity Nabs Another $15M to Bring More Interactivity to Online Education. Retrieved from https://gigaom.com/2012/10/25/udacity-nabs-another-15m-to-bring-more-interactivity-to-online-education/. Accessed online February 21, 2016.

Ifrah, G. (1998). *The Universal History of Numbers: From Prehistory to the Invention of the Computer*. London: Harvill Press.

Langton, C.G. (1989). Artificial Life. *Proceedings of an Interdisciplinary Workshop on the Synthesis and Simulation of Living Systems* (vol. 6, pp. 1–47). Santa Fe Institute Studies in the Sciences of Complexity. Boston, MA: Addison-Wesley Longman Publishing.

Langton, C.G. (1995). *Artificial Life: An Overview*. Cambridge, MA: MIT Press.

Mansel, T. (2013). How Estonia Became E-stonia. Retrieved from www.bbc.com/news/business-22317297. Accessed online February 21, 2016.

Marks, L.U. (2010). *Enfoldment and Infinity: An Islamic Genealogy of New Media Art*. Cambridge, MA: MIT Press.

Molnar, V. (1991). Red Squares. Retrieved from www.openprocessing.org/sketch/209391. Accessed online February 21, 2016.

Ng, A. and Widom, J. (2014). *Origins of the Modern MOOC (xMOOC)*. Retrieved from Center for Benefit-Cost Studies of Education, New York: http://cbcse.org/wordpress/wp-content/uploads/2014/05/MOOCs_Expectations_and_Reality.pdf. Accessed online February 21, 2016.

Pappano, L. (2012). The Year of the MOOC. *The New York Times*. Retrieved from www.nytimes.com/2012/11/04/education/edlife/massive-open-online-courses-are-multiplying-at-a-rapid-pace.html. Accessed online February 21, 2016.

Pink, D.H. (2005). *A Whole New Mind: Moving from the Information Age to the Conceptual Age*. New York: Riverhead Books.

Rodowick, D.N. (2007). *The Virtual Life of Film*. London: Harvard University Press.

Saunders, R. (2002). *Curious Design Agents and Artificial Creativity: A Synthetic Approach to the Study of Creative Behaviour. (Doctor of Philosophy)*, University of Sydney, Sydney.

Sterling, L. (2015). An Education for the 21st Century Means Teaching Coding in Schools. Retrieved from http://theconversation.com/an-education-for-the-21st-century-means-teaching-coding-in-schools-42046. Accessed online February 21, 2016.

Wesley, N. (2014). Molnar. Retrieved from https://www.openprocessing.org/sketch/151341. Accessed online February 21, 2016.

PART V

CRITICAL PEDAGOGY

9

Process and Outcome Paradigms in Media Arts Pedagogy

NANCY E. PATERSON

Abstract: This chapter explores process and outcomes paradigms in media arts pedagogy in the context of new media information and communications technologies (ICTs) and the "contested" Internet – the highly controlled, surveilled, and commercialized networks we use. The paradigmatic notions of pedagogy as either process-based (Dewey) or outcomes-oriented (Niebuhr) are discussed in connection to studio-based learning. Process-based approaches to education have been dominant in the twentieth century and were developed by Dewey, Vygotsky, Schön, Kolb, and many others, while outcomes-oriented education developed later in the period. Originating with sociologist William Spady, outcomes-based education (OBE) (1994) has been implemented as an administrative tool both for measuring individual performance as well as course or program level assessments. Performance "metrics" in outcomes initiatives emphasize peer review and measurement, de-emphasizing flexible approaches such as allowing individual students to assess according to their own goals. This chapter draws on Niebuhr rather than Dewey for expanding OBE frameworks for the use of ICTs in media arts project-based learning. Students are technologically enabled in project-based learning to become agents of their own goals and learning agendas since ICTs provide capabilities for individually tailored learning experiences which contextualize knowledge and assist in developing informed Internet citizenship.

Keywords: process-based pedagogy, outcomes-based education, John Dewey, Reinhold Niebuhr, William Spady, experiential learning, transrationalism, contested Internet

This chapter explores process and outcomes paradigms in media arts pedagogy in the context of new media information and communications technologies (ICTs) and the "contested" Internet – the highly controlled, surveilled, and commercialized network(s) we use. Utilizing ICT technologies, educators, in their teaching practices; administrators, applying "performance metrics" and exerting pressure on educators to change; policy makers, looking to cut funding or gain efficiencies; educational technology designers, seeking to expand markets or online learning units; and instructional designers, porting face-to-face courses into an online format, all face commensurate technical and theoretical considerations regarding how to foster creative and engaged learners through learning technologies. Focused primarily on educators themselves in their teaching practices, this discussion considers process-oriented and outcomes-based teaching and learning conceptual models in the context of the multiplicity of communications platforms, Internet protocols, and commercial software controls which create challenges and opportunities for the use of ICTs in media arts education.

At a high level, pedagogical approaches are grounded in the contrasting paradigms as either process-oriented or outcomes-based. Dewey and Niebuhr in particular are chosen as theoretical sources, in part to reappraise them in light of the context of new communications technologies with which they would not have been familiar, and other theorists such as Vygotsky, Schön, Kolb Galloway, and Cubitt will be drawn from to help explicate these contrasting paradigms for the contemporary moment.

PROCESS AND OUTCOMES MODELS

Evaluative comparisons between process and outcomes paradigms are not common. Typically comparisons occur in critiques of outcomes-based education (OBE) where process is discussed as a previous theoretical model which has been replaced. Process-oriented learning places emphasis on the subjective, motivational, open-ended, and discovery dimensions of learning. Generating information and making meaning is framed as a contextually defined social and personal experience. Dewey's experiential learning pedagogy, often applied as general problem solving, required the learner to actively participate in personal or authentic experiences to make meaning through personal engagement and inquiry. The process of problem solving is a recurring theme in Dewey: "Thinking is objectively discoverable as that mode of serial responsive behavior to a *problematic situation* in which transition to the relatively settled and clear is effected" (cited in MacKinnon, 1985, p. 273, emphasis added).

Dewey's instrumentalist theory and later Kolb's cycle of experience and reflection argued that each learner constructs knowledge individually and socially in pragmatic situations. These theories were oriented toward mutual understanding among learners and teachers, where the role of teachers was to assist students in understanding their own cognitive processes as they apply concepts in active, problem-centered, and experiential contexts. Vygotsky stressed social interaction in addition to the act of solving problems as a critical component of cognitive development.

With intellectual roots in behaviorism, OBE was developed in the work of William Spady (1994). OBE is referred to by a variety of different names including systemic education restructuring, performance-based education, standards-based education, competency-based education, and others. As a result of the wide nomenclature in this area, this text utilizes the term "outcomes-based" and OBE to describe this paradigm for learning. OBE places strong emphasis on measurement techniques to formally assess the results of the learning process.

OBE has been implemented as a relatively recent administrative tool for assessment, evaluation, and comparison. Learning is objectified as the measurement of specific goals, often stated as "learning outcomes" or "educational goals." Outcomes-based assessment is becoming a new mainstay in administrative practices alongside the traditional (since the 1960s) use of course evaluations, which have been controversial over the years, for example often claimed to be the main driver of grade inflation, and argued by many to measure not students' learning or teaching effectiveness but rather general features of students' experience (Brawley et al., 2013). The idea of "performance metrics" originated in business practices, migrated to governmental administration, and now has been imported into academia:

> The severity of the global economic crisis has put the spotlight firmly on measuring academic and research performance and productivity, and assessing its contribution, value, impact and benefit. While traditionally, research output and impact was measured by peer-publications and citations, there is increased emphasis on a "market-driven approach," which favours the bio-, medical and technological sciences, and helped reinforce a disciplinary hierarchy in which arts and humanities research (A&HR) has struggled for attention. (Hazelkorn, 2014, p. 25)

The contemporary context of teaching and learning has become decidedly quantitative in its core assumptions and epistemes, and the rolling out of learning outcomes regimes has faced considerable backlash and resistance in many institutions particularly from arts, humanities, and social science faculties. Today's media arts educators have to contend with both paradigms, in that creative pedagogies have a strong process-oriented tradition behind them, while their institutional overseers increasingly demand quantified evidence of learning.

PROCESS AND REFLEXIVE LEARNING

Process-oriented pedagogy in North America, characterized by "social process – a process of living and not a preparation for future living" (Dewey, 1897) – had its most ardent proponent in John Dewey with his philosophy of pragmatism and instrumentalism. Dewey proposed that experimental science and democracy were inherently guiding social processes and his instrumentalism proposed that truth (or certainty) could never be epistemologically fixed for all time but needed testing against real-world applications. Although Dewey was recognized more widely for his educational reforms than for his instrumentalist philosophy, his assertions that education was key to understanding and that advancements in science and democracy were instrumental to liberal democracy were widely known (Rice, 1993, p. xii). Vygotsky, Schön, and Kolb further developed "experiential learning" as active, participatory, and distinct from didactic learning in which the learner plays a comparatively passive role. In "Experiential Learning from a Constructivist Perspective," Mughal and Zafar summarize:

> The school of thought emphasizing learning through reflection on experience considers individuals to gain and construct knowledge by interacting with their environment through a set of perceived experiences (Fenwick, 2001). Works of Kolb (1984), Piaget (1966), Dewey (1938), and Wells (1995) have greatly contributed to the constructivist view of experiential learning. The theory of constructivism implies that the learners or the individuals are constructors of their own knowledge which is generated by interacting with their sociocultural environment (Mughal and Zafar, 2011, p. 28; Vygotsky, 1978).

Lev Vygotsky's approach to learning and collaboration through interactive learning contexts asserted that consciousness is the product of socialization, and the role of play both by the child alone and with others was emphasized:

> Every function in the child's cultural development appears twice: first, on the social level, and later, on the individual level; first, between people (inter-psychological) and then inside the child (intra-psychological). This applies equally to voluntary attention, to logical memory, and to the formation of concepts. All the higher functions originate as actual relationships between individuals. (Vygotsky, 1978, p. 57)

In language learning, children's speech is for the purpose of communication but once mastered becomes internalized speech and consciousness. According to Vygotsky, humans use cultural tools such as speech and writing to mediate their social environments and the internalization of these tools leads to higher thinking skills.

Donald Schön's (1983) reflective practice and improvisation in the work of Elliot Eisner (1979) both critiqued technical rationality and had a significant base in process (Smith, 2012). Eisner advocated that education had much to learn from the arts and creativity, asserting that improvisation was integral to learning. Schön's "The Reflective Practitioner" explored cyclic patterns of experience and conscious application of learning experiences. Mughal and Zafar (2011) added that experiential learning has always been mistakenly used interchangeably with experiential education:

> Experiential learning refers to 'making meaning from direct experience.' Experiential learning plays a supporting role in experiential education which facilitates the process of knowledge creation, sense-making and knowledge transfer in teaching, training and development. Since its conception by John Dewey in the mid 1930s, experiential education has been used in multiple disciplines including sociology, anthropology, science and research due to its interdisciplinary nature (Carver, 1996). However, David Kolb's (1984) theory of experiential learning has greatly contributed to the expanding philosophy of experiential education.

> The theory of constructivism implies that the learners or the individuals are constructors of their own knowledge which is generated by interacting with their socio-cultural environment (Vygotsky, 1978). Constructivists like David Kolb whose book entitled, "Experiential Learning" was published in 1984, [focus] more on individual development through reflection on its past experiences. (Mughal and Zafar, 2011, p. 28)

With the four-part experiential learning cycle termed the "Learning Styles Inventory" (LSI), Kolb offered both a way to understand individual learning styles and an explanation of a cycle of experiential learning that applies to all learners, "a learning spiral of ever-increasing complexity" (Lewis and Williams, 1994, p. 7). In their 1995 paper "Experiential Learning: Theoretical Underpinnings," Beaudin and Quick detail the process of experience and integration:

> Kolb describes experiential learning as a four part process, where the learner is asked to engage themselves in a new experience, actively reflect on that experience, conceptualize that experience, and integrate it with past experiences. Furthermore, they must make decisions based on their created concepts. In the process of learning, one moves in varying degrees from actor to observer, and from specific involvement to general analytic detachment. (Beaudin and Quick, 1995, p. 11)

Experiential learning analysis in Ferry and Ross-Gordon (1998) documented the use of reflection-in-action by adult educators in problematic situations. Their study results supported Schön's theory that reflective practitioners use constructivist problem solving and nonreflective practitioners use an instrumentalist approach. Their findings demonstrated that reflecting educators, whether novice or experienced, use reflection-in-action and reflection-on-action as a means to develop expertise. The presence of experienced educators exhibiting minimal reflection and the inclusion of one highly reflective novice indicated that experience alone is not the sole source of the reflective process.

DISENTANGLING OUTCOMES – IDEALS AND MEASURES

Dewey was a generation older than Reinhold Niebuhr yet since the 1930s the two had long-standing ideological rivalry in many areas of philosophy. Dewey provides the modernist process-oriented approach to pedagogy with his left-leaning positivist views while Niebuhr's realism and transrationalism were philosophical forerunners of today's outcomes-based paradigm in pedagogy, with the primary "outcome" in this sense being the development of a citizen fully participating in a democratic society, which is a much more expansive conception of "educational outcomes" compared to today's measurement of quantified learning. The primary outcome in this sense is "freedom."

> [A] free and open society is justified more than any other because it gives latitude to the creative expression of the vitalities of life – creative vitalities that such a society leave open to ever-expanding opportunities. Democracy best reflects and conforms to man's "essential" nature; namely, to that freedom that is the self's "capacity for indeterminate transcendence over the processes and limitations of nature." (Rice, 2009, p. 126)

For contemporary media arts, Niebuhrian concepts of transrationalism and self-transcendence (Niebuhr, 1932, intro) can provide theoretical support for understanding online identity and distributed intelligence. These Niebuhrian concepts facilitate understanding general pedagogical requirements that can enable active citizenship in cyberspace, since "intelligence that transcends rationality" (Harries and Platten, 2010, p. 13) and transrationalism are analogous to users' projected identity, while intelligence becomes "data" in networks.

Niebuhr's theological explorations of crisis and responsibility countered Dewey's philosophy for decades but had a relatively minor impact on North American pedagogical theory in the twentieth century, when Dewey's ideas were dominant. Transrationalism is the perspective that rationalism on its own is limited and can only go so far, and that beyond the limits of rationalism other means such as wisdom and intuition to understand the world and existential conditions are required.

Niebuhr held the view that society is a formed sociopolitical instrument with democracy as a chosen structure which must be developed and maintained (Harries and Platten, 2010, p. 10) and it is proposed here that his freedom of identity and consciousness provides a starting point for pedagogy in the context of global communications networks and citizenship. Niebuhr's self-transcendence is the dimension of the eternal in the human spirit that is reflected in the ability of the self to transcend both the processes of nature and one's own interest and rationality. According to Niebuhr, "the ideal is never simply rooted in the realm of the real and that the real reflects the ideal. The conflict is between creativity and resistance" (Rice, 1993, p. 4). Niebuhr argued for an intelligence that transcended rationality and restored the imaginative spiritual dimension in life:

> We are living in a world . . . in which a higher degree of technological achievement and to a certain degree, a higher intelligence, brings us in closer and closer contact with all the world but we haven't the intelligence by which we may make our common life sufferable. (Rice, 1993, p. 11)

While admittedly these concepts, originating in the discipline of theology, are quasi-mystical in tone, they prefigure a kind of preliminary notion of the electronically networked self which is useful for conceptualizing today's online citizen in search of self-realized freedom through democratic participation in open networks.

Contemporary theorists such as Sean Cubitt (2009) have criticized the commercial ideologies and biases in technology which are obstacles for democratic citizenship today, providing support for the claim that the Internet is neither rhizomatic nor organic but highly controlled, surveilled, and commercialized. Cubitt argues that there is no single or simple digital aesthetics, but there is or can be a digital ethics (Creeber and Martin, 2009, p. 29). Creeber asserts that there is no set method or theoretical framework for studying new media (p. 11).

It is this interest in digital ethics and in the hidden embedded nature of protocols which govern and regulate online interactivity, which offers challenges and opportunities for developing critical analysis in media arts pedagogy. Communications through networked technological mediation, including interactivity, virtual reality, and the Internet, which includes the World Wide Web, e-mail services, bulletin boards (BBS), file-transfer services, etc., are in effect a network of networks, four-fifths of it or more lie hidden below the surface (Creeber and Martin, 2009, p. 26). At the routing level, especially in wireless networks, the commercial controls and protocols that Cubitt and Galloway (2004) have analyzed are now found to incorporate surveillance by governments and commercial entities as well as the networks themselves. Transport controls and protocols function invisibly to users and serve to control Internet data in a finely grained manner based on user's metadata – data embedded at the head of user data packets which describe and control the user's packets – and various unattended-to settings and preferences. Metadata tracks the individual user, monitors, and controls data traffic by "tunneling" end-user communications. As this happens, on-screen content is readily available to the user, providing real-time automatic adjustment according to the user's specific selections and preferences.

> It is worth mentioning Alex Galloway's . . . thesis, derived from the work of French philosophers Foucault and Deleuze, that while modern societies were characteristically societies of discipline and postmodern societies of control, digital society is characterized by protocols, the invisible but ubiquitous codes which simultaneously enable and constrain what can and cannot be done in a given system. (Creeber and Martin, 2009, p. 29)

Online experiences are co-created as users interact with each other, commercial software, network controls, and government agencies, in the context of the embedded nature of technological protocols and controls. Niebuhr's concept of self-transcendence is analogous to the transduction of users' identity and intelligence into networks. Despite all the popular rhetoric of today's youth being "digital natives," they are not necessarily "digital citizens" in the sense of operating under classic Enlightenment principles of freedom and autonomy. In spite of their intimacy with the dynamics of the digital culture and technical skills, many students

> may not always be informed by important considerations about the technical, political, and artistic dimensions of new media. Perhaps this is because the technologies through which they access these media are embedded in their lives and almost rendered "invisible." (Freire and McCarthy, 2014, p. 28)

PROJECT-BASED LEARNING, ICTS, AND THE CONTESTED INTERNET

Media arts technologies enable a broad perspective on issues associated with the rapidly evolving digital landscape and are characterized by interdisciplinarity as well as distributed, collaborative scholarship that transcends textual sources. One of the aims of media arts pedagogy is to produce graduates who are ready to take up roles as citizens in cyberspace yet the idea of "citizenship" is a very receding theme as the terrain has shifted more toward outcomes-based pedagogy which, especially in its newer guise as "competency-based learning," emphasizes, as one pithy and scything phrase has it, "earners not learners." Nonetheless, ICTs do provide the capability and flexibility for the innovative development of outcomes-based pedagogy in media arts and humanities through addressing the challenges and opportunities that arise from the "contested" Internet.

Outcomes-based learning considers goals and outcomes in context-free ways, as the quantified measurement of specific and objectified educational goals. This lack of context is difficult in media arts pedagogy because we live in and through media. Internet users are borderless citizens of "Facebook nation" or "Google nation" as much as they are national citizens of geo-delimited state formations. Users define themselves in terms of their online interests as much or more than their connection with the country they inhabit in the offline world. Especially among young users, online interaction in specialized applications and communities occurs with a level of frequency comparable to the offline physical world. In part as a response to the general surveillance afforded by online networks, some users seek anonymity through elusive and hard-to-find software settings, websites, and software. Some users seeking anonymity have been driven further away from mainstream commercial applications into the "deep web" via websites such as *4chan*.

In 2014, Judith Donath, founder of the Sociable Media Group at MIT, discussed the website *4chan*, which originated in October 2003 for posting pictures, manga, and anime but was later adopted for wide-ranging discussion and hacktivism. *4chan* provides users with anonymity in postings with no required registration process. "[4chan] provides the ability to have a social identity without leaving the basement . . . identities are created by history, [it is] hard to follow an identity over time in [online] communities" (Donath, 2014).

Burdick, Drucker, Lunenfeld, Presner, and Schnapp (2012) discuss project-based learning and experimentation as necessary for learning outcomes:

> Metrics for evaluating the quality and impact of Digital Humanities projects combine traditional assessment methods in the humanities with new factors. Peer review remains fundamental to processes of assessment, but now draws as much from the community of leading Digital Humanities practitioners as from field-based peers. A less risk-averse culture is the

prerequisite for a more innovation- and experimentation-driven model. (pp. 121–36)

Project learning and experimentation provide opportunities for learners to contextualize learning through participating in fluid communities of practice, addressing questions that cannot be reduced to a single genre, medium, discipline, or institution. In their preface to *Digital Humanities*, these authors outline broad pedagogical requirements to enable ideal citizens in cyberspace, arguing that digital humanities

> represents a major expansion of the purview of the humanities, precisely because it brings the values, representational and interpretive practices, meaning-making strategies, complexities, and ambiguities of being human into every realm of experience and knowledge of the world. It is a global, trans-historical, and transmedia approach to knowledge and meaning-making. (Burdick, Drucker, Lunenfeld, Presner, and Schnapp, 2012, p. vii)

CHmaps[1] and IXmaps[2] are Internet infrastructure research projects that encourage critical thinking and experimentation in media arts in which students and faculty researchers formulated interactive ways to explore the underlying architectures of social networks, apps, and websites. CHmaps was the original project visualization created by the present author and the collaborative project IXmaps arose from it. The IXmaps team was comprised of David J. Phillips, Andrew Clement, and myself.

These projects originated as a means to contextualize knowledge regarding traffic exchange over the Internet infrastructure and how the Internet physically routes data. The hidden controls and surveillance used in the technical routing of Internet networks were familiar from the work of Cubitt, Galloway, and others but not yet visualized in ways that included relevant sociopolitical information. The projects most similar in scope to IXmaps were the DIMES project at Tel Aviv University, Kahunaburger Traceroute, the Gtrace project, the Geographical Traceroute project, and the xtraceroute project,[3] all of which (except DIMES) measured and

---

[1] www.vacuumwoman.com/hidden/url/

[2] www.ixmaps.ca

[3] DIMES (Distributed Internet MEasurements & Simulations). Tel-Aviv University EE-Systems. Retrieved online from www.netdimes.org/about.html; Kahunaburger traceroute. Retrieved online from www.kahunaburger.com/2009/03/28/google-earth-as-a-traceroute-viewer/; Gtrace project. Retrieved online from http://freecode.com/projects/gtrace; Geographical Traceroute project. Retrieved online from https://sourceforge.net/

illustrated solely bandwidth capacities. Unlike these comparator academic visualization research projects, CHmaps and IXmaps make sociopolitical information such as network ownership, interconnection, and surveillance available publicly. Employing the analogy that network interconnections are similar to personal interconnections, with the exchange of information adding complexity and value, the precursor project CHmaps focused on visualizing network "interconnection" rather than network "capacity." CHmaps utilized a map of North America (in Google Earth) on which Internet "exchange points" or "carrier hotels" are displayed as interactive labeled highlighted icons. When the icon is clicked, information about that interconnection point and the building where it is physically located becomes available. This includes ownership, Internet Service Providers (ISPs), as well as known links or alliances among the building owners, clients, and government or corporate entities.

IXmaps research was designed to be more dynamic, providing Internet users' capability to see the route that specific user's data packets take across North America. IXmaps is distinct as it employs a unique traceroute visualization from the user's system to the final destination on a map of North America, also displayed in Google Earth, and presents information about Internet exchange points transited along the way. Project goals included rendering visible to users' interesting aspects of Internet infrastructure related to everyday usage, e.g., NSA surveillance, deep packet inspection (DPI), and carrier hotel ownership in order to counteract the tendency to regard the Internet core as an immaterial, virtual, placeless "cloud" (Paul, 2015). IXmaps development involved geolocating the latitude and longitude of network core routers inside interconnection exchange facilities by trace-routing the path of users' Internet requests. Custom software (TRgen – traceroute generation), once downloaded by users and executed, populated project databases with Internet core routing "hops" (network interconnection points) of users Internet website requests. These routers were located and visualized on maps of North America along with relevant sociopolitical information.

By showing the Internet's geographical and physical concreteness and contingency, an understanding of the Internet core amenable to informed Internet citizenship and public policy engagement was created. The availability of visual information regarding Internet flows assists researchers in

---

projects/geotrace/; xtraceroute project. Retrieved online from http://gnu.gds.tuwien.ac.at/directory/xtraceroute.html

developing public policy in the areas of privacy, communications risk, and infrastructure. The potential benefits to Canada are in the area of international oversight of the Internet as a resource:

> One project underway to redress this situation involves expanding the number of Internet Exchange Points (IXPs) in Canada. These switching stations, usually shared among a consortia of providers, act like large data intersections. Canada currently has four such stations: in Ottawa, Toronto, Vancouver and, just recently, Montreal. This is three to 30 times fewer than other similarly developed nations, according to an independent research report on Canadian Internet traffic exchange commissioned by the Canadian Internet Registration Authority (CIRA). In contrast, there are 85 IXPs in the U.S., 11 in Australia and five in New Zealand. Canada, says the report, is in the "laggard" category with respect to the provision of domestic IXPs . . . Bell Canada, says the CIRA report, does not participate in current Canadian IXP sites, "preferring to force its Canadian counterparts to meet it in Seattle, New York, or San Jose." It will clearly take pressure on providers to change some current routing practices. (Moll, 2013)

These examples of project-based learning strengthen multidisciplinary approaches and collaborations among learners in the art and information science fields and assist with contextualizing knowledge as it makes concrete the general notions of the ethereal Internet "cloud" created, maintained, and monitored by private network companies and governments. Students working on the projects had previously used the Internet as an opaque tool or service and upon participating in the project found that geopolitical differences are diminished by the Internet once a better understanding of network materiality is achieved. Discoveries included new notions of how state borders are physically challenged by communications networks that route data traversing geopolitical borders which are physically undermined and redrawn by inter-network routing. Specific project outcomes showed that networks in Canada are controlled, contested spaces with surveillance by government and commercial entities, proving that routing rendered user data available to government agencies outside Canada:

> [The] IXmaps project, which has been studying Internet routing practices, [found] one in four messages travel through U.S. data space on their way to and fro across the country. They call it "boomerang routing." So, depending on the carrier, a message originating in Toronto can go to New York and then to Montreal on its way to Health Canada in Ottawa. Another message, originating in Abbotsford B.C., will end up at Lakehead University only after passing through San Jose, San Francisco,

Kansas City and Chicago. In this transparent transaction space, it is easy to forget that Internet traffic, just like highway traffic, falls under U.S. law when it passes through U.S. territory. That leads us to the problem of surveillance. (Moll, 2013)

As the Internet develops with applications and content flowing freely over borders, research into information flows and transnational network(s), has become "urgent":

[B]orders, which are dependent on transnational ICT networks, are permitting state actors to re-scale border controls in a way that transcends the territorial framework of the nation-state system . . . [expanding] the boundaries of the informational state beyond its geopolitical borders. (Shields, 2014)

POSSIBILITIES OF LEARNING ANALYTICS – EXPANDING OBE FRAMEWORKS

Through performance metrics in outcomes initiatives, educators are in effect forced to reshape their goals and reconfigure students' experiences to match specific demands and competency measures. Particular challenges for media arts pedagogy include barriers to the use of open-source software or hardware. When students create unique hardware and software, using technologies such as Arduino, Lily Pad, wearables, Ladybug, hackerbots, etc., getting these projects onto commercially controlled networks for deployment can be difficult. Teaching the critical use of ICTs involves difficulties of getting innovative projects and products to wider audiences:

Imaginative use of digital technologies could be transformational for teaching and learning, taking us well beyond the incremental value of more accessible lecture presentations. The problem is that transformation is more about the human and organizational aspects of teaching and learning than it is about the use of technology. We have the ambition. We have the technology. What is missing is what connects the two. If education leaders were fully engaged with this, it would be strategy, and we would have a top-down change process. If practitioners were fully engaged it would be experimental innovation, and we would have a bottom-up change process. Better to have both, but too many educational institutions still lack serious leadership engagement with the innovative application of digital technologies. (Beetham and Sharpe, 2013)

To prepare for work-related skills that are applicable in the rapidly changing environment of ICTs and the Internet, learning experiences which are not characteristic of OBE such as unpredictability and transient learning experiences should be included in project-based learning to develop critical problem solving (Burdick et al., 2012, pp. 121–36). Internet-connected and rapidly developed and deployed technologies can increase the opportunities for the students to individualize their learning through problem-centered processes for discovery in experiential and pragmatic contexts. The contemporary regime of measured learning outcomes, typically mandated by the accrediting organizations to which our academic institutions are beholden, call for some kind of "translation" of these process-oriented approaches, if only to fulfill the annual departmental compliance rituals handed down to us by our metric-minded administrative overseers.

Pedagogy redolent of classic twentieth-century process-based approaches, whose "demise" in the current institutional context is exaggerated in the managerial and administrative discourse, is as relevant today as it ever has been, given the manner in which technology is constantly disrupting all professional fields. Educating for open-ended, unpredictable, and uncertain problems and domains remains vital. Students are technologically enabled in project-based learning to become agents of their own goals and learning agendas as ICTs provide capabilities for individually tailored interactive learning experiences which contextualize knowledge and assist in developing informed Internet citizenship as its more legitimate outcome.

REFERENCES

Beaudin, B. and Quick, D. (1995). *Experiential Learning: Theoretical Underpinnings.* Fort Collins, CO: High Plains Intermountain Center for Agricultural Health and Safety, Colorado State University. Retrieved from http://users.ugent.be/~mvalcke/LI_1213/experiencial_learning.pdf. Accessed online February 1, 2016.

Beetham, H. and Sharpe, R. (2013). *Rethinking Pedagogy for a Digital Age: Designing for 21st Century Learning.* London: Routledge.

Brawley, S., Clark, J., Dixon, C. et al. (2013). Learning Outcomes Assessment and History: TEQSA, the After Standards Project and the QA/QI Challenge in Australia. *Arts and Humanities in Higher Education*, 12(1), 20–35. http://doi.org/10.1177/1474022212460745. Accessed online December 7, 2016.

Burdick, A., Drucker, J., Lunenfeld, P., Presner, T., and Schnapp, J. (2012). *Digital Humanities.* Cambridge, MA: MIT Press. Retrieved from http://mitpress.mit.edu/sites/default/files/titles/content/9780262018470_Open_Access_Edition. Accessed online December 7, 2016.

Carver, R. (May/June 1996). Theory for Practice: A Framework for Thinking about Experiential Education. *Journal of Experiential Education*, 19(1), 149–58. Retrieved from https://rampages.us/utaproject/wp-content/uploads/sites/6546/2015/04/Carver-1996_Experiential-Education-Framework.pdf. Accessed online February 1, 2016.

Creeber, G. and Martin, R. (Eds.) (2009). *Digital Culture: Understanding New Media*. Berkshire, England: Open University Press.

Cubitt, S. (2009). Digital Theory. Case Study: Digital Aesthetics. In G. Creeber and R. Martin (Eds.), *Digital Culture: Understanding New Media*. Berkshire, England: Open University Press, pp. 23–9.

Dewey, J. (1897, January). My Pedagogic Creed. *School Journal*, 54, 77–80.

(1938). *Experience and Education*. New York: Collier Books.

Donath, J. (2014, November 8). The Social Machine: Designs for Living Online. Boston Book Festival panel: Howard Gardner, Judith Donath, Vikram Chandra, host Jason Pontin. Boston Old South Church. *Book TV* air date November 8, 2014 C-SPAN2, www.booktv.org. Original date October 25, 2014.

Eisner, E.W. (1979). *The Educational Imagination: On the Design and Evaluation of School Programs*. New York: Macmillan.

Fenwick, J.T. (2001). "Experiential Learning: A Theoretical Critique from Five Perspectives," ERIC Information Series No. 385.

Ferry, N.M. and Ross-Gordon, J.M. (1998). An Inquiry into Schon's Epistemology of Practice: Exploring Links between Experience and Reflective Practice. *Human Relations June 1*, 2015, 68, 973–1000.

Freire, M. and McCarthy, E. (March 2014). Four Approaches to New Media Art Education. *Art Education*, (67.2), 28–31.

Galloway, A.R. (2004). *Protocol: How Control Exists after Decentralization*. Cambridge, MA: MIT Press.

Harries, R. and Platten, S. (2010). *Reinhold Niebuhr and Contemporary Politics: God and Power*. New York: Oxford University Press.

Hazelkorn, E. (2014). Making an Impact: New Directions for Arts and Humanities Research. Articles. *Arts and Humanities in Higher Education*, 2013. Pre-print article. Retrieved from http://arrow.dit.ie/cserart/51. Accessed online December 7, 2016.

Kolb, D.A. (1984). *Experiential Learning: Experiences as a Source of Learning and Development*. Englewood Cliffs, NJ: Prentice-Hall.

Lewis, L.H. and Williams, C.J. (Summer 1994). Experiential Learning: Past and Present. *New Directions for Adult and Continuing Education* (62) pp. 5–16. Retrieved from www.sunyjcc.edu/files/Experiential%20Learning%20-%20Past %20and%20Present.pdf. Accessed online March 3, 2016.

MacKinnon, B. (1985). *American Philosophy: A Historical Anthology*. Albany, NY: State University of New York Press.

Moll, M. (2013, September 26). Do You Know Where Your Data Have Been? *Ottawa Citizen*. Retrieved from http://maritamoll.ca/content/do-you-know-where-your-data-have-been. Accessed online December 7, 2016.

Mughal F. and Zafar A. (2011). Experiential Learning from a Constructivist Perspective: Reconceptualizing the Kolbian Cycle. *International Journal of Learning and Development*, (1), 27–37. Retrieved from http://eprints.lancs.ac.uk/62024/1/952.pdf. Accessed online February 1, 2016.

Niebuhr, R. (1932). *Moral Man and Immoral Society: A Study in Ethics and Politics*. New York: Charles Scribner.

Paul, C. (2015, December 11–January 30). *Little Sister (is Watching You, Too)*. Exhibition catalog. Pratt Manhattan Gallery, New York City.

Piaget, J. and Beth, E.W. (1966). *Mathematical Epistemology and Psychology.* Holland: Dordrecht.

Rice, D. (1993). *Reinhold Niebuhr and John Dewey: An American Odyssey.* Albany, NY: State University of New York Press.

(2009). *Engagements with an American Original.* Grand Rapids, MI: Wm. B. Eerdmans Publishing.

Schön, D. (1983). *The Reflective Practitioner. How Professionals Think in Action.* London: Temple Smith.

Shields, P. (2014). Borders as Information Flows and Transnational Networks. *Global Media and Communication,* 10(1), 3–33.

Smith, M.K. (2012). What is Pedagogy? *The Encyclopedia of Informal Education.* Retrieved from http://infed.org/mobi/what-is-pedagogy/. Accessed online December 7, 2016.

Spady, W.G. (1994). *Outcome-Based Education: Critical Issues and Answers.* Arlington, VA: American Association of School Administrators.

Vygotsky, L.S. (1978). *Mind in Society.* Cambridge, MA: Harvard University Press. Retrieved from www.instructionaldesign.org/theories/social-development. html. Accessed online December 7, 2016.

Wells, G. (1995). Language and the Inquiry-Oriented Curriculum. *Curriculum Inquiry,* 25(3), 233–48.

10

Citizens of the Cognisphere

DANIEL SAUTER

Abstract: To become citizens of the cognisphere, a new generation of students requires a modified intellectual immune system with the social and cultural competencies to rein in technical affordances – a form of anthropotechnic autoimmunity. A liberal arts education that provides coding and machine learning capacity alongside humanistic competency prepares students to perform daily Turing tests on automated systems that have the capacity to learn and evolve, and reflect on how we are interpolated and disciplined by machine cognizers. The computational regime transgresses geopolitical sovereignty, for it predominates traditional governmental structures and systems of control. In the labor market of the computational regime, work follows information – to discrete information hubs and havens where infrastructure and conditions are opportune. The variety of praxes discussed in this article from the extreme ends of the planetary spectrum illustrate computational thinking through scientific breakthroughs such as CRISPR, geopolitical jurisdiction as in the case of Safe Harbor, and control systems exemplified by telematics. Following seminal sources such as N. Katherine Hayles's scholarship on the cognisphere and Benjamin Bratton's notion of the planetary computing stack, this chapter examines how students can engage the world as citizens of the cognisphere rather than 24–7 mercenaries operating an accidental planetary megastructure made of stacks and protocols. To that end, social and cultural competencies of the humanities remain critical, and must step up to the technological issues of our time.

Keywords: computational intelligence, critical pedagogy, human–computer interaction, information networks, student teaching, machine learning, coding theory

INTRODUCTION

> Research and the raising of consciousness have turned man into the
> idiot of the cosmos; he has sent himself into exile and expatriated him-
> self from his immemorial security in self-blown bubbles of illusions into
> a senseless, unrelated realm that functions on its own. With the help of
> its relentlessly probing intelligence, the open animal tore down the roof
> of its old house from the inside. Taking part in modernity means putting
> evolved immune systems at risk.
>
> (Sloterdijk, 2011, p. 23)

As we prepare a new generation of students for the computational regime
(Brueck, 2016), we need to make room for cultural examination and critical reflection – not just to transcribe a liberal arts agenda in "an obligation
to develop their abilities to think and live" (Deresiewicz, 2015) – but also
to re-instill astonishment and wonder in the "resolutely wonder-free zone"
(Sloterdijk, 2016, p. 3) of institutionalized philosophy and social sciences.
We need to notice how we are "interpolating humans with machines that,
as they become intelligent, increasingly interpenetrate and indeed constitute human bodies" (Hayles, 2005, p. 62). We require new conceptual tools
to acquire our own anthropotechnic immune system. The core liberal arts
"ability to make autonomous choices" (2015) often succumbs to the pressures of credit hours and learning outcomes – so much to cover, so many
voices. In such circumstance, comprehensive ignorance can be mistaken as
expertise, and tunnel vision as a form of professional aptitude. We end up
peddling "real-world" skills to an idealized workforce of producers, only to
find out in the real world that the number one career skill for knowledge
workers remains the capacity to self-assess and learn incessantly.

Within or without computation at the core of classroom instruction,
how can we be satisfied graduating students into the cognisphere without
providing them the opportunity to examine their own machinic interpolation, and what role it plays in making autonomous choices? How can we
accept the human-centric fallacy that we merely use tools to make our lives
more convenient, instead of acknowledging the many ways in which our
digital unconscious impacts all aspects of our emotional and creative lives?
Autonomous thinking can only become a foundation for lifelong learning
and sustained practice if we create space for it and demonstrate its value.
The praxes discussed in this chapter from the extreme ends of the planetary spectrum are chosen to instill astonishment and wonder, and also to
illustrate lateral and computational thinking through the lens of seminal

scholarship on information and matter, cognition and agency, and geopolitics and infrastructure. I have given those primary voices a prominent place in this chapter, so they can inspire as primary sources for further study and classroom instruction.

In what follows, I will argue that the computational regime transgresses geopolitical borders and jurisdictions, for it predominates traditional governmental structures and control. As we cohabit the cognisphere alongside nonconscious machine cognizers of different scale, complexity, and kinetic ability, we need to close current thermodynamic loopholes for machine cognizers, and bring them out of the cloud shadows to enjoy agency and accountability. I will refer to a diverse range of such machine cognizers simply as "cogninodes." We might afford cogninodes varying degrees of consideration and empathy. As they actively redraw geopolitical boundaries and interpolate our selves into the machinic, they nonetheless deserve a closer look. We already find ourselves running daily Turing tests to decipher increasingly sophisticated machine learning systems, reverse-engineering their inherent humanity. The capacity to decipher, and to do so with ease, becomes our anthrophotechnic immune system. This also points to a new digital divide between cognicitizens and noncitizens – who are more vulnerable to exercise basic rights and more susceptible to be disciplined by the computational regime.

CUSTOMS IN THE COGNISPHERE

The shift from "thinking" to "cognizing" in this model is significant, for it blurs the boundary between conscious self-awareness and nonconscious processes.

(Hayles, 2006a, p. 139)

The cognisphere, a concept coined by Thomas Whalen (1994), is a critical resource for this chapter, defined by Katherine Hayles in her excellent elaboration of Haraway's cyborg as "the globally interconnected cognitive systems in which humans are increasingly connected" and "not the only actors within the system: machine cognizers are crucial players as well" (2006b, p. 161). Hayles sets the stage for this analysis in her seminal book *My Mother was a Computer: Digital Subjects and Literary Texts* (2005) where she demonstrates the inherent linguistic properties of code as a form of natural language, its ability to form multiorder systems of emergences, and relationship to ideology – critical notions on which I rely heavily. Along with

How We Became Posthuman (1999), it offers an expanded context that I recommend to anyone seeking answers as to why coding technology "becomes central to understanding the human condition" (2005, p. 192). Networked things already outnumber humanity, and sightings of autonomous vehicles have become commonplace not only in the skies over conflict areas (Singer, 2009), but also domestically – hauling shipping containers and cargo ("Freightliner," 2015), driving cautiously (Gibbs, 2015), crashing ski races (Willemsen, 2015), and presidential lawns (Schmidt and Shear, 2015). Instead of autonomous vehicles and networked things, let us focus instead on less tangible and able-bodied descendants of the DARPA family tree (DARPA, 2014) – artificial organisms constituted solely based on electric differences reverberating through data networks. Machine bodies without organs (Deleuze and Guattari, 1987), if you will.

We interpolate our selves into machine cognizers and extend our abilities and senses through devices and digital infrastructure. By wearing head-mounted displays and EyeTap devices for over three decades, Steve Mann, "the father of the wearable computer" (2004), has demonstrated how the addition of a sixth and seventh sense can look and feel like. Decades before Google adopted and abandoned the idea, Mann's fascinating research and lived experience point directly to the tensions between interpolated bodies and personal rights, subverting panoptic surveillance through "souveillance" – his personal and democratized counterpiece (Lynch, 2002). To fathom the cognisphere, we first need to come to terms with our own posthuman condition and not succumb to an oversimplified technophile or technophobe dichotomy. It would leave us with the old and unsavory dilemma: resist the information stack and its implications while becoming increasingly disenfranchised and less competitive, or concede our quantified selves to the "inverse-panopticon," trading "cognitive capital . . . in exchange for global infrastructural services" (Bratton, 2014). It is a choice we have already made. Under the cloak of convenience and the spell of access, we exchange cognitive feedback for doses of dopamine (Berridge and Robinson, 1998) in a transaction that adds urgency to the idea of cogninodes agency and accountability, closing some ethical and thermodynamic loopholes currently afforded to them. Will we allow cogninodes to claim insanity in a courtroom?

> As it is true for other forms of ideology, the interpolation of the user into the machinic system does not require his or her conscious recognition of how he or she is being disciplined by the machine to become a certain kind of subject. As we know interpolation is most effective when it is largely unconscious. This conclusion makes abundantly clear why we

cannot afford to ignore code or allow it to remain the exclusive concern of computer programmers or engineers. (Hayles, 2005, p. 61)

To establish a sense of cognisphere scale and material variance, I will begin by outlining two types of cogninodes that are in many ways scalar opposites, before returning to critical geopolitical aspects of the cognisphere. Both examples demonstrate fundamental computational principles, and show how planetary computing transcends both geopolitical and metaphysical boundaries.

Life-changing on a molecular level is the discovery of a natural defense mechanism in bacteria-turned editing technology called clustered regularly interspaced short palindromic repeats (CRISPR) – a bacterial DNA database that stores virus mug-shots within its very own genetic code. This memory mechanism allows the microorganism to match exogenous DNA exactly, and then applies molecular blades to cut and eliminate intruders with precision (Resnick, 1994). The underlying principle of this immune system, combined with a natural genetic repair pathway, has become the highly influential CRISPR-Cas9 gene editing technology – a "programmable" (Jinek et al., 2012; Liao et al., 2015) and cost-effective cut-and-paste technology for manipulating the genetic code of virtually any organism: fish, flies, mice, monkeys, and many more. Recognized as the 2015 Science Magazine Breakthrough of the Year, CRISPR-Cas9 represents a new era in molecular biology. Deemed unethical for use on human DNA by one of the technology's inventors, for once inherited, it constitutes a permanent and irreversible change to human evolution (Abumrad and Krulwich, 2015b), it took just about 2 years until the first research lab edited a non-viable human embryo – with mixed success (Cyranoski and Reardon, 2015). The possibilities and implications are enormous: cure cancer and HIV, eradicate malaria, pluck invasive species, bring back creatures of the past, engineer human life without hereditary disease, and these are some of the initial ideas. Technically it is possible, and bio-ethicists can barely keep up with the exponential growth of research and patents in this area, with more than 1,200 CRISPR-Cas9 citations since the key paper was published in 2012 (Lewis, 2015). As a volatile domain for investment, it is also heavily invested in the protection of intellectual property – a dynamic familiar to us from the GMO monopolies of the agricultural sector. The monetary value of the investment resides the genetic code, the software of life. Sequencing genetic code has already progressed to an inexpensive mail-order business; Cas9 added the capacity to rewrite DNA for double-digit dollars per edit.

> If, as Stephen Wolfram, Edward Fredkin, and Harold Morowitz maintain, the universe is fundamentally computational, code is elevated to the lingua franca not only of computers but of all physical reality. (Hayles, 2005, p. 15)

This brief discussion of CRISPR-Cas9 already highlighted the enormous stakes involved in this new technology. When a group of scientists moved to regulate "gene drives" (Oye et al., 2014), a CRISPR-based technique to edit the reproductive capacity of an entire species, gene drive capacity did not exist. A year later, Californian scientists engineered a gene drive in fruit flies, which was adapted to mosquitos the same year, one step closer to eradicating malaria or in other words to eradicate the species that carries the disease (Callaway, 2015). There are few technological advances more impactful than gene drives. There peril of unforeseen consequence is stark, and the need for safety precautions is obvious. So what are we to do to ensure that an accident in the research lab does not result in an escape and the accidental eradication of an entire species? The computational answer for a safety measure is a kill switch or circuit breaker – a principle familiar to anyone who operates hazardous machinery. CRISPR-based DNAi "kill switches" (Caliando and Voigt, 2015) program genes to survive only when a particular synthetic substance is present, i.e., in the lab. If that substance is absent, it renders the modified genetic material irreversibly obsolete within minutes. The convenient side effect is also "useful to degrade the associated DNA to reduce environmental release and protect intellectual property . . . You just plug in all the systems you want erased, and when the system is turned on it will erase that DNA and largely leave the other DNA in place" (Brandom, 2015).

Independent of Wolfram's and Morowitz's claim that the universe is fundamentally computational, computationally trained scientists draw naturally from computational solutions afforded by the regime of computation. CRISPR's contribution to genetic biology further tightens the feedback loop between information and matter. Moving forward, we will make health and reproductive care decisions involving CRISPR/Cas9 technology in a ubiquitous space where computational and ethical competencies merge. When promise meets conscience, cautionary voices can easily sound conservative and seem irrelevant. Even if the voice belongs to the creator of the aforementioned mosquito gene drive, "It's not going to go anywhere until the social science advances to the point where we can handle it," he says. "We're not about to do anything foolish" (Ledford and Callaway, 2015).

> Whereas the "human" has since the Enlightenment been associated with rationality, free will, autonomy and a celebration of consciousness as the seat of identity, the posthuman in its more nefarious forms is construed as an informational pattern that happens to be instantiated in a biological substrate. (Hayles, 2006b, p. 16)

Let us journey Powers of Ten from the fundamental principles of molecular immune systems to a telescope of planetary scale, adding the computational significance of synchronicity to the discussion, to illustrate how cogninodes can be made up recursively of smaller autonomous units. The Event Horizon Telescope – "a telescope as big as the world" (Overbye, 2015, para 1) – seeks the unseeable at the center of the Milky Way. Astronomers suspect a massive black hole named Sagittarius A* behind a haze of gases "about 50 million miles across . . . into which the equivalent of four million suns has evidently disappeared" (2015). Since Albert Einstein formulated the general theory of relativity a hundred years ago, there was no actual proof of the theory up to this point. The Event Horizon Telescope was conceived with the fundamental goal to finally proof the theory by determining the exact dimension of Sagittarius A*. An individual telescope on Earth is unable to penetrate the haze as its wavelength is too long to see through it. To reduce the wavelength, a quantum shift in magnitude was necessary. The solution was to create a planetary telescope megastructure, a network of individual telescopes that could be synchronized. The effort involved "20 universities, observatories, research institutions and government agencies" (2015). Each telescope got a new short-wavelength receiver and an atomic clock accurate to 1 second every 100 million years to ensure synchronicity. Bursts of data were then captured individually during matching time intervals, and then transported to a super computer at M.I.T., tasked to find collective interference patterns months after the data was gathered from the remote areas of the planet. When the first composite image of the black hole emerges, Sagittarius A*'s size and shape would "provide a judgment on general relativity" (2015, para 73).

Judgment day for Einstein's general theory of relativity finally came by listening rather than looking, on September 14, 2015, when a pair of L-shaped antennas in Hanford, Washington and Livingston, Louisiana detected the collision of two black holes from about 1.2 billion years ago. Forty years in the making, this successful and groundbreaking effort by the LIGO Laser Interferometer Gravitational-Wave Observatory (Abbott et al., 2016) is now going planetary scale, moving out into space. The new LISA program is ongoing and aims to improve previous LIGO results by "two orders of magnitude" (European Space Agency, 2016).

These dynamics make unmistakably clear that computers are no longer merely tools (if they ever were) but are complex systems that increasingly produce the conditions, ideologies, assumptions, and practices that help to constitute what we call reality. (Hayles, 2005, p. 6)

Rooted in fundamental research, the molecular and planetary systems discussed so far demonstrate machine cognizers in a range of scales, contexts, and applications. Resulting data can be captured and synchronized in a time continuum, enabling computational processes to unfold at any consecutive point in time and at the speed of Moore's law – until a particular inference pattern can be corroborated. Computational inference generally builds on captured data, or capta, which is "taken not given, constructed as an interpretation of the phenomenal world, not inherent in it" (Drucker, 2014, p. 128) – upon which qualitative knowledge production can ensue. Visual forms of knowledge production have a long history – the most well-known historic artifact being John Snow's 1854 map of cholera outbreaks in London (Rogers, 2013). "Art as visual research" using "thinking machines" began in 1961, "a little-known story" (Rosen, Weibel, Fritz, and Gattin, 2011) about the New Tendencies movement in the advent of computation that began in Zagreb, Yugoslavia. It exceeds the scope of this chapter.

In a sphere seemingly unfazed by geopolitical or economic constraints, fundamental research by international research conglomerates suits as case study to illustrate the principles of planetary computing. Individuals and geopolitical subjects, in contrast, are likely more familiar with inference patterns through consumer data and communication (DoJ, 2016), perhaps voting behavior (Biesecker and Bykowicz, 2016), and potentially law enforcement (*Facial Recognition*, 2015) and national security (Ackerman and Thielman, 2016). It is an opaque space, occasionally resold to new stakeholders if privately owned (Abumrad and Krulwich, 2015a). The stark differences in regards to jurisdiction and geopolicy come into critical focus when we consider the private domain of the computational regime, which we will do next.

MAPPING THE COGNISPHERE

The 21st century will rather be a conservative century . . . human conservatism can no longer be denied in the long term. In the 20th and also the 19th century, people tried to identify themselves with progress. Not only to experience progress, but to be progress. The individual of the 20th century was the self-revolutionary, the self-progressive, the self-liberal. In the 21st century, all people will be conservative – based on the fact that truly progressive will only be the devices and algorithms. And man will lag behind like an old cumbersome biomass as an eternal rearguard of development.

(Peter Sloterdijk, 2014)

To understand computationally redefined geopolitical boundaries and control structures at a deeper level, we will consider closely two thorough and far-reaching sources: Alexander Galloway's *Protocol* (2004) and Benjamin Bratton's *(Black) Stack* (2016). Galloway examines "how control exists after decentralization," and the power structures that he sees expressed in the technical protocols governing data networks, which becomes particularly relevant to us geopolitically. Bratton illuminates aspects of "geography, jurisdiction, and sovereignty" within the "platform-as-totality" and its users, an "accidental megastructure . . . that produces new territories in its image" (2014, para 2). He uses the scalar of "the Stack" dissected into "six interdependent layers: Earth, Cloud, City, Address, Interface, User" (2016, p. 11). Both authors conceptualize the computational regime by way of topology.

In Bratton's view, it all fits together. The megastructure that he outlines takes the form of "a vast (if also incomplete), pervasive (if also irregular) software and hardware Stack" (2014, para 1). The Stack redefines transnational jurisdiction and labor, rewires memory and pedagogy, and refocuses natural resources. He sees a conflict over the geometry of political geography "bound by the territorial integrity of the state," where Cloud platforms are "displacing, if not also replacing, traditional core functions of states" (2014, para 7). There is a lot in there. The "dire inevitability" of the "computational totality-to-come" seems infinitely more discrete and all-encompassing than most incrementalist optimization theories would let us think. The Stack adds hierarchy to the cognisphere and reminds us how each information layer might "grind against the grain" of the other (2014, para 6). Parallel to Hayles notion of software as "interpolated ideology," Bratton sees platforms not only as a "technical architecture; they are also institutional form." He seeks geopolitical theory to develop "models for the organization of durable alter-totalities which command the force of law, if not necessarily its forms and formality" (2014, para 12).

> Planetary-scale computation takes different forms at different scales: energy grids and mineral sourcing; chthonic cloud infrastructure; urban software and public service privatization; massive universal addressing systems; interfaces drawn by the augmentation of the hand, of the eye, or dissolved into objects; users both overdetermined by self-quantification and exploded by the arrival of legions of nonhuman users (sensors, cars,

robots). Instead of seeing the various species of contemporary computational technologies as so many different genres of machines, spinning out on their own, we should instead see them as forming the body of an accidental megastructure. (Bratton, 2014, p. 1)

The "durable alter-totalities which command the force of law" are governed by 47 US Code § 230: "No provider or user of an interactive computer service shall be treated as the publisher or speaker of any information provided by another information content provider" ("47 US Code § 230," 1996) This is a core US Statute that holds platforms harmless, extended to other nations through distributed data centers. The "safe harbor" agreement (*Safe Harbor*, 2015) that governs data exchange between data centers between the United States and Europe essentially redraws territorial boundaries – undermining the sovereignty of states through clandestine surveillance programs such as PRISM (Scott, 2015). The key principle of 47 US Code § 230 is to immunize web services and content providers from the harms committed by third-party users. Its litigation history ("Section 230," 2015) shows how broadly immunity is granted since it became law in 1996 ("Reno vs.," 1997). Formulated before networked things inhabited the World Wide Web, this statute no longer fits the requirements of a globally distributed network of machine cognizers and cloud software services.

The contradiction at the heart of protocol is that it has to standardize in order to liberate. It has to be fascistic and unilateral in order to be utopian. (Galloway, 2004, p. 95)

In fact, the global information map was redrawn with very broad strokes on October 6, 2015, when the European Court of Justice declared a US-EU Safe Harbor Framework (*Safe Harbor*, 2015) invalid (Scott, 2015) – illustrating the ideological differences on privacy and speech. The ruling affects personal data and social media and highlights the territorial dimension of data flows, giving new relevance to the location of data infrastructures and the investments that go along with it (*Europe's Top*, 2016).

The Right to be Forgotten provides evidence of the contested geopolitics of personal data. Tackling some of the most cherished ideological values – freedom of expression and the right to privacy, a French court asserted the human right of an individual to determine their life in an autonomous way and ordered Google to remove search results deemed misleading and inappropriate by an individual user (Hern, 2015). Google complied locally on google.fr, but refused to do so on the main google.com domain, appealing the ruling (CURIA – Documents, 2014; "InfoCuria," 2015). Regulators justified their verdict this way: "Contrary to what Google has stated, this decision does not show any willingness on the part of the CNIL to apply French law extraterritorially. It simply requests full observance of European legislation by non European players offering their services in Europe" (2015). The Right to be Forgotten breaks new ground in the dispute between information and territory, illuminating the distinct intercontinental interpretations of freedom and expression, reminding us also that data packets do flow not only in and out of tax havens but also into contested safe harbors, transgressing local jurisdictions in the process ("Facebook's Data," 2011). Safe Harbor was declared invalid because a 27-year-old Austrian graduate student argued that "Europeans' online data was misused when Facebook was said to have cooperated with the N.S.A.'s PRISM program" (Scott, 2015). However, what looks like a decisive move back toward territorial sovereignty makes also clear that courts have no adequate tools to deter violators. For platforms worth tens of billions, "the agency's one-off maximum financial penalty of 150,000 euros, or about $160,000, is essentially a mere rounding error" (*Europe's Top*, 2016). It confirms that the platform overwhelms the territory, and the protocol hollows the territory's sovereignty.

Legal scholar Lawrence Lessig ascertains that "code is law" (2010, p. 1), because it regulates the changing landscape of cyberspace in a way that is less free and anonymous. Lessig argues against a false choice between regulation and no regulation, identifying code itself as the potential agent of change. He suggests the World Wide Web Consortium's P3P project as one approach to fill the void. P3P enables web sites to standardize privacy practices in a way that can be retrieved and interpreted easily by a user, allowing them to be informed and automate decision-making based on these practices (Wenning and Schunter, 2006, para 1). In the end, Lessig makes clear that it always comes down to the fact that it is people who write code. Choosing no regulation and self-government as the preferred and predominant paradigm of the commercial web, he argues, leaves the determination of collective values to expert coders. The collective has no role in the matter. When the government plays no role, private interests take its place. In his argument, Lessig questions why private interests should be considered any better than the flawed character of government regulation (2010, p. 255).

In an information society run by coders and knowledge workers, routing information to new harbors and havens also has the consequence of rerouting information labor. According to McKenzie Wark, the growing separation of territory and information produces an abstract new terrain which he calls "third nature" – manifested in finance, copyright, and supply chains. It extends the notion of second nature, industry, which in turn has redefined first nature through "flows of energy, labor, and raw materials"

(2015). In third nature, economic activities become vectors within a network of flows that can be re-routed any time if "supply becomes erratic," "labor at the processing site becomes difficult," or profit margins become too slim (2015, para 29). Wark's "vectoralist class . . . does not control land or industry anymore, just information" (2015, para 30). The content creators who "inform" third nature, "the hacker class" (2015, para 35), are an information elite with stock options, followed by some specialized workers in control positions who run information infrastructure, and a broader third tier of knowledge workers who engage in "in-sourcing" (2015, para 39) labor. Wark constructs his topology on the vector space from "the dense network of information that overlays the territory which enables the landscape to be stretched, compressed, folded, and twisted into new shapes" (2015, para 27).

> If outsourcing sends a worker's job overseas to another worker, insourcing assigns the hacker's job to anyone who will perform the task for free. Thus the cooperative effort and the commons of information is itself treated as a resource from which to extract interest. (Wark, 2015)

Assigning a hacker's jobs to anyone who does the task for free in a cooperative effort should ring a bell for anyone who has written code recently as part of a team or in a public context. Github, the predominant code in-sourcing platform – with the occasional contribution from journalism, science, and policy – is a free-range pasture where cogninodes are born and raised. Defaulting to public, code can be private for a monthly fee. Synchronizing asynchronous labor is no trivial task. The platform's exponential growth indicates its popularity and also the size of the growing class of hackers. It works so well that even Google shut its own service and moved over to the platform (DiBona, 2015). On Github, code gets a chance to grow up and be popular, in a highly coordinated ballet of push and pull, commit, review, and merge (*Github Help*, 2016).

Interest can be extracted from the information commons by starring and forking projects, submitting bug fixes and pull requests – logged exactly, character by character. Deleting content also adds a copy to the version stack, in keeping with Github's archival totality. Precise and systematic feedback signals to the commons individual proficiency and productivity, by itself incentive and motivation to maintain free labor in exchange for status currency. As a platform, Github is a great example for the positive feedback loop that Bruno Latour sees to "get under way as soon as one is able to muster a large number of mobile, readable, visible resources" (1981, p. 12). Github makes inscriptions "combinable, superimposable and could, with only a minimum of cleaning up, be integrated" (1981, p. 4) in whatever you are coding on. Latour sees inscriptions as "immutable mobiles" (1981, p. 7), media objects that can travel "without withering away . . . immutable, presentable, readable and combinable with one another" (1981, p. 7). Designed for standardizing inscriptions, dissemination, and positive feedback, Github fulfills all of Latour's criteria for immutable mobiles, with the effect that "no matter how inaccurate these traces might be at first, they will all become accurate just as a consequence of more mobilization and more immutability. A mechanism is invented to irreversibly capture accuracy" (1981, p. 12).

As a platform, Github tracks contribution traffic and frequency through charts and graphs, including a punch card that shows individual contributions down to hourly patterns. This is new currency valued by an emerging hiring industry called work-force science. It hires knowledge workers directly based on automated indicators provided by platforms like Github (Richtel, 2013).

> Next to states and markets, platforms are a third form, coordinating through fixed protocols while scattering free-range Users watched over in loving, if also disconcertingly omniscient, grace. (Bratton, 2014)

What are the motivations to write code in a commons? Free and open source software (F/OSS) plays a significant role in the creation and dissemination of economic value. Because gift economies are lacking the immediate monetary exchange of wages, freelance work, or human intelligence tasks ("Amazon Mechanical Turk," 2005, para 2), it is also a constant source of free market fascination. F/OSS depends and thrives on protocolean standardization. It enables flexibility through standardized application interfaces and licensing agreements. Significant effort goes into documenting and contextualizing code, so the source can be read against a particular need, building trust, and adding value. In an early and widely quoted report commissioned by the European Commission that surveyed and analyzed F/OSS in regards to policy, market implications, and security, motivations to engage in F/OSS included: "learn and develop new skills" (79 percent), "share knowledge and skills" (50 percent), "participate in a new form of cooperation" (35 percent), "improve OS/FS products of other developers" (34 percent), "participate in the OS/FS scene" (31 percent), "think that software should not be a proprietary good" (30 percent), "improve my job opportunities" (24 percent), and "get help in realizing a good idea for a software product" (24 percent) (Aiyer, Glott, Krieger, and Robles, 2002). F/OSS is a gift economy that still exchanges economic value, along with the social norms and customs put forth by the information commons.

FROM PERSON TO PER CAPITA

Labor practices grounded in territory have shifted not only in regards to recruitment practices, but also through data-driven performance analysis assessed near real time based on sensor data from machine cognizers. In her account on "gamification of performance management," using "big data and the cloud," Esther Kaplan investigates the change in labor practices since the implementation of telematics, a telecommunication and informatics approach for the UPS fleet base using "more than 200 sensors on each delivery truck that track everything from backup speeds to stop times to seat-belt use" (2015). Kaplan shadows a driver, whose delivery quota and timing is set by UPS's algorithm, exceeded by many drivers – in some cases up to 4 hours. "These days, on an average shift, Rose makes 110 stops and delivers 400 packages. He leaves his house at seven in the morning and seldom gets home before nine-thirty at night, when he is so exhausted that he rarely makes it to bed – he grabs dinner and passes out on the couch." It is a glimpse into the other side of premium delivery culture. To the supervisor, the person zipping through intersections, rushing, and jaywalking looks like this:

> For every driver within his purview, he can monitor a neighborhood map with the driver's route traced in teal and the stops marked and numbered. Another window shows a complete list of addresses on the route and the number of packages per address. A third window shows the driver's speed, whether the engine is off or on, whether the bulkhead – the massive, rolling rear door – is open or closed, whether the seat belt is engaged, whether the driver is backing up, and more. In the center of the screen, a fourth window shows the number of minutes allotted per stop and whether the driver is under or over that target. (Kaplan, 2015, p. 33)

Advertised as a safety technology that tracks seat-belt compliance and backing speeds, UPS credits telematics to have "lifted seat-belt compliance to an 'almost perfect' 98.8 percent," explained by one driver's approach that "he will buckle the seat belt behind him and not wear it" (Kaplan, 2015, p. 34). Posthumans should not be underestimated in their creative capacity to counteract machine discipline. Rose, the driver, describes the inverse-panoptic discipline signaled by telematics this way: "People get intimidated and they work faster . . . 'It's like when they whip animals. But this is a mental whip'" (2015, p. 34). Beyond UPS, readily available vehicle systems plug directly into our car's telematics port, where a comprehensive log of vehicle data is available for transmission (NASA's Toyota Study, 2011). It is used by some insurance companies to track clients (Wingfield, 2015), and by some of us to track teenage drivers. Any platform with read and write access has inherent security risks also, shown by security experts who "[i]n a controlled test, they turned on the Jeep Cherokee's radio and activated other inessential features before rewriting code embedded in the entertainment system hardware to issue commands through the internal network to steering, brakes and the engine" (Bilton, 2013). The metrics that workers in the field feed into centralized management systems are also used to discipline the growing number of teleworkers who work from home. "Studies show that people tend to work more hours at home than when they're in the office, he said, but watching their employees work gives managers 'a sense of security'" (2013, p. 38). Typically, supervisors have access to a teleworker's computer screen, and teleworkers who speak with clients are audio monitored as well.

Kaplan goes on to investigate the leading freelance portal now called Upwork (Upwork, 2015) which is coordinating work relations for about 10 million freelancers. Freelancers are drawn to the platform because it gives them guaranteed payment in exchange for a 10 percent fee. Similar to a teleworker employee who uses company equipment to track every keystroke, Upwork's hourly wage guarantee entails that the freelancer "must allow the company deep inside your personal computer" (Steyerl, 2010). The company uses a Work Diary that records a screenshot every 10 minutes, independent of what's on the screen, including "minute-by-minute keystroke and mouse data, along with a productivity rating" (2015, p. 38). Proclaimed not to be a surveillance system – because freelancers can choose to delete any screenshot that shows inappropriate content – the 10 minutes of work attached to that screenshot is deleted along with the fee. Nolan, a graphic designer interviewed by Kaplan, reflects on the Work Diary this way: "knowing that someone's watching the process, it's harder to take risks." Nolan's interpolates consciously, recognizing how the machine disciplines his creative process.

> If the panopticon effect is when you don't know if you are being watched or not, and so you behave as if you are, then the inverse panopticon effect is when you know you are being watched but act as if you aren't. (Bratton, 2014, p. 9)

Payment Protection assures clients who hire freelancers on the platform that they "only pay the work [they] approve," with the advertised premise to "work together, effortlessly . . . stress-free." It is a business model that builds on a trust vacuum, outsourcing the enforcement of discipline to the algorithm. Sherry Turkle sees this dynamic as part of a greater contemporary phenomenon that "we expect more from technology and less from each other" (2011). As of this writing, the highest average hourly rate posted on the platform across more than 22 thousand jobs was less than $25 USD, featured categories averaged just above $16 (*Job Search Results*, 2015) – bringing the median hourly wage for the skilled labor featured on the site in proximity to what some US cities have declared minimum wage. Hito Steyerl compares the "freelance" to the figure of the medieval mercenary, detached from a master or government. She counters common liberal ideas of freedom, through expression and pursuit of happiness, with the negative freedoms from regulation and public goods, such as the "freedom from social bonds, freedom from solidarity, freedom from certainty or predictability, freedom from employment or labor, freedom from culture, public transport, education, or anything public at all" (2013, para 5).

While the "lance-for-hire" (Steyerl, 2013, para 13) in the Upwork model still follows to the traditional model of currency exchange for approved time and rendered services, "the artificial artificial intelligence" model of Amazon's Mechanical Turk labor platform deliberately goes where computation cannot or will not ("Amazon Mechanical Turk," 2005). The tagline "artificial artificial intelligence" points to a reversal of roles, equivalent to human farmers hand-pollinating fruit trees (Pearson, 2014). The Mechanical Turk facilitates micro-compensation for minute tasks. Highly paid human intelligence tasks typically ask for transcribing audio or video. Sometimes a HIT is more idiosyncratic, like finding a billionaire aviator gone missing in stacks of satellite images (*Steve Fossett*, 2007). The platform's name is a play on the seventeenth-century Mechanical Turk chess playing automaton who beat unsuspecting Napoleon Bonaparte and Benjamin Franklin. The automaton was in fact operated by a human chess grandmaster sitting inside the machine's body. As of this writing, HITs averaged hourly less than $3.

> The Cloud Polis draws revenue from the cognitive capital of its Users, who trade attention and microeconomic compliance in exchange for global infrastructural services, and in turn, it provides each of them with an active discrete online identity and the license to use this infrastructure. (Bratton, 2014, p. 4)

Continuous feedback and platform-enhanced productivity represents in Jonathan Crary's view "the end of sleep," a sign of extended 24–7 consumerism, with new labor pressures depleting times of rest and regeneration. Citing Deleuze's "continuous interface," he argues that the seamless "engagement with illuminated screens of diverse kinds that unremittingly demand interest or response" (2014, p. 75) is in conflict with the need for a balance between "the exhaustion resulting from labor or activity in the world, and the regeneration that regularly occurs within an enclosed and shaded domesticity" (2014, p. 22), in reference to Hannah Arendt. Besides the end of sleep, the focus of Crary's argument is directed at the accelerated tempo of consumption and cognitive exchange.

OUR DAILY TURING TEST

The odds are not in favor of humans when individuals are stacked against fast, sophisticated, multimillion dollar machine cognizers (Sang-hun and Markoff, 2016). Human supervision is increasingly coerced or left to agree with a computed prediction, especially when time is short and the stakes are high. Hayles has shown that "the interpolation of the user into the machinic system does not require his or her conscious recognition of how he or she is being disciplined by the machine to become a certain kind of subject" (2005, p. 61). This assessment is further substantiated by the "robotic revolution" in which P.W. Singer illustrates numerous friendly fire incidents, where decisions have to be made in hostile contexts within seconds (2009, p. 125).

> Everyday interactions replay the Turing Test over and over. Is there a person behind this machine, and if so, how much? In time, the answer will matter less, and the postulation of human (or even carbon-based life) as the threshold measure of intelligence and as the qualifying gauge of a political ethics may seem like tasteless vestigial racism, replaced by less anthropocentric frames of reference. (Bratton, 2014)

Friendly fire of a different kind occurred in the financial industry during the so-called flash crash of 2010, where more than 1 trillion dollars moved through the markets in 36 minutes (Kirilenko, Kyle, Samadi, and Tuzun, 2015). Since then, the US Securities and Exchange Commission (SEC) has "voted to require the national securities exchanges and the Financial Industry Regulatory Authority (FINRA) to establish a market-wide consolidated audit trail that will significantly enhance regulators' ability to monitor and analyze trading activity" (SEC Approves, 2012). The protocolean rule of standardization across exchanges, applied with the goal to bring oversight and accountability to an opaque market for algorithmic trading, remains largely unrealized and challenged in court – along with many other parts of the Wall Street Reform and Consumer Protection Act ("State National," 2014). The mantra of human supervision becomes a fantasy in situations where algorithmic volatility escalates at imperceptible speed, as evidenced by 14 seconds on May 6, 2010, where "[b]etween 2:45:13 and 2:45:27, HFTs traded over 27,000 contracts, which accounted for about 49 percent of the total trading volume" ("Findings regarding," 2010). Human oversight over algorithmic speed will further deteriorate at the rate of Moore's law times the scale of the cloud. Comparisons tend toward the abstract, but when DeepMind thinks about 10,000 Go moves per second, human mastery over such a particular task is called into question (Sang-hun and Markoff, 2016). To compensate, one posthuman option is extensive record keeping, so human oversight can account for systemic failures in hindsight through archival totality. SEC's analysis of the high-frequency trade transactions over 36 minutes in 2010 took 5 years. Alternatively, the kill-switch comes to mind again, using a circuit breaker approach for financial markets – as illustrated by the suspension of the Chinese stock exchange for 15 minutes when the market plunged by 5 percent, or even suspending trade entirely for the rest of the day at 7 percent (Kim and Wang, 2016). Both options absorb significant resources and reduce trust in the financial system, resulting in further losses. Because heavy-handed human oversight in automated markets only provides temporary relief, the circuit breaker approach for financial markets was quickly abandoned.

When Goldman Sachs hired Sergey Aleynikov to improve the speed of its HFT trading platform, he encountered an "amalgamation" of estimated "sixty million lines of code in it" (Lewis, 2014, p. 136). Since Goldman is located just across the street of Nasdaq, Aleynikov knew that there was friction in Goldman's platform. He set out to rewrite it from scratch, sending code to himself on a weekly basis to his repository (2014). The jurors who found him guilty "lacked experience programming computers" (2014, p. 245). Lewis, the author of *Flash Boys*, assembled a group of experts from the industry to assess what Aleynikov had done, "[A]ll of them had followed the case in the newspapers and noted the shiver it had sent through the spines of Wall Street's software developers . . . 'Every tech programmer out there got the message: Take code and you could go to jail. It was huge'" (2014, p. 247). Aleynikov got sentenced to 8 years in jail because he did something that "was common practice for Wall Street programmers" (2014) – to use a "repository to store code and deleting one's bash history" (2014, p. 248). Both of those aspects were convincing the jury that he was stealing code and that he was covering his tracks. After a year in jail, federal and state courts overturned the verdict and determined that due to a lack evidence and probable cause, the arrest was illegal.

> [C]ode is the only language that is executable (Galloway, 2004, p. 165).
> Code is the first language that actually does what it says – it is a machine
> for converting meaning into action. (2004, p. 166)

"The next 100 startups are going to be like the last 100, just with AI," proclaimed a presenter at a startup convention in Manhattan. Used as a marketing device, artificial intelligence is often equated to the "secret sauce" in a startup concept, automatically searching for categories, patterns, and insights. The focus on big consumer data, versus more generalized cybernetic notions of intelligent machines, has propelled data science to the top of popular career choices. The vocational online education platform Udacity guarantees tuition back if a student does not get hired within 6 months of graduating their *Nanodegree Plus* machine learning offering (*Nanodegree Plus*, 2016). Google demonstrates its artificial neural networks through "inceptionism" (Mordvintsev, Olah, and Tyka, 2015), the visual results of image classification tasks, illustrating how classification bias plays a role in any machine learning process. In a typical machine learning task, a perceptron (Minsky and Papert, 1969) weighs the algorithmic output in an adaptive feedback loop, which can occur unsupervised, semi-supervised, supervised, or reinforced. In a supervised setting, the inceptionist bias relies inherently on the teacher's input. In an unsupervised setting, the topological structure of an adaptive neural network still retains the "hand" of the network designer who implies how a network node transforms the stimulating signal.

In a neural network such as Facebook's M messaging service, training can be conducted by the collective cognitive effort of more than a billion daily users. Competing with Siri and Now, M integrates seamlessly into the social media platform by getting rid of UI distinctions between a Facebook friend and M. People interact with M "as if it were one of their friends" (Dredge, 2015), leaving Facebook's real-name policy only for human users (*Facebook: What*, 2015). M is "artificial intelligence that's trained and supervised by people" (2015) echoing a familiar mantra that there will always be a human in the loop (Singer, 2009). Inspired by the central nervous system of a biological brain, the computational model of a neural network goes back to second-order cybernetics and the school of thought attributed to Heinz von Foerster, who answered the question "whether there is a relation between the human brain and the computer with 'yes and no.'" Then he added: "No computer is a brain, but all brains are computers." "Second-order or 'new' cybernetics of the 1970s which revolved around biology and organisms supplanted 'old' cybernetics, focused on physics and control systems to construct a model of the mind" (1982). Cognitive scientist and AI pioneer Marvin Minsky built the first neural network learning machine in 1951 and coined the notion of the perceptron in 1969.

Machine cognizers trained by the collective cognitive labor of humans are making it increasingly difficult to decipher as the output is artificial. Turing's 30 percent threshold is put to the test in the yearly Loebner price challenge ("Home Page," 2015) – won by Thomas Whalen in 1994 who coined the term cognisphere. Rollo Carpenter, the creator of the online chatbot Cleverbot (*Talking to Machines*, 2015), put it this way: "The day will come not to far down the road, where Cleverbot becomes so interesting to talk to that people will be talking to it all day every day" (Abumrad and Krulwich, 2015a). Cleverbot's speech output is generated in its entirety based on human interactions. His comment is based on how some users talk to Cleverbot 11 hours straight (2015). Trained by 3 million monthly teachers, it is a quaint number compared to the number of Facebook trainers. Facebook's Trust Engineering Group (*The Trust Engineers*, 2015), renamed Protect and Care Team after its large-scale experiments in manipulating user emotions through selectively biased images (2015), is aware of its cognitive potential and research value. Sample sizes of this magnitude are unheard-of in the social sciences, and not available to the public due to its monetary value (Parker and Corasaniti, 2014).

> Are all proxy composite users one User? Is anything with an IP address a User? If not, why not? If this throne is reserved for one species – humans – when is any one animal of that species being a User, and when is it not? Is it a User anytime that it is generating information? If so, that policy would in practice crisscross and trespass some of our most basic concepts of the political, and for that reason alone it may be a good place to start. (Bratton, 2014)

The machine learning principles in supervised and unsupervised settings illustrate that machine cognizers should not be mistaken as neutral, impartial, or unbiased. Nor should machine learning platforms be held harmless, shruggingly pointing to user bias when their artificial intelligence products fail: "Google has apologized after its new photo app labelled two black people as 'gorillas'" (Kasperkevic, 2015). The mantra in automation – that there will be always a human in the loop when supervision is desired, and there will be no human in the loop when private emails are data-mined – is indicative of the opportunistic interpretation of machine agency. The rogue trader or software engineer becomes the rogue machine learning algorithm. Since digressions are protected by trade secrets and intellectual property, antidiscrimination circuit breakers and oversight cannot be deployed from the outside. Still, when cogninodes act, speak, or take lives on our behalf (Grothoff and Porup, 2016), we remain implicated.

PASSPORT TO THE COGNISPHERE

Lev Manovich has shown that "[s]oftware has become our interface to the world, to others, to our memory and our imagination – a universal language through which the world speaks, and a universal engine on which the world runs" (2013, p. 2). The path to cognicitizenship requires coding capacity and machine learning literacy, so we can effectively run our daily Turing tests on interpolated systems that have the capacity to evolve (Sims, 1994). Those anthropotechnic competencies are one part of the story. Its humanist counterpart balances how we address a new form of digital divide between cognicitizens and noncitizens. In the cognisphere, work follows information – to discrete information hubs and havens where conditions are opportune. As labor platforms become increasingly standardized and employer risk democratized, the much larger group of non-cognicitizens is more vulnerable and disenfranchised – free from labor, bound to geopolitical territory. All of us are disciplined by machines and protocols to some degree, but we have choices to make as it comes to propagating telematics as the new normal at work and in our private lives. As experts working longer hours we might compensate for less time to rest, run chores, and regenerate by way of premium subscriptions and prime delivery. A new generation of cognicitizens requires the social and cultural competencies that rein in technical proficiency if necessary – let us call it anthropotechnic autoimmunity – which can be attained through a liberal arts education that takes both technical capacity and humanist competencies seriously. "Design as innovation just isn't strong enough of an idea by itself. We need to talk a lot more about design as immunization, actually preventing certain innovations that we don't want from happening" (Bratton, 2013).

> Education sees the psychology of the student as analogous to a computer whose software should be continually updated to function inside contemporary information networks, to survive all possible virus attacks from the outside world, to incorporate the viruses coming from the outside into his or her own software, and-in the best sense of modernism's subversive ambition-even to start a hacker attack against the software of the others. (Groys, 2009, p. 28)

Cyberneticist Norbert Wiener pointed already in 1961 to the need for a shared language among experts: "The mathematician need not have the skill to conduct a physiological experiment, but he must have the skill to understand one, to criticize one, and to suggest one. The physiologist need not be able to prove a certain mathematical theorem, but he must be able to grasp its physiological significance and to tell the mathematician for what he should look" (1961, pp. 3–4). Why should this insight not be relevant today? Since Peter Sloterdijk first stirred public debate on the ethical dimensions of "antrophotechne" – showing the philosophical and ethical dimensions of genetic modification and "betterment" – we have had a chance to catch up and make it public discourse. Instead, cutting-edge scientists today claim that their research is "not going to go anywhere until the social science advances to the point where we can handle it" (Ledford and Callaway, 2015). As a consequence, the social and cultural competencies of the humanities remain critical, and must step up to the technological issues of our time.

> To remain a humanist, one must become a cyberneticist. A technohuman culture that wants to be more than successful barbarism requires above all two things: psychological education, and cultural translatability. Mathematicians must become poets, cyberneticists religious philosophers, doctors composers, computer scientists shamans. But was humanity ever anything different than the art to create intersections? (Sloterdijk, 2007).

REFERENCES

47 U.S. Code § 230 – Protection for private blocking and screening of offensive material. (1996). Retrieved August 20, 2015, from www.law.cornell.edu/uscode/text/47/230. Accessed online March 3, 2016.

Abbott et al. (2016). Observation of gravitational waves from a Binary Black Hole Merger. *Physical Review Letters*, 116(6). Retrieved from http://link.aps.org/doi/10.1103/PhysRevLett.116.061102. Accessed online March 3, 2016.

Abumrad, J. and Krulwich, R. (2015a, June 18). *Eye in the Sky*. Retrieved March 12, 2016, from www.radiolab.org/story/eye-sky/. Accessed online March 3, 2016.

 (2015b, June 6). *Antibodies Part 1: CRISPR*. Retrieved August 15, 2015, from www.radiolab.org/story/antibodies-part-1-crispr/. Accessed online March 3, 2016.

Ackerman, S. and Thielman, S. (2016, February 09). *US intelligence chief: We might use the internet of things to spy on you*. Retrieved February 09, 2016, from www.theguardian.com/technology/2016/feb/09/internet-of-things-smart-home-devices-government-surveillance-james-clapper. Accessed online March 3, 2016.

Aiyer, G.R., Glott, R., Krieger, B., and Robles, G. (2002, June). *Free/Libre and open source software: Survey and study FLOSS*. Retrieved February 05, 2016, from http://flossproject.org/report/Final4.htm#_Toc13908258. Accessed online March 3, 2016.

Amazon Mechanical Turk. (2005). Retrieved February 15, 2016, from www.mturk.com/mturk/help?helpPage=overview. Accessed online March 3, 2016.

Berridge, K.C. and Robinson, T.E. (1998). What is the role of dopamine in reward: Hedonic impact, reward learning, or incentive salience? *Brain Research Reviews*, 28(3), 309–69.

Biesecker, M. and Bykowicz, J. (2016, February 11). *Cruz app data collection helps campaign read minds of voters.* Retrieved February 22, 2016, from http://bigstory.ap.org/article/2db0fc93cf664a63909e26e708e91c67/cruz-app-data-collection-helps-campaign-read-minds-voters. Accessed online March 3, 2016.

Bilton, N. (2013, August 11). *Disruptions: As new targets for hackers, your car and your house.* Retrieved February 15, 2016, from http://bits.blogs.nytimes.com/2013/08/11/taking-over-cars-and-homes-remotely. Accessed online March 3, 2016.

Brandom, R. (2015, May 19). *Scientists develop new 'kill switch' to destroy genetically-modified organisms that escape.* Retrieved February 05, 2016, from www.theverge.com/2015/5/19/8625623/gmo-crispr-kill-switch-self-destructing-dna. Accessed online March 3, 2016.

Bratton, B.H. (2013, December 30). *New perspectives – What's wrong with TED talks?* Benjamin Bratton at TEDxSanDiego 2013 – Re:Think. Retrieved August 12, 2015.

(2014, March). *The black stack.* Retrieved www.e-flux.com/journal/the-black-stack/. Accessed online August 23, 2015.

(2016). *The stack: On software and sovereignty.* Cambridge, MA: MIT Press.

Brueck, H. (2016, February 26). *Here's why Chicago just made computer science a graduation requirement.* Retrieved March 07, 2016, from http://fortune.com/2016/02/26/chicago-computer-science/. Accessed online March 3, 2016.

Caliando, B.J. and Voigt, C.A. (2015). Targeted DNA degradation using a CRISPR device stably carried in the host genome. *Nature Communications*, 6, 6989.

Callaway, E. (2015). Mosquitoes engineered to pass down genes that would wipe out their species. *Nature.* Retrieved from http://www.nature.com/news/mosquitoes-engineered-to-pass-down-genes-that-would-wipe-out-their-species-1.18974. Accessed online February 5, 2016.

Carpenter, R. (2011, September 3). *Cleverbot comes very close to passing the Turing Test.* Retrieved February 16, 2016, from www.cleverbot.com/. Accessed online March 3, 2016.

Crary, J. (2014). *24/7: Late capitalism and the ends of sleep* (p. 144). London: Verso.

CURIA – Documents. (2014, May 13). Retrieved August 31, 2015, from http://curia.europa.eu/juris/document/document.jsf?docid=152065&mode=req&pageIndex=1&dir=&occ=first&part=1&text=&doclang=EN&cid=341631. Accessed online March 3, 2016.

Cyranoski, D. and Reardon, S. (2015, April 22). *Chinese scientists genetically modify human embryos.* Retrieved August 16, 2015, from www.nature.com/news/chinese-scientists-genetically-modify-human-embryos-1.17378. Accessed online March 3, 2016.

DARPA (2014). Defense Advanced Research Projects Agency: Where the future becomes now. Retrieved March 09, 2016, from www.darpa.mil/about-us/darpa-history-and-timeline. Accessed online March 3, 2016.

Deleuze, G. and Guattari, F. (1987). *A thousand plateaus: Capitalism and schizophrenia.* Minneapolis, MN: University of Minnesota Press.

Deresiewicz, W. (2015, September 1). The neoliberal arts: How college sold its soul to the market. *Harper's Magazine*, 25–32. Retrieved August 16, 2015, from http://harpers.org/archive/2015/09/the-neoliberal-arts/. Accessed online March 3, 2016.

DiBona, C. (2015, March 12). *Bidding farewell to Google Code*. Retrieved September 21, 2015, from http://google-opensource.blogspot.com.es/2015/03/farewell-to-google-code.html. Accessed online March 3, 2016.

DoJ. (2016, February 19). *Government's motion to compel Apple inc. to comply with this court's February 16, 2016 order compelling assistance in search*. Retrieved February 22, 2016, from https://assets.documentcloud.org/documents/2715926/Motion-to-Compel-Apple-Compliance.pdf. Accessed online March 3, 2016.

Dredge, S. (2015, August 27). *Facebook M virtual assistant will compete with Siri and Google Now*. Retrieved August 31, 2015, from www.theguardian.com/technology/2015/aug/27/facebook-m-virtual-assistant-siri-google-now. Accessed online March 3, 2016.

Drucker, J. (2014). *Graphesis: Visual forms of knowledge production*. Cambridge, MA: Harvard University Press.

European Space Agency. (2016, February 12). *LISA Pathfinder overview*. Retrieved February 21, 2016, from www.esa.int/Our_Activities/Space_Science/LISA_Pathfinder_overview. Accessed online March 3, 2016.

Facebook: What types of ID does Facebook accept? (2015, December). Retrieved February 16, 2016, from www.facebook.com/help/1590964641162185. Accessed online March 3, 2016.

Facebook's Data Pool (2011). Retrieved August 20, 2015, from http://europe-v-facebook.org/EN/Data_Pool/data_pool.html. Accessed online March 3, 2016.

Peter Sloterdijk interview (2014, June 12). Retrieved February 01, 2016, from www.youtube.com/watch?v=N8x-cp7SXAs. Accessed online March 3, 2016.

Findings regarding the market events of May 6, 2010. (2010, September 30). Retrieved August 31, 2015, from www.sec.gov/news/studies/2010/marketevents-report.pdf. Accessed online March 3, 2016.

Foerster, H.V. (1982). To know and to let know: An applied theory of knowledge. *Canadian Library Journal, 39*, 277–82.

Freightliner (2015). Retrieved February 23, 2016, from www.freightlinerinspiration.com/. Accessed online March 3, 2016.

Galloway, A. (2004). *Protocol how control exists after decentralization*. Cambridge, MA: MIT Press.

Gibbs, S. (2015, November 13). *Google's self-driving car gets pulled over for driving too slowly*. Retrieved February 05, 2016, from www.theguardian.com/technology/2015/nov/13/google-self-driving-car-pulled-over-driving-too-slowly?INTCMP=sfl. Accessed online March 3, 2016.

GitHub Help. (2016). Retrieved March 12, 2016, from https://help.github.com/articles/fork-a-repo/. Accessed online March 3, 2016.

Grothoff, C. and Porup, J.M. (2016, February 16). *The NSA's SKYNET program may be killing thousands of innocent people*. Retrieved February 29, 2016, from http://arstechnica.co.uk/security/2016/02/the-nsas-skynet-program-may-be-killing-thousands-of-innocent-people/. Accessed online March 3, 2016.

Groys, B. (2009). Education by infection. In H. Madoff (Ed.), *Art school: Propositions for the 21st century* (pp. 26–32). Cambridge, MA: MIT Press.

Hayles, N.K. (1999). *How we became posthuman: Virtual bodies in cybernetics, literature, and informatics*. Chicago, IL: University of Chicago Press.

(2005). *My mother was a computer: Digital subjects and literary texts*. Chicago: University of Chicago Press.

(2006a). Traumas of code. *Critical Inquiry*, 33(1), 136–57.

(2006b). Unfinished work: From Cyborg to cognisphere. *Theory, Culture & Society*, 23(7–8), 159–66. Doi:10.1177/0263276406069229.

Hern, A. (2015, July 30). *Google says non to French demand to expand right to be forgotten worldwide*. Retrieved February 10, 2016, from www.theguardian.com/technology/2015/jul/30/google-rejects-france-expand-right-to-be-forgotten-worldwide. Accessed online March 3, 2016.

Home Page of The Loebner Prize in Artificial Intelligence. (2015). Retrieved August 31, 2015, from www.loebner.net/Prizef/loebner-prize.html. Accessed online March 3, 2016.

InfoCuria. (2015). Retrieved from http://curia.europa.eu/juris/recherche.jsf?cid=716879. Accessed online March 3, 2016.

Jinek, M., Chylinski, K., Fonfara, I. et al. (2012). A programmable dual-RNA-guided DNA endonuclease in adaptive bacterial immunity. *Science*, 337(6096), 816–21. Retrieved from http://science.sciencemag.org/content/337/6096/816. Accessed online March 3, 2016.

Job Search Results. Retrieved Labor Day, 2015, from www.upwork.com/o/jobs/browse/t/o/. Accessed online March 3, 2016.

Kaplan, E. (2015, March 1). The spy who fired me: The human costs of workplace monitoring. *Harper's*, 31–40.

Kasperkevic, J. (2015, July 01). *Google says sorry for racist auto-tag in photo app*. Retrieved February 16, 2016, from www.theguardian.com/technology/2015/jul/01/google-sorry-racist-auto-tag-photo-app. Accessed online March 3, 2016.

Kim, K. and Wang, C. (2016, January 4). *China's seven-minute selling Frenzy that shook global markets*. Retrieved February 15, 2016, from www.bloomberg.com/news/articles/2016-01-04/china-s-seven-minute-selling-frenzy-shows-circuit-breaker-risks. Accessed online March 3, 2016.

Kirilenko, A.A., Kyle, A.S., Samadi, M., and Tuzun, T. (2015, December 28). *The Flash Crash: The impact of high frequency trading on an electronic market*. Available at SSRN: http://ssrn.com/abstract=1686004 or http://dx.doi.org/10.2139/ssrn.1686004. Accessed online March 3, 2016.

Latour, B. (1981). Visualisation and cognition: Drawing things together. In R.A. Jones and H. Kurlick (Eds.), *Knowledge and society: Studies in the sociology of culture past and present* (Vol. 6, 1–40). Greenwich, CT: Jai Press.

Ledford, H. and Callaway, E. (2015). 'Gene drive' mosquitoes engineered to fight malaria. *Nature*. Retrieved February 5, 2016, from www.nature.com/news/gene-drive-mosquitoes-engineered-to-fight-malaria-1.18858?WC.mc_id=TWT_NatureNews. Accessed online March 3, 2016.

Lessig, L. (2010). *Code: Version 2.0*. Retrieved February 15, 2016, from http://codev2.cc/download remix/Lessig-Codev2.pdf available at http://codev2.cc/download+remix/Lessig-Codev2.pdf. Accessed online March 3, 2016.

Lewis, M. (2014). *Flash boys: A wall street revolt.* New York, London: W.W. Norton & Company.

Lewis, R. (2015, December 03). *A conversation with CRISPR-Cas9 inventors Charpentier and Doudna|DNA Science blog.* Retrieved February 19, 2016, from http://blogs.plos.org/dnascience/2015/12/03/a-conversation-with-crispr-cas9-inventors-charpentier-and-doudna/. Accessed online March 3, 2016.

Liao, H.K., Gu, Y., Diaz, A. et al. (2015). Use of the CRISPR/Cas9 system as an intracellular defense against HIV-1 infection in human cells. *Nature Communications* 6. Article number: 6413. DOI: 10.1038/ncomms7413. Retrieved from www.nature.com/articles/ncomms7413. Accessed online August 15, 2015.

Lynch, P. (Director). (2002). *Cyberman* [Motion picture on DVD]. Canada.

Mann, S. (2004). *EyeTap personal imaging lab.* Retrieved February 20, 2016, from www.eyetap.org/about_us/hilab/index.html. Accessed online March 3, 2016.

Manovich, L. (2013). *Software takes command: Extending the language of new media.* New York, NY: Bloomsbury Academic.

Minsky, M. and Papert, S. (1969). *Perceptrons: An introduction to computational geometry.* Cambridge, MA: MIT Press.

Mordvintsev, A., Olah, C., and Tyka, M. (2015, June 17). *Inceptionism: Going deeper into neural networks.* Retrieved February 16, 2016, from http://googleresearch.blogspot.com/2015/06/inceptionism-going-deeper-into-neural.html. Accessed online March 3, 2016.

NASA's Toyota Study released by Dept. of Transportation. (2011, February 8). Retrieved August 27, 2015, from www.nasa.gov/topics/nasalife/features/nesc-toyota-study.html. Accessed online March 3, 2016.

Nanodegree Plus – Get a job guaranteed|Udacity. (2016). Retrieved February 15, 2016, from www.udacity.com/nanodegree/plus. Accessed online March 3, 2016.

Overbye, D. (2015, June 8). *Black hole hunters.* Retrieved August 16, 2015, from www.nytimes.com/2015/06/09/science/black-hole-event-horizon-telescope.html. Accessed online March 3, 2016.

Oye, K.A., Esvelt, K., Appleton, E. et al. (2014). Regulating gene drives. *Science,* 345(6197), 626–8.

Parker, A. and Corasaniti, N. (2014, October 30). *Data-driven campaigns zero in on voters, but messages are lacking.* Retrieved February 01, 2016, from www.nytimes.com/2014/10/31/us/politics/data-driven-campaigns-zero-in-on-voters-but-messages-are-lacking.html. Accessed online March 3, 2016.

Pearson, G. (2014, May 20). *Will we still have fruit if bees die off?* Retrieved September 7, 2015, from www.wired.com/2014/05/will-we-still-have-fruit-if-bees-die-off/. Accessed online March 3, 2016.

Reno v. American Civil Liberties Union, 117 S.Ct. 2329, 138 L.Ed.2d 874 (1997). (1997, March 19). Retrieved August 20, 2015, from www.law.cornell.edu/supct/html/96-511.ZS.html. Accessed online March 3, 2016.

Resnick, M. (1994). *Turtles, termites, and traffic jams: explorations in massively parallel microworlds.* Cambridge, MA: MIT Press.

Richtel, M. (2013, April 27). *How big data is playing recruiter for specialized workers.* Retrieved September 6, 2015, from http://nyti.ms/18JCAYS. Accessed online March 3, 2016.

Rogers, S. (2013, March 15). *John Snow's data journalism: The cholera map that changed the world.* Retrieved February 26, 2016, from www.theguardian.com/news/datablog/2013/mar/15/john-snow-cholera-map. Accessed online March 3, 2016.

Rosen, M., Weibel, P., Fritz, D., and Gattin, M. (2011). *A little known story about a movement, a magazine and the computer's arrival in art: New Tendencies and Bit international, 1961–1973.* Karlsruhe, Germany: ZKM/Center for Art and Media.

Safe Harbor: Advisory. (2015, February 11). Retrieved February 15, 2016, from www.export.gov/safeharbor/. Accessed online March 3, 2016.

Sang-hun, C. and Markoff, J. (2016, March 09). *Master of go board game is walloped by Google Computer Program.* Retrieved March 12, 2016, from www.nytimes.com/2016/03/10/world/asia/google-alphago-lee-se-dol.html. Accessed online March 3, 2016.

Schmidt, M.S. and Shear, M.D. (2015, January 26). *A Drone, Too Small for Radar to Detect, Rattles the White House.* Retrieved February 05, 2016, from www.nytimes.com/2015/01/27/us/white-house-drone.html?_r=0. Accessed online March 3, 2016.

Scott, M. (2015, October 06). *Data transfer pact between U.S. and Europe is ruled invalid.* Retrieved February 10, 2016, from www.nytimes.com/2015/10/07/technology/european-union-us-data-collection.html. Accessed online March 3, 2016.

(2016, January 24). *Europe's top digital – Privacy watchdog zeros in on U.S. Tech giants.* Retrieved January 28, 2016, from www.nytimes.com/2016/01/25/technology/europes-top-digital-privacy-watchdog-zeros-in-on-us-tech-giants.html. Accessed online March 3, 2016.

SEC approves new rule requiring consolidated audit trail to monitor and analyze trading activity. (2012, July 11). Retrieved August 30, 2015, from www.sec.gov/News/PressRelease/Detail/PressRelease/1365171483188. Accessed online March 3, 2016.

Section 230 of the Communications Decency Act (2015). Retrieved August 20, 2015, from https://en.wikipedia.org/wiki/Section_230_of_the_Communications_Decency_Act#Case_law. Accessed online March 3, 2016.

Sims, K. (1994, July 1). *Evolving virtual creatures.* Retrieved August 17, 2015, from www.karlsims.com/papers/siggraph94.pdf. Accessed online March 3, 2016.

Singer, P.W. (2009). *Wired for war: The robotics revolution and conflict in the twenty-first century.* New York: Penguin Press.

Sloterdijk, P. (2007, November 25). *Optimierung des Menschen?* Retrieved February 15, 2016, from www.tele-akademie.de/begleit/video_ta110116.php. Accessed online March 3, 2016. SWR Fernsehen Tele-Akademie.

(2011). *Bubbles: Microspherology* (W. Hoban, Trans.). Los Angeles, CA: Semiotext(e).

(2016). *Stress and freedom.* Cambridge: Polity.

State National Bank of Big Spring v. Jacob J. Lew. (2014, November 19). Retrieved from http://harvardlawreview.org/2016/01/state-national-bank-of-big-spring-v-lew/. Accessed online August 31, 2015.

Steve Fossett – Mechanical Turk results. (2007, September 24). Retrieved September 7, 2015, from http://s3.amazonaws.com/fossett/index.html. Accessed online March 3, 2016.

Steyerl, H. (2010). Politics of art: Contemporary art and the transition to post-democracy. *E-flux Journal.* Retrieved from www.e-flux.com/journal/21/67696/politics-of-art-contemporary-art-and-the-transition-to-post-democracy/. Accessed online August 5, 2015.

(2013). *Freedom from everything: Freelancers and mercenaries.* Retrieved September 6, 2015, from www.e-flux.com/journal/freedom-from-everything-freelancers-and-mercenaries/. Accessed online March 3, 2016.

Talking to Machines. (2015). Retrieved www.radiolab.org/story/137407-talking-to-machines/. Accessed online August 31, 2015.

The Trust Engineers. (2015, February 9). Retrieved www.radiolab.org/story/trust-engineers/. Accessed online August 31, 2015.

Turkle, S. (2011). *Alone together: Why we expect more from technology and less from each other.* New York: Basic Books.

Upwork, the world's largest online workplace. (2015). Retrieved http://upwork.com/. Accessed online February 15, 2016.

Wark, M. (2015, August 29). E-flux journal 56th Venice Biennale – SUPERCOMMUNITY – *The vectoralist class.* Retrieved September 21, 2015, from http://supercommunity.e-flux.com/texts/the-vectoralist-class/. Accessed online March 3, 2016.

Wenning, R. and Schunter, M. (2006, November 13). *The platform for privacy preferences 1.1 (P3P1.1) specification.* Retrieved February 22, 2016, from www.w3.org/TR/P3P11/#Introduction. Accessed online March 3, 2016.

Whalen, T. (1994). *My experience with the 1994 Loebner competition.* Retrieved January 29, 2016, from http://thomwhalen.com/nonfiction/ThomLoebner1994.html. Accessed online March 3, 2016.

Wiener, N. (1961). *Cybernetics; or, control and communication in the animal and the machine* 2nd ed. New York: MIT Press.

Willemsen, E. (2015, December 23). *Ski federation bans drones after camera nearly hits racer.* Retrieved February 19, 2016, from http://bigstory.ap.org/article/9680a8b4a3934750a8eeacd6594996cb/ski-federation-bans-drones-after-camera-nearly-hits-racer. Accessed online March 3, 2016.

Williams, T. (2015, August 12). *Facial recognition software moves from overseas wars to local police.* Retrieved August 16, 2015, from www.nytimes.com/2015/08/13/us/facial-recognition-software-moves-from-overseas-wars-to-local-police.html. Accessed online March 3, 2016.

Wingfield, N. (2015, June 10). *How's my driving? The insurer knows.* Retrieved September 5, 2015, from http://bits.blogs.nytimes.com/2015/06/10/hows-my-driving-the-insurer-knows/. Accessed online March 3, 2016.

PART VI

TRANSDISCIPLINARY

11

From Growing Tools to Designing Organisms: Changing the Literacies of Design

ORKAN TELHAN

Abstract: Contemporary design problems continuously challenge us to think about new skills, methods, tools, and techniques that often cannot be addressed with the expertise of a single discipline. Design problems have always been multifaceted and complex. But compared to the past, global challenges such as social inequality, environmental pollution, food scarcity, and climate change have had cascading effects on local conditions, demanding artists and designers to be more agile and aware of the social, cultural, and political realities of their times. In this chapter, I propose ways for augmenting design pedagogy to embrace a broader understanding of design that can address these challenges. Instead of reinforcing template paradigms used to educate the conventional design professions – such as product design, architecture, or graphic design – I propose a literacy-oriented pedagogy that is centered around acquiring knowledge, methods, and skills developed across different disciplines. I suggest that tool-making methods, computational thinking, or research-oriented learning are literacies that cannot be grasped from a singular approach; instead, they have to be studied as interdisciplinary foundational domains of knowledge that help designers orient their interests, find their own voices, and decide what skills to specialize in.

Keywords: design literacy, tool-making, design research, materiality, biological design, interdisciplinary design

INTRODUCTION

There has been an increasing effort to cross knowledge, experience, and skills among different disciplines in the past few years. Artists and designers have worked along with social scientists, engineers, historians, or policy makers on multidimensional and complex challenges where no single disciplinary perspective can adequately provide enough expertise, know-how, and methodology. Design problems have always been multifaceted and complex; but compared to the past, global challenges such as social inequality, environmental pollution, food scarcity, and climate change have started to exhibit cascading effects on local conditions. The shifting nature of such challenges sets pressure on designers for better agility and awareness of the social, cultural, and political realities of our times (Buchanan and Margolin, 1995).

In comparison to recent past, contemporary design pedagogy is equipped with a deeper understanding of materials and a much diverse set of fabrication technologies. Advancements in various fields have quickly translated into design methods and have shown immediate impact on designs. For instance, as DNA sequencing techniques became cheaper, we began to learn more about the genetic makeup of living organisms. These dynamics led to the discovery of many additional microbial species in unexpected places such as the interior of our bodies, houses, buildings, hospitals, and larger urban infrastructures. Such know-how has quickly changed the ways we study surrounding environments in relation to organisms we share these with, and the ways in which these organisms influence human behavior. The technical and scientific knowledge behind these studies has quickly turned into a prevailing design paradigm which influenced disciplines involved in designing products, buildings, and cities. Planners of urban infrastructure suddenly came to realize the necessity of knowing biology for the understanding of how microbes move around in the city through door handles, turnstiles, or subway cars (Cameron, Corne, Mason, and Rosenfeld 2013). Microbial maps of cities allowed researchers to figure out the ways in which good bacteria can help us eliminate pathogens in the environment and significantly contribute to the well-being of citizens. Furniture, fashion, and makeup designers started to look closely toward design practices with microbial organisms. From microbial materials to furniture, probiotic clothing, food, and cosmetics, the microbial landscape has been suddenly transformed into a design space of interest to numerous disciplines besides life sciences.

Contemporary designers are not limited to applied knowledge, but may find creative applications of a new technology based on comprehension from other disciplines. As creative and critical thinkers, designers can make propositions to design challenges, but have also become increasingly interested in contributing to the production of knowledge and advancement of their fields' research repository. Thus, many designers are involved in creating technologies – fabrication tools, materials, design software – or work with scientists and scholars toward the invention of new theories and methodologies that can expand the role of the designer into a public intellectual. With the recent spawning of design biennials that exhibit an interdisciplinary survey of design[1] and the emphasis of exhibiting designed artifacts at prominent art shows,[2] contemporary design is shaping the broader cultural discourse in non-mainstream venues and audiences.

In this chapter, I propose ways for the augmentation of design pedagogy so that it can facilitate a broader understanding of design beyond individual disciplines. Instead of reinforcing template paradigms used in conventional design education, I propose a literacy-centered pedagogy that is centered around transdisciplinary knowledge, methods, and skills. I suggest that tool-making methods, computational thinking, or research-oriented learning are literacies that cannot be developed following a singular approach. They can be studied as interdisciplinary foundational domains of knowledge which help designers orient their interests, find their own voices, and decide what skills to cultivate, what to delegate, and what to ignore within the flux of academic trends. Thus, I identify three literacies central to transdisciplinary art and design practices. These form the essence of this chapter.

LITERACIES FOR DESIGN

The term literacy is often used as a measure of competence with respect to a domain of knowledge. Like the ability to read and write, the term literacy has grown to include competencies related to electronics, programming, and biology among others. Similar to expertise, the term signifies an accumulation of awareness, know-how, and skillsets related to tools, technologies, or conceptual thinking. Unlike expertise, however, literacies work on a continuum – they do not dismiss specialization or advancement in a specific domain, but also do not require a specific domain as a measure of affiliation with a discipline. Literacies are open to the accumulation of different kinds and degrees of knowledge without the need of committing to a single discipline. One can become a programmer, learn the syntax and semantics of programming languages, apply techniques of reasoning, and become proficient in the use of certain tools without becoming an engineer or computer scientist. Similarly, computational literacy can be obtained without

---

[1] As opposed to singular design streams dedicated to Furniture, Architecture, or Fashion Design.

[2] Examples of such art shows include Documenta, Gwanji, and Sharjah Biennials.

commitment to a single discipline. While there is a wide variety of literacies involved in contemporary design practices, there is also the question of synthesizing these to a manageable level. In the following sections, I propose three high-level literacies foundational for computation and design practices: (1) tool-making, (2) research, and (3) literacy in matter and material.

TOOL-MAKING

There is a wide variety of tools and media available to contemporary designers. Ranging from print and screen-based interfaces, to mobile apps, to fabrication tools, to responsive materials, to lab protocols that program the behavior of living organisms, a plethora of tools and frameworks navigate designers through the conception, simulation, fabrication, and study of their designs. In design pedagogy, teaching the tools of the trade often parallels the teaching professional foundations. Mastery of the tools is often associated with the creative capacity of the maker.

With the advancement of computational technologies, software tools invaded almost every discipline. Design disciplines have become increasingly rooted in media and information-centric thinking. Consequently, the operational logic of tools often triggered the formation of new styles among designers as tools not only inform but also impose certain capacities of form making and material manipulation. A course in digital fabrication, for instance, cannot dismiss the use of laser cutters, 3D printers, or CNC mills, which can automate processes and extend the limits of manual labor by taking care of repetitive and precise tasks. Scripting tools help designers generate forms that cannot be sculpted through software but rather by manipulating algorithms. Designers either initiated or participated in the building of open source tools where the features of tools were shifted toward designers' own needs. 3D design and image-making software became more versatile and accessible. In contrast to the early 2000s, many design fields can be entirely taught using free software where designers can switch between alternative image editing, rendering, layout, or web design programs instead of being confined to a monopoly of design suites.

Every tool inevitably introduces its own frame of thinking, assumptions, and constraints from the beginning to the end of the design process. A thorough understanding of the foundations of tools allows artists and designers to challenge those limits. The design of a new tool can also be an integral part of solving a design challenge by simply structuring production processes, eliminating logistical needs, or facilitating ways for the inclusion of local materials and labor.

With the ability to write code, many designers have created computational design platforms (e.g., Processing) and hardware prototyping platforms (e.g., Arduino) with a fundamental transitioning from digital software to customizable computational platforms. Such tools not only enable individual designers, but also build entire communities that regularly work together to update, revise, and generate new versions of these platforms.

We can observe similar transformative dynamics happening in the fields of biological studies. DIY and open-source biology tools allow non-experts to practice and experiment with living organisms outside labs and specialized environments [site]. Designers organize around makerspaces and community biolabs such as Hackteria[3] and Genspace[4] to build low-cost alternatives to expensive hardware. As bioart, biological design, or synthetic biology garner more interest among artists and designers, the demand for more accessible tools drive many designers to rethink entire workflows and invent novel design not foreseen even by the specialists in the fields. Open Trons,[5] Bento Labs,[6] and Biorealize,[7] for instance, are all artist- or designer-driven initiatives that propose countertop or portable biology labs allowing for safe biology-related practices in design studios. These DIY tools not only focus on lowering the barriers of entry to Biological Design but also work on cultivating collective approaches where biological knowledge can be automated, networked, and practiced in distributed ways. Instead of enabling individual users, biological design tools address communal needs and allow designers to collectively explore complex challenges. The #Violacein Factory and Open Insulin (Di Franco et al., 2015) projects demonstrate that designers can even contribute toward the development of cancer medicines or insulin – a dynamic challenging the approaches pursued by leading pharmaceutical companies.

The literacy toward tool-making is an initial step in teaching students the necessity to challenge established paradigms in design. Such a literacy also poses two fundamental questions: (1) What can be designed by whom? and (2) How can it be distributed or made accessible to those who need it? These two questions are central to cultivating critical thinking in design

[3] http://hackteria.org
[4] http://genspace.org
[5] http://opentrons.com
[6] http://bento.bio
[7] http://biorealize.com

pedagogy and facilitating designers' contribution to knowledge, skills, and technologies within broader cultural domains.

RESEARCH

One important distinction between a computer scientist and a programmer might lie in their personal commitment to a discipline. Whether it is the social or natural sciences, engineering or the arts, the advancement of knowledge happens through the dissemination of new research pursued by those who are invested into their fields. A computer scientist may respond to the historical context of their research area and contribute novel knowledge to their domain of study, whereas a programmer may utilize the knowledge in a very specific way and advance the work not as a contribution to the discipline but rather as providing access to those who are outside the disciplinary communities. These dynamics are overtly exemplified by the open source software, hardware, or the DIY biology communities, where experts and nonexperts collectively generate specialized forms of knowledge available to broader users. Fields grow, expand, and interconnect with each other through these formal and informal exchanges. What we refer to as interdisciplinarity today is an outcome of the mixing of different research interests and methods.

The idea of research, however, is not limited to production and dissemination of knowledge by members of a discipline. At its very core, research is an intellectual tool that enables continuous learning and sharing of what has been learned. Whether it is through academic publications or research conducted and disseminated through Research & Development (R&D) departments of companies, the ability to do research is an important asset for contemporary artists and designers. Latest research helps artists and designers keep up-to-date with most current know-hows in their fields. This is especially the case for individuals who have completed their studies and have been out of school.

As a platform for developing methods of learning and sharing knowledge, research is often understood as the acquisition of specific methodologies to conceptualize ideas, pose questions, hypothesize claims, and find the means to justify these claims. Over time, different disciplines developed their unique strategies to produce knowledge. If the objective of a research endeavor is to explain phenomena and generalize knowledge so it can be further reused, scientific methods and deductive reasoning provide a reasonable framework. However, not every research question lends itself to such line of reasoning. Sometimes knowledge cannot be generalized.

It has to be local, partial, opinionated, and grounded in human experience. Instead of conducting empirical experiments, researchers utilize interviews, surveys, or field work in which they get exposed to the subjectivities and multiplicity of human existence. Similarly, by adopting sociological and anthropological methods, designers get a chance to learn how their work is perceived, utilized, and consumed (Gupta and Ferguson, 1997). In contrast to social scientists who try to minimize their influence on the studied subjects, artists and designers can explore deliberate interventions and focus on the effects of their designs on people. Such research has the potential to become the basis of user feedback as designers develop artifacts in response to the identified needs of the user. Artists can utilize similar methods as part of evaluating the social consequences of their practice or work with communities.

By learning mixed approaches from different disciplines, art and design students can gain an interdisciplinary understanding of research that lies beyond disciplinary boundaries (Creswell, 2013). Developing a literacy toward interdisciplinary research involves an equal understanding of pragmatic approaches geared toward finding feasible solutions – whether for fashion design or building bridges, as well as an appreciation of scientific methods that assist the understanding of protocols and procedures behind quantifiable, measurable, and data-driven facts. Research literacy should also include a sensitivity toward socially constructed knowledge and perspectives from queer, feminist, and disability studies which serve as a reminder that knowledge always operates in a network of power dynamics, funding models, and conflicting sociopolitical interests.

Research literacy also develops a strong sensibility toward engagement with history and equips students with a sense of criticality: understanding not only the history of a particular artifact, aesthetic style, or artistic movement, but also the broader cultural and political contexts that have contributed to its emergence. Often designers are well versed in their own disciplinary backgrounds, but less informed about the histories of scientific and technological paradigms. Research literacy suggests an engagement with history as an integrative model responsible for cross-referencing developments in mathematics, language, and use of scientific tools in the progression of time. This allows designers from different domains to develop critical sensibilities not only through form, aesthetics, technologies, or visual style, but also through developing a deeper understanding of the human condition, ideologies, politics, and values as they shift over time.

A comparative study of "radios" from different periods reveals how designers invested in different values can pursue design "criticism" through a multitude of approaches. From portable sound players to deconstructed radios, Gourgechon's printed radio, Posch and Kurbak's Knitted Radio (2014), Joe Davis's bacterially grown radio (2011), and finally Spotify's digital radios, each artifact demonstrates a critical response to what has preceded it. These not only challenge the boundaries of what radios can be, but also broaden the design discourse by proposing shifts in ideology, business plans, material use, and technologies. The varieties of these artifacts also show how radio design can be reconsidered when different artists and design fields get involved. While Sanyo's Boombox demonstrates advancements in hardware engineering, Radio in a Bag (Weil, 1981), Knitted Radio (Kurbak and Posch, 2014), and paper printed radios (Gourguechon, 2013) show how product and graphic designers can introduce new materials and fabrication processes. Artist Joe Davis's Bioradio offers, for example, not only a thought provocation, but also an exposition of the assumptions behind the materiality of sound transmission and how these can be altered by growing sound emitting circuits via bacteria. Today, as Spotify becomes a ubiquitous online service mostly conceived by software engineers and user interface and experience designers, the design of the radio still holds an important benchmark in relation to creative and critical thinking within art and design discourse. Imagining the future of any design artifact requires research skills along with a profound engagement with the historical discourse of the continuum within which values, design, methods, technologies, and pedagogy develop.

LITERACY IN MATTER AND MATERIAL

Certain materials have historical precedence in art and design pedagogy: wood, foam, metal, and clay are all exemplary in the study of form in architecture and product design; paper and cardboard – in graphic and print design; various soft materials and fabrics – in fashion design. The list of materials – included or excluded from teaching curricula – defines the conceptual foundations of the fields. Traditionally, the foundation classes of most design fields have focused on low-cost, solid materials easily manipulatable by human labor. Students sketch, model, and prototype with such materials due to their availability and ease of use. In addition, facilities in art and design departments have already been organized to support such pedagogy.

The past 20 years have marked advancements in digital design and fabrication techniques where prices of computer-controlled machinery have been increasingly decreasing. At the same time, the choice of materials that can be manipulated and fabricated has been growing at an exponential speed. As CNC mills, 3D printers, laser cutters, automated wire benders, drones, and robotic arms claim more space in fabrication labs, designers face the need for developing new strategies to incorporate these into their work in more creative and critical ways. The fabrication revolution has also challenged designers to shift their attention from tools to reconsidering the role of matter and materiality in their designs.

Additive fabrication tools such as 3D printers provide alternative ways for combining solid and liquid materials into one and the same designs. Designers can make their own filaments and customize printing heads to incorporate syringes and pumps that can deposit liquids, gels, or flexible polymers and print soft structures and surfaces.

The shift from solid to liquid materials suggests a profound transformation in design thinking where artists and designers become a part of the biochemical design space. Knowledge on chemical processes such as polymerization, crystallization, and gelling allows designers to work with a vast variety of new materials while using chemical reactions, assembly, and bonding processes together with electronics and computation. The Artificial Jellyfish (Nawroth et al., 2012), for example, demonstrates how animal cells grown on a soft polymer can be electrically controlled to form a "medusoid" which moves in a jellyfish-like manner.

Another aspect of the biochemical design space includes direct work with micro- or macroorganisms which incorporates living processes into designs. The ability to "design like nature" has always been a familiar benchmark shaping the ideals of artists and designers. It has introduced many different styles or art movements that observed and mimicked forms, appearances, and behaviors of living organisms – from plants, to seashells, to dolphins. The Streamline movement of the 1930s, for example, demonstrates this biomimetic desire as an aspiration to building forms as efficient as Nature. Anatomical studies of animals have introduced a deeper interest in understanding fluid dynamics and eventually informed the design of trains, planes, and buses (Bush, 1975). Designs that aspire for energy efficiency and sustainability have inspired designers to build structures and surfaces that imitate the patterns created by plants and leaves as they emerge in nature. The assumption that millions of years of evolution should yield "better" results than what humans can come up with is still a prominent style of not only thinking, but also making. Ideas originating from natural entities have shaped many design artifacts – from bridges to robots that "move like snakes" or "crawl like centipedes."

Working directly with living matter, on the other hand, varies greatly from these approaches. Methods for designing bacteria, yeast, and mycelium are becoming accessible to nonexperts who can explore the creative uses of these organisms at their homes, garages, or design studios. DIY Biology tools allow designers to grow biological artifacts at different scales from food packaging to cosmetics, fashion, furniture, and architectural design. Designers can also develop hybrid approaches while working with living matter and thus avoid the dichotomy between human-made and Nature-born artifacts. For instance, living matter can also be programmed "like machines" to synthesize chemicals while still exhibiting vitality for exercising different functions and behaviors. Similar to learning the basics of programming, design students can learn to assemble DNA with standardized genes, insert them inside bacteria, and grow various biochemical products that can range from dyes to food flavors, fuels, and novel materials. A more integrative literacy toward matter and materiality allows designers to see their research and practice in a continuum. Designers can directly engage with biological processes such molecular synthesis, fermentation, self-assembly, and growth which can inform design principles and be applied to different design challenges.

INTEGRATIVE DESIGN STUDIO

The three literacies discussed earlier – (1) tool-making, (2) research, and (3) literacy in matter and material – lay the foundations of an integrative design studio, that we have been teaching at the University of Pennsylvania's School of Design. We work with graduate and undergraduate students from fine arts, digital media design, product design, or architecture and help them develop projects in response to a theme. In this chapter, I refer to two different courses – Cultures of Making and Biological Design – where students formulate design questions and make propositions that lay outside their major field of study.

The integrative design studio starts with questioning the traditional approaches and spaces of design pedagogy. Throughout the semester, students work in different environments, such as the electronics and hardware prototyping lab, printmaking facilities, digital fabrication lab, and a biosafety level (BSL) 2 biology lab. When exposed to different work environments, students not only develop literacies toward using tools and technologies integral to these spaces, but also learn how to use tools in unconventional ways. A printmaking tool can suddenly become an indispensable tool for working with biological organisms, or electronic components can be combined with chemical designs to grow organisms that can synthesize electricity.[8]

---

[8] https://sciencehack.synbiota.com/

Students start their semester by developing a series of assignments that investigate the idea of "circuit making." Circuit making relies on two frameworks. The first one is a conceptual framework which organizes students' ideas around computational, systems-oriented, and constructivist design principles. The second one is a technical framework that exposes the diversity of tools and technologies for making circuits: using conductive threads, printing graphics with conductive inks, and growing genetic circuits using microogranisms.

At its very core, thinking through circuits provides an abstract framework to introduce many foundational concepts such as controlling the flow of information or materials, interactivity, input and output, sensing and actuation. The students are exposed to the ubiquity of this vocabulary through a variety of examples ranging from musical instruments to automatic doors, urban plans, or transportation infrastructure. The intention behind this is to make students move beyond familiar applications of machines, computers, or software. Assigning different material contexts to the concepts also helps them understand their role in different design applications and treat these as principles used to compose new systems as machines, materials, or living organisms.

In the second half of the semester, the course transitions from assignments to developing projects and concrete responses to course materials. Based on their interests, students are expected to develop ideas and make propositions that respond to a design challenge. During this process, we introduce students to different research methodologies that will help them formulate ideas, make proposals, and develop their studies by engaging with potential users and audiences. In contrast to certain traditions of studio discourse which emphasize thinking through digital representations, 3D renders, and animations, we require students to develop their work by building physical artifacts. Starting from the idea sketches to system diagrams, scale models, and full-scale prototypes, we emphasize the importance of thinking within the material domain by creating handmade or digitally fabricated objects. While working without drawings or renders imposes originally a certain challenge and a limit to structuring ideas, it eventually helps students think closer with matter and materiality. This approach differs from traditional approaches that privilege visuality as a form of embodiment for an idea, function, or product. As students go through a number of iterations, they quickly learn how to talk about their work both with its capabilities and limits instead of simply relying on visual representations which often offer an idealized version of the project. When working with microorganisms or mycelium, we encourage students to think through the capabilities and needs of the living organisms. Estimating how organisms would grow and become functional in a specific design context depends on a multitude of factors. Students often benefit more from running experiments parallel instead of pursuing single ideas – they can evaluate multiple options and anticipate the time frame required for their designs to grow.

Building enclosures for a mycelium-based lamp for instance helps students compare and contrast different traditions of design. Mycelium is a relatively cheap and fast-growing organism that can be incubated inside hollow forms to design various objects. The organisms can quickly grow around a carrier material such as corn or wood scraps and take the shape of the forms they are molded in. Students can use these molds in a variety of ways, for instance, by sketching the form in freehand and fabricating it out of clay, or modeling it in software and then printing it out using a 3D printer. However, mycelium can also be grown inside an active or living mold using bacteria. The interaction between the species can be controlled so that mycelium can be grown in specific areas at specific amounts instead of passively filling hollow spaces. Molding with mycelium, for example, can be grown into various "tools" based on different tectonic and biological principles. Mycelium growth can be spatially driven by visual patterns, as the organism can follow gaps or marks on the surfaces through "contact sensing." By growing together inside the same mold, mycelium can also be "actively" driven by bacteria, which can slow it down or limit its growth in certain areas of the design. Brought into a classroom, the exercise allows students to grow their own tools and to manipulate living designs. But more importantly, it demonstrates that not every design can be predictably modeled or studied through digital tools.

Thinking through experiments and prototypes also helps students explore ways to intersect biological and chemical systems. For instance, once they learn how electrical circuits work, students can substitute the energy source – typically a battery – with a biochemical circuit. In some instances, a microbial fuel cell can source enough power to an electrical circuit that powers up a microcontroller which then plays sound using a low-power transducer. The microcontroller in turn powers up an electrochromic display which projects information or wirelessly connects to the Internet. Instead of a final project, students are required to provide a critical response to course materials – a response which also engages with broader cultural and historical discourses shaped by human needs and desires. Students spend about a month pursuing their own subject-, brief-, problem-, or question-driven interests and work on transforming their explorations into functional prototypes. We expect these prototypes to work at multiple levels; besides embodying a history of engagement with different literacies introduced in the class, we expect students to contribute their own commentary toward a social, cultural, or environmental challenge.

The final outcomes of the studio are often culminated through an end-of-year exhibition. However, the research behind the prototypes is communicated and disseminated further through additional writing, media, and online presence. The course blog from Fall 2015 – www.biologicaldesign.info – has attracted more than 3,000 visitors.

CONCLUSION

Today's designers need new strategies to cope with the complex challenges shaping society. Designers need to be equipped with a diverse set of skills, utilize different research methodologies, and be able to apply a multitude of design and fabrication methods for prototyping and realizing their designs. In this chapter, I suggested three design literacies – tool-making, research, and matter and materiality – as domains that can provide artist and designers with the skills and knowledge that can be seamlessly applied in the design of widely different artifacts, from products to buildings to living organisms. This literacy-driven approach does not suggest disciplinary, interdisciplinary, or anti-disciplinary positions, as these notions are typically conceived, but rather emphasizes the importance of acquiring knowledge across a continuum as it is developed through different perspectives or methodologies. Today's designers should be able to develop their own tools and methodologies of design and also be part of broader research networks where they can contribute to the production and dissemination of knowledge. We foresee that designers going through this type of pedagogy will not only be able to address some of the most pressing challenges of the twenty-first century but also be influential in designing new literacies, and perhaps even entirely new disciplines that currently lie outside our imagination.

REFERENCES

Buchanan, R. and Margolin, V. (Eds.) (1995). *Discovering Design: Explorations. Design Studies*, 1st edn. Chicago: University of Chicago Press.

Bush, D.J. (1975). *The Streamlined Decade*, 1st edn. New York: George Braziller.

Cameron, P., Corne, D.W., Mason, C.E., and Rosenfeld, J. (2013). Crowdfunding Genomics and Bioinformatics. *Genome Biology* 14(9): 134. Retrieved from https://genomebiology.biomedcentral.com/articles/10.1186/gb-2013-14-9-134. Accessed online November 20, 2016.

Creswell, J.W. (2013). *Research Design: Qualitative, Quantitative, and Mixed Methods Approaches*, 4th edn. New York: SAGE Publications, Inc.

Davis, J. (2011). Joe Davis: The Mad Scientist of MIT? Retrieved from www.new scientist.com/blogs/culturelab/2012/03/the-mad-scientist-of-mit.html. Accessed online November 20, 2016.

Di Franco, A., Zayner, J., Shi, Y. et al. (2015, July 27). Open Insulin. Retrieved from: https://experiment.com/projects/open-insulin. Accessed online January 17, 2016.

Gourguechon, C. (2013). Paper Electronic Modules. Retrieved from www.coraliegour guechon.fr/Paper-electronic-modules-1. Accessed online November 20, 2016.

Gupta, A. and Ferguson, J. (1997). *Culture, Power, Place: Explorations in Critical Anthropology*. Raleigh-Durham: Duke University Press.

Kurbak, E. and Posch, I. (2014). Knitted Radio. Retrieved from http://ebrukurbak .net/the-knitted-radio/. Accessed online November 20, 2016.

Nawroth, J.C., Lee, H., Feinberg, A.W. et al. (2012). A Tissue-Engineered Jellyfish with Biomimetic Propulsion. *Nature Biotechnology* 30(8): 792–7. Doi:10.1038/ nbt.2269.

Weil, D. (1981). Radio in a bag. Retrieved from http://collections.vam.ac.uk/item/ O85208/radio-in-a-bag-radio-weil-daniel/. Accessed online November 20, 2016.

12

Pedagogical Experiments in Creative Coding

ANGUS G. FORBES

Abstract: This chapter aims to contribute new ideas and encourage new approaches to facilitating effective teaching at the intersections of new media arts and computer science. It introduces pedagogical experiments that were developed for a series of "creative coding" courses taught over the last 6 years at public research institutions, and which are currently being used in interdisciplinary classes taught at the Electronic Visualization Laboratory at University of Illinois at Chicago. Each of these courses emphasizes different material, but all are designed to provide students with the technical ability and creative opportunity to think critically about contemporary intersections between technology and culture. Interdisciplinary courses are challenging to teach: students are drawn from different backgrounds and have different interests; they have different technical and creative proficiencies; and they may or may not have experience or enthusiasm for working collaboratively. In addition to providing the motivations for particular pedagogical choices, this chapter discusses specific, pragmatic classroom exercises that have sparked successful research activity and creative exploration.

Keywords: creative coding, art and science, interdisciplinary methodology, student research, studio critique, tree criticism, techne, episteme

INTRODUCTION

The study of media arts is inherently interdisciplinary. The media arts engage with the discourse and practice of multiple fields, with a hybrid focus on both technical and aesthetic concerns. One of the primary challenges of a media arts practitioner, in whatever form the practice takes, is the need to solve complex engineering problems while simultaneously maintaining an awareness of design considerations and cultural impact. The "meaning" of media arts practice (as distinct from, for example, theoretical computer science or more traditional fine arts projects) is located precisely within this interplay between craft and science, the *techne* and the *episteme*. Likewise, the challenges in teaching media arts involve fostering an awareness of this interplay, even while necessarily focusing on the various foundational aspects of the disciplines that the student must draw from and move between. That is, in addition to providing a thorough working knowledge of another discipline (or perhaps multiple disciplines), an instructor must also promote the mediation between disciplines – a skill that is independent of any particular discipline. This skill is ultimately the more useful. Technologies will evolve and new forms of scientific and cultural inquiry will emerge; the ability to forge meaningful connections between disparate scientific and cultural models will always be needed in order to participate and innovate in contemporary research and practice.

The Creative Coding Research Group (CCRG)[1] promotes applied research in interactive data visualization and experimental explorations of creative concepts grounded in techniques related to human–computer interaction, scientific and information visualization, computer vision, immersive environments, machine learning, and other computational topics. A core philosophy of the CCRG is that by integrating research methodologies from media arts, design, and computer science, we can develop novel solutions to interdisciplinary problems. Another core tenet is that the creative outputs generated at the intersections of artistic and empirical research can meaningfully elucidate issues in science and technology relevant to contemporary culture. This hybrid approach has led to successful academic publications and creative presentations that were collaboratively developed by students and faculty. Recent projects have been published in or presented at top-tier journals and conferences in computer science and new media arts, including Transactions on Visualization and Computer Graphics (Forbes, Hollerer, and Legrady, 2010), Computer Graphics & Applications (Forbes, Burbano, Murray, and Legrady, 2015), Information Visualization (Etemadpour and Forbes, 2016), Multimedia (Villegas and Forbes, 2014), Computational Aesthetics (Forbes, Höllerer, and Legrady, 2013; Forbes and Villegas, 2015), and SIGGRAPH (Forbes, 2015).[2] Computational artworks have been shown at galleries, museums, and festivals throughout the world, such as the Beall Center for Art+Technology in Irvine, California, the

[1] The Creative Coding Research Group is a team of interdisciplinary researchers and artists working in the Electronic Visualization Laboratory, housed within the Department of Computer Science at University of Illinois at Chicago.
[2] See http://creativecoding.evl.uic.edu/publications.php for a full list of recent publications.

Lawrence Hall of Science in Berkeley, California, the Mediations Biennale in Poznan, Poland, the Todaiji Cultural Center in Nara, Japan, and the Bogota International Book Fair, among others.[3]

Interdisciplinary approaches that embrace artistic and computational methodologies contribute to meaningful outputs, each relevant to multiple disciplines and collaborators (West et al., 2015). Roger Malina discusses increasingly problematic issues in contemporary scientific practice and explores how new forms of collaboration may lead to new techniques and methodologies for approaching such issues. He explains that a primary motivation for the "art–science movement" is the "epistemological inversion" that has occurred due to the exponential acceleration in data that is available, whereby the sciences have become "data rich and meaning poor" (Malina, 2011). Moreover, the complexity of the data has changed; rather than working solely with "snapshots" of data, researchers strive to make sense of temporal "streams" and dynamic "data systems." Science is largely conducted through data analysis rather than through empirically sensing the world and, because there are no obvious or standard ways to represent probabilistic, fleeting, or otherwise unintuitive data, this necessitates the attention of the artistic sensibility that is skilled at thinking about issues of representation, or what Malina calls "re-sensing." He writes, "visualization and sonification technologies from computer science are a rich terrain of art–science practice and should be viewed as projects in translation" (Malina, 2012). Moreover, this "deluge" of data creates potential "blind spots," areas within and interpretations of datasets that are ignored because the amount of available information exceeds our ability to analyze it. The solutions to complex, global issues require diverse skill sets and the involvement of experts from multiple disciplines, and thus art–science collaboration is necessary. Similar to the notion of "transdisciplinarity" developed by Gale Moore and Danielle Lottridge in their investigation of interactions between disciplines (Moore and Lottridge, 2010), Malina imagines a "shared language" which "entails shared ontologies and eventually connected epistemologies" and that can "contribute to creativity and innovation." However, building this shared language necessitates a perpetual negotiation between different perspectives, a process of "trade and barter and not assimilation" (Malina, 2012).

Ben Shneiderman similarly advocates for effective collaborations, characterizing the importance of different methodological approaches

---

[3] See http://creativecoding.evl.uic.edu/projects.php for a full list of selected creative projects.

to knowledge using an interdependent "seed–root–flower" metaphor in which scientific, engineering, and design strategies all have a role to play in achieving "breakthrough collaborations" (Shneiderman, 2015). He describes the need for creativity support tools that enable researchers to come to new understanding or to make discoveries during different stages of research, from the "early stages of gathering information, hypothesis generations, and initial production through the later stages of refinement, validation, and dissemination" (Shneiderman, 2007).

Media artists continue to introduce new platforms for enabling original interdisciplinary research. Linda Candy sees the media artist as especially well situated to develop tools for creative expression. She explains that media arts projects present a way to harness the various "complex social, organizational, and cultural factors" that are required for innovation. Candy describes the artist as a "power user" who pushes the boundary of existing frameworks and tools in order to discover new forms of expression (Candy, 2007). Zafer Bilda also explores how media arts installations function as proving grounds for techniques that are helpful for understanding how different forms of interaction promote increased engagement and creativity (Bilda, Edmonds, and Candy, 2008). Pamela Jennings and Elisa Giaccardi further extend the idea of the creativity support tool as a framework for pervasive computing. They recognize that any tool is part of "a sociotechnical architecture deeply interwoven with the physical environment and social fabric of local communities" and call for a more "pervasive" outlook on creativity when "investigating and promoting situated and distributed aspects of creativity, particularly in relation to temporal, spatial and conceptual distribution across multiple interaction spaces" (Jennings and Giaccardi, 2005).

These issues – related to novel approaches to data representation, hybrid collaboration, tool building, and self-critical reflection – indicate areas at the intersections of technology and creativity that a contemporary media arts curriculum must address. The landscape is ever-changing and there is no surefire recipe to follow for training students to become competent practitioners and creative interdiscipinarians. Nonetheless, certain pedagogical goals can be prioritized that promote creative and critical practice.

PEDAGOGICAL GOALS

The pedagogical goals of the CCRG are deeply influenced by my time spent at University of Arizona's School of Information: Science, Technology, and

Arts (SISTA),[4] the University of California, Santa Barbara's Media Arts and Technology (MAT) program,[5] and the Electronic Visualization Laboratory (EVL) at University of Illinois at Chicago[6] (which the CCRG is part of). Each of these centers fosters interdisciplinary thinking by bringing together researchers and students with different interests and expertise into the same physical and institutional space. For instance, SISTA is comprised of a diverse core faculty of applied computer scientists whose interests span computational linguistics, computer vision, machine learning, information visualization, and media arts. Likewise, every faculty member in the MAT program has a joint appointment in a second department, such as studio arts, music, computer science, or electrical engineering. EVL was jointly founded in 1973 by two forward-thinking professors – one in computer science and the other in electronic art – and its core and affiliated faculty are currently drawn from the areas of virtual reality, visualization, human–computer interaction, communications, design, and media arts, among others.

Bringing together people with diverse research interests fosters interdisciplinary conversations, but also introduces new problems. The artist George Legrady explores some of the challenges in leading interdisciplinary classrooms (Legrady, 2006). Specifically, he discusses an experimental course that included students from different fields who were tasked with working together on conceiving and implementing novel interdisciplinary projects. In observing the development of these interdisciplinary projects, he noticed different roles that tend to be played by the artist and engineering members of the projects. For instance, artists tended to focus on "cultural aspects of media," to look for various kinds of "subtext," and were more comfortable when working with noisy data, while the engineering students were interested in "problem-solving opportunities," were more comfortable with "purer signals," and sought reliable, measurable collections of data. Legrady posits that artists are by nature "generalists" who incorporate a "wide spectrum of sources" to come up with a unique approach that cannot be reduced or replicated without dissolving "essential qualities." Ultimately, Legrady concludes that these differences in approach could be somewhat detrimental to short-term engineering goals; but, at the same time, that the artist's insight may "have an impact . . . by opening up new vistas" (Legrady, 2006).

---

[4] http://sista.arizona.edu; after a restructuring in 2015 it was rebranded as the School of Information (https://si.arizona.edu).

[5] http://mat.ucsb.edu

[6] http://evl.uic.edu

Designing a curriculum that successfully prepares students for success in mediating these two worlds requires a commitment to communication and a willingness to change directions when appropriate, as the intended outcomes of wrestling with contemporary practice is inherently in flux. Educational activities at the CCRG thus revolve around developing collaborative projects in interdisciplinary seminars and developing new research projects for academic conferences and media arts venues, as well as learning new technical skills.

CODING AS A FUNDAMENTAL SKILL FOR CREATIVE RESEARCH

Although the field of media arts continues to expand into many areas, such as bio-computing and physical computing, the CCRG focuses on programming as a core competency. An important side effect of learning software engineering is the awareness of the relationship between syntax and expression. That is, the student learns to wrestle with the necessary tensions between technological constraints and the infinite creative potential available through these technologies. A creative media arts concept cannot be implemented without some mastery of implementation tools. On the other hand, the mastery of implementation tools does not of course guarantee successful creative output. In order to learn a technology, a student is forced to reason about the small, exact, and purposeful steps it takes to define functionality. There is a carryover from this "low-level" reasoning into thinking about creative projects. Similarly, the act of developing software fundamentally requires the modeling of pertinent aspects of a system, which naturally develops the more abstract skill of identifying and defining appropriate models for meaningful projects. An auxiliary effect that develops through the processes of reducing ideas into small steps and creating models of systems is the deeper understanding of the interplay between the various technical and design issues involved in interdisciplinary research.

Courses taught in the CCRG tend to be language agnostic, though certain languages are used for particular courses: C or C++ for graphics, GLSL and CUDA for hardware-accelerated GPU programming, JavaScript for web programming, and Python for data analysis. Other languages, such as Processing/Java, MATLAB®, R, or SQL, are also used in some contexts. Although students having a computer science background are experienced with data structures and algorithms, most media arts students are less familiar with software engineering best practices and computational thinking. Rather than try to build up a student's knowledge from scratch, we utilize the creative projects as a springboard for this type of investigation. For example, in the context of a computer graphics course, a wide range of algorithmic thinking can be introduced through examining many different flavors of collision detection, many of which require an understanding of fundamental data structures and commonly used algorithms for spatial hashing. Similarly, techniques for generating shadows can lead students to grapple with more fundamental computer science concepts. That is, although it is generally not possible to be comprehensive in introductory courses with students with different technical and creative backgrounds, it is still possible to be thorough.

PROMOTING ART–SCIENCE ACUMEN

A previous survey examined the roles of media arts activities within scientific and engineering research contexts (Forbes, 2015), loosely categorizing these activities into four interrelated areas: generation, augmentation, provocation, and mediation. In addition to emphasizing specific coding skills and a holistic computational approach to problem solving, the CCRG curriculum aims to provide students with awareness of these roles and the skills to navigate within each of these areas.

Generation

Media artists function as *generators* of research agendas in which art exploration leads to and helps define the contours of interesting research problems or applications of research. Simply by following an artistic inclination, a media artist will quickly run up against personal and disciplinary limitations. Many times what the artist wants to do is not possible or is inaccessible. Through a bottom–up approach, media arts projects can generate valid, interesting research questions. Moreover, the exploration of a particular area of interest can serve as a way to explicitly trace the contours and boundaries of the research – which is not known or is not yet easily accessible. In addition to surveying the research topic, media artists, who are often experts at particular engineering tasks or generating creativity support tools, can switch hats and turn from idea generation to research and implementation. Of course, it is generally not possible to be an expert in everything, and this may be a point where the media artist now has a precise enough understanding of what they do not know in order to seek out appropriate collaborators.

Augmentation

Media artists function as *augmenters* of research, enhancing the representation, interaction, tool-building, or narrative components of the research in order to make it more effective for domain experts and more accessible to outsiders. A fundamental activity of art is thinking about representation; research into visualization and sonification are obvious areas in which media artists can make contributions. Similarly, it makes sense for media artists to explore ways to augment research through investigations into immersion and interactivity. The creation of artworks, whether static or interactive, involves issues of engagement and how to use the "language of art" to tell stories and provide context and narrative; media artists could apply this know-how to make research both more accessible and more meaningful. Additionally, the tool-building interests of media artists can also serve to augment research, as media artists apply their creativity to novel ways of working with data representation and interaction.

Provocation

Media artists function as *provokers*, questioning assumptions and introducing alternative perspectives and interpretations. The theme of provocation involves the idea of challenges to the status quo, introducing alternative perspectives and interpretations. New thinking can arise by questioning assumptions from different points of view: Why are the stated goals of a project important? Are there other more interesting or useful goals? Are the methods being used to achieve these goals ideal? Provocation is inextricably linked to the questioning of and experimenting with methodology. Through provocation, media artists can introduce an interpretive element to research and can provide new formulations through exploring cultural implications embedded in research questions. Some potential activities include identifying areas that are underrepresented in research, exploring the meaning and implications of those areas (not just their pragmatic functionality), and explicitly introducing guiding metaphors and aesthetic modalities in order to try to frame research in alternative ways. Provocation may initially introduce new complications, but ultimately promotes dialogue leading to more integrated and more relevant research.

Mediation

Media artists function as *mediators*, creating systems that bridge perspectives and languages, promoting knowledge-sharing across different communities, and helping investigators prioritize research goals. Media arts projects often create collisions between different disciplines, bringing together the everyday and the rarefied, the natural and the unreal, and the public and the private. Interesting projects, almost by definition, make new knowledge through combining perspectives and interpretations informed by multiple disciplines or ways of thinking. Thus it is important to create processes and strategies that support effective knowledge-sharing. What if this was an explicit goal of a project rather than a side effect? In order to function in collaborative contexts, Victoria Vesna writes that "negotiating the gap between the canon of rationality and the fluid poetic is ultimately the goal of artists who work with communication technologies" and that the act of "bridging and synthesizing" is itself an art form (Vesna, 2001). Emphasizing this important yet often unarticulated focus of media arts projects is a valuable way for media artists to explicitly position themselves as builders of tools that can help mediate between different research communities participating in art–science collaborations. Some potential media arts activities include creating projects to represent or externalize thinking and understanding, exploring ways to translate concepts from one domain to another, and creating projects that facilitate communication.

PRAGMATIC EXERCISES FOR DEVELOPING INTERDISCIPLINARY RESEARCH SKILLS

In the remainder of this chapter, I describe details about three exercises that have been used effectively across a range of courses, each made up of students with different levels of expertise in new media arts and computer science. Each of these exercises aims to foster expertise within the four thematic areas described earlier. The first exercise, writing "state-of-the-art" reports, teaches students how to navigate the vast archives of scholarship made available via article databases and aggregators such as Project Muse,[7] ACM Digital Library,[8] and Google Scholar.[9] The second exercise asks students to emulate existing works so that they can focus on technical skills without the initial burden of needing to be original or interesting (outside of choosing what work to mimic). The third exercise trains students to more incisively articulate their thoughts about other people's works and to more confidently defend their own choices. These exercises enhance a

[7] https://muse.jhu.edu
[8] http://dl.acm.org
[9] https://scholar.google.com

student's research prowess, technical skills, and communication. Moreover, they can be flexibly applied across a range of topics and used for group projects to give students further experience in collaborative settings. Each of these exercises aims to provide a rapid, yet thorough pathway to mastering fundamental concepts of scholarship, making, and critical thinking.

Writing "STAR" Reports

As a way to have students gain an understanding of the seminal and current concepts in a particular field, students are asked to present a state-of-the-art (or "STAR") report that provides an overview of that field. This exercise is based on STAR reports that have been published in the EuroGraphics series of conferences[10] (top-tier conferences in visualization and graphics). These reports aim to summarize the research done on a particular subarea of the field as well as to enumerate gaps in literature and to articulate a road map of future research that could fill those gaps. Depending on the level of the course, an individual student or group of students is asked to choose an area related to the course that they are interested in.

The instructor provides an overview of how to access journal and conference papers available online via the University's library and Google Scholar. Many students, including graduate students, are unfamiliar with how to use these resources effectively. For instance, most students are not aware that they can not only use the references in the paper to see what previously published articles were cited by an article, but also use Google Scholar to see which papers published at a later date have cited the article they are reading. Knowing this allows students to navigate through a collection of articles both backward and forward in time, observing how themes grow and fade in popularity and how concepts evolve and are refined.

In order to make sense of the articles, some of which use unfamiliar terminology, figures, or mathematical notation, students are asked to conduct a close reading of a small number of the articles that are influential (i.e., highly cited), controversial (e.g., that explicitly challenge prior work), or that were most recently published. As a first step, students are asked to use three differently colored highlighters to identify sentences in the paper that describe the main goals of the paper (as stated directly by the authors), and its main contributions (which can be either implicitly or explicitly articulated in the text), and that introduce terms or concepts that they do not

---

[10] www.eg.org

understand. Students assigned to read the same paper can then be asked to meet in small groups in order to compare notes and to share knowledge or to strategize how to make sense of unfamiliar parts of the article. A particularly useful aspect of this exercise is that it introduces students to the concept of thinking about their own ideas in terms of their contributions, which are often characterized as a response to or an outgrowth of previous work.

A recent, more elaborate version of this exercise that I created asks students to answer the following set of questions in greater detail:

Describe the CONTEXT of the paper. What problem does it explore? Why is exploring this problem important? Who does this problem affect? Who would benefit from reading this paper?

What are the CONTRIBUTIONS of the paper? What specifically does it present that is new and interesting?

Summarize the STRUCTURE of the paper. How do the authors present their ideas? What steps do they take to present their contributions and then convince you of the validity of these contributions?

Discuss the RESULTS of the paper. What specific conclusions does it make? What advice does it give it to the target audience?

What are the METHODS used to yield these results? Is it a user study, a survey, or an interview? Does it use statistical analyses? Do the methods used make sense for the problem? Is there anything that may have been left out? What assumptions did the authors make when they chose these methods? How many people were involved in the user study or interview? Do you think the addition of more studies would help convince you that their results were meaningful?

What TECHNOLOGIES does the paper explore? Does the paper make sense only in terms of a specific device or technology, or would the contributions of the paper apply to a range of technologies or to future technology?

Describe the FIGURES in the paper. Do they help explain the main ideas of the paper? Could you redesign the figures so that they are more useful or more clear?

List any words or ideas that you do not understand or that cause CONFUSION. Look up the meaning of these words. Do the references help you make sense of technical phrases or jargon? Provide the definition of the words that's relevant to the paper. If you can't figure it out, what is your best guess?

How would you EVALUTE the effectiveness of this paper and the research it describes? How do you think the authors could build upon or improve the contributions of the paper? Is there anything that was left out? Can you think of future research that would build upon this paper?

Explain the RELEVANCE of the article towards your research interests in general and especially towards the articles that you are writing in conjunction with this class. Before the mid-point of the semester, the papers you choose should be important precursors that can be discussed in the "related work" section of your articles.

These instructions can of course be modified depending on the experience of the students and the focus of the class. In answering these questions, the student will gain a very thorough understanding of the papers they are reading as well as deeper insight into how to express and present their own research ideas. The exercise has proven to be effective for examining a range of different topic areas, including visualization, human–computer interaction, computer graphics, and media arts. By comparing publications from the different areas, students working at the intersections of these fields become aware of the different disciplinary approaches to what "counts," for example, as effective evaluation or a meaningful contribution. It might seem somewhat counterintuitive to have students spend so much effort on reading and analyzing academic articles (rather than on creating new research projects), but in almost all cases, I have found that students are much better able to define, articulate, and defend their own ideas after only a few weeks of engaging in this exercise. Furthermore, having a thorough, albeit not comprehensive, exposure to tools of and approaches to scholarship is very empowering. Students begin to see themselves as having the ability to comment articulately on contemporary topics and the authority to make their own contributions to these topics.

Emulation and Extension of Existing Works

Another exercise that has also proven to be successful asks students to focus on recreating existing work rather than on generating original projects. For example, in a class on information visualization, students mimic an existing visualization technique or implement an existing layout algorithm; in a media arts course they implement an existing media arts project, perhaps using a more modern software language. Often the advances in technology make it relatively easy to make a new version of a project that originally could have been challenging to create. For instance, a project such as Camille Utterback's *Text Rain* (Utterback, 2004) originally required designing a novel approach to interpreting camera input but now can be much more easily implemented in a few lines of Processing using built-in functionality provided by the OpenCV or BoofCV libraries.[11]

---

[11] https://processing.org/reference/libraries

This exercise provides many advantages. Determining what work to re-implement forces students to rigorously explore threads in the history of media arts and to think about why particular projects are (or once were) considered innovative or provocative. Additionally, it provides students with an opportunity to assess their current skill set and to think about what technical abilities they need in order to achieve particular results. Furthermore, it allows students to focus on building these technical skills without the additional pressure of feeling the need to be original. By removing this pressure, students are more inclined to help each other and to share insights, rather than focusing inwardly on a creative idea that they feel territorial about. It is important to emphasize this camaraderie in a class early on and to create a space where students feel like their ideas are being nurtured and respected, especially in courses that include a critique component.

The emulation exercise can be extended by asking students to elaborate upon their initial output. For instance, in a recent class in introductory computer graphics, I first asked students to investigate and emulate early modernist paintings by creating 2D sketches using WebGL. Specifically, they were asked to choose an artist featured from MOMA's *Inventing Abstraction* exhibition and to mimic one of their works.[12] This alone is an interesting exercise, as it forces students to think deeply about what makes a particular artwork relevant and to recognize how complex in terms of texture, color, and composition even an apparently minimalistic work – such as Mondrian's series of paintings with rectangular forms – actually is. A follow-up to this project asks students to extend their initial efforts by adding interactivity, animation, and/or to refigure their work by adding in a third dimension. Again, the goal of these exercises is primarily to help students to increase their mastery of multimedia tools and interactive graphics programming, rather than to have the students create original artworks of their own. Similar exercises could be created to increase other aspects of programming or to focus instead on other modalities, such as sound or interactivity.

Tree Criticism

A staple of studio art education is the critique (Klebesadel and Kornetsky, 2009). A studio critique generally includes a public dialogue between a teacher and a student or a group of students with a student who is

---

[12] www.moma.org/inventingabstraction

"being critiqued." The role of the critiquer involves assessing the overall competency of the student, helping the student recognize and sort through elements of his or her work that are unclear, and identifying cultural or academic reference points that could inform and strengthen future work (Motley, 2015). Additionally, the student being critiqued may, in some settings, be expected to use the critique as an opportunity to defend his or her creative choices or design decisions. However, many students are wholly unfamiliar with critiquing, uncomfortable with expressing their opinions publically, and feel as though they lack the knowledge or authority to form an opinion (Barrett, 2000). This is true especially of students with a background in engineering or computer science rather than studio art or design. Even in art and design studio courses, critique sessions are often run in an informal manner without explicit structure and may not provide students with the skills to defend their own work or to helpfully judge the work of others (Inman, 2015). For this next exercise, I introduce students to a form of critiquing that gives them clear instructions for how to translate their initially vague or overly critical opinions into valuable assessments of each other's work. In this formulation of the critique, a main goal is to encourage students to identify and articulate their aesthetic principles. A critique session can be used to investigate how an aesthetic or design philosophy is able to embrace or fails to embrace different kinds of works and trains students to be able to effectively defend their work, educating those who fail to appreciate it. That is, the critique session is reframed, rather than as an exercise in passing judgment, as a springboard for conversations about the aesthetic principles of both the critiquer and the critiqued, as well as the observed and intended meanings in the work. This reframing is thus emotionally or intellectually less risky for the student, providing a collegial environment in which to introduce and challenge hypotheses about the goals of the creative endeavor.

An issue for students when first participating in critiquing is that it may appear as though commentary is entirely made up of subjective interpretations, or that opinions are justified entirely in terms of a jargon in which the student is unfamiliar. Indeed, in some cases an effective presentation at a critiquing session requires, for better or worse, mimicry of terminology rather than the clear explication of ideas (Rule and Levine, 2012). To combat this, and to jumpstart more interesting conversations, this exercise describes a shorthand for thinking about how to comment on an art or research artifact. This shorthand, called *tree criticism*, asks students to engage in an iterative exploratory process in which the student first offers an interpretive comment and then is asked to quantify that interpretation on a simple numerical scale that ranges from one to ten. For instance, a common response from an inexperienced student asked to reflect on a classmate's user interface project, to take a recent example from a human–computer interaction course, is to say something maddeningly nebulous, such as "I like it" or "it's pretty cool." Getting a student to elaborate on their comment can feel like pulling teeth, and guiding the student to be more verbose can have the unfortunate effect of putting words in his or her mouth. With tree criticism, the student is encouraged to "dive in" to their initial qualitative responses by making a concrete decision through assigning a numerical weight to it. They are then asked to justify the rating, usually leading to another qualitative response, which in turn leads to another rating, and so on. The process is referred to as a "tree" since often times a qualitative response will have multiple aspects to it, and the student will have to choose one branch of the response to quantify, but can return to the other branch as needed. Somewhat surprisingly, this simple set of instructions quickly leads the student to identify a more detailed actionable observation that frames their opinion in terms of an aesthetic or philosophical principle. This principle may turn out to be shared by the student being critiqued, in which case the conversation can shift to suggestions for clarifying how to emphasize this principle in the work. Or it may not be shared, in which case an even more interesting conversation about the reasoning behind each student's opinions can take place.

As a simple example, we show how the first steps of the tree criticism process are carried out (using the user interface project mentioned earlier). Here the instructor initiates the process with a question (in italics), making sure that the student's response (in quotation marks) provides an answer that can be quantified with a numerical rating (and if not, asking a follow-up question). In cases where the response does not provide a fruitful response, the process can rewind to an earlier step where multiple "branches" were indicated. The process can continue indefinitely; here we stop when we have the first actionable observation. Comments that show the instructor's thought process are provided parenthetically; the numbering indicates the current depth of the questioning, where each deeper level indicates a refinement of the student's previous opinion.

Response: *What is your first thought about the system?* "I like it."
    Rating: *How much do you like it on a scale of 1–10?* "I give it a 7."
    Response: *Why do you give it a 7?* "It's really neat."
        Rating: *How neat is it on a scale of 1–10?* "About an 8."
        Response: *Why do you give it an 8?* "I like the sliders." (This answer doesn't lead to a rating, so a follow-up question is asked)

Follow-up: *Why do you like the sliders?* "They are really useful."
  Rating: *How useful is it on a scale of 1–10?* "A 6."
  Response: *Why is it useful?* "It helps me understand the range of data
    in the query."
  Rating: *How helpful is it on a scale of 1–10?* "I just told you!" (This line
    of inquiry isn't going well, so we can go back up a level)
  Response: *Why else is it useful?* "That's the main reason." (Again,
    this line of inquiry isn't going well, so we can jump back up [for
    brevity, we skip over some steps here].)
Response: *Why else is it neat?* "Because the graphic design is really clean."
  Rating: *How clean is it on a scale of 1–10?* "Oh, probably about a 9
    or a 10."
  Response: *Why is it clean?* "The cool clear borders on the side of all the
    tables, the fonts, the overall layout." (Three branches are indicated,
    the one about the fonts is chosen here.)
  Rating: *How cool are the fonts on a scale of 1–10?* "Hmm, that's not
    really my area of expertise." (Instead of persisting with this line of
    inquiry, we go up a level to revisit a previous branch.)
Response: *Why else is it neat?* "Um, didn't I just tell you?" (We back-
    track yet another level.)
Response: *Why else do you like it?* "That's the main thing I like about it."
  (At this point, the student indicates that they are finished talking about
  the positive aspects of the work.)
Response: *What else do you think about the system?* "It seems actually a bit
  limited."

Rating: *How limited is it on a scale of 1–10?* "A 10."
Response: *Why is it limited?* "I can't really see it being applied to any other
  data, not even data that's in the same format!"
  Rating: *How would you rate how it can't it be applied?* "Huh?" (This
    poorly formulated question doesn't make sense to the student.)
Response: *Why else is it limited?* "You can't transform the data."
  [Etcetera]

At the end of this process, the student has clearly articulated a number
of things about the project they are critiquing. In this case, the student has
pointed out things they like about the layout (the design of the sliders and
the use of borders), identified an area where they are less knowledgeable
and may want to learn more about (typography), and clearly articulated a
statement about their belief that it is important for tools to be: (a) able to

effectively transform data in interesting ways and (b) easily generalizable to multiple datasets. Of course, any of these comments could be explored more deeply, but the last ones especially were, in this case, sufficient to spark a discussion about whether or not generalizability was an important goal for user interface design.

Although this process appears highly artificial and is indeed quite stilted, it nonetheless has proven to be successful in getting students who might otherwise remain silent to formulate and express critical responses. After seeing it acted out one or two times, the student can then go through the process on their own, even graphically presenting their internal conversation as a tree diagram, using it to identify a list of thoughts and observations. In a short amount of time, students internalize the process and are able to contribute meaningful commentary without going through this process explicitly. However, they are still able to fall back on it when a critique falters. The exercise works well when applied to different types of content, such as artworks, installations, user interfaces, visualization projects, and research papers, across a range of classrooms.

CONCLUSION AND FUTURE WORK

The media arts student is being trained in a highly relevant set of skills: the awareness to identify novel and culturally significant aspects of multiple areas of research; the ability to communicate and collaborate successfully on interdisciplinary projects requiring technical and artistic proficiencies; and the confidence to describe and defend the importance of rigor and creativity in interdisciplinary research. This chapter articulated the main goals of an interdisciplinary research lab that has a dual focus on generating novel research in interactive visualization and fostering the creation of new artistic installations. Specifically, it introduced pragmatic exercises that are broadly useful in helping students to engage deeply and critically with contemporary research. Although each of the exercises may seem painfully obvious to more experienced practitioners, they nonetheless nurture core aspects of critical thinking relevant to interdisciplinary research projects. After including these exercises in a range of educational contexts over the last few years (and after much adjustment and refinement), they have proven to be effective pedagogical techniques. However, more work needs to be done to define an appropriate evaluation process in order to more thoroughly determine where and when these techniques are most usefully introduced.

REFERENCES

Barrett, T. (2000). Studio critiques of student art: As they are, as they could be with mentoring. *Theory into Practice*, 39(1), 29–35.

Bilda, Z., Edmonds, E., and Candy, L. (2008). Designing for creative engagement. *Design Studies*, 29(6), 525–40.

Candy, L. (2007). New media arts and the future of technologies. *Communications of the ACM*, 50(12), 30–1.

Etemadpour, R. and Forbes, A.G. (2017). Density-based motion. *Information Visualization*, 16(1), 3–20.

Forbes, A.G. (2015). Articulating media arts activities in art–science contexts. *Leonardo*, 48(4), 330–7.

Forbes, A.G., Burbano, A., Murray, P., and Legrady, G. (2015). Imagining Macondo: Interacting with García Márquez's Literary Landscape. *IEEE Computer Graphics and Applications*, 35(5), 12–19.

Forbes, A.G., Hollerer, T., and Legrady, G. (2010). Behaviorism: A framework for dynamic data visualization. *Transactions on Visualization and Computer Graphics*, 16(6), 1164–71.

(2013). Generative fluid profiles for interactive media arts projects. In *Proceedings of the Symposium on Computational Aesthetics in Graphics, Visualization, and Imaging* (pp. 37–43). New York, NY: ACM.

Forbes, A.G. and Villegas, J. (2015). Video granular synthesis. In *Proceedings of the Workshop on Computational Aesthetics* (pp. 195–201). Aire-la-Ville, Switzerland: Eurographics Association.

Inman, J. (2015). Teaching through critique: An extra-disciplinary approach. *The National Teaching & Learning Forum* 24(2), 6–8.

Jennings, P. and Giaccardi, E. (2005). Creativity support tools for and by the new media arts community. In *NSF Workshop Report on Creativity Support Tools* (pp. 37–52). Washington, DC: National Science Foundation.

Klebesadel, H. and Kornetsky, L. (2009). Critique as signature pedagogy in the arts. In *Exploring Signature Pedagogies: Approaches to Teaching Disciplinary Habits of Mind* (pp. 99–120). Sterling, VA: Stylus Publishing.

Legrady, G. (2006). Perspectives on collaborative research and education in media arts. *Leonardo*, 39(3), 215–18.

Malina, R. (2011). Is art–science Hogwash? *Leonardo*, 39(1), 66–7.

(2012). Non-Euclidian translation: Crossing the river delta from the arts to the sciences and back again. *Leonardo Reviews Quarterly*, 1(3), 6–8.

Moore, G. and Lottridge, D. (2010). Interaction design in the university: Designing disciplinary interactions. In *CHI'10 Extended Abstracts on Human Factors in Computing Systems* (pp. 2735–44). New York: ACM.

Motley, P. (2015). Learning – To and from – The visual critique process. *New Directions for Teaching and Learning*, 2015(141), 77–86.

Rule, A. and Levine, D. (2012). International Art English. *Triple Canopy*, 16. www.canopycanopycanopy.com/issues/16/contents/international_art_english. Accessed online December 7, 2016.

Shneiderman, B. (2007). Creativity support tools: Accelerating discovery and innovation. *Communications of the ACM*, 50(12), 20–32.

(2015). *The New ABCs of Research: Achieving Breakthrough Collaborations.* Oxford: Oxford University Press.

Utterback, C. (2004). Unusual positions-embodied interaction with symbolic spaces. In Wardrip-Fruin, N. and Harrigan, P. (Eds.), *First Person: New Media as Story, Performance, and Game* (pp. 218–26). Cambridge, MA: MIT Press.

Vesna, V. (2001). Toward a third culture: being in between. *Leonardo*, 34(2), 121–5.

Villegas, J. and Forbes, A.G. (2014). Analysis/synthesis approaches for creatively processing video signals. In *Proceedings of the ACM International Conference on Multimedia* (pp. 37–46). ACM.

West, R., Malina, R., Lewis, J. et al. (2015). DataRemix: Designing the datamade. *Leonardo*, 48(5), 466–7.

Interviews

Scott Snibbe, Jussi Ängeslevä, and Dimitri Nieuwenhuizen were interviewed separately by e-mail or Skype. Their responses below have been edited together for purposes of clarity, connection to the original questions, and flow.

Michael Filimowicz (MF):
This book is intended to address what I see as a gap in the articulation of pedagogies for interactive technologies. One of the things we train our students for is the general space of technological disruption. That's the word we always hear about in relation to Society and Technology – new technologies "disrupt" previously formed social patterns. So in a sense we are saying to our students, "Go forth into the space of disruption. Disrupt, and be disrupted yourselves!" But a space of disruption is also a space of anxiety, and so students are sometimes anxious as they approach the end of their studies. My first question is to get your sense of what you make of disruption and anxiety (that is, if you even agree with this notion! Feel free to disagree).

Scott Snibbe (SS):
I think disruption is the key force in interaction design and technological innovation today. I started my career with some buddies making a disruptive product called After Effects (acquired by Adobe). At the time the nearest competitor for doing digital compositing cost $100,000 or 1,000 bucks an hour. We made a product that was 1,000 bucks and ran on the first color Macs. Craigslist is another colossal example, where a crafty, ugly classifieds site destroyed the newspaper industry.

Lately, what I've been noticing, and am excited about, is the movement of digital art into products. Once the iOS app store opened (and later others), all of a sudden there were no more gatekeepers to releasing interactive software. I was finally able to release my "useless programs" Gravilux, Bubble Harp, and Autograph into the App Store, and a couple of them reached number one, and started a new phase in my life leading to Björk: Biophilia, Philip Glass: REWORK_, and other "app albums." And now culminating in a new platform I'm creating called Eyegroove, that lets people instantly create interactive music videos.

Digital art projects are evolving into mass media mobile products. Imagine 15 years ago someone saying, "My project will let everyone in the world write one beautiful or subversive sentence a day and share it with the world." It would have been popular in Ars Electronica and the subject of some intellectual dialogue. Today it's Twitter. For years people with these bulky Rolliflex cameras staring down into a square viewfinders were the nerdiest of photographers, and now there are 200 million people on Instagram. I'd encourage people to look at this unique opportunity, and the vehicle of the startup as the most creative act one can do today, far beyond exhibiting something "controversial" in a gallery to a few dozen friends.

In terms of anxiety, that's generally caused by ego – thinking too much about oneself. There are two flavors – "I am the greatest." And "I suck." It's helpful to avoid those extremes. There's a great quote from the Buddha who says, "Have no hope and no fear." No hope that one will succeed, and no fear that one won't. On top of that, if you can frame your work as a way to benefit others, rather than advance your own ego, then I think one can be quite free of anxiety regardless of one's position in life or the challenges one faces.

Jussi Ängeslevä (JA):
Anxiety and disruption . . . well, yes, it can be seen at different levels. On one hand, critical thinking about the technological status quo, what it presents us right now, and how we can disrupt it, use it for something unintended. In this context, I think Levi Strauss's words about how every technology embodies at some level its original purpose, is as true as ever, seeing what's happening online. As for students, in their own perception of the world toward the end of their degree, I haven't sensed any internal anxiety. Of course, as always, there are those who are confident, and those who aren't, but I don't think in general new media art/design has any more anxiety inducing challenges than others.

MF:
When do you think we will ever overcome the medieval notion that a person's identity is tied to mastery of one particular narrowly defined craft? While

the old linguistic connections between surnames and occupations are typically forgotten these days, there is still this "Jack of all trades, Master of none" hang-up that produces various forms of identity crises among students, and perhaps less so with more established practitioners. What would it take, e.g., what sorts of institutional changes could be made, to lessen what is almost a kind of stigma associated with being able to do many different things creatively and technically?

SS:

I think specialization is a modern but not a medieval phenomenon. Until even the mid-twentieth century broad knowledge of a wide variety of subjects was considered, for a member of the educated class, a mainstream achievement. For example, they say somewhere in the seventeenth or eighteenth century humanity passed the point where it was possible for one person to "know everything." And there are even candidates for this person, such as Athanasius Kircher. I'm not sure how much he knew about Chinese poetry or African dance though.

So then it's only with the highly refined academic and corporate specialization of today that people get pegged so precisely into a subdomain. My experience with design and media grads, though, in the last 20 years is the opposite – a broadening and shallowing of knowledge. Before there were hybrid media programs where you had to choose one specialization, such as design, animation, film, etc., and then you added on top of that other skills – you went deep in one area and shallow in others.

Today, the problem I find, especially when trying to hire, is that people have not taken one area to deepen to mastery, but have dabbled across many domains – programming, animation, web design, etc. I find this a terrible shame for both the students and those of us trying to hire them, because that person has not had the pleasure of learning what it is to master something. That's the advice I normally give to students: take one subject and master it, so you know what mastery is, and then you can claim mastery as one of your talents. Also, ultimately, you've gotta do something all day. That's the question, again, I often ask these shallow job candidates – what exactly are you going to do all day? (if you can't competently program, design, etc.)

So, to be succinct, I think the institutional change that would be beneficial is actually to go back and require people in multidisciplinary programs to take one skill to mastery, but then to broadly educate themselves in many other fields at the same time, so they have a great creative soup in their heads, and a vocabulary for talking to collaborators who are experts in other fields. The CalArts Center for Integrated Media program does this, where students have a "home department."

JA:
Well, the thing is, I feel strongly the same: Master of none. But luckily, I get to work with many masters, and that way together we can create great things. So, again, I don't think media artists should be by definition generalists, and avoid specialization. In today's world, bigger things tend to be collaborations, and in that, all roles are necessary.

But yes, perhaps there's a bit of such a stigma in air, which means that media artists tend to overcompensate by claiming to be experts in various fields, even if their skills just scratch the surface. I guess, inherently, media implies technology of some sort, and hence such mastery tends to be a central feature, and therefore often overstated.

From my own point of view, I think having a strong base in some field helps a lot in understanding others.

MF:
There is a general identity or definitional problematic. For instance, I teach in "SIAT," which has to be explained as "The School of Interactive Arts and Technology" and then that longer phrase in turn usually has to be unpacked and further explained in the form of multiple paragraphs (assuming a willing listener!) for an outsider who doesn't know the school. Many jobs are ill-defined or poorly understood, and often a job title has nothing to do with the actual work to be done, e.g., in naming a position "interaction design" that is really "software engineering," etc. What's your take on these kinds of definitional difficulties in the field? Is it just a matter of the need for more time for the different practices to become better articulated, or is there something fundamentally fluid and hybrid about computational media and design generally? Any thoughts for better definitions?

SS:
If one's job can be clearly defined, then it's likely it can be immediately outsourced to Pakistan or India via oDesk, eLance, etc. To be a first world creative worker, one needs to be a synthesizer of information and fields. I read this great blog post by A.J. Kessler, that was titled "If You Can Easily Describe What You Do, You're Fucked." He said, "The people that will thrive are the ones who can figure out what needs to be done next and why." So it's good that you can't explain the meaning of your program – you're on the right track to creating people who can think on the fly and fill holes that don't exist yet.

JA:

I think it's really a matter of time. I mean, when I started my master's degree it was called Computer Related Design. But when I graduated, I got a degree in Interaction Design. Now the course is called Design Interactions – Multimedia, Hypermedia, New Media Design, Experience Design, Information Design, Information Architecture. They're surely different foci, some are already outdated, but still they're connected. And the tool side of things, let's say "using algorithms to inspire or solve problems" has very many application fields. I mean, philosophy used to mean many things, but over the years things have gotten more defined. Give new media a few centuries, and I am sure things will get clearer.

Dimitri Nieuwenhuizen (DN):

It's a big question. I think maybe it's the most relevant question. I really think we're in the middle of this transformation age. Let's say starting around 1991 with www when the web really took off and became accessible to everyone, and here we are 24 years later, and probably we need another 24 years to really redefine these kinds of things that you're talking about right now. We're probably exactly half way; we're still having all this luggage with us that basically started around with, let's say the fifteenth century when the Gutenberg press came, the first time that we could share information on a large scale, and now 500 years later and within 20 years the world went totally upside down in the amount of information we can share now, it's just insanely large. I think we first have to figure out how we're going to deal with it as a society before we can redefine the professions that are needed to shape this society. So I guess we have to go back a few levels and first ask ourselves how are we going to deal with these things as a community? I mean just the fact of this conversation, you send me an e-mail, now we're on Skype, already the amount of information I have gotten from you is pretty impressive if you would compare it to not so long ago. So I guess I would call it undefined; we can't define it yet because we also don't know where it's going. For sure I know the tools that we have right now, the laptops and smartphones and like C++ or OpenFrameworks, they're all very temporary things, in 5, 10, or 15 years we're going to laugh at those and say, "Oh, I remember those laptops, haha." So it's really hard to say something about it.

I think, for me, when I turned 18, and I knew I wanted to create things, I moved to Amsterdam and started to study philosophy. Because I felt that if you want to make things, you have to understand things. And it didn't work out because we started with Plato and I don't know what, it was super boring, and I thought I needed a place that can teach me the tools, and then

I can do the thinking myself. Well, that kind of worked, but for sure I think we have to go back to a level where we start understanding things first, and then define the tools for the things we need to do and define the kinds of people around us that can help us make those things and then maybe we can slowly start defining these new professions. And probably, if you ask me, the profession of the future is always a collaboration. Like the old model of being an individual professional is kind of like an old-fashioned thought, it comes from craftsmanship, you know, the master painter, who had all the students and blah blah. And I think right now, if you are the master painter, then you, together with your students, together you are this one entity that is this one profession, and all these students they shouldn't just know one skill, they all should have different skills, which can be quite diverse actually. If you take design as an example, then maybe you need an architect and you need a biologist or maybe you need a psychologist or psychiatrist, and maybe you need someone who's good at making data vis-ualizations, and someone who's really good at making databases, you need a whole team. If you want to make the world around us look more simple you need actually a more complex system to get that to work. For us at LUST it really works. You know, having this team of people that operates as one entity, as one person almost, where everybody has their own fascinations and their own skills, then you're really able to think things through very thoroughly and attempt to create something new.

MF:
What do you see as the primary professional organizations that can bring clarity of scope to this field, and perhaps act as a bridge between education and professional practice? If you were in charge of this project, what institu-tional bridges would you seek to create between education and professional practice?

SS:
I think the groups that drive people's passions, and touch their hearts, are the most likely to bridge educational and professional practice. A few great examples are: the openFrameworks community, the Eyeo Festival, the (now defunct) Creator's Project, the New Inc. incubator at New Museum, Maker Faire, Future of Storytelling, Sundance New Frontiers, etc. These commu-nities are driven by people's passions to create, connect, and impress each other. Something particularly exciting to me is how talks by creative tech-nologists have become something that now plays alongside big bands in festivals. I just got back from a talk at Moogfest where you'd have parallel

tracks with digital artist talks, an interview with Giorgio Moroder, and a Kraftwerk concert.

JA:

Well, at UdK (Universität der Künste Berlin), we've got currently a project together with TU (the Berlin University of Technology), attempting to build such bridges. We call it a hybrid platform, and it attempts to bring people together to initiate transdisciplinary projects, find ways of financing them, and disseminate the results. But inherently, I've learned that the motivations of research between arts and sciences are pretty far apart, and to attempt such collaboration, one needs to truly appreciate these motivations in order to make these collaborations work.

Between education and professional work, there's this "creative technologist" as a new meme, but it's definitely a tricky balance too. Mostly such individuals do stunts in marketing, where the use of some new technology is already a big part of the message, whatever one does with it.

I think in a long run, when new media designers and artists are seen as a core value within the organization, instead of "hired guns" for special stunts, things will change. And such people then will most certainly have to have a strong generalist approach, not be defined by the tools they use, but define the tools by what they want to achieve.

MF:

Probably most of us can look back at advice that we were given when we were students ourselves or just starting out that actually turned out to be true. Or at least continuously relevant. In my case, I can count maybe three or four specific moments of having been given advice as a student that were pretty accurate and useful. Do you have any such "past advice moments" in your own personal history that you still find ring true, and that you would be willing to share with today's students of "computational media + design" (to give a label to this group)?

SS:

One of the best pieces of advice I recall came from Michael Naimark – I remember, while we were working at Interval Research, asking him how I should go about getting into the digital art scene, and how do you eventually get successful? He said that in your 20s maybe there are hundreds of thousands of young artists; in your 30s tens of thousands, in your 40s, thousands, and then dwindling thereafter. The key is to hang in there. As my parents often said to me, "Patience is a virtue."

I also remember seeing Chuck Close speak in college, and something that really stuck with me was when he said, "If you're doing good work in grad school, you're doing the wrong thing." I think that's been lost on people today – to take real risks and push oneself beyond the edge of failure. Real lessons come from taking real risks. But today people polish their work too early and have these pretty websites with projects that look the same as everyone else's. It's better to fail big, to take on something insurmountable, than to fit in as a bland mediocrity.

MF:

What technologies, including software and programming languages, are you yourself most proficient in? What would you say is the ratio in your skills between those that were formally learned versus self-taught?

SS:

I started programming at age 10, first on a Commodore PET in the public library that had no disk or tape drive, so I'd have to write my programs out on paper, work on them until the library closed, then transcribe changes back to paper. That was a great lesson. Then I worked on an Apple II+ from age 10 to 17, making interactive audiovisual programs much like I make today, though simpler. By the time I got to college I knew at least seven or so programming languages, self-taught from manuals, hobby magazines like Byte, and so on: BASIC, Pascal, Forth, 6502 Assembly, etc.

I went to Brown University and got bachelor's and master's degrees in Computer Science, and parallel degrees in Art and Film/Animation. In Computer Science departments, they actually never teach you any programming language. They teach you higher-level principles like algorithm design, operating systems, compilers, computer graphics, and then it's up to the students to learn languages on their own, or even choose a language of choice. At that time, C and C++ were the main languages. Later I got into Java and Objective-C.

I think you would say all my programming languages are "self-taught" but that's a bit misleading, because it's the same with most fields at an advanced level. When you study English in college they're not teaching you what a verb is, you're learning how to tell stories, to convey emotion. It's the same thing with Computer Science. The people who don't have a chance to formally study Computer Science miss out on this study into the deep abstractions underlying computation, though nowadays you can learn them yourself on Coursera or Wikipedia, as long as you know to look in the first place.

The most important skills I've learned though aren't technical. They are managerial and financial. The world runs on spreadsheets and presentations, so learning to articulate ideas in those forms so they can be supported and funded has been a long, essential part of my education. The other is management, which is kind of the opposite of academics. In academics you get in trouble for collaborating, but in the real world, collaboration is beyond important, it's the essence of civilization. My main guiding principles in management are to give people big chunks of a project that they will be able to point to with pride and say, "I did this." The other key principle is to let people use the tools and methodologies they are comfortable with to accomplish their work. Finally, I articulate ethical principles about how we hope to treat one another, and the positive impact we hope to have on the world – why are we doing what we are doing?

JA:
I'm not really proficient. Mostly self-taught.

MF:
What is the typical size of teams involved in the projects you work on, and how many skill areas would you say are represented on these teams? With regard to these skill areas, do you think interactive media and design curricula should try to cover most of these, so that students get exposure to the full set of possible recombination of media and technology? Or if not, to what extent (what are the main areas that should be covered)?

SS:
The main skills are software development, interaction design, visual design, creative direction, art direction, production/project management, and quality assurance. People usually embody one or more of these talents. We don't hire engineers who don't have some kind of art, design, or musical sensitivity, for example. Team sizes are usually 4–6 people, that's an ideal size. You can make Instagram with a team that size! Bigger teams don't necessarily work better or faster.

JA:
Every project is different; different teams, different projects, different skills. I think teaching is all about metaskills, learning about how to learn, and strategically deciding what to learn. Of course, it means that one needs to teach practical skills to understand what the learning is, but the tools of the day, what one learns, are almost irrelevant. There are bound to be trendy

tools of the day, and therefore surely useful, but that won't last, and therefore knowing about how to learn, and deciding when to learn is what matters.

DN:
It depends. You know the way it works here, there's LUST, which is formally a company, and there's also LUSTlab, and those are two entities and they're actually in two separate buildings, but pretty close to each other. And the purpose of the lab is that we need to do these ongoing continuous experiments, trying both new theories, new methodologies, also new technologies that come out. We're not just trying to play with these things but conduct experiments with them. And usually that work ends up as an autonomous installations which end up in museums all over the world, and we can put all our skills into that, all our thoughts, etc. And then, of course, as you can imagine, that delivers a lot of knowledge, and a lot of ideas, so that we actively try to look for interesting institutes or companies or whatever, that we can use these ideas and technologies for. And by doing so, we often manage to find the clients that we want to work for, so then the teams that form themselves when starting such projects, it's a very organic process. So sometimes there's something that everyone is enthusiastic about and there are 10 people working on it, and there are other projects that are really very specific and there may be only three people working on it, and so it's very diverse and actually we don't really try to steer that too much, we try to just let it happen. For example, I don't care what time people start in the morning or when they go home, or how many holidays they take, as long as at the end of the road, the thing is there. And it's fine, and that usually works really well because it just kind of creates this vibe, this kind of wave where you just go and then suddenly it's there and that's such a great moment that nobody wants to miss. You get this fantastic synergy that makes things work, and so the size of the team is very diverse in that sense.

MF:
A lot of students feel that specialization gives them more, I'm not sure what to call it, let's say "survivability" in the workforce. There's an impression that being a generalist makes one more vulnerable to not obtaining a foothold in the field. What is your view about relatively unvalorized generalist skills versus a strong sense of narrow specialization?

DN:
Usually I advise students to go a few steps further before they specialize, so for example before focusing only on C++ or Open Frameworks or any

programming language, go to some old garbage place and take an old computer and then start taking it apart and try to understand how that machine actually works. You know, what does the microprocessor actually do, how does it come up with these calculations, and how does it respond to different programming languages? It's more like understanding what kinds of materials your tool is actually made from, before you start making something with it. There's a nice program at Delft, in the computer science area, where basically what they teach the students is how to build a computer. But the nice thing about that is when you know how to do that, then you can program in any language. It doesn't matter anymore, then you understand how the machine responds to different programming languages. And it makes you very aware that each design or each artwork, whatever you want to make, can be done in another programming language. These languages, they're tools, and they're not always sufficient for what you have in mind.

I mean, remember Flash, you know, 10 years ago, for everybody, Flash was the thing, so everyone was teaching ActionScript, and it was such a big influence on the visual language that you could find it on the web or anywhere actually, because it was vector-based. It was pretty limited in its visual power, so you could see that it delivered a lot of work that had a hard time representing the real thoughts of the maker, and was more representing the capabilities of this specific programming language. So I think that, as a student, so long as you're aware of the limitations of your tool it's ok to specialize, but you have to be open and always be sure that it's temporary, because probably in 2 or 5 years, who knows, there's going to be something else that's better or faster or more relevant. So as long as you're open to that, it's ok to specialize, as long as you promise to yourself in 2 or 5 years, "I'm going to specialize again," then it's ok.

SS:
I think I articulated this clearly before, but I believe it is essential that people master one talent. Malcolm Gladwell writes about this in *Outliers*. Except I don't think the lesson is for outliers, it's for anyone who wants to accomplish something with their life. A human being is missing out on what it means to be human if one doesn't learn to master something in one's lifetime, whether it be a CEO, a mother, a yogi, a meditator, or a designer. Ultimately, we're all trying to master being a human being – to make the most of the off-the-charts potential of the human mind. If you just skip stones across the depths of human knowledge, you've really missed the point of being alive.

But again, I don't think this means people should narrowly focus on one specialty their whole lifetime, or even from the get-go. If you master one thing, you have mastered mastery. And then you can transfer that ability again-and-again in your life. Learning languages is like that – it's far easier to learn a third language than a second. I really believe this is the fundamental problem with these media programs today. I had thought that I missed out on these programs that didn't exist when I was in school. But actually I got a much better education because I had to independently master computer science, art, and animation. That was a different time, though, before the Internet, when you would lie low for 7 to 10 years before you made much of a public debut. Young people now are sometimes trying to craft a public persona before their brains have matured, and before they have much of meaning and depth to say.

JA:
Well, as said before, we need both, and I feel that the generalists have less of a defined path how to go about the work life planning, etc. If you've got fixed skills, you know what works to apply, what is needed, etc. On the other hand, generalists need good people to work with, and to get to that position is also not so easy.

MF:
What are the "Big Ideas" that inspire you, either as a thinker or a maker? By "Big Ideas" I mean something from the history of ideas, art, philosophy, or science. For example, for me systems theory is an important theoretical lens for a range of considerations in the way that I think about creating and understanding interactive systems or analyzing society and culture. What conceptual ground do you find yourself continuously coming back to in your work?

SS:
The main guiding principle in my work is the concept of interdependence (what they call Emptiness in Buddhism), that nothing exists independent of anything else. There's a quote from the Buddha, who says, "You are only made of non-you elements." This can be first understood physically – we're tiny bits of our parents combined with everything we ever ate and breathed, including breathing in little bits of every person we ever were in a room with together. We're ultimately the remnants of stellar explosions – all the heavy elements are "second-generation" solar detritus.

But then more important is on a mental level. Neither you nor I have written words we made up in this interview. We're articulating concepts we learned from others. We have our parents and teachers to thank for the way we behave, the knowledge in our heads, and so on. It's an awful, sad moment when you hear wealthy, famous, and powerful people claiming they achieved their success due to their own efforts. It's only due to the kindness of our parents, teachers, every writer we've ever read, every movie we've ever seen, the people who invented our languages, the humans who invented tools, the creatures that we evolved from, and so on, that we exist and thrive.

So that's the biggest idea to see that things only exist in relation to other things. A nice conceptual framework for how things exist is as: mind, parts, causes. But let's start with parts: everything has parts, nothing is solidly, atomically existing – your body can be broken into organs, cells, atoms, etc. Thoughts and ideas can be broken down into individual subthoughts, ideas, moments of consciousness. Everything dissolves upon analysis into smaller and smaller parts, never finding the indivisible. And then all parts have causes – material causes like gravity or weather, as well as the mental causes like ideologies, motivations, inspiration, etc., each with their own causes you can trace back forever. Finally, it's the mind that projects a unitary idea onto a bundle of parts and causes, for example, the bundle of meat, bones, thoughts, and causes you to be called Michael.

Before I became a Buddhist, I had some thoughts like this as a kid, both from Christian Science Sunday school, and also spontaneous "meditations." For example, sometimes I'd sit and try and imagine what the people were doing in the houses next door to me, then the block, the neighborhood, the state, the world. To try and hold that totality in my head (which of course I couldn't). Or little meditations on perception, like I used to set up my camera on a time and take a picture of my arm moving very fast behind an object. My arm wasn't visible, but then when I got the picture back from the lab I'd know that I had a picture of my moving arm.

JA:
Well, I'm pretty down on earth with that. Currently looking into Arts and Crafts, where the actual making is central, not just what comes out. Also, perceptual psychology follows in most places where I go. Actor-network theory (ANT) from Latour helps with many things too. But again, I think I'm too scatterbrained to be able to define momentous ideas as the core of my work. What I am very grateful about is that when I was kid, my family built a house, and when it was ready, the remaining construction material became toy-making material, and the tools the means for that. And that sort of hands on making of things, sometimes hacking, sometimes building from scratch has probably most fundamentally influenced my career.

DN:

Well formally, it's definitely taking the process as a base, that's definitely something that keeps coming back. But that's more of a "commandment" or something. It's a methodology, of which, you know, when you follow it, you'll find the inspiration. But in general you can say that we're [LUST] 20 very different people, so everyone gets their inspiration from very different things. So for me, I may be into more philosophical kinds of things, but I'm also very interested in evolution, or how people communicate with each other. Or what happens in the world of art. But it could also be, like whatever weird new television program comes up that just tries something, in a way any experiment could be an inspiration. But I think the way to measure it is this kind of undefined feeling, then you know it really inspired you. But it's hard to put that into categories or something. I guess it's a mix.

MF:

What parts of interaction media and design curricula do you feel tend to be the first in line to be sacrificed in order to gain various efficiencies, by being deemed 'inessential,' and probably shouldn't be?

SS:

Probably some of the basics, like color theory, formal design principles, art and architectural history, typography, etc. I'm not sure you guys teach these as dedicated special courses anymore? I think it's very helpful to go deep and people need to actually do week over week of exercises for these kinds of ideas to sink in. If you master the basics of design, the way an architect does, then you can design anything from an app to a city. Also very useful are fiction writing; film history (the only mature visual time-based medium); and filmmaking, animation, and theater, particularly the principles of staging – how to direct people's attention. Studying magic I bet would help too, like J.J. Abrams did.

DN:

I think it can be tempting, I think it started 8 or 9 years ago here in the Netherlands, where there was this movement in the art academies where theory became more important than practice, let's say, which on the one hand was interesting because it forced students to think more about the why questions, like why do we do things? But then you saw in the graduation shows for example that they weren't able to translate this or communicate this to an audience anymore. So I think that what is essential, things that have traditionally been part of an art academy for example, is the skill to make that bridge between something that you thought of into something that can tell this thought to a wider audience. I guess it's more like a methodology than literally like a skill, but it could actually be very useful to teach people how to make a silk screen or something like that, just to understand the process from the thought and the limitations of the medium that you're using, and then where does it end up, like on a wall or wherever, to really get a grip on the whole A to Z from where the thought starts to where it ends up on a wall or on a website, and then how that's being interpreted. And for that, the process of old media doesn't differ that much from the new media, well, unless you can say, ideas like from Nicholas Negroponte's about "medium-lessness," where before, McLuhan for instance wrote about the importance of the media for information, and now it's more like information can end up anywhere. So for example, when you're designing with information, you're not really sure where it's going to end up. Is it going to end up on an app, on a website, or maybe just in a tweet, or on a poster or wherever? It could be anything. And maybe soon it's going to end up in a table or a chair or I don't know, with the Internet where things are going. So that's definitely a big change but we can still learn a lot from the old skills, just understanding the process of creating something that communicates in an individual way.

MF:
It seems like a lot of what you describe (@DN) depends on some fundamental act or notion of communication, in completing the circuit toward communicating to others in the work.

DN:
Yeah, well, it's not like the main goal or anything, but I think it's interesting to observe what happens with something once it has been communicated. I don't think it should be like a starting point, like in advertising or something, but it's definitely something interesting to observe people viewing whatever is being communicated and understanding how they make their interpretations and then compare those to what you intended.

MF:
Do you involve your students in your professional projects, or do you report back to the classroom on things that you've been doing?

DN:
We always have three or four interns walking around, in total we're about 20 people. We have what we call a horizontal structure in the company,

which means that no matter whether you are an intern or whether you have worked here for 10 years, everyone has the same responsibilities and shares the same tasks, etc. So like these students, they get a nice insight into how things work. The other way of course is the teaching, which has several levels. I am teaching in a master's program, so on the one hand it's a bit more theoretical, more like design thinking, but at the same time I invite them to the studio session, working with the people who work here. For me it's really important that the process of thinking about things and making things are parallel processes. So it's not that first you think about things and then you decide how you're going to make them. But I think it's important when you start thinking about a specific topic that you also start experimenting with it. Experimenting with new tools, with new technologies, or it could also be new methodologies. What is a big problem is lot of students lack the really good skills to do such things, so that is very helpful to bring together a group of multidisciplinary people so they can fill the gaps that they have. And then together create something way beyond what they could have done by themselves. And a third way, for example, my colleague Thomas, he is the head of a design school in an art academy, I was the head of the design academy for a few years, so also on the level of shaping education, we're pretty involved. But you know how it is, I think all of us remember how important that was, that small amount of time that you got 4 years of education, it makes a big difference in who you become later on. So I think it's something that's really important to always give back, but of course as a studio we also get a lot back from the students, you know they make crazy stuff and it's very inspiring, so it's a two-way thing. And I think if you treat students equally, then they get the most out of you, and you get the most out of them.

MF:
How common is that approach in the Netherlands? Is that an approach that you and your colleagues have developed at the institutions that you are a part of, or do you see that as more of the norm in Northern Europe, or becoming more of a norm?

DN:
No, I wish. It's definitely something you have to fight for almost. You know, art academies became institutes; they are not like the kind of free places that they used to be. And there's only a few left that are really independent but most of them are part of a bigger system of education that covers all kinds of disciplines. You tend not to get an art education, but you get

an education that makes you into a graphic designer or a fashion designer or a photographer which in my opinion are not professions, but just ways of capturing your thoughts. So it started pretty well, a hundred years ago with the Bauhaus, with the idea that experimenting is a really cool way to educate people, but you should never be limited to a certain toolset, which is what happened when these academies started to divide all of these professions so that graphic designers need these tools, or photographers need those tools, etc. while I think it's actually really nice to be open to any kind of tool that you can use to do something with your thoughts, independent of the medium that you're using. So I'm really trying to push this more anti-disciplinary idea into the art academies, that it should be way more like, you know, things like serendipity or something. Where it's more like you're trying to find a way to express yourself, but you don't have any tools to do that, and the search is more interesting than the end result. The end result should come by itself, by doing stuff, by doing the search, you know the whole idea behind process-based design. You know, if you do such an extensive research, and you dive so deep into the topic that there's nothing you can mix anymore, that you know so much about it, and parallel to that you start experimenting, you start making things, you start visualizing things, then at a certain moment those two things cross. And when they cross then you know you're on the right track and you've created something that you couldn't have thought of before. So you need this process. I think it's way more important within education to teach students how to start a process, rather than, you know, learn the rules of the professions, let's say, or what's going to be expected of them when they are graduating. Because what's actually being expected of them is that they are going to surprise people, that they're going to come up with new thoughts and new ideas. I mean, anybody can make a poster, and that's not a big deal. But making something that innovates in a really cool and unique way is a different thing. It's a big challenge, it's not easy!

Afterword: Toward a Curricular Synthesis

MICHAEL FILIMOWICZ AND
VERONIKA TZANKOVA

As we stated in the Introduction, the idea for this volume was a response to the lack of literature directly related to our professional practices as educators in the intersecting fields of interactive media, design, and computation. The chapters present practical and theoretical considerations around pedagogies across the connected disciplines. As a way of concluding our journey, we offer a high-level curricular map that addresses the transdisciplinary considerations required for computational creativity. Our model has three "meta-pedagogical" areas:

- Technical Domains – groupings of competencies organized around a general field of application, comprised of the domain knowledge associated with digital craft and also mastery of the required tools.
- Discursive Skills – the combination of communication, reading, writing, critical, analytic, and research skills which enable students to conceptualize their creative work at higher levels of abstraction and in relation to already existing scholarship in the relevant disciplines.
- Transdisciplinary Studio – an open experimental space for multidisciplinary teams who respond to new themes each semester, and in which students are asked to integrate the diversity of technical and discursive skills they have acquired throughout their learning. This teaches creative, design, and systems processes as well as teamwork and communication skills in a regularly recurring manner.

We map these concepts over a 2-year period in a semester-based system in Table A.1.

This curricular synthesis models the following:

1. Technical Domains typically require strict laddering of prerequisite courses in order to develop a sufficient level of mastery. This

TABLE A.1. *High-level meta-pedagogical mapping of curriculum over a 2-year period*

Timeline and curricular area	Fall 1	Spring 1	Summer (virtual semester)	Fall 2	Spring 2
Technical Domain	Pre-req 1	Pre-req 2	Pre-req 3	Pre-req 4	Summative Capstone of Skillset
Technical Domain	Pre-req 1	Pre-req 2	Pre-req 3	Pre-req 4	Summative Capstone of Skillset
Transdisciplinary Studio	Theme 1	Theme 2	Open	Theme 3	Theme 4
Writing, Theory, Research Methods, History	Flexible	Flexible	Open	Flexible	Flexible
Elective	Elective	Elective	Open	Elective	Elective

curricular area is not conceived to be tool-specific but would comprise general application areas such as audiovisual media, web development, industrial design, games, multimedia programming, and so on, as makes sense for the particular school or program.

2. Technical Domains are envisioned as requiring two school years of learning to achieve depth, connected by an online Summer "virtual semester" which fosters self-learning, continuous practice (i.e., no gap in learning the domain's skillset over the Summer) and allows the Fall 2 semester to pick up at a higher level than where Spring 1 has left off. Summer online semesters also develop the pedagogical and communication skills of faculty for online delivery formats.

3. Each Technical Domain ends with a Capstone semester-long project that is summative of the five-term skillset.

4. Depending on the students' use of the Electives space, they can complete 4–6 Technical Domain specializations in a hypothetical 4-year full-load sequence of a Bachelor's degree.

5. Discursive abilities – such as reading and writing; use of research methodologies; histories of media, art, design, and technology; and theoretical explorations. These support a very different kind of learning relative to making and production-oriented skills. Such courses do not need to be as strictly laddered in sequence and so provide

significant flexibility in the timing of course offerings vis-a-vis a school's teaching capacity and students' choice.

6. Similarly, the Elective space is another source of flexibility and exploration for the student and the school. Students could also use the Elective space to develop additional technical specializations, as noted earlier.

7. The Electives area can feature courses that do not need to be part of five-course domain sequences, or courses that intersect multiple technical domains. For example, a course in Narrative Design could be a stand-alone elective, but also be shared by both a gaming and an audiovisual media domain. Another example of course type that can work as either stand-alone or integrated into a Technical Domain sequence is User Experience, which can apply to a range of expressions such as interface design, installations, tangibles, and wearables.

8. The Transdisciplinary Studio would occur every semester and be the curricular site where the multiplicity of domains along with the integration of technical and discursive skills would come together via multidisciplinary teams. Each semester, different themes can be selected for the transdisciplinary studio, ensuring that there is always a new challenge and constraint space which provides some scope to the projects. Examples of themes might be: Sustainability, Social Enterprise, Performance, Architectural Scale, Virtual Worlds, Entrepreneurship, Global Culture. Summers are kept open for any variety of typical activities, such as work, travel, self/directed studies, taking additional courses, etc.

9. Finally, this configuration of an undergraduate curriculum can close some of the cultural gap that may occur between the undergraduate and graduate programs, opening up space in the undergrad area for intersections with research activities.

We should be clear that this model presents an ideally synthesized high-level concept. Certain specific details or modules can be shifted in actual implementations. For example, the five-semester sequences starting in a Fall term and linked by a Summer virtual semester can be shifted to a Spring start time if additional sections are created, in order to allow for more flexibility for students and their completion rates. Such shifts would vary of course by a school's needs and capacities. In principle, a self-paced online virtual semester can be offered anytime as it supports additional flexibility.

A comparative analysis of curricula at seven institutions[1] yielded the following thematic groupings, which could form the basis of a general framework for Technical Domains as we describe here:

Virtual Worlds, Animation & Gaming
Graphic & Communication Design
Coding, Programming, Computer Science
Artificial Intelligence & Advanced Computation
Human Computer Interaction & User Experience
Audiovisual Media
Physical Computing
Industrial Design
Robotics & Hardware
Informatics
Data

In the same analysis, we identified the following Discursive Domains:

Writing, Communication, Collaboration
Theory and History
Narrative
Research Methods
Science (e.g., Representation and Modeling)
Mathematics
Social & Cultural Theory

We would group the following domains under what we have defined the Elective space:

Business
Professional Practice
Experimental and Artistic Approaches
Security
Education
Speech Recognition
Health
Sustainability

---

[1] School of Interactive Arts and Technology at Simon Fraser University, UCLA Design Media Arts, University of Indiana Informatics, Carnegie Mellon University Human–Computer Interaction, University of Southern California Interactive Media, Northeastern University Games, MIT Media Arts.

Achieving breadth and depth in the kinds of highly multidisciplinary curricula that are becoming more typical of today's creative technology-rich programs has always presented a primary and critical challenge. For many students with a narrow focus on an ideal "dream" or "glamour" job as a professional outcome, the favoring of a "hands-on" education can co-equate to "brain-off" tendencies in learning, such as an avoidance of reading and writing. General intellectual skills – such as qualitative and quantitative analysis or argument-based reasoning – are sometimes underappreciated in making-oriented programs. Our vision is for a curriculum that is both hands-on and brain-on! Our model accounts for both strict prerequisite course sequences needed to achieve in-depth technical skills, and also supporting flexibility and exploration through the discursive, team project studio, and elective program areas. While the epistemes, tools, methodologies, and applications can vary considerably if not dramatically (in exciting and always changing ways), we would argue that these three curricular constructs of Technical Domains, Discursive Skills, and Transdisciplinary Studio satisfy the needs of computational creativity for our information age.

Index

4chan, 221
1 Squares (Molnar), 202
3-D printing technology, 134–36, 267
200 lines: in space/of code, 98

Abrams, J. J., 306
ACM Digital Library, 281
ActionScript, 51–52, 54, 60, 303
Ader, Bas Jan, 37
Adobe, 82
Adobe After Effects, 293
Adobe Animate, 51
Adobe Creative Suite, 84
Adobe Dreamweaver, 29
Adobe Flash, 51–53, 57–58, 59–60, 303
Adobe Photoshop, 29
advice for students, 299–300
"Advice from an Old Programmer" (Shaw), 171
affordance and style, 167
affordance theory, 165–66
After Effects, 293
agency. *See* ARRAY[ ]; interactivity, teaching
agile model, 100–101, 102–4
AI (artificial intelligence), 15, 95, 142, 198, 244, 246–47
Aleynikov, Sergey, 246
algorithmic thinking, 12, 196–97
Amanita Design, 37
Amazon, 244
American College Dance Association, 145
analysis phase in process framework, 99
Analytical Engine, 80
Android Development Toolkit, 120
Ängeslevä, Jussi, 293, 294, 296–97, 299, 301, 304, 305

anthropotechnic autoimmunity, 249
anthropotechnic immune system, 229
Anthropy, Anna, 37
Apache Cordova, 102
app interface, 137
Appalachian Spring, 149
Apple Computers, 79, 82, 111
Arduino, 39, 60–62, 64, 110, 124, 150, 153
AREA, 64–67, 70
Arizona's School of Information: Science, Technology, and Arts (SISTA), 276
ARRAY[ ]
  basic coding with processing, introduction to, 86–93
  code .edu hype, 79–82
  code as contemporary art and design medium, 83–85
  code as specialized field, 82–83
  code is not easy, 77–79
  Coding Slowly, 85–93
  conclusion, 93
  example from, 85–86
  introduction to, 75–77
  resistances to code in new media art and design foundations, 79–83
art/design students, introducing computation to
  AREA, 64–67
  case study, Michael, 63–64
  case study, Saam, 51–52
  case study, Ting, 57
  conclusion, 70–71
  farm town, 52–54
  introduction to, 48–51
  out there in the void, 67–70
  puppet face-off, 60–63

art/design students, introducing
computation to (*cont.*)
  puppet show, 57–60
  retirement, 54–57
art and design foundation. *See* ARRAY[ ]
art, introducing computation to, 48–71
artificial intelligence (AI), 15, 95, 142, 198, 244,
246–47
Artificial Jellyfish, 267
Artist is Present, The (Barr), 37
art-science acumen, promotion of, 279–81
AUDFIT, 145
audience experience and perception, 150
audiovisual complementarity, 185
augmentation, 279–80
Augmented Reality (AR), 118, 119–20, 122
autoethnographic method, 164–65, 180
Autograph, 293
autonomous thinking, 229–31
avant-garde movement, 67

Babbage, Charles, 80
Barr, Pippin, 37
basic coding with processing
  instructional narrative, 89–93
  intentions, 87–89
  project narrative, 86
  starting points, 86–87
  structure and timing, 89
  vocabulary, 89
behaviorism, 215
Bento Labs, 263
Big Ideas, 304–6
Bilda, Zafer, 276
biochemical design, 267–68
biological design, 263, 267–68, 268–71
Bioradio, 265
Biorealize, 263
Bishop, Claire, 82–83
Black Stack (Bratton), 237–38
blood glucose measurement, 131–32, *See also*
  Sango project
BlueGriffon, 29
Bogost, Ian, 53–54
BoofCV library, 284
Boombox, 265
Bratton, Benjamin, 229, 237–38
bricolage approach, 26
browser, coding in, 167–70
browser, coding outside, 170–71
browsing, 186
Bubble Harp, 293
building and opening, 186

Byrne, David, 26
Byron, Ada, 80

Cage, John, 148, 202
Canadian Internet Registration Authority
  (CIRA), 224
Candy, Linda, 276
Carclay, Christian, 37
Carpenter, Rollo, 248
Cave of the Heart, 149
Cheng, Liang, 77
Chick-fil-A, 30
CHmaps, 222–23
circuit making, 268–69
Cirino, Rafael, 133
citizenship, 220–21
Cleberbot, 248
Clement, Andrew, 222
Clock, The (Marclay), 37
Close, Chuck, 300
Cloud platforms, 237
Cloud Polis, 244
clustered regularly interspaced short
  palindromic repeats (CRISPR), 233–34
code .edu hype, 79–82
Code Academy, 167, 171, 172, 175
code as medium
  ARRAY coding slowly, 75–93
  design singularity, teaching for, 95–104
  introduction to, 9–10
code learning platforms. *See* online code
  learning environments
Code School, 167, 171, 172
code-based design curriculum, 95–104
CodeSkulptor, 168
coding as fundamental skill for creative
  research, 278–79
coding in another browser window, 168–70
coding in the browser, 167–68
coding MOOC, developing
  background, 193–95
  conclusion, 207–8
  Creative Coding MOOC, 195–97
  evaluating MOOCs as an education
    platform, 204–7
  introduction to, 191–93
  social learning, 201–4
  technical and cultural prism, 197–204
coding outside the browser, 170–71
Coding Slowly
  instructional narrative, 89–93
  intentions, 87–89
  introduction to, 85–86

project narrative, 86
   starting points, 86–87
   structure and timing, 89
   vocabulary, 89
coding, overview of, 15
cogninodes, 231, 232–33, 235
cognisphere, citizens of
   customs in the cognisphere, 231–36
   from person to per capita, 241–45
   introduction to, 229–31
   mapping the cognisphere, 236–41
   our daily turing test, 245–48
   passport to the cognisphere, 248–50
Cognition in the Wild (Hutchins), 163
coherence principle, 175
collaborative research, 147–49
communication, 307
communication/implementation phase in
   process framework, 99
computation literacy. *See* interactivity,
   teaching
computational creativity, interdisciplinary
   nature of, 5–6
computational creativity, teaching
   code as medium, 9–10
   critical pedagogy, 12–13
   curricular synthesis, 311–15
   introduction to, 1–8
   new foundations, 8–9
   online learning, 11–12
   physical computing, 10–11
   transdisciplinary, 13–14
computational literacy, 49, *See also* ARRAY[ ]
computer science, 84, 87, 98, 140, 264
"conceptual economy", 195
conditioning, 88
"Conference on Design Methods", 114
constructivism, 216, 218
consumerist mindset, 25
contemporary art and design medium, code
   as, 83–85
contemporary maker movement. *See* maker
   movement
contested Internet, 213, 220–25
contextualizing knowledge, 222
contiguity principle, 175
conventional process, 103–4
Cordova, 102
costume design, 151
course design, 41–63
course readings, in Technology in Art
   Education course, 29
Coursera, 168, 171, 172–73, 194

Cow Clicker, 53
Craigslist, 293
Crary, Jonathan, 244
Crawford, Chris, 52
creative classroom. *See* digital literacies,
   developing for the creative
   classroom
creative coding. *See* ARRAY[ ]
Creative Coding MOOC, 195–97, *See also*
   coding MOOC, developing
Creative Coding Research Group, 274,
   276, 278
creativity, 16
Creator's Project, 298
CRISPR (clustered regularly interspaced short
   palindromic repeats), 233–34
critical coding. *See* ARRAY[ ]
critical pedagogy
   cognisphere, citizens of, 229–50
   introduction to, 12–13
   media arts pedagogy, process and outcome
   paradigms in, 213–26
critique sessions, 285–89
Cross, Nigel, 109, 114, 115
Csikszentmihalyi, Mihaly, 66
Cubitt, Sean, 219
culture-jamming project, 30–34
Cunningham, Merce, 148
curricula collection. *See* ARRAY[ ]
curriculum mapping, 311–14
cycle of experience and reflection, 214
cycles of code, 80–81

dance movement capture, 144
Databases, 194
data-driven performance analysis,
   242–43
Davis, Joe, 265
DCog (Distributed Cognition),
   163–67, 180
DeepMind, 245
Deleuze, Gilles, 48–49
delivery culture, 242–43
democratization of technology, 96, *See also*
   design singularity, teaching for
design curricula, 103, 306–7
design literacy. *See* literacies of design,
   changing
design pedagogy. *See* literacies of design,
   changing
design process, 50–51, *See also* design
   singularity, teaching for
design programs, 4

design scenes of online coding environments
　affordance and style, 167–78
　coding in another browser window, 168–70
　coding in the browser, 167–68
　coding outside the browser, 170–71
　conclusion, 187–88
　DCog, 163–67
　design parameters, 185–87
　multimedia cognition, 171–77
　note taking, 177–78
　three screen scene, 178–85
design singularity, teaching for, 95–104
design-build. *See* design singularity, teaching for
designer, role of. *See* design singularity,
　　　teaching for
"design-then-build" paradigm, 99
Dewey, John, 214–15, 216, 217, 218–19
digital art pedagogy, 25–26
"digital citizens", 220
digital divide, 249
"Digital Divide" (Bishop), 82–83
digital ethics, 219
digital fabrication, 262
Digital Humanities (Burdick et al), 222
digital literacies, developing for the creative
　　　classroom
　future impact of course design, 41–63
　introduction to, 21–24
　projects, 30–41
　syllabus development, 24–30
digital media in the classroom, 40
"digital natives", 82, 220
digital objects, creative potential of, 25
digital systems, 21
DIMES project, 222
discursive skills, 311, 312
disruption, 293–94
disruptive products, 293
Distributed Cognition (DCog), 163–67, 180
distributed design scene, 182
distributed intelligence, 218
DNA, 233–34
DNA sequencing, 260
Donath, Judith, 221
"draw your name" exercise, 203–4
Driessens, Erwin, 202
Dynabook, 78
Dys4ia (Anthropy), 37

Eclipse, 120
Eclipse development environment for Android
　　　devices, 136–37
Ede, Siân, 148

Einstein, Albert, 235
Eisner, Elliot, 217
electives, 313
Electronic Visualization Laboratory (EVL), 276
Embattled Garden, 149
enactive learning, 49
Erp, Jean, 202
Errand into the Maze, 149
evaluation phase in process framework, 99
Event Horizon Telescope, 235
existing works, emulation or extension of, 284–85
expanded context, experimenting with, 186
expectations, 89
experience, 88
experience-based knowledge, 146
experiential education, 217
experiential learning, 216–18
Experiential Learning (Kolb), 217
"Experiential Learning from a Constructivist
　　　Perspective" (Mughal and Zafar), 216
"Experiential Learning: Theoretical Under-
　　　pinnings" (Beaudin and Quick), 217
expertise effect, 176
expression, vs. syntax, 278
expressive interactive experience, 50, 51
Eyeo Festival, 298

Facebook, 247, 248
Falling series (Ader), 37
Farm Town, 52–54
FarmVille, 53
feelings, 89
Fernandez, Eduardo, 77
Final Cut, 79
Financial Industry Regulatory Authority
　　　(FINRA), 245
financial markets, 245–46
Flash, 51–53, 57–58, 59–60, 303
Flash (ActionScript), 50, 51–52, 54, 57–58
flash crash of 2010, 245
flow, 66, *See also* interactivity, teaching
Flux Ping-Pong (Maciunas), 69
Fredkin, Edward, 234
free and open source software (F/OSS), 241
freedom, 218
freelancers, 243–44
Frontier, 149
Fuller, Buckminster, 114
Future of Storytelling, 298
FutureLearn, 196, 201, 204, 205, 206

Galloway, Alex, 220, 237
Game Art, 67, 70

game design. *See also* digital literacies,
    developing for the creative classroom;
    interactivity, teaching
  AREA, 64–67
  case study, 51–57
  Farm Town, 52–54
  Puppet Show, 57–60
  Retirement, 54–57
game development, 31, 35–40
GameMaker, 29, 35, 39
gatekeeping, 186
Geertz, Clifford, 164
gender, 21, 27
gendered clothing, 31
"General Purpose User" of digital technology, 26
general theory of relativity, 235
generation, 279
generation phase in process framework, 99
generative art, 198–201, 202
Genspace, 263
Geographical Traceroute project, 222
Giaccardi, Elisa, 276
Gibson, J. J., 165, 166
GIMP, 29, 40
Gimsewski, James, 148
Github, 240–41
Gladwell, Malcolm, 303
glycemic index reading, 132
Goldman Sachs, 246
Google, 238, 240, 247
Google Android mobile platform, 119, 134
Google docs, 177
Google Scholar, 281, 282
graffiti painting, 121, *See also* Tinta Solta project
Graffitti Research Lab, 124
Graham, Martha, 149
Graham, Paul, 84–85
graphical user interface (GUI), 49, 111
Gravilux, 293
Gtrace project, 222
guerrilla communications. *See* digital literacies,
    developing for the creative classroom

Hackteria, 263
hacktivism, 221
Hayles, N. Katherine, 229, 231–32, 245
high culture, 6
high-fidelity prototype, 101, 102–3, *See also*
    design singularity, teaching for
Hot Throttle (Söderström), 37
"How Big is Coding Right Now? A
    Programming School Just Sold for
    $36m", 80

How We Became Posthuman (Hayles), 231
human intelligence tasks (HITs), 244
human-computer interaction (HCI), 183–84
humanities, culture of, 5
Hutchins, Edwin, 163
Hwang, Indae, 197
hybrid platform, 299

I am sitting in a room (Lucier), 199
I Ching, 148
IATI (Interactive Technology and Arts
    Initiative), 142, 158
iconic learning, 49
identity and definitional issues, 296–98
"If You Can Easily Describe What You Do,
    You're Fucked" (Kessler), 296
Igoe, Tom, 110–11
ImogenHeap, 145
iMovie, 29, 35
implementation phase in process framework, 99
In the Shadow performance, 154–55
information and communications technologies
    (ICTs), 213, 220–25, 225–26
information labor, 239, 242
Instagram, 294
instrumentalist theory, 214
integrated curriculum. *See* design singularity,
    teaching for
Integrated Development Environment (IDE),
    15, 60, 168, 169, 170
integrative design studio, 268–71
interaction design, 98–101, 101–4, 107, 140, *See
    also* physical computing initiative in
    Brazil
interactive dance performance, art and
    technology collaboration
  background, 145–49
  challenges, 156–58
  collaborative research, 147–49
  conclusion, 158–59
  course activities, 150–56
  course design, 149–56
  creative activities, 144–45
  In the Shadow performance, 154–55
  interactive performances, 145–46
  introduction to, 142–43
  learning objectives, 149
  overview of course, 143–45
  practice-based research, 146–47
  proximity, 153–54
  research, 144
  roles of participating faculty, 149–50
  students' collaborations, 151–53

interactive dance performance, art and technology collaboration (*cont.*)
  students' projects, 153–56
  teaching, 143–44
  Zwischenkörper Performance, 155–56
interactive design, 57–58, *See also* interactivity, teaching
interactive media, 5, 57–63
interactive multimedia programming. *See* digital literacies, developing for the creative classroom
interactive performances, 145–46, 149–56
interactive systems, 144
interactive technology, 3, 4, 5
Interactive Technology and Arts Initiative (IATI), 142, 158
Interactive Telecommunications Program (ITP), 110
interactivity, teaching
  AREA, 64–67
  case study, Michael, 63–64
  case study, Saam, 51–52
  case study, Ting, 57
  conclusion, 70–71
  farm town, 52–54
  introduction to, 48–51
  out there in the void, 67–70
  puppet face-off, 60–63
  puppet show, 57–60
  retirement, 54–57
interdependence, 304–5
interdisciplinarity, 6, 275–76
interdisciplinary collaborations, 147–49
interdisciplinary research, 264–66
interdisciplinary research skills, exercises for developing
  emulation and extension of existing works, 284–85
  "STAR" reports, writing, 282–84
  tree criticism, 285–89
interface design, 58
Internet Exchange Points (IXPs), 224
Internet infrastructure, 220–25
interviews, 289–90, 293–311
Introduction into Artificial Intelligence, 194
Inventing Abstraction exhibition, 285
iOS app store, 293
iPad, 77–78
iteration, 88
ITP (Interactive Telecommunications Program), 110
IXmaps, 222–23, 224

Java programming language, 120, 137
Jennings, Pamela, 276
Jiang, Zhen, 77
Jobs, Steve, 111
Joy, Bill, 80

K-12 art education/educators, 21–23, 24, 27, *See also* digital literacies, developing for the creative classroom
Kahunaburger Traceroute, 222
Kaplan, Esther, 242–44
Kay, Alan, 48, 49–50, 77–78, 78, 81
Kessler, AJ, 4, 296
Ketai Sensor Library, 119, 134
kill-switch, 245
Kinect sensor, 126–27, 150, 156
Kircher, Athanasius, 295
Knitted Radio, 265
Knuth, Donals, 97
Kolb, David, 214, 216, 217
Kopas, Merritt, 37
Kurzweil, Ray, 4, 95
Kwasteck, Katja, 69

language literacy, 49
Le Corbusier, 114
learnable programming. *See* ARRAY[ ]
"Learnable Programming" (Victor), 77, 78–79, 80
learner control principle, 176
learning analytics, possibilities of, 225–26
Learning Styles Inventory (LSI), 217
LED Dress Research Project, 144
Legrady, George, 277
Lessig, Lawrence, 239
Lewis, Michael, 246
LeWitt, Sol, 198, 202
Lialina, Olia, 26
LIFE Lab, 107, 108, 110, 113, 117, 124, 131, 132–33
LIGO Laser Interferometer Gravitational-Wave Observatory, 235
Lilypad Arduino, 150
LIM (Kopas), 37
literacies, 261
literacies of design, changing
  conclusion, 271
  integrative design studio, 268–71
  introduction to, 259–61
  literacy in matter and material, 266–68
  overview of, 261–62
  research, 264–66
  tool-making, 262–64
literacy in matter and material, 266–68

looping, 88
low culture, 6
low-fidelity prototyping, 101
Lucier, Avlin, 199
LUST, 302
LUSTlab, 302
Lynda.com, 170, 174

M messaging service, 247
Machinarium (Amanita Design), 37
Machine Learning, 194
Macintosh personal computer, 96
Maciunas, George, 69
Madsen, Rune, 97–98
Maker Faire, 298
maker movement, 95, 96, 97
Makey Makey, 39, 42
Malina, Roger, 275
Manifesto for Agile Software Development, 100
Mann, Steve, 232
Manovich, Lev, 63, 249
Marks, Laura, 208
Massive Open Online Courses (MOOC), 171,
     172, 204–7, *See also* coding MOOC,
     developing
mastery, 294–96, 303–4
Mauricio, Gabriela Schirmer, 118
McLuhan, Marshall, 173
Mechanical Turk, 244
Media Arts and Technology (MAT) program, 276
media arts pedagogy
   ideals and measures, 218–20
   introduction to, 213–14
   learning analytics, possibilities of, 225–26
   OBE frameworks, expanding, 225–26
   process and outcomes models, 214–15
   process and reflexive learning, 215–18
   project-based learning, ICTs and the
        contested Internet, 220–25
mediation, 280–81
Mei, Rafael, 133
Menkman, Rosa, 26
metadata, 219
meta-design, 96–97
Metaio Augmented Reality Library, 120
microbial maps, 260
Microsoft ExpressionWeb, 29
Mindstorms (Pappert), 70
Minsky, Marvin, 247
modality principle, 174
Molnar, Vera, 202–3
Mondloch, Kate, 62
mono screen scene, 181

Moogfest, 298
Moore's Law, 236, 245
Moroder, Giorgio, 298
Morowitz, Harold, 234
movement session, 144
multi-disciplinarity, 6
multimedia cognition, 171–77
My Mother Was a Computer (Hayles), 231
mycelium, 270

Naimark, Michael, 299
narrational context, 185
National Coalition for Core Arts Standards, 24
national curriculum, 193–94
National Dance Educator Organization, 145
Negroponte, Nicholas, 306
neural networks, 246–47
new foundations
   art/design students, introducing
        computation to art, 48–71
   digital literacies, developing for the creative
        classroom, 21–63
   introduction to, 8–9
New Inc. incubator at New Museum, 298
new media artists, 34, 37
New Tendencies movement, 236
NEXT Tridimensional Experimentation Lab,
     135, 136
Ng, Andrew, 194
Niebuhr, Reinhold, 214, 218–19, 220
Nielsen, Jakob, 2
Nieuwenhuizen, Dimitri, 293, 297–98, 302–3,
     305–6, 306–7, 307–9
Night Journey, 149
nine "9 Evenings: Theatre and Engineering", 85
Noguchi, Isamu, 149
Norman, Donald, 165
Norvig, Peter, 194
note taking, 177–78
numerical systems, 191–93

O'Sullivan, Dan, 110–11
OBE (outcomes-based education), 215, 218, 221,
     225–26
Oliveira, Jhonnata, 131, 133, 134, 137
online code learning environments
   affordance and style, 167–78
   coding in another browser window,
        168–70
   coding in the browser, 167–68
   coding outside the browser, 170–71
   conclusion, 187–88
   DCog, 163–67

online code learning environments (*cont.*)
   design parameters, 185–87
   multimedia cognition, 171–77
   note taking, 177–78
   three screen scene, 178–85
online identity, 218, 220
online learning
   creating coding MOOC, developing, 191–208
   introduction to, 11–12
   learning environments, design scenes of, 163–88
Open Insulin, 263
Open Trons, 263
OpenCV library, 284
openFrameworks community, 298
Out There In The Void (OTITV), 67–70
outcome paradigms. *See* process and outcome paradigms in media arts pedagogy
outcomes-based education (OBE), 215, 218, 221, 225–26
outdoor installations, 157
Outliers (Gladwell), 303

P3P project, 239
Pappert, Seymour, 70
pedagogical experiments in creative coding
   art-science acumen, promotion of, 279–81
   augmentation, 279–80
   coding as fundamental skill for creative research, 278–79
   conclusion, 289–90
   generation, 279
   interdisciplinary research skills, exercises for developing, 281–89
   introduction to, 273–76
   mediation, 280–81
   pedagogical goals, 276–78
   provocation, 280
"Pedagogical Pattern for Teaching Computer Programming to Non-CS Majors, A" (Jiang, Fernandez, and Cheng), 77
peer assessments, 206
Penny, Simon, 26
performance capture, 144, 145
performance metrics, 213, 215
Perpetual Motion, 145
Personal Computer for Children of All Ages, A (Kay), 77–78
personalization effect, 173–74
personalization principle, 176
Phillips, David J., 222
physical computing. *See also* digital literacies, developing for the creative classroom
   Brazilian teaching initiative, 107–48
   definition of, 109
   goals of, 62
   interactive dance performance, art and technology collaboration, 142–64
   introduction to, 10–11
   overview of, 110–13
physical computing initiative in Brazil
   case studies, 118–37
   conclusion, 137–40
   examples of projects, 113
   introduction to, 107–10
   LIFE lab, 113
   methodological considerations, 116–24
   physical computing, 110–13
   reflective practice learning experience, 114–16
Physical Computing: Sensing and Controlling the Physical World with Computers (O'Sullivan and Ioge), 110–11
Pink, Daniel, 195
Pixlr, 29
Polanyi, Michel, 116
Pontifícia Universidade Católica do Rio de Janeiro, 107, 108
Popper, Karl, 5–6
practice context, 185
practice-based research, 146–47
pre-built interface components, 102
pre-service art education. *See* digital literacies, developing for the creative classroom
pre-training principle, 176
Printed Radio, 265
PRISM, 238
procedurality. *See* interactivity, teaching
procedure, connecting with, 88
process and outcome paradigms in media arts pedagogy
   ideals and measures, 218–20
   introduction to, 213–14
   learning analytics, possibilities of, 225–26
   OBE frameworks, expanding, 225–26
   process and outcomes models, 214–15
   process and reflexive learning, 215–18
   project-based learning, ICTs and the contested Internet, 220–25
process and outcomes models, 214–15
process and reflexive learning, 215–18
process framework in creative disciplines, 99
Processing, 60–62, 64, 66, 98, 101–3, 110, 119, 120, 134, 137, 138–39, 153, 284, *See also* Coding Slowly
Processing (Java), 50
process-oriented pedagogy, 216, 218
professional organizations, 298–99

professional projects, and students, 307–9
"Programming Design Systems", 97–98
programming languages, 278, 300–301, 303
Project Muse, 281
project-based learning, 220–25
Projection Mapping, 118
Protocol (Galloway), 237
protocols, 219–20
prototyping. *See* high-fidelity prototype;
    low-fidelity prototyping
provocation, 280
Proximity performance, 153–54
Psychology of Everyday Things, The (Norman), 165
Puppet Face-Off, 60–63
Puppet Show, 57–60, 63
Python, 168, 170, 171

QuantumSound, 145
QuickTime VR, 110

Radio in a Bag, 265
redundancy principle, 176
reflection-in-action, 218
reflection-on-action, 218
reflective practice, 115–16, 116, 139–40
"Reflective Practitioner, The" (Schön), 217
research, 264–66
research literacy, 265
resistances to code in new media art and
    design foundations, 79–83
responsive environment design, 151
Retirement, 54–57, 62
Rhizome, 85
Right to be Forgotten, 238
Rittel, Horst, 115
Rozin, Daniel, 34
rules, connecting with, 88
Rushkoff, Doug, 25
Ryle, Gilbert, 116

safe harbor agreement, 238–39
Salonen, Essi, 148
Salter, Anastasia, 82
Sango project, 131–37, 140
Schiffman, Daniel, 66
scholarship of teaching and learning
    (SoTL), 7
Schön, Donald, 109, 115–16, 116, 216, 217, 218
School of Information: Science, Technology,
    and Arts (SISTA), 276
science, technology, engineering, art, and math
    (STEAM), 22
Sciences of the Artificial, The (Simon), 115
Scientific Management (Taylor), 2

Screening the Hello World! Processing
    Documentary, 87
segmenting principle, 175
self-transcendence, 218, 219, 220
Senses Considered as Perceptual Systems
    (Gibson), 165
Seven on Seven Conference, 85
Shaw, Zed, 170, 171, 174
Shneiderman, Ben, 275
Shrank, Brian, 68–69
signaling principle, 175–76
Signature Track, 172–73
Simon, Herbert, 109, 115
simulation. *See* interactivity, teaching
singularity, 95
Singularity is Near, The (Kurzweil), 95
sketch, 102
skill development, 301–2
Sloterdijk, Peter, 249
Smalltalk, 49
Snibbe, Scott, 4, 293–94, 295–96, 296, 298–99,
    299–300, 300–301, 301, 303–4, 304–5, 306
Snow, C. P., 5
Snow, John, 236
So Kanno, 124
social constructivist paradigm, 166
social in/formality, 186
social learning, 201–4
social networking, 29–30
sociology of scientific knowledge (SSK), 166
Söderström, Jonatan, 37
Soft Circuit, 144
software used in Technology of Art Education
    course, 29
sound sculpture, 43
Spady, William, 213, 215
spatial memory, 181–84
specialization, 295, 302–3, 303–4
specialized field, code as, 82–83
spinning top example, 196–97
Spotify, 265
Springer, P. W., 245
Stanford University, 194
state-of-the-art (STAR) reports, 282–84
Status of Arts Education in Ohio's Public
    Schools, The, 24
STEAM (science, technology, engineering, art,
    and math), 22
Steyerl, Hito, 243
Strauss, Levi, 294
Streamline movement, 267
sublated video, 168–70
Sundance New Frontiers, 298
surveillance, 219, 221, 222–23, 224–25, 232, 238

326Index

syllabus development, 24–30
symbolic learning, 49
synchronicity, 235
syntax, vs. expression, 278

Tacit Dimension, The (Polanyi), 116
tacit knowledge, 116
talking/identity mask, 44
Target, 80
TattooAR project, 118–21, 140
Taylor, Frederick, 2
teaching games, 43
technical domains, 311–12
technical skillsets, 2
Technology in Art Education course
    development of, 26–30
    future impact of course design, 41–63
    introduction to, 21–24
    projects, 30–41
    student evaluations, 41–60
    syllabus development, 24–30
Technology Student Association (TSA), 40
technoscience, culture of, 5
telematics, 242–44
telemedicine, 135
Text Rain (Utterback), 284
TextWrangler, 170
"third culture", 5
third wave human-computer
    interaction, 6
three screen scene, 178–85
Thrun, Sebastian, 194
Tiger Leap Foundation, 194
Tinta Solta project, 121–31, 140
tool-making, 262–64
transdisciplinarity, 6
    introduction to, 13–14
    literacies of design, changing, 259–71
    pedagogical experiments in creative coding,
        273–90
transdisciplinary studio, 311, 313
transrationalism, 218–19
tree criticism, 285–89
TRgen – traceroute generation, 223
Trust Engineering Group, 248
Turing Test, 245–48
Turkle, Sherry, 243
Twitter, 294
"Two Dimensions of Collaboration" (Pisano
        and Verganti), 148
typing vs. handwriting, 177–78

US Securities and Exchange Commission
        (SEC), 245

US-EU Safe Harbor Framework, 238–39
Udacity, 194, 247
Unity (C#), 50
UPS, 242–43
Upwork, 243–44
usability, history of, 2–4
User Interface: A Personal View (Kay), 49
Utterback, Camille, 284

variables and conditions, connecting
        with, 88
vector graphics, 51
Venn Diagram, 166
Verstappen, Maria, 202
Vesna, Victoria, 148, 280
Victor, Bret, 77–78, 78–79, 79, 81
video production, 35
Vieira, Amanda, 130
Villaça, Matheus, 133
Violacein Factory, 263
virtual tattoo. See TattooAR project
visualizations, 144
Viz-a-Go-Go public exhibition, 145
Vygotsky, Lev, 216–17

Waco Dance Fest, 145
Wall Street Reform and Consumer Protection
        Act, 245
Wark, McKenzie, 239–40
waterfall model, 99–100
wearable technology, 150, 156, 232
web design, 31
Webber, Melvin, 115
Whalen, Thomas, 231, 248
What is Creative Coding?, 199
Whitaker, João, 121, 122–24, 125–28, 128–31
Widom, Jennifer, 194
Wiener, Norbert, 249
Wii, 150
Windows and Mirrors (Bolton and Gromala), 70
Windows Movie Maker, 29
Wolfram, Stephen, 234
words, 88
"World 3", 5–6
World Wide Web Consortium, 239

xtraceroute project, 222

"Year of Code", 80, 82
Yo-Yo Games, 29

Zanini, Gabriel, 133
Zwischenkörper performance, 155–56
Zynga, 53